TEXT MINING AND VISUALIZATION

Case Studies Using Open-Source Tools

Chapman & Hall/CRC
Data Mining and Knowledge Discovery Series

SERIES EDITOR
Vipin Kumar
University of Minnesota
Department of Computer Science and Engineering
Minneapolis, Minnesota, U.S.A.

AIMS AND SCOPE

This series aims to capture new developments and applications in data mining and knowledge discovery, while summarizing the computational tools and techniques useful in data analysis. This series encourages the integration of mathematical, statistical, and computational methods and techniques through the publication of a broad range of textbooks, reference works, and handbooks. The inclusion of concrete examples and applications is highly encouraged. The scope of the series includes, but is not limited to, titles in the areas of data mining and knowledge discovery methods and applications, modeling, algorithms, theory and foundations, data and knowledge visualization, data mining systems and tools, and privacy and security issues.

PUBLISHED TITLES

ACCELERATING DISCOVERY : MINING UNSTRUCTURED INFORMATION FOR
HYPOTHESIS GENERATION
Scott Spangler

ADVANCES IN MACHINE LEARNING AND DATA MINING FOR ASTRONOMY
Michael J. Way, Jeffrey D. Scargle, Kamal M. Ali, and Ashok N. Srivastava

BIOLOGICAL DATA MINING
Jake Y. Chen and Stefano Lonardi

COMPUTATIONAL BUSINESS ANALYTICS
Subrata Das

COMPUTATIONAL INTELLIGENT DATA ANALYSIS FOR SUSTAINABLE
DEVELOPMENT
Ting Yu, Nitesh V. Chawla, and Simeon Simoff

COMPUTATIONAL METHODS OF FEATURE SELECTION
Huan Liu and Hiroshi Motoda

CONSTRAINED CLUSTERING: ADVANCES IN ALGORITHMS, THEORY,
AND APPLICATIONS
Sugato Basu, Ian Davidson, and Kiri L. Wagstaff

CONTRAST DATA MINING: CONCEPTS, ALGORITHMS, AND APPLICATIONS
Guozhu Dong and James Bailey

DATA CLASSIFICATION: ALGORITHMS AND APPLICATIONS
Charu C. Aggarawal

DATA CLUSTERING: ALGORITHMS AND APPLICATIONS
Charu C. Aggarawal and Chandan K. Reddy

DATA CLUSTERING IN C++: AN OBJECT-ORIENTED APPROACH
Guojun Gan

DATA MINING FOR DESIGN AND MARKETING
Yukio Ohsawa and Katsutoshi Yada

DATA MINING WITH R: LEARNING WITH CASE STUDIES
Luís Torgo

EVENT MINING: ALGORITHMS AND APPLICATIONS
Tao Li

FOUNDATIONS OF PREDICTIVE ANALYTICS
James Wu and Stephen Coggeshall

GEOGRAPHIC DATA MINING AND KNOWLEDGE DISCOVERY,
SECOND EDITION
Harvey J. Miller and Jiawei Han

GRAPH-BASED SOCIAL MEDIA ANALYSIS
Ioannis Pitas

HANDBOOK OF EDUCATIONAL DATA MINING
Cristóbal Romero, Sebastian Ventura, Mykola Pechenizkiy, and Ryan S.J.d. Baker

HEALTHCARE DATA ANALYTICS
Chandan K. Reddy and Charu C. Aggarwal

INFORMATION DISCOVERY ON ELECTRONIC HEALTH RECORDS
Vagelis Hristidis

INTELLIGENT TECHNOLOGIES FOR WEB APPLICATIONS
Priti Srinivas Sajja and Rajendra Akerkar

INTRODUCTION TO PRIVACY-PRESERVING DATA PUBLISHING: CONCEPTS
AND TECHNIQUES
Benjamin C. M. Fung, Ke Wang, Ada Wai-Chee Fu, and Philip S. Yu

KNOWLEDGE DISCOVERY FOR COUNTERTERRORISM AND
LAW ENFORCEMENT
David Skillicorn

KNOWLEDGE DISCOVERY FROM DATA STREAMS
João Gama

MACHINE LEARNING AND KNOWLEDGE DISCOVERY FOR
ENGINEERING SYSTEMS HEALTH MANAGEMENT
Ashok N. Srivastava and Jiawei Han

MINING SOFTWARE SPECIFICATIONS: METHODOLOGIES AND APPLICATIONS
David Lo, Siau-Cheng Khoo, Jiawei Han, and Chao Liu

TEXT MINING AND VISUALIZATION
Case Studies Using Open-Source Tools

Edited by
Markus Hofmann
Andrew Chisholm

CRC Press
Taylor & Francis Group
Boca Raton London New York

CRC Press is an imprint of the
Taylor & Francis Group, an **informa** business

A CHAPMAN & HALL BOOK

Dedication - Widmung

Für meine Großeltern, Luise and Matthias Hofmann - Danke für ALLES!

Euer Enkel, Markus

To Jennie

Andrew

Contents

II   KNIME   61

3 Introduction to the KNIME Text Processing Extension   63

Kilian Thiel

4 Social Media Analysis — Text Mining Meets Network Mining   81

Kilian Thiel, Tobias Kötter, Rosaria Silipo, and Phil Winters

Contents

Foreword

Data analysis has received a lot of attention in recent years and the newly coined data scientist is on everybody's radar. However, in addition to the inherent crop of new buzz words, two fundamental things have changed. Data analysis now relies on more complex and heterogeneous data sources; users are no longer content with analyzing a few numbers. They want to integrate data from different sources, scrutinizing data of diverse types. Almost more importantly, tool providers and users have realized that no single proprietary software vendor can provide the wealth of tools required for the job. This has sparked a huge increase in open-source software used for professional data analysis.

The timing of this book could not be better. It focuses on text mining, text being one of the data sources still to be truly harvested, and on open-source tools for the analysis and visualization of textual data. It explores the top-two representatives of two very different types of tools: programming languages and visual workflow editing environments. R and Python are now in widespread use and allow experts to program highly versatile code for sophisticated analytical tasks. At the other end of the spectrum are visual workflow tools that enable even nonexperts to use predefined templates (or blueprints) and modify analyses. Using a visual workflow has the added benefit that intuitive documentation and guidance through the process is created implicitly. RapidMiner (version 5.3, which is still open source) and KNIME are examples of these types of tools. It is worth noting that especially the latter stands on the shoulders of giants: KNIME integrates not only R and Python but also various libraries. (Stanford's NLP package and the Apache openNLP project, among others, are examined more closely in the book.) These enable the use of state-of-the-art methods via an easy-to-use graphical workflow editor.

In a way, the four parts of this book could therefore be read front to back. The reader starts with a visual workbench, assembling complex analytical workflows. But when a certain method is missing, the user can draw on the preferred analytical scripting language to access bleeding-edge technology that has not yet been exposed natively as a visual component. The reverse order also works. Expert coders can continue to work the way they like to work by quickly writing efficient code, and at the same time they can wrap their code into visual components and make that wisdom accessible to nonexperts as well!

Markus and Andrew have done an outstanding job bringing together this volume of both introductory and advanced material about text mining using modern open source technology in a highly accessible way.

Prof. Dr. Michael Berthold *(University Konstanz, Germany)*

Preface

When people communicate, they do it in lots of ways. They write books and articles, create blogs and webpages, interact by sending messages in many different ways, and of course they speak to one another. When this happens electronically, these text data become very accessible and represent a significant and increasing resource that has tremendous potential value to a wide range of organisations. This is because text data represent what people are thinking or feeling and with whom they are interacting, and thus can be used to predict what people will do, how they are feeling about a particular product or issue, and also who else in their social group could be similar. The process of extracting value from text data, known as *text mining*, is the subject of this book.

There are challenges, of course. In recent years, there has been an undeniable explosion of text data being produced from a multitude of sources in large volumes and at great speed. This is within the context of the general huge increases in all forms of data. This volume and variety require new techniques to be applied to the text data to deal with them effectively. It is also true that text data by their nature tend to be *unstructured*, which requires specific techniques to be adopted to clean and restructure them. Interactions between people leads to the formation of networks, and to understand and exploit these requires an understanding of some potentially complex techniques.

It remains true that organisations wishing to exploit text data need new ways of working to stay ahead and to take advantage of what is available. These include general knowledge of the latest and most powerful tools, understanding the data mining process, understanding specific text mining activities, and simply getting an overview of what possibilities there are.

This book provides an introduction to text mining using some of the most popular and powerful open-source tools, *KNIME*, *RapidMiner*, *Weka*, *R*, and *Python*. In addition, the *Many Eyes* website is used to help visualise results. The chapters show text data being gathered and processed from a wide variety of sources, including books, server-access logs, websites, social media sites, and message boards. Each chapter within the book is presented as an example use-case that the reader can follow as part of a step-by-step reproducible example. In the real world, no two problems are the same, and it would be impossible to produce a use case example for every one. However, the techniques, once learned, can easily be applied to other problems and extended. All the examples are downloadable from the website that accompanies this book and the use of open-source tools ensures that they are readily accessible. The book's website is

```
http://www.text-mining-book.com
```

Text mining is a subcategory within data mining as a whole, and therefore the chapters illustrate a number of data mining techniques including *supervised learning* using classifiers such as *naïve Bayes* and *support vector machines*; *cross-validation* to estimate model performance using a variety of performance measures; and *unsupervised clustering* to partition data into clusters.

Data mining requires significant preprocessing activities such as cleaning, restructuring, and handling missing values. Text mining also requires these activities particularly when text data is extracted from webpages. Text mining also introduces new preprocessing techniques such as tokenizing, stemming, and generation of n-grams. These techniques are amply illustrated in many of the chapters. In addition some novel techniques for applying network methods to text data gathered in the context of message websites are shown.

What Is the Structure of This Book, and Which Chapters Should I Read?

The book consists of four main parts corresponding to the main tools used: RapidMiner, KNIME, Python, and R.

Part 1 about RapidMiner usage contains two chapters. Chapter 1 is titled "Rapid-Miner for Text Analytic Fundamentals" and is a practical introduction to the use of various open-source tools to perform the basic but important preprocessing steps that are usually necessary when performing any type of text mining exercise. RapidMiner is given particular focus, but the MySQL database and Many Eyes visualisation website are also used. The specific text corpus that is used consists of the inaugural speeches made by US presidents, and the objective of the chapter is to preprocess and import these sufficiently to give visibility to some of the features within them. The speeches themselves are available on the Internet, and the chapter illustrates how to use RapidMiner to access their locations to download the content as well as to parse it so that only the text is used. The chapter illustrates storing the speeches in a database and goes on to show how RapidMiner can be used to perform tasks like tokenising to eliminate punctuation, numbers, and white space as part of building a word vector. Stop word removal using both standard English and a custom dictionary is shown. Creation of word n-grams is also shown as well as techniques for filtering them. The final part of the chapter shows how the Many Eyes online service can take the output from the process to visualise it using a word cloud. At all stages, readers are encouraged to recreate and modify the processes for themselves.

Chapter 2 is more advanced and is titled "Empirical Zipf-Mandelbrot Variation for Sequential Windows within Documents". It relates to the important area of authorship attribution within text mining. This technique is used to determine the author of a piece of text or sometimes who the author is not. Many attribution techniques exist, and some are based to a certain extent on departures from Zipf's law. This law states that the rank and frequency of common words when multiplied together yield a constant. Clearly this is a simplification, and the deviations from this for a particular author may reveal a style representative of the author. Modifications to Zipf's law have been proposed, one of which is the Zipf-Mandelbrot law. The deviations from this law may reveal similarities for works produced by the same author. This chapter uses an advanced RapidMiner process to fit, using a genetic algorithm approach, works by different authors to Zipf-Mandelbrot models and determines the deviations to visualize what similarities there are between authors.

Additionally, an author's work is randomised to produce a random sampling to determine how different the actual works are from a random book to show whether the order of words in a book contributes to an author's style. The results are visualised using R and show some evidence that different authors have similarities of style that is not random.

Part 2 of the book describes the use of the Konstanz Information Miner (KNIME) and again contains two chapters. Chapter 3 introduces the text processing capabilities of KNIME and is titled "Introduction to the KNIME Text Processing Extension". KNIME is a popular open-source platform that uses a visual paradigm to allow processes to be rapidly assembled and executed to allow all data processing, analysis, and mining problems to be addressed. The platform has a plug-in architecture that allows extensions to be installed, and one such is the text processing feature. This chapter describes the installation and use of this extension as part of a text mining process to predict sentiment of movie reviews. The aim of the chapter is to give a good introduction to the use of KNIME in the context of this overall classification process, and readers can use the ideas and techniques for themselves. The chapter gives more background details about the important preprocessing activities that are typically undertaken when dealing with text. These include entity recognition such as the identification of names or other domain-specific items, and tagging parts of speech to identify nouns, verbs, and so on. An important point that is especially relevant as data volumes increase is the possibility to perform processing activities in parallel to take advantage of available processing power, and to reduce the total time to process. Common preprocessing activities such as stemming, number removal, punctuation, handling small and stop words that are described in other chapters with other tools can also be performed with KNIME. The concepts of documents and the bag of words representation are described and the different types of word or document vectors that can be produced are explained. These include term frequencies but can use inverse document frequencies if the problem at hand requires it. Having described the background, the chapter then uses the techniques to build a classifier to predict positive or negative movie reviews based on available training data. This shows use of other parts of KNIME to build a classifier on training data, to apply it to test data, and to observe the accuracy of the prediction.

Chapter 4 is titled "Social Media Analysis — Text Mining Meets Network Mining" and presents a more advanced use of KNIME with a novel way to combine sentiment of users with how they are perceived as influencers in the Slashdot online forum. The approach is motivated by the marketing needs that companies have to identify users with certain traits and find ways to influence them or address the root causes of their views. With the ever increasing volume and types of online data, this is a challenge in its own right, which makes finding something actionable in these fast-moving data sources difficult. The chapter has two parts that combine to produce the result. First, a process is described that gathers user reviews from the Slashdot forum to yield an attitude score for each user. This score is the difference between positive and negative words, which is derived from a lexicon, the MPQA subjectivity lexicon in this case, although others could be substituted as the domain problem dictates. As part of an exploratory confirmation, a tag cloud of words used by an individual user is also drawn where negative and positive words are rendered in different colours. The second part of the chapter uses network analysis to find users who are termed leaders and those who are followers. A leader is one whose published articles gain more comments from others, whereas a follower is one who tends to comment more. This is done in KNIME by using the HITS algorithm often used to rate webpages. In this case, users take the place of websites, and authorities become equivalent to leaders and hubs followers. The two different views are then combined to determine the characteristics of leaders compared with followers from an attitude perspective. The result is that leaders tend to score more highly on attitude; that is, they are more positive. This contradicts the normal marketing wisdom that negative sentiment tends to be more important.

Part 3 contains five chapters that focus on a wide variety of use cases. Chapter 5 is titled "Mining Unstructured User Reviews with Python" and gives a detailed worked example of mining another social media site where reviews of drugs are posted by users. The site, pillreports.com, does not condone the use of drugs but provides a service to alert users to potentially life-threatening problems found by real users. The reviews are generally short text entries and are often tagged with a good or bad review. This allows for classification models to be built to try and predict the review in cases where none is provided. In addition, an exploratory clustering is performed on the review data to determine if there are features of interest. The chapter is intended to be illustrative of the techniques and tools that can be used and starts with the process of gathering the data from the Pill Reports website. Python is used to navigate and select the relevant text for storage in a MongoDb datastore. It is the nature of Web scraping that it is very specific to a site and can be fairly involved; the techniques shown will therefore be applicable to other sites. The cleaning and restructuring activities that are required are illustrated with worked examples using Python, including reformatting dates, removing white space, stripping out HTML tags, renaming columns, and generation of n-grams. As a precursor to the classification task to aid understanding of the data, certain visualisation and exploration activities are described. The Python Matplotlib package is used to visualise results, and examples are given. The importance of restructuring the data using grouping and aggregation techniques to get the best out of the visualisations is stressed with details to help. Moving on to the classification step, simple classifiers are built to predict the positive or negative reviews. The initial results are improved through feature selection, and the top terms that predict the class are shown. This is very typical of the sorts of activities that are undertaken during text mining and classification in general, and the techniques will therefore be reusable in other contexts. The final step is to cluster the reviews to determine if there is some unseen structure of interest. This is done using a combination of k-means clustering and principal component analysis. Visualising the results allows a user to see if there are patterns of interest.

Chapter 6 titled "Sentiment Classification and Visualization of Product Review Data" is about using text data gathered from website consumer reviews of products to build a model that can predict sentiment. The difficult problem of obtaining training data is addressed by using the star ratings generally given to products as a proxy for whether the product is good or bad. The motivation for this is to allow companies to assess how well particular products are being received in the market. The chapter aims to give worked examples with a focus on illustrating the end-to-end process rather than the specific accuracy of the techniques tried. Having said that, however, accuracies in excess of 80 percent are achieved for certain product categories. The chapter makes extensive use of Python with the NumPy, NLTK, and Scipy packages, and includes detailed worked examples. As with all data mining activities, extensive data preparation is required, and the chapter illustrates the important steps required. These include, importing correctly from webpages to ensure only valid text is used, tokenizing to find words used in unigrams or bigrams, removal of stop words and punctuation, and stemming and changing emoticons to text form. The chapter then illustrates production of classification models to determine if the extracted features can predict the sentiment expressed from the star rating. The classification models produce interesting results, but to go further and understand what contributes to the positive and negative sentiment, the chapter also gives examples using the open-source Many Eyes tool to show different visualisations and perspectives on the data. This would be valuable for product vendors wanting to gain insight into the reviews of their products.

Chapter 7 "Mining Search Logs for Usage Patterns" is about mining transaction logs containing information about the details of searches users have performed and shows how unsupervised clustering can be performed to identify different types of user. The insights could help to drive services and applications of the future. Given the assumption that what a user searches for is a good indication of his or her intent, the chapter draws together some of the important contributions in this area and proceeds with an example process to show this working in a real context. The specific data that are processed are search transaction data from AOL, and the starting point is to extract a small number of features of interest. These are suggested from similar works, and the first step is to process the logs to represent the data with these features. This is done using Python, and examples are given. The open-source tool Weka is then used to perform an unsupervised clustering using expectation maximization to yield a candidate "best" clustering. As with all clustering techniques and validity measures, the presented answer is not necessarily the best in terms of fit to the problem domain. However, there is value because it allows the user to focus and use intelligent reasoning to understand what the result is showing and what additional steps would be needed to improve the model. This is done in the chapter where results are considered, alternative features are considered and different processing is performed with the end result that a more convincing case is made for the final answer. On the way, the importance of visualising the results, repeating to check that the results are repeatable, and being sceptical are underlined. The particular end result is of interest, but more importantly, it is the process that has been followed that gives the result more power. Generally speaking, this chapter supports the view that a process approach that is iterative in nature is the way to achieve strong results.

Chapter 8, "Temporally Aware Online News Mining and Visualization with Python", discusses how some sources of text data such as newsfeeds or reviews can have more significance if the information is more recent. With this in mind, this chapter introduces time into text mining. The chapter contains very detailed instructions on how to crawl and scrape data from the Google news aggregation service. This is a well-structured website containing time-tagged news items. All sites are different, and the specific instructions for different sites would naturally be different; the instructions in the chapter would need to be varied for these. Detailed instructions for the Google site are given, and this, of necessity, drills into detail about the structure of HTML pages and how to navigate through them. The heavy lifting is done using the Python packages "scrapy" and "BeautifulSoup", but some details relating to use of XPath are also covered. There are many different ways to store timestamp information. This is a problem, and the chapter describes how conversion to a common format can be achieved. Visualizing results is key, and the use of the open-source SigmaJS package is described.

Chapter 9, "Text Classification Using Python", uses Python together with a number of packages to show how these can be used to classify movie reviews using different classification models. The Natural Language Toolkit (NLTK) package provides libraries to perform various processing activities such as parsing, tokenising, and stemming of text data. This is used in conjunction with the Scikit package, which provides more advanced text processing capabilities such as TF-IDF to create word vectors from movie review data. The data set contains positive and negative reviews, and supervised models are built and their performance checked using library capabilities from the Scikit learn package. Having performed an initial basic analysis, a more sophisticated approach using word n-grams is adopted to yield improvements in performance. Further improvements are seen with the removal of stop words. The general approach taken is illustrative of the normal method adopted when performing such investigations.

Part 4 contains three chapters using R. Chapter 10, titled "Sentiment Analysis of Stock Market Behavior from Twitter Using the R Tool", describes sentiment analysis of Twitter messages applied to the prediction of stock market behaviour. The chapter compares how well manually labelled data is predicted using various unsupervised lexical-based sentiment models or by using supervised machine learning techniques. The conclusion is that supervised techniques are superior, but in the absence of labelled training data, which is generally difficult to obtain, the unsupervised techniques have a part to play. The chapter uses R and well illustrates how most data mining is about cleaning and restructuring data. The chapter includes practical examples that are normally seen during text mining, including removal of numbers, removal of punctuation, stemming, forcing to lowercase, elimination of stop words, and pruning to remove frequent terms.

Chapter 11, titled "Topic Modeling", relates to topic modeling as a way to understand the essential characteristics of some text data. Mining text documents usually causes vast amounts of data to be created. When representing many documents as rows, it is not unusual to have tens of thousands of dimensions corresponding to words. When considering bigrams, the number of dimensions can rise even more significantly. Such huge data sets can present considerable challenges in terms of time to process. Clearly, there is value in anything that can reduce the number of dimensions to a significantly smaller number while retaining the essential characteristics of it so that it can be used in typical data mining activities. This chapter is about topic modeling, which is one relatively new technique that shows promise to address this issue. The basic assumption behind this technique is that documents contain a probabilistic mixture of topics, and each topic itself contains a distribution of words. The generation of a document can be conceived of as the selection of a topic from one of the available ones and from there randomly select a word. Proceed word by word until the document is complete. The reverse process, namely, finding the optimum topics based on a document, is what this chapter concerns itself with. The chapter makes extensive use of R and in particular the "topicmodels" package and has 'worked examples to allow the reader to replicate the details. As with many text mining activities, the first step is to read and preprocess the data. This involves stemming, stop word removal, removal of numbers and punctuation, and forcing to lowercase. Determination of the optimum number of topics is a trial and error process and an important consideration is the amount of pruning necessary to strike a balance between frequent and rare words. The chapter then proceeds with the detail of finding topic models, and advanced techniques are shown based on use of the topicmodels package. The determination of the optimum number of topics still requires trial and error, and visualisation approaches are shown to facilitate this.

Chapter 12 titled "Empirical Analysis of the Stack Overflow Tags Network", presents a new angle on exploring text data using network graphs where a graph in this context means the mathematical construct of vertices connected with edges. The specific text data to be explored is from Stack Overflow. This website contains questions and answers tagged with mandatory topics. The approach within the chapter is to use the mandatory topic tags as vertices on a graph and to connect these with edges to represent whether the tags appear in the same question. The more often pairs of tags appear in questions, the larger the weight of the edge between the vertices corresponding to the tags. This seemingly simple approach leads to new insights into how tags relate to one another. The chapter uses worked R examples with the igraph package and gives a good introductory overview of some important concepts in graph exploration that this package provides. These include whether the graph is globally connected, what clusters it contains, node degree as a proxy for importance, and various clustering coefficients and path lengths to show that the graph differs from random and therefore contains significant information. The chapter goes on to show how to reduce the graph while trying to retain interesting information and using certain node importance measures such as betweenness and closeness to give insights into tags. The interesting problem of community detection is also illustrated. Methods to visualise the data are also shown since these, too, can give new insights. The aim of the chapter is to expose the reader to the whole area of graphs and to give ideas for their use in other domains. The worked examples using Stack Overflow data serve as an easy-to-understand domain to make the explanations easier to follow.

About the Editors

Markus Hofmann

Dr. Markus Hofmann is currently a lecturer at the Institute of Technology Blanchardstown, Ireland, where he focuses on the areas of data mining, text mining, data exploration and visualisation, and business intelligence. He holds a PhD from Trinity College Dublin, an MSc in Computing (Information Technology for Strategic Management) from the Dublin Institute of Technology, and a BA in Information Management Systems. He has taught extensively at the undergraduate and postgraduate levels in the fields of data mining, information retrieval, text/web mining, data mining applications, data preprocessing and exploration, and databases. Dr. Hofmann has published widely at national as well as international level and specialised in recent years in the areas of data mining, learning object creation, and virtual learning environments. Further, he has strong connections to the business intelligence and data mining sectors, on both academic and industry levels. Dr. Hofmann has worked as a technology expert together with 20 different organisations in recent years for companies such as Intel. Most of his involvement was on the innovation side of technology services and for products where his contributions had significant impact on the success of such projects. He is a member of the Register of Expert Panellists of the Irish Higher Education and Training Awards council, external examiner to two other third-level institutes, and a specialist in undergraduate and postgraduate course development. He has been an internal and external examiner of postgraduate thesis submissions. He also has been a local and technical chair of national and international conferences.

Andrew Chisholm

Andrew Chisholm holds an MA in Physics from Oxford University and over a long career has been a software developer, systems integrator, project manager, solution architect, customer-facing presales consultant, and strategic consultant. Most recently, he has been a product manager creating profitable test and measurement solutions for communication service providers. A lifelong interest in data came to fruition with the completion of a masters degree in business intelligence and data mining from the Institute of Technology, Blanchardstown, Ireland. Since then he has become a certified RapidMiner Master (with official number 7, which pads nicely to 007) and has published papers, a book chapter relating to the practical use of RapidMiner for unsupervised clustering and has authored a book titled *Exploring Data with RapidMiner*. Recently, he has collaborated with Dr. Hofmann to create both basic and advanced RapidMiner video training content for RapidMinerResources.com. In his current role, he is now combining domain knowledge of the telecommunications industry with data science principles and practical hands-on work to help customers exploit the data produced by their solutions. He fully expects data to be where the fun will be.

List of Contributors

Editors

- **Markus Hofmann**, Institute of Technology Blanchardstown, Ireland
- **Andrew Chisholm**, Information Gain Ltd., UK

Chapter Authors

- **Nelson Areal**, Department of Management, University of Minho, Braga, Portugal
- **Patrick Buckley**, Institute of Technology, Blanchardstown, Ireland
- **Brian Carter**, IBM Analytics, Dublin, Ireland
- **Andrew Chisholm**, Information Gain Ltd., UK
- **David Colton**, IBM, Dublin, Ireland
- **Paul Clough**, Information School, University of Sheffield, UK
- **Paulo Cortez**, ALGORITMI Research Centre/Department of Information Systems, University of Minho, Guimarães, Portugal
- **Pavlina Davcheva**, Chair of Information Systems II, Institute of Information Systems, Friedrich-Alexander-University Erlangen-Nuremberg, Germany
- **Kyle Goslin**, Department of Computer Science, College of Computing Technology, Dublin, Ireland
- **Tobias Kötter**, KNIME.com, Berlin, Germany
- **Nuno Oliveira**, ALGORITMI Research Centre, University of Minho, Guimarães, Portugal
- **Alexander Piazza**, Chair of Information Systems II, Institute of Information Systems, Friedrich-Alexander-University Erlangen-Nuremberg, Germany
- **Tony Russell-Rose**, UXLabs, UK
- **John Ryan**, Blanchardstown Institute of Technology, Dublin, Ireland
- **Rosaria Silipo**, KNIME.com, Zurich, Switzerland
- **Kilian Thiel**, KNIME.com, Berlin, Germany
- **Christos Iraklis Tsatsoulis**, Nodalpoint Systems, Athens, Greece
- **Phil Winters**, KNIME.com, Zurich, Switzerland

Acknowledgments

Many people have contributed to making this book and the underlying open-source software solutions a reality. We are thankful to all of you.

We would like to thank the contributing authors of this book, who shared their experience in the chapters and who thereby enable others to have a quick and successful text mining start with open-source tools, providing successful application examples and blueprints for the readers to tackle their text mining tasks and benefit from the strength of using open and freely available tools.

Many thanks to Dr. Brian Nolan, Head of School of Informatics, Institute of Technology Blanchardstown (ITB); and Dr. Anthony Keane, Head of Department of Informatics, ITB for continuously supporting projects such as this one.

Many thanks also to our families. MH: A special thanks goes to Glenda, Killian, Darragh, Daniel, SiSi, and Judy for making my life fun; My parents, Gertrud and Karl-Heinz Hofmann, for continuously supporting my endeavours. Also a huge thank you to Hans Trautwein and Heidi Krauss for introducing me to computers and my first data related application, MultiPlan, in 1986. AC: To my parents for making it possible and to my wife for keeping it possible.

The entire team of the Taylor & Francis Group was very professional, responsive, and always helpful in guiding us through this project. Should any of you readers consider publishing a book, we can highly recommend this publisher.

Open-source projects grow strong with their community. We are thankful to all contributors, particularly, text analysis — related open source-tools and all supporters of these open-source projects. We are grateful not only for source code contributions, community support in the forum, and bug reports and fixes but also for those who spread the word with their blogs, videos, and word of mouth.

With best regards and appreciation to all contributors,

Dr. Markus Hofmann, Institute of Technology Blanchardstown, Dublin, Ireland

Andrew Chisholm, Information Gain Ltd., UK

List of Figures

List of Tables

Part I

RapidMiner

Chapter 1

RapidMiner for Text Analytic Fundamentals

John Ryan

Blanchardstown Institute of Technology, Dublin, Ireland

1.1 Introduction

The objectives of this chapter are twofold: to introduce you to the fundamentals of building a text-based repository; and to explain how you can apply text mining techniques to documents, such as speeches, in order to discover any valuable insights and patterns that may be contained within their content. This chapter is strictly focused towards a novice or start-up level; thus, techniques and processes are explained in a more detailed and visual manner than would otherwise be necessary.

1.2   Objectives

There are two objectives that should be achieved by the end of this chapter: an *education objective* and a *text analysis objective*. Every text analysis research needs to have an aim or a goal; this then informs the researcher on the types of data sources they should seek, the tools (and data cleaning) required, and the types of patterns they should be aspiring to uncover.

1.2.1   Education Objective

After this chapter has been read, you should have, at the very minimum, a foundation-level knowledge of how to build a text corpus and to be able to apply some basic, but fundamental, text analysis to that corpus and subsequently visualise the results, all using open-source software.

1.2.2   Text Analysis Task Objective

In this chapter you, the student, are applying text analysis to *American Presidential Inaugural Speeches* [1] in order to summarise and therefore compare the most frequently used words in those speeches. Thus, without having to actually read the documents or listen to them online, you (or your companions and colleagues) should be able to gain an understanding of the key terms by quickly glancing at the visual output.

1.3   Tools Used

You should be familiar with the database software MySQL (knowing a GUI-based application, such as HeidiSQL, would be beneficial), data analytics suite RapidMiner 5.3, online visualization tool Wordle (`http://www.wordle.net/`), and spreadsheets in order to accomplish the tasks within this chapter.

Note: Ensure to have the following plug-ins installed within your copy of RapidMiner: *Information Extraction*, *Text Processing*, and *Web Mining*. The *Information Extraction* extension provides operators to perform preprocessing of the text-based corpus in order to facilitate specific extractions of text-based data, such as fragments within sentences [2]. The *Text Processing* extension provides all necessary text mining operators to fully extrapolate and statistically review text-type data within a corpus (e.g., reducing words to their stem, adding stopword filtering). The *Web Mining* extension operates in tandem with the *Text Processing* extension; thus, this needs to be installed with it. The *Web Mining* extension provides operators (such as *Get Pages*) in which you can retrieve online based information, for example, by means of web scraping. All of these functions are comprehensibly explained and demonstrated in Sections 1.4.3 through 1.6.3.

Note: Create a MySQL database called *inauguralspeeches*. Do not create any tables within it, as they will be generated automatically within RapidMiner processes (detailed in Section 1.5). This database will be used to store the required speech-related attributes.

Note: Create a new local repository within RapidMiner called *Chapter*. This will be used to store the required processes detailed within this chapter; particularly referenced in Sections 1.4.3 through 1.6.3.

1.4 First Procedure: Building the Corpus

1.4.1 Overview

The overall objective is to build a corpus that can be mined in later sections. So in order to do this, you need to obtain a list of functioning URL address links that can be eventually downloaded, their content mined, analyzed, and produced in visual reports. This section concentrates on that initial step: creating a viable list of URLs that can be downloaded. In order to accomplish this task, you require each speech's unique reference tag to be gathered (labelled as *pid* in the address URL structure) and assigned to a fixed URL address to facilitate appropriate online access to each of the presidential speeches.

1.4.2 Data Source

The source to achieve the text mining objectives of this chapter (outlined in Section 1.2) is *The American Presidency Project* website [1], in particular the web page that contains indexes to all U.S. presidents inaugural speeches: `http://www.presidency.ucsb.edu/inaugurals.php`.

The initial task for any text mining analyst is to understand the corpus. This particular web page lists speeches you can read to gain an appreciation of the corpus's context. This web page also lists the approximate number of words beside each speech; this is valuable information as it allows you to gauge the quantity of the tokens in your analysis. To understand the structure of the HTML content, you should also select *View Source* for the web document. This knowledge is essential for your extraction text mining model as it informs you of the types of retrieval methods that will be necessary to collect the fragments of data required for your analysis by viewing the HTML structure of where those data items are located.

The language in all the presidential speeches is English, though the terminology and verbal construction change over the different periods. All speeches are stored, from April 30, 1789 (George Washington) up until the present day (the current American president).

1.4.3 Creating Your Repository

1.4.3.1 Download Information from the Internet

The first procedure in building your repository is solely related to gathering a list of URLs with unique identifiers (represented by the variable *pid* in the URL address) that distinctly tag each speech; these IDs allow for the identification and extraction of the speech's content in Section 1.5.

In order to achieve this, a number of RapidMiner operators are required, and are referenced in Figure 1.1.

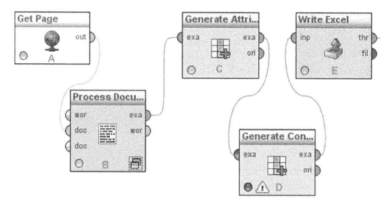

FIGURE 1.1: Creating your repository: Overall process.

> Note: The alphabetical steps that label each RapidMiner process (A, B, C...) in the relevant operator based *Figures* are outlined by the steps in the appropriate sections. They are organized in alphabetical order.

> Note: It is critical to name each of your processes in a manner that allows you to refer back to them over time and enables you to instantly recognise what they represent. Text analysis can create numerous processes due to the type of content involved and outputs required. Throughout each procedure in this chapter, a text process name will be suggested.

> Note: Save the following process within the local repository *Chapter* as *Step1-ObtainPresidentUrls*.

Step A (Figure 1.2): In order to discover what the range of unique identifiers are for the speeches, you first have to download and extract information from `http://www.presidency.ucsb.edu/inaugurals.php`, which contains these values within its HTML content code. The *Get Page* operator is used to retrieve these values, whose HTML content contains the necessary identifiers that reference all the inaugural US presidential speeches, for example:

- `http://www.presidency.ucsb.edu/ws/index.php?pid=46366`

- `http://www.presidency.ucsb.edu/ws/index.php?pid=44`

In summary, *Get Page* retrieves the web page via HTTP, and produces the information as an HTML source code document. This document can then be sliced and mined for the reference numbers that you wish to retrieve; it should be noted from viewing the source code that these are in the HTML structure format of

```
<tr>
  <td nowrap class="ver12">
        <strong>Grover Cleveland - I </strong>
    </td>
  <td align="right" nowrap bgcolor="#FFFFFF" class="ver12">
  <p>
```

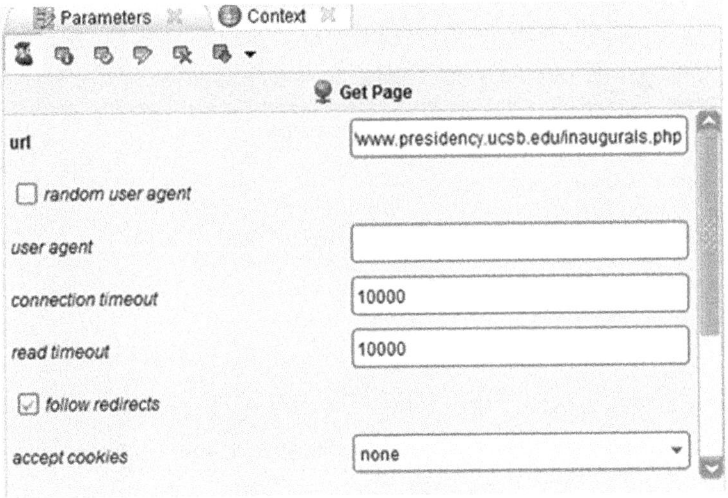

FIGURE 1.2: Creating your repository: Step A – Get Page operator.

```
<a href="http://www.presidency.ucsb.edu/ws/index.php?pid=25824">
      March 4, 1885
      </a>
      </p>
      </td>
      <td width="80" align="center" bgcolor="#FFFFFF"
            class="ver12">1686</td>
   </tr>
```

Step B (Figure 1.3): The element where you can extract the reference number is

`pid=25824"`

To achieve this extraction, you next select the *Process Documents* operator within Rapid-Miner, and select a *Cut Document* process within that operator's *Vector Creation* window (Figure 1.4).

The *Cut Document* operator slices the HTML source into segments using specific criteria that can be based on a range of query type mechanisms including *String Matching, Regular Region, Regular Expression*; for full reference of these terms, select the *query type* drop-down menu within the *Cut Document*. It should be noted that *Regular Region* and *Regular Expression* are explained further within Section 1.5.

Note: The core difference between the *Cut Document* operator and the *Extract Information* operator is essentially that the cut document mechanism slices a document, such as a speech, with a beginning and end tag, usually stipulated by regular expressions, whereas the *Extract Information* operator extracts information anywhere within a structured document. So you could often cut a document and then, within the cut operator's segment-processing window, extract information from that sliced portion.

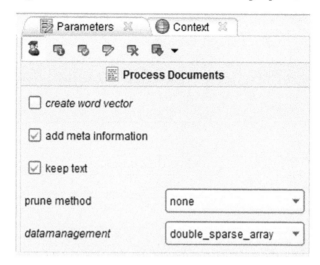

FIGURE 1.3: Creating your repository: Step B.

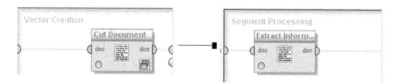

FIGURE 1.4: Creating your repository: Step B – vector window.

Note regarding *query type* within both *Cut Document* and *Extract Information* operators:

- *String Matching*: Specifies a beginning and ending for a string search and extracts anything that is between those two parameters.

- *Regular Region*: This query type is essentially a user-friendly way of adding 2 regular expressions to stipulate a beginning tag, and an end tag in order to retrieve what is between those two parameters.

- *Regular Expression*: These are expressions used to match a group and extract appropriate information. They require detailed set-up and knowledge of various command words and symbol functions. They tend to be more flexible than other query types.

For this example, *String Matching* is used as it is deemed the most efficient, where the query expression states to parse the text string from "*http://www.presidency. ucsb.edu/ws/index.php?pid*" to "*>*" (Figure 1.5). This means that for *http: //www.presidency.ucsb.edu/ws/index.php?pid=25824*"¿, the segmented source code would be sliced into fragments of reference numericals, for example *=25824*.

The next process is to extract those numeric values using an *Extract Information* process that is nested within the *Cut Document* operator's *Segment Processing* window, previously outlined in Figure 1.4. This operator extracts the required information from the structured content for each reference number from all the inaugural speeches. Using *String Matching* again, an attribute, labelled *URL* is created with a query expression stating, extract values from between = and " (Figure 1.6). Thus, the value *25824* is retrieved from the source text.

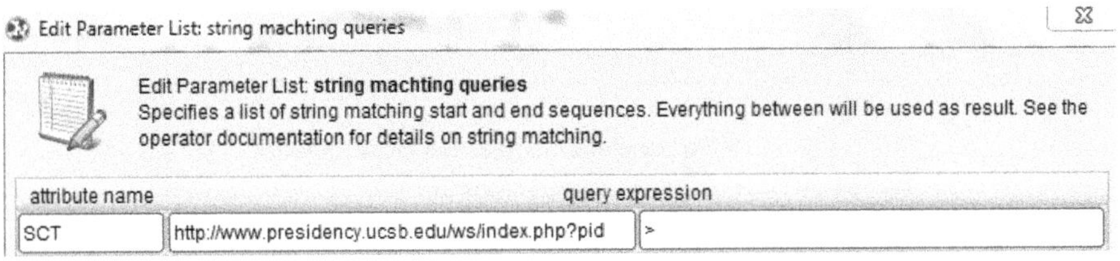

FIGURE 1.5: Creating your repository: Step B – Cut Document operator.

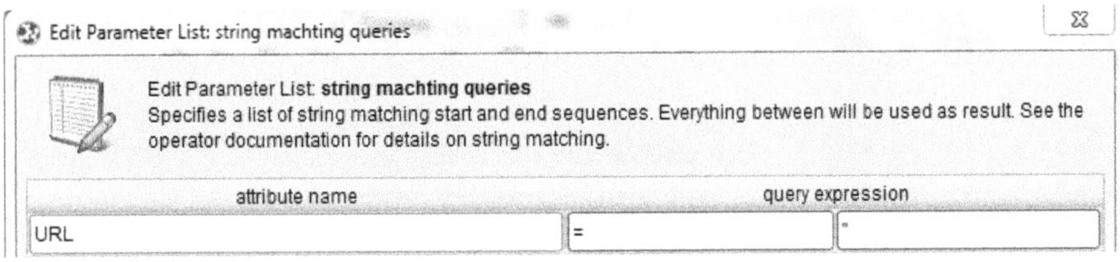

FIGURE 1.6: Creating your repository: Step B – Extract Information operator.

Step C (Figure 1.7): The next step is to create an attribute that contains the address link for each speech in which you wish to crawl and analyze. Select the *Generate Attributes* operator within RapidMiner and label it as in Figure 1.8. The content of the attribute should be *http://www.presidency.ucsb.edu/ws/index.php?pid*. The attribute should be titled *LINK* (Figure 1.8).

Step D (Figure 1.9): You now want to join the extracted reference number contained within *URL* with the HTTP link *LINK* to create a full URL address for each speech and store this list within a spreadsheet. The *Generate Concatenation* operator achieves this requirement by joining these two attributes *LINK* and *URL*, with an = sign, as can be referenced from the following output example: *http://www.presidency.ucsb.edu/ ws/index.php?pid=25824*.

Step E (Figure 1.10): Finally, the *Write Excel* operator allows you to store the generated speech address URLs within a spreadsheet; it should be noted that you should ensure that the file format is XLS.

Ultimately you should have a spreadsheet report, saved as *getlist.xls*, that resembles Table 1.1, Table 1.2, and Table 1.3.

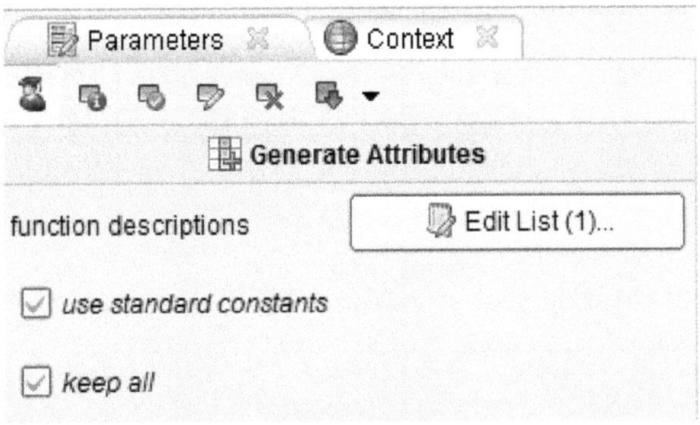

FIGURE 1.7: Creating your repository: Step C – create attributes.

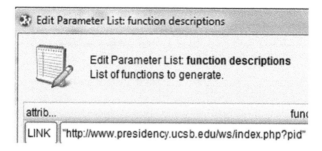

FIGURE 1.8: Creating your repository: Step C – attribute name.

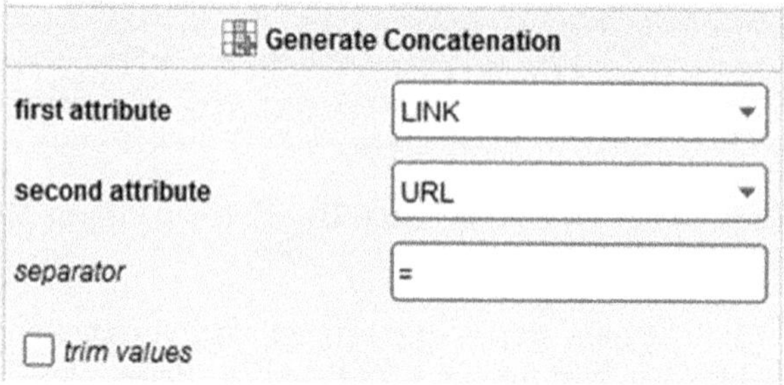

FIGURE 1.9: Creating your repository: Step D.

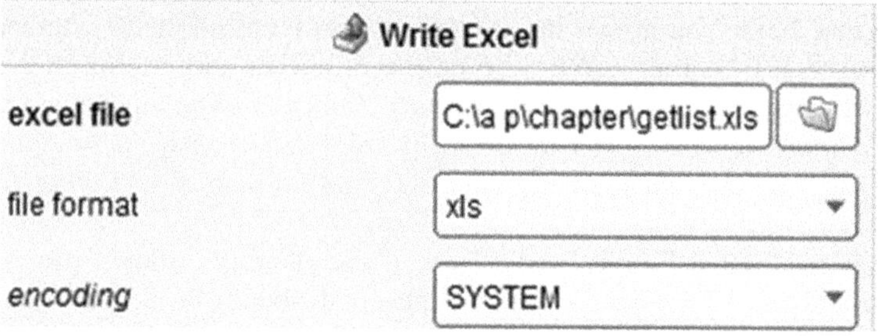

FIGURE 1.10: Creating your repository: Step E – Write Excel operator.

TABLE 1.1: Creating your repository: Step E – report snapshot I.

text	URL	Response-Code	Response-Message	Content-Type
=25800"	25800	200	OK	text/HTML

TABLE 1.2: Creating your repository: Step E – report snapshot II.

Content-Length	Date	Last-Modified	Expires
	2014-03-31 14:33:25		

TABLE 1.3: Creating your repository: Step E – report snapshot III.

query_key	LINK	LINK=URL
SCT	http://www.presidency. ucsb.edu/ws/index.php? pid	http://www.presidency. ucsb.edu/ws/index.php? pid=25800

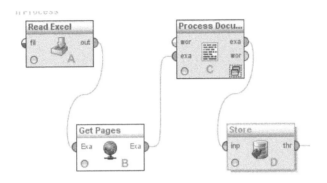

FIGURE 1.11: Build a token repository: Process I.

1.5 Second Procedure: Build a Token Repository

1.5.1 Overview

The main requirement of this section is to collect each speech's core relevant details, extracting key information for new attributes such as the president's name, the speech's date, and the content of the speech itself. This extracted information is then stored within a database repository once successfully retrieved.

The required RapidMiner processes are referenced in Figure 1.11.

1.5.2 Retrieving and Extracting Text Information

Note: Save the following process within the local repository *Chapter* as *Step2-RetrieveallSpeeches*

Step A (Figure 1.12): Now that the spreadsheet *getlist.xls* is created and stored from Section 1.4.3, you can actively import and mine the HTML structure of the inaugural speeches. The first process is to access the spreadsheet using the *Read Excel* operator. Click on the *Import Configuration Wizard* button as displayed in Figure 1.12. Select your file *getlist.xls* and click the [Next] button. There are four steps within this process; press [Next] until you get to the fourth step and click [Finish].

Step B (Figure 1.13): So now that you have a connection to the spreadsheet containing the URLs, you use the *Get Pages* operator to retrieve the speeches using the list of speech HTML addresses. This operator should not be confused with the *Get Page* operator within Section 1.4.3, which retrieves just the one page. *Get Pages* works by examining the attribute *Link=URL* and using the data value (i.e., the Web URL links for the speeches) within this

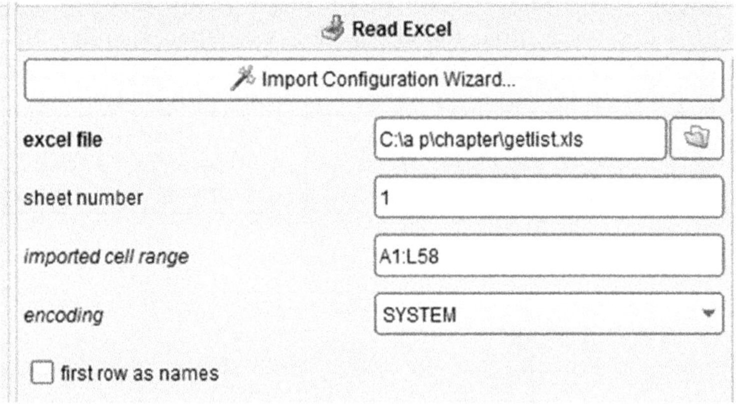

FIGURE 1.12: Build a token repository: Process I Step A – Read Excel operator.

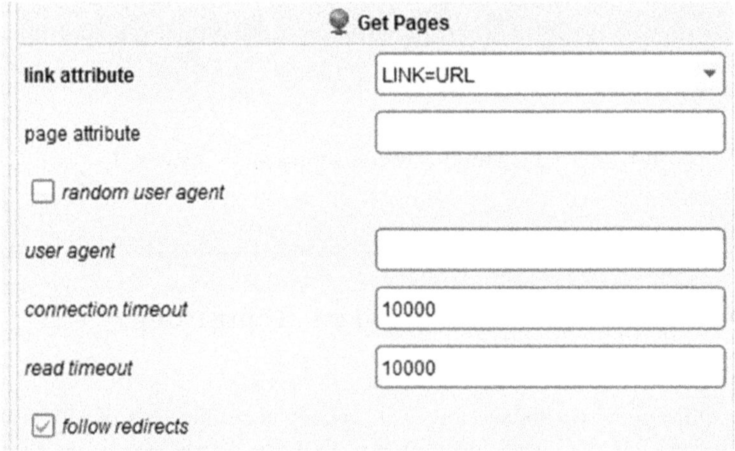

FIGURE 1.13: Build a token repository: Process I Step B – Get Pages operator.

attribute to determine the example set and thus the extraction of appropriate information. Thus, the spreadsheet data itself contained within *Link=URL* determines and therefore controls the information that is retrieved for future analysis when using the *Get Pages* operator. It functions within a loop by going through each row of the attribute *Link=URL* and selecting the next value of that attribute until there are no more available to be called. Ensure that the link attribute is *Link=URL* as in Figure 1.13.

Step C (Figure 1.14): You now need to extract the key elements of the president's name, date of speech, and the speech itself from the raw source document for each inaugural speech. Select the *Process Documents from Data* operator and have the following processes within its *Vector Creation* window (referenced in Figure 1.15).

- *Extract Information* operator (Figure 1.16): The year of the inaugural speech is within <span class="docdate" >January 20, 1981 <\span >. Use a *Regular Expression* to extract the core element by stating

```
((?<=docdate">).*?(?=<))
```

Essentially what this regular expression statement means is that you want to extract

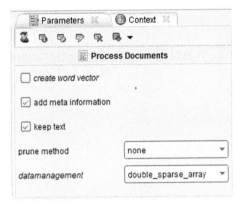

FIGURE 1.14: Build a token repository: Process I Step C – Process Documents operator.

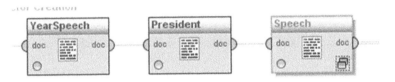

FIGURE 1.15: Build a token repository: Process I Step C – vector window.

anything that is between *docdate"* > and < (Figure 1.17). Thus, in this case that text string would be *January 20, 1981*. Label the attribute as *Inaugural Date*.

- *Extract Information* operator: The president's name is within <*title* >*Ronald Reagan: Inaugural Address* <*title* >. So similar to the previous extraction, use a regular expression (Figure 1.18)

```
((?<=title>).*?(?=:))
```

In this case take anything that is between *title* > and *:*; retrieving *Ronald Reagan* for this example. Label the attribute as *President*.

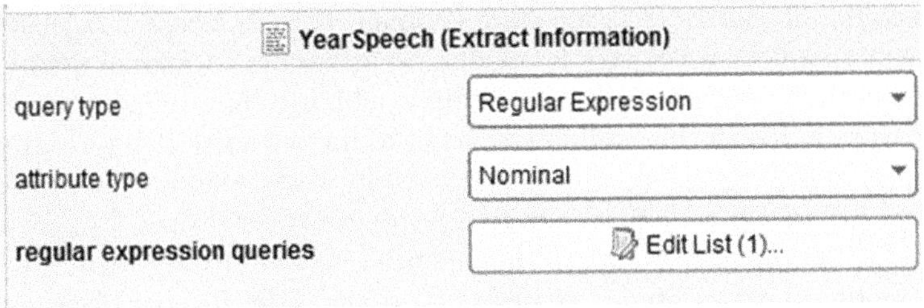

🖾 **YearSpeech (Extract Information)**	
query type	Regular Expression ▾
attribute type	Nominal ▾
regular expression queries	🖉 Edit List (1)...

FIGURE 1.16: Build a token repository: Process I Step C – Extract Information operator.

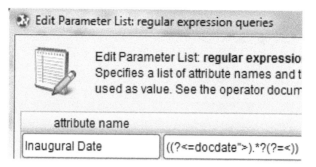

FIGURE 1.17: Build a token repository: Process I Step C – extracting date.

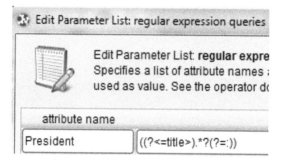

FIGURE 1.18: Build a token repository: Process I Step C – extracting president's name.

Note: *Regular Expression* contains many symbols and formats (some not very intuitive) to enable you to write an appropriate text retrieval expression. There are lots of variations of regular expressions to achieve the token extraction. In the case of the president's name, the most flexible method you could use is *Grouping* and *Capturing* the required information; in particular using a variation of this category, broadly labelled as *Lookaround* grouping, where the matching only keeps the specific token and not the criteria parameters. In this case, ?<=title >is considered as a *look behind*; it informs the system to match anything that is matching after *title*>. In this case that includes .* meaning all arbitrary characters following from the <title >tag. This matching is narrowed as a further criterion for matching is included: a *positive lookahead*. In this instance ?(?=:), matches anything that is before :, so Reagan: would match, but if it was Reag:an, then only Reag would be extracted. You could, of course write the expression as *((?<=>).*?(?=:))*, meaning group anything between >and: however this is opening your results to matching any other tag that has >and :, so the President's name attribute would also contain incorrect data. There are many more ways in which this could be written to further restrict the results outcome, such as adding \S, which means include only non-white space character data, so ((?<=title>).*?(?=:))\S. Other types of options include \w (a word letter) and [a-z] meaning show lowercase. RapidMiner includes plenty of documented help regarding regular expressions, so it is worth reading that reference material. Use the *Edit Regular Expression: query expression* window, activated from the *magnifying glass* icon in Figure 1.18 to trial your *Regular Expression*, as referenced in Figure 1.19. Within *Grouping* and *Capturing* there are four main categories, two of which are previously covered. There is also a *negative lookbehind* represented as *(?! ....)* and *negative lookahead* represented as *(?<!....)*, both of which state what to avoid or exclude. As a final note, aside from RapidMiner's help files, there is numerous reference material available online, which is worth researching, such as http://www.rexegg.com/, http://www.regular-expressions.info/, and http://www.regexlib.com/.

FIGURE 1.19: Build a token repository: Process I Step C – extracting regular expression.

- *Cut Document*: Finally the speech is extracted from a particular span class and is extracted using regular regions as referenced in Figure 1.20, with a *region delimiter* of *<span class="displaytext" >)* and *(\span >)* (Figure 1.21), meaning that all text within that span is captured. Label the attribute as *text*.

Note: When configuring the *Cut Document* operator, ensure that nodes *seg* and *doc* (within its *Segment Processing* window) are joined as in Figure 1.22.

Step D (Figure 1.23): The final step in this process is to store the information using the *Repository Access:Store* operator, in this case into a RapidMiner Repository called *Speeches*, as referenced in Figure 1.23.

Note: Save the following process within the local repository *Chapter* as *Step3-StoreMySQL*

The next requirement within this second procedure element is to create a process that writes to the MySQL database, *inaugurualspeeches*, that was referred to in Section 1.3 (as

	📊 Speech (Cut Document)	
query type	Regular Region	▼
attribute type	Nominal	▼
regular region queries	📝 Edit List (1)...	

FIGURE 1.20: Build a token repository: Process I Step C – regular region.

Edit Parameter List: regular region queries				💢

Edit Parameter List: regular region queries
Specifies a list of attribute names and their corresponding regular expressions. Two regular expressions might be specified in order to define the start and the end of a region. Everything in between the two matches will be delivered as result.

attribute name		region delimiter	
text	(<span class="displaytext">)	🔍	(/span>)	🔍

FIGURE 1.21: Build a token repository: Process I Step C – cutting speech content.

FIGURE 1.22: Build a token repository: Process I Step C – cut document nodes.

	📦 Store	
repository entry	Speeches	📁

FIGURE 1.23: Build a token repository: Process I Step D – store repository.

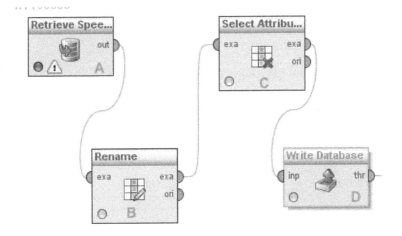

FIGURE 1.24: Build a token repository: Process II.

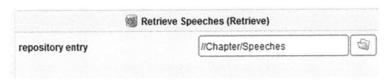

FIGURE 1.25: Build a token repository: Process II Step A – Retrieve operator.

referenced in Figure 1.24). This enables the data to be accessed, manipulated, and queried using SQL in the following sections of this chapter.

Step A (Figure 1.25): Use the *Repository Access: Retrieve* operator to access the stored speeches repository *Speeches*.

Step B (Figure 1.26): The next operator you require is the *Rename* operator, as you wish to change the names of two attributes, as in Figure 1.26 and Figure 1.27. These renaming attribute changes improve the readability of your output.

Step C (Figure 1.28): Out of all the attributes in the repository, you wish to store only three: *InauguralDate, President,* and *Speech.* In order to do this you use the *Select Attributes* operator, and select your subset as in Figure 1.29.

Step D (Figure 1.30): Finally, to store this information into your MySQL database, you need to connect to it using the *Write Database* operator. Within this, establish a *connection* configuration to the *inauguralspeeches* database that you set up in Section 1.3. Finally input a table name *tblSpeeches* and select the option *overwrite first, append then.* Once you run your process, that table will be created and populated with all available indexed speeches.

1.5.3 Summary

After this section you now have a fully populated table stored within a MySQL database that contains three attributes: *Speech, InauguralDate*, and *President.* You should understand and be aware of the differences between regular expressions, string matching, and regular regions. You should also be familiar now with the differences between *Information Extraction* and *Cut Document* operators.

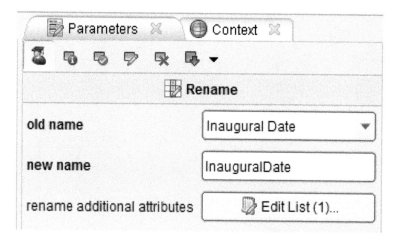

FIGURE 1.26: Build a token repository: Process II Step B – Rename operator.

FIGURE 1.27: Build a token repository: Process II Step B – additional attributes.

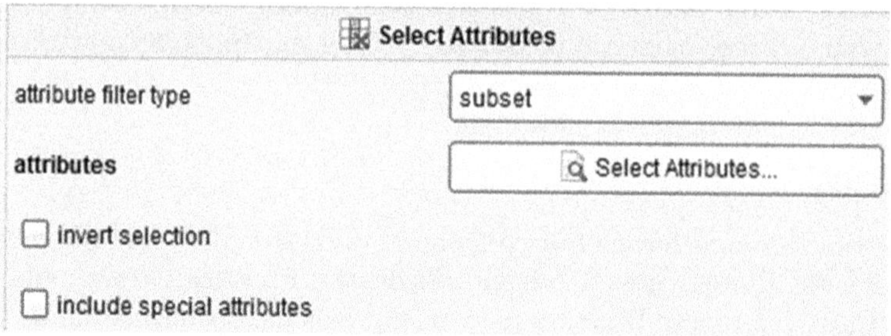

FIGURE 1.28: Build a token repository: Process II Step C – Select Attributes operator.

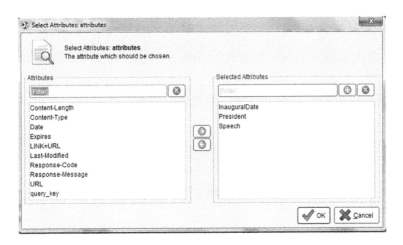

FIGURE 1.29: Build a token repository: Process II Step C – subset attributes.

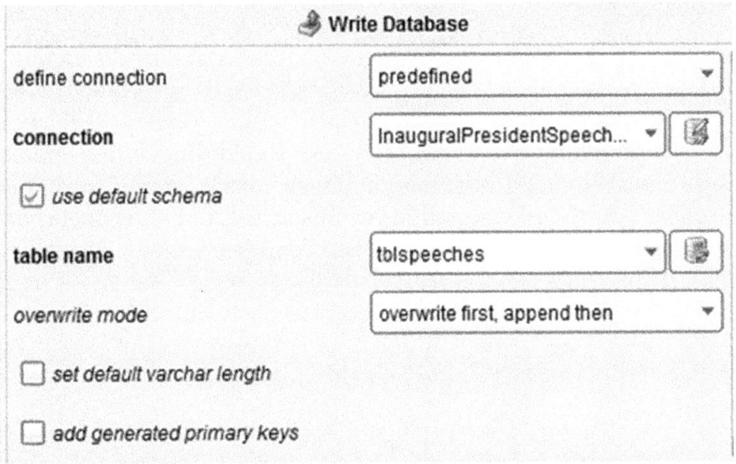

FIGURE 1.30: Build a token repository: Process II Step D – Write Database operator.

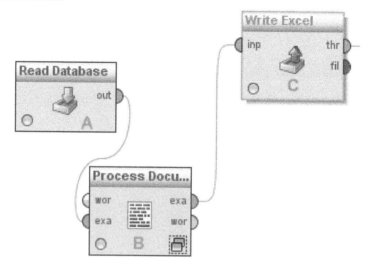

FIGURE 1.31: Analyzing the corpus: Process I.

The following section, moves away from this preparing and building corpus stage into the areas of analyzing the raw data and subsequently visualizing its output.

1.6   Third Procedure: Analyzing the Corpus

1.6.1   Overview

Now that you have gathered all your information, you want to do something with it. There are a plethora of ways in which you can search and, subsequently, analyze your content. In the case of this example, you will write a standard query to retrieve President Barack Obama's 2009 inaugural speech and then use RapidMiner's text mining processes to perform various functions to it, including applying tokens, stopword dictionaries, and n-grams. These results will then be stored in a spreadsheet and subsequently summarized into the most frequently used words which are then displayed using a visualization method called *word clouds*. Thus, with *word clouds* you wish to review the most frequent use of words; to do this in RapidMiner, you need to tokenize the document explained within this section.

The required RapidMiner processes are referenced in Figure 1.31.

1.6.2   Mining Your Repository — Frequency of Words

Note: Save the following process within the Local Repository *Chapter* as *Step4-TextAnalysis*.

Step A (Figure 1.32):   As can be referenced from Figure 1.32, you initially have to query and retrieve relevant information from *tblSpeeches* using the *Read Database* operator.

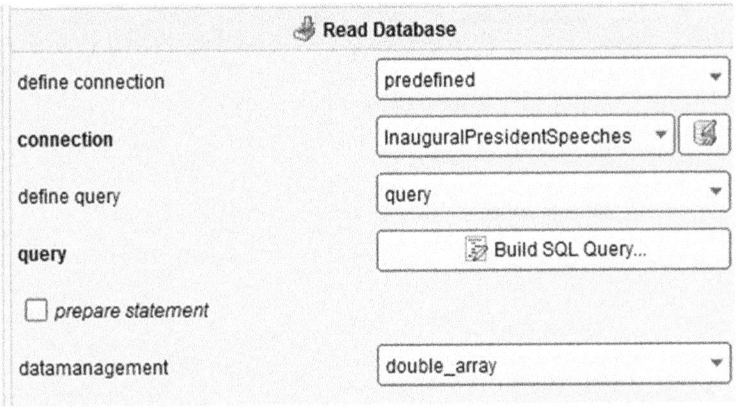

FIGURE 1.32: Analyzing the corpus: Process I Step A – Read Database operator.

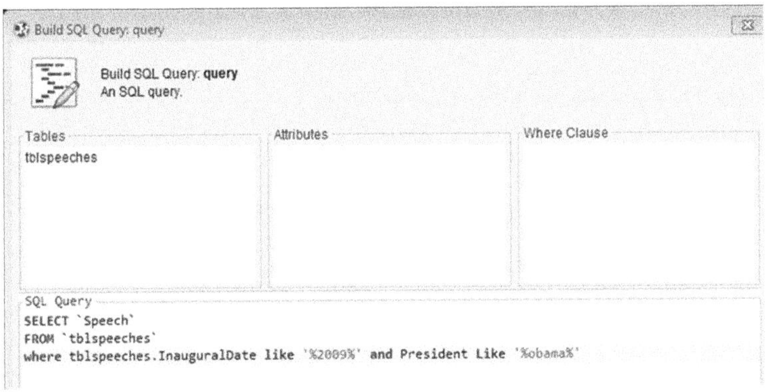

FIGURE 1.33: Analyzing the corpus: Process I Step A – SQL.

Click on the [Build SQL Query] button once you have established a connection labelled *InauguralPresidentSpeeches*.

As can be referenced from Figure 1.33, you wish to extract the speech by President Barack Obama in 2009, using the following SQL statement:

```
SELECT `Speech`
FROM `tblspeeches`
WHERE tblspeeches.InauguralDate like '%2009%' AND
President like '%Obama%'
```

Note: The attribute *Speech* that is used within this query was generated through a re-naming procedure included within the process *Step3-StoreMySQL*.

Step B (Figure 1.34): Once this query-specific statement is complete, the processed speech has to be extracted and transformed into tokens; this is achieved using the *Process Documents from Data* operator. As referenced in Figure 1.34, *Term Occurrences* is selected to ensure that the number of recurrent tokens (words) is calculated. There are multiple text token processes required within this operator's *Vector Creation* window, which can be

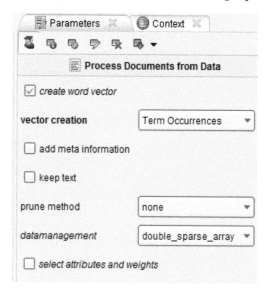

FIGURE 1.34: Analyzing the corpus: Process I Step B – term occurrences.

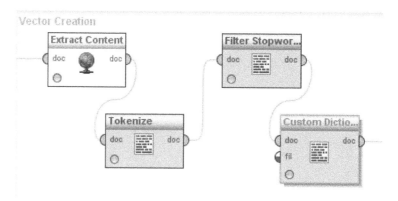

FIGURE 1.35: Analyzing the corpus: Process I Step B – vector creation window.

viewed in Figure 1.35.

> Note: *Tokenization* breaks the raw source document into individual words, these list formatted words are labelled as *Tokens* [3].

Since this data is HTML sourced, you have to remove the HTML tags such as <p >etc., so you include the *Extract Content* operator within the *Process Documents from Data* vector window (Figure 1.36). From this, you have to break the cleaned source document into individual words (also called tokens) using the *Tokenize* operator (Figure 1.37).

There are standard English stopwords such as *the* and *is* which you do not want cluttering your analysis; to automatically remove these words, you include a RapidMiner dictionary operator called *Filter Stopwords (English)* (Figure 1.38).

> Note: *Stopwords* are regular English words that add no benefit to the analysis such as *the* and *as*.

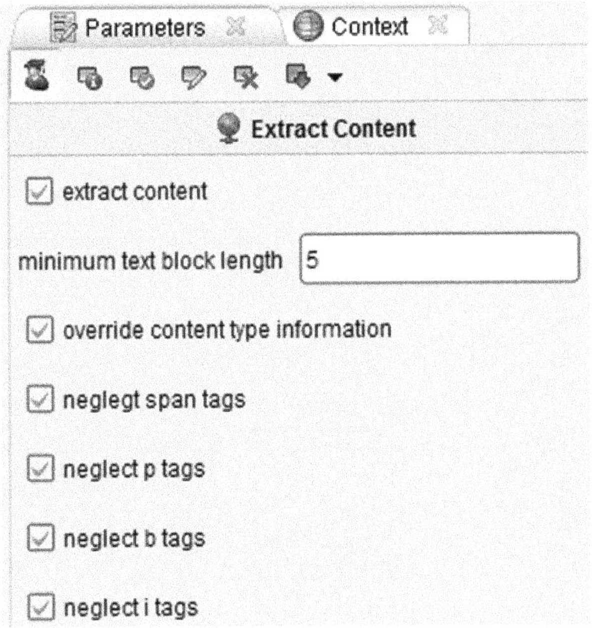

FIGURE 1.36: Analyzing the corpus: Process I Step B – Extract Content operator.

FIGURE 1.37: Analyzing the corpus: Process I Step B – Tokenize operator.

Finally, the last operator, *Filter Stopwords (Dictionary)*, is a customized list of words that you create in which to remove tokens that clutter the results and have no benefit in their inclusion. This custom dictionary is created via Windows Notepad, and is saved as a .txt file extension. In this case, the custom stopword dictionary is saved as *speechstop.txt* (a copy of which is included with the processes for this chapter) and contains the words represented within Table 1.4 (which are subsequently excluded from the analysis output).

Simply list the words one line after another that you wish to exclude. Figure 1.39 contains the required configuration information you need to properly establish a custom dictionary.

Step C (Figure 1.40): To output these results use a *Write Excel* operator to write to a spreadsheet (Figure 1.40) called *outputanalysis.xlsx*. The data is represented with the words in Row 1, and the frequency of their occurrences in Row 2. For analysis with *word clouds*, these need to be copied and transposed into a new worksheet so that the words are in Column A (labelled *Token*) and the frequency values in Column B (labelled *Amount*), as referenced in Figure 1.41.

This outputted report will be transformed into a *word cloud* within Section 1.7

FIGURE 1.38: Analyzing the corpus: Process I Step B – Filter Stopwords (English) operator.

TABLE 1.4: Speechstop.txt content.

Term
President
America
God
Bless
United
States
Nation
American
Americans

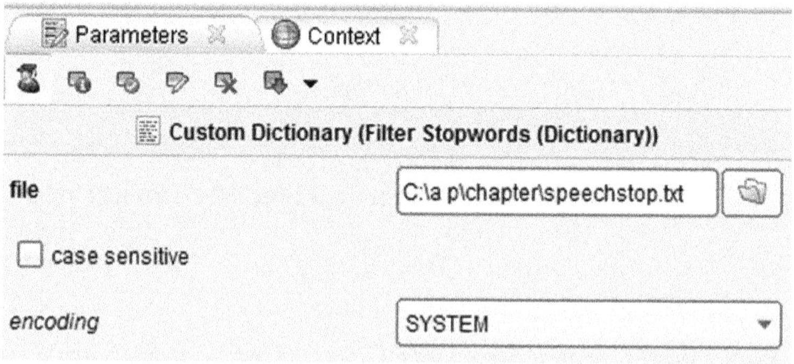

FIGURE 1.39: Analyzing the corpus: Process I Step B – custom dictionary.

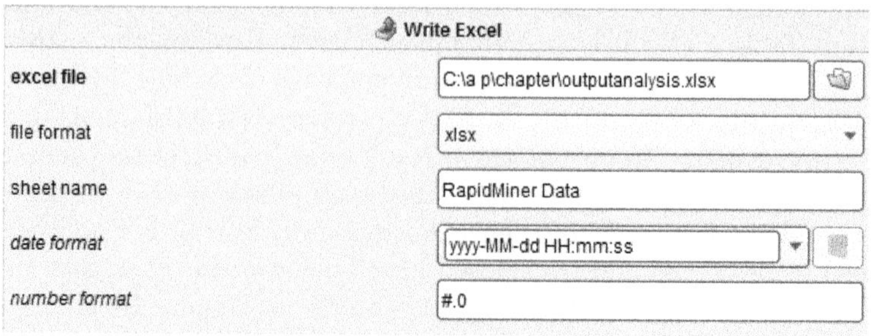

FIGURE 1.40: Analyzing the corpus: Process I Step C – Write Excel operator.

	A	B
1	Token	Amount
2	Afghanistan	1.0
3	Arlington	1.0
4	Bush	1.0
5	Capital	1.0
6	Christians	1.0
7	Concord	1.0

FIGURE 1.41: Analyzing the corpus: Process I Step C – transposed report.

1.6.3 Mining Your Repository — Frequency of N-Grams

Note: Save the following process within the Local Repository *Chapter* as *Step4-TextAnalysis-NGRAM*.

Listing words by their recurrence frequency, as in Section 1.6.2, provides basic summarization of topics by calculating the most repeated individual words (tokens) in a speech. However, this type of analysis can lack overall clarity of context. A method to try and gain this level of nuance is obtained by analyzing words that traditionally could be considered to be combined together, called *n-grams* [4]. Examples of these would be *United States* and *Founding Fathers*. In fact, combined tokens (multi words) can enhance the output's interpretation [3]. Research has also indicated that people tend to prefer viewing a combination of words instead of single terms [5].

Note: *n-gram (terms)* are used for combining words.

N-grams can be combinations of two, three, four, or more words. For this section, a two consecutive-word combination is used.

Note: You will see in literature that 2 n-gram term processes are also referred to as *bigrams* [5].

As in Section 1.6.2, Steps A and B are the same procedures. Step B contains two additional operators within the *Vector Creation* window, as referenced in Figure 1.42. These two operators are specifically related to the bigrams process. These are *Generate N-Grams (Terms)* (Figure 1.43) which has a *max length* value set at 2 indicating that you are seeking a bigrams (or two combined tokens) and *Filter Tokens (By Content)* (Figure 1.44) which has its *condition* configured as *contains* and *string* set at _. This operator thus ensures that all non-n-grams are excluded from the final output, as you only wish for words that are joined by _.

As in Step C from Section 1.6.2, write the results to a spreadsheet called *outputanalysisng.xlsx*, and transpose those results to another worksheet; the exact same process as in Section 1.6.2 (Figure 1.45). These results will be transformed into a visualization report using *word clouds* in Section 1.7.

Vector Creation
Extract Content
doc
doc
Tokenize
doc
doc
Filter Stopwor...
doc
doc
N-Gram Proceses
Filter Stopwor...
doc
fil
doc
Generate n-Gr...
doc
doc
Filter Tokens ...
doc
doc

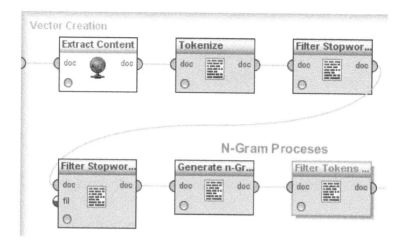

FIGURE 1.42: Analyzing the corpus: Process II Step B.

Generate n-Grams (2) (Generate n-Grams (Terms))
max length
2

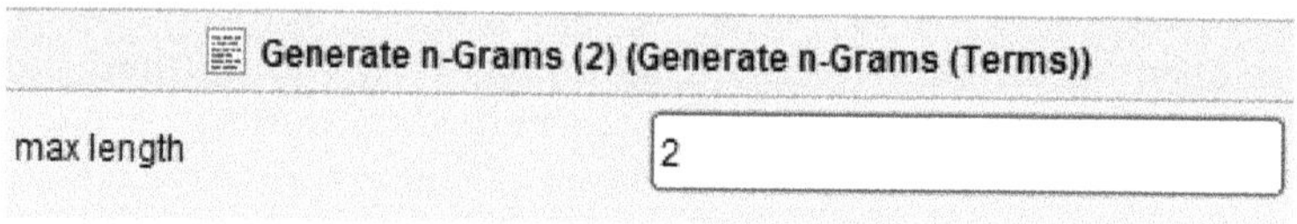

FIGURE 1.43: Analyzing the corpus: Process II Step B – Generate n-Grams (Terms) operator.

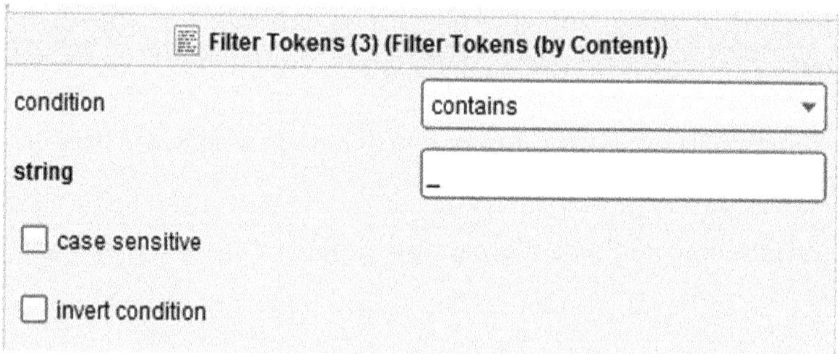

Filter Tokens (3) (Filter Tokens (by Content))
condition
contains
string
_
case sensitive
invert condition

FIGURE 1.44: Analyzing the corpus: Process II Step B – Filter Tokens (by Content) operator.

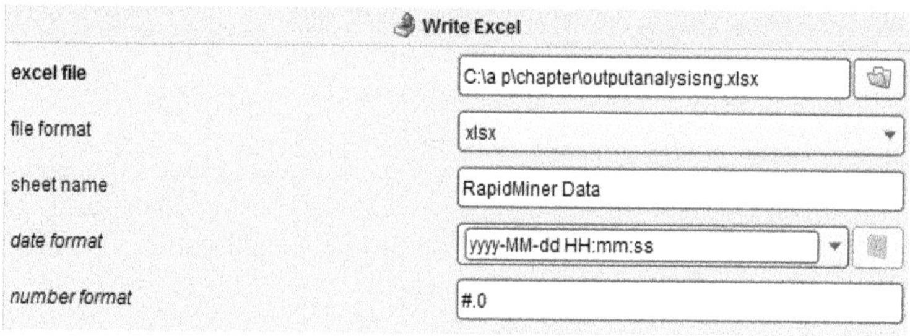

Write Excel
excel file
C:\a p\chapter\outputanalysisng.xlsx
file format
xlsx
sheet name
RapidMiner Data
date format
yyyy-MM-dd HH:mm:ss
number format
#.0

FIGURE 1.45: Analyzing the corpus: Process II Step C.

1.6.4 Summary

After this section, you should be entirely familiar with the basic concepts of retrieving information using SQL, how to remove HTML code, tokenize the speech documents, and output them to a spreadsheet. You should also be familiar with the difference in output of using n-grams and not using them. You should also experiment with different types of n-grams and also alternative customize stopword dictionaries to understand how that changes your results. In the next section, the spreadsheet reports that you generated from your analysis will be converted into *word cloud* visualization representations.

You could also vary your results by applying different operators within the *Process Documents from Data* operator including filtering by length (*Filter Tokens (by Length)* operator) checking parts of speech such as nouns or verbs (*Filter Tokens (by POS Tags)* operator), or stemming words (*Stem (Porter)* operator). However, the key point to take from this is not to show how sophisticated your text mining model is or how many operators you include; it is solely what adds benefit to your overall analysis.

Note: You also have to be extremely careful that you do not lose patterns. For example, filtering tokens out by length is useful to avoid unnecessary polluting of results; however, you may also lose key terms. For example, you may configure when analyzing a financial document to exclude three-letter words; if that is the case then you may lose words such as *IMF (International Monetary Fund)*. Thus, the key is to read your document(s), understand the content, note the key points, and only then build your model. The same applies to stemming, where you truncate a word to its core, such as *political* to *polit* and *politic* to *polit*. An over-enthusiastic stemmer could potentially lose valuable insights [5].

1.7 Fourth Procedure: Visualization

1.7.1 Overview

In the previous sections, all the analysis was based within the RapidMiner software application environment, and the reports that were produced were text-based. In this section, you want to visualise those spreadsheet reports. You could use many online environments to achieve this. For this section, you will produce your *word clouds* within the *Wordle* www.wordle.net online tool.

1.7.2 Generating word clouds

The first *word cloud* that you will produce sources its dataset from the transposed report generated within Section 1.6.2.

Note: *word clouds* are a quick reference visualization representation of a document (such as speech), displaying the most frequently used words within its content; the actual font size of the token within the cloud indicates its frequency [5].

1.7.2.1 Visualize Your Data

1. Open your transposed worksheet from within *outputanalysis.xlsx* and input the following formula into Cell C2:

| C2 | ▼ | ◦ | f_x | =REPT((A2 & " "),B2) |

	A	B	C
1	Token	Amount	String
2	**people**	7.0	people people people people people people people
3	**world**	7.0	world world world world world world world
4	**common**	6.0	common common common common common common

FIGURE 1.46: Visualization: Layout of transposed worksheet.

```
=REPT((A1 & " " ),B1)
```

The *Token* should be stored within Cell A2, and the *Number of Times* that it appears throughout the document is within Cell B2 (Figure 1.46). The formula in Cell C2 recreates the number of times that this token is mentioned in the original source document by repeating the word (*Wordle* requires this in order to generate a *word cloud* visualization of its frequency). Drag this formula down Column C until you reach the last token row.

2. Once complete, open www.wordle.net (Figure 1.47), select *Create*, and within the subsequently displayed grid box (Figure 1.48) area, copy and paste the string data stored within the C column. If limited by processing, it would be best to sort the rows by the most frequent to the least, and only select the top one hundred most frequent tokens for your *word cloud*.

3. Once this task is complete, press the *Go* button, to generate the *word cloud* represented within Figure 1.49.

4. There are many editing and filtering options for layout (Figure 1.50), colouring (Figure 1.51), limiting the number of tokens on display (Figure 1.52) and changing font types (Figure 1.53). You are free to experiment here, but remember that the benefit and aim of your analysis is not to display the best, most flashiest, graphic visualization. Your goal is always to create a clear and insightful report, nothing more. For example, Figure 1.54 represents the dataset with a limit of 20 maximum-value tokens (avoids cluttering), a horizontal layout (easy to read), and wild variance in the colouring palette (allows tokens to be distinct from one another).

5. The initial *word cloud* contains words that do not add much to the analysis. You can *right click* on a word to remove it (Figure 1.55). For this report, remove *people, common, day, world, calls, things, generation, generations, time, come, and know* and review the difference (Figure 1.56). It is clear now that *economy, peace*, and *crisis* are tokens that have prominence in the speech.

6. At the end of the *word cloud* (Figure 1.57), you will see that you can change the layout of the *word cloud* (*Randomize*), open it as a separate window (*Open In Window*), print your image (*Print*), or save it as a file on your desktop (*Save as PNG*).

Note: *REPT((A1 & " "),B1)* is an Excel formula that repeats a string fragment (your tokens) by a defined number of times (the number of occurrences RapidMiner registered its frequency). You need to concatenate the original string token with a space character in order for *Wordle* to recognise it as multiple words as opposed to a single word term, so *hope hope* instead of *hopehope*.

Wordle™ Home   Create   Credits   News   Forum   FAQ   Advanced

Wordle is a toy for generating "word clouds" from text that you provide. The clouds give greater prominence to words that appear more frequently in the source text. You can tweak your clouds with different fonts, layouts, and color schemes. The images you create with Wordle are yours to use however you like. You can print them out, or save them to your own desktop to use as you wish.

Create your own.

View some examples created by others...

   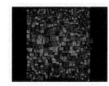

English notebook cover
by Ace Acedemic!
5 years, 9 months ago

Period G
by Meredith
5 years, 9 months ago

US Constitution
by Jonathan
5 years, 6 months ago

Most Common Crossword Answers
by Jonathan
6 years, 6 months ago

© 2013 Jonathan Feinberg   Terms of Use

build #1455

FIGURE 1.47: Visualization: Wordle menu.

Note: With Wordle *word cloud* generation you need to have Java-enabled. Please note that Google Chrome browsers stopped supporting NPAPI which is required to run Java applets.

You can apply the same steps to the report (*outputanalysisng.xlsx*) that you generated from Section 1.6.3, to understand the differences between counting individual tokens and calculating multi words that are combined in their context (Figure 1.58). Instead of the formula used for the single tokens, use the following instead, as *Wordle* does not recognise the underscore marker and thus would separate the words as if they were independent tokens instead of combined tokens:

```
=SUBSTITUTE(REPT((A2 & " " ),B2), "_", ":")
```

Figure 1.59 is limited to 40 tokens, and is further filtered in Figure 1.60 with removal of *I* related tokens such as *I_say*. From both of the visual representations you can understand that there is a focus on health-related terminology.

Note: *SUBSTITUTE(REPT((A2 & " "),B2), "_", ":")* is an Excel formula that repeats a string fragment (your tokens) by a defined number of times (the number of times Rapid-Miner registered its frequency) and then substitutes (replaces) the underscore _ with :. This is required as *Wordle* does not recognise _ and thus treats words (tokens) such as *Founding_Fathers* as *Founding* and *Fathers*. With :, *Wordle* recognises the bigram as *Founding:Fathers*.

FIGURE 1.48: Visualization: Copy and paste data into create section.

FIGURE 1.49: Visualization: Speech represented as a word cloud.

FIGURE 1.50: Visualization: Word cloud layout.

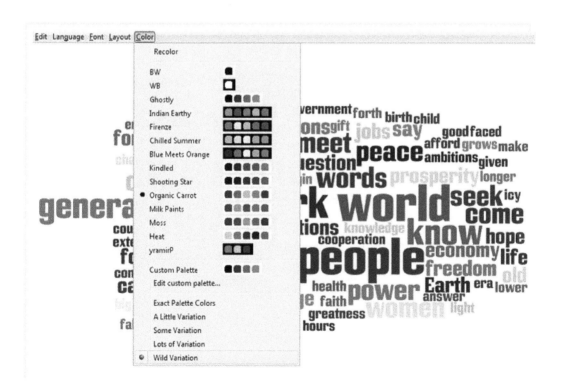

FIGURE 1.51: Visualization: Word cloud colour.

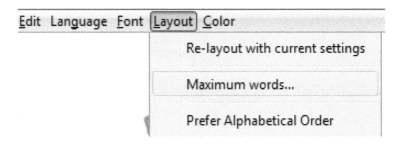

FIGURE 1.52: Visualization: Word cloud token limit.

FIGURE 1.53: Visualization: Word cloud font types.

FIGURE 1.54: Visualization: Word cloud remove tokens (filtered to 20 tokens).

FIGURE 1.55: Visualization: Word cloud filter option (remove token).

FIGURE 1.56: Visualization: Word cloud filtered (specific tokens removed).

FIGURE 1.57: Visualization: Word cloud options (print, save, new window, randomize).

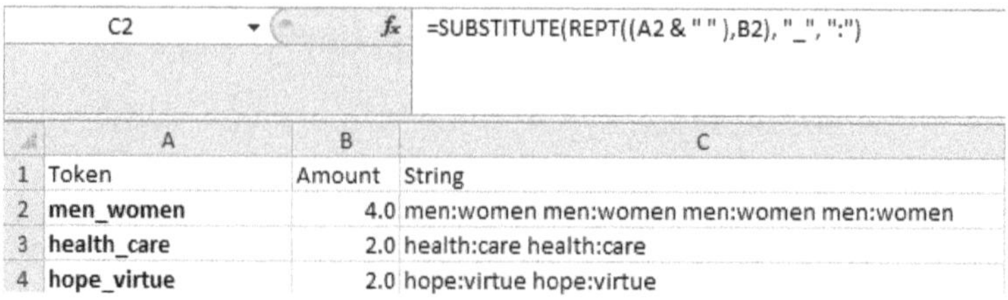

C2		f_x =SUBSTITUTE(REPT((A2 & " "),B2), "_", ":")	
	A	B	C
1	Token	Amount	String
2	men_women	4.0	men:women men:women men:women men:women
3	health_care	2.0	health:care health:care
4	hope_virtue	2.0	hope:virtue hope:virtue

FIGURE 1.58: Visualization: Layout of transposed bigram worksheet.

FIGURE 1.59: Visualization: Word cloud bigrams.

FIGURE 1.60: Visualization: Word cloud bigrams filtered (removal of tokens).

1.7.3 Summary

Within this section you created visualization reports of the worksheets produced within Section 1.6. You will be aware of how to upload a data set, generate a *word cloud*, exclude tokens and change the layout of your imagery.

1.8 Conclusion

This chapter has covered the basic tools that you require to start gathering text sources and exploring their content using software such as RapidMiner Version 5.3 and online visualization environments such as *Wordle*. You should experiment with checking for parts of speech and different visualizations. You should also do further reading around the whole topic area; http://scholar.google.com/ is a notable resource for text mining research papers. Mastering the core techniques outlined in this chapter should enable you to build upon and enhance your expertise, knowledge and skills by adding to this base using different corpus, experimenting with other text mining methods and RapidMiner operators.

Bibliography

[1] G Peters. The American Presidency Project [online] http://www.presidency.ucsb.edu/ inaugurals.php. Last Accessed: October 2015.

[2] F Jungermann. Information extraction with rapidminer. In *Proceedings of the GSCL Symposium Sprachtechnologie und eHumanities*, pages 50–61. Citeseer, 2009.

[3] S.M. Weiss, N. Indurkhya, and T. Zhang. *Fundamentals of predictive text mining*, volume 41. Springer, 2010.

[4] RapidMiner 5.3 Software. Text sourced within the Help Module: Generate n-Grams (Terms) operator [online] http://rapid-i.com/wiki/index.php?title=text:generate_n-grams_(terms)&oldid=2554. Last Accessed: October 2015.

[5] G de Hollander and M Marx. Summarization of meetings using word clouds. In *Computer Science and Software Engineering (CSSE), 2011 CSI International Symposium on*, pages 54–61. IEEE, 2011.

Chapter 2

Empirical Zipf-Mandelbrot Variation for Sequential Windows within Documents

Andrew Chisholm

Information Gain Ltd., UK

2.1 Introduction

Word rank–frequency distributions are often used as input to various authorship attribution investigations. This chapter uses advanced RapidMiner processes to fit the Zipf-Mandelbrot distribution to sequential fixed-size windows within a single document to create a summary of observed fluctuations for an author. These are compared with random samples of the same size from the same document. Different works by the same author as well as different authors are assessed to determine if there is a consistent pattern for individual authors. Some initial evidence of a consistent variation for different works by the same author is observed.

The study of word rank–frequency distributions (hereafter referred to as rank–frequency distributions) within documents (see [1] for an extensive and detailed overview) has found applications in understanding the differences between texts to determine authorship (see [2] and [3]). The assumption behind this is that authors have unique styles that can be revealed by the analysis of these distributions. The distributions are observed to follow power law like behaviour and various empirical distributions, such as Zipf's law, can be fitted to the data. The act of fitting to a distribution generates numerical measures that summarise the fit and these are assumed to relate to stylistic features.

It is observed that as more and more text is written, new unique words continue to be created. The rate of creation tends to zero as the text increases, but it never reaches it. A sample of an author's entire work, such as a book, will contain words with a certain frequency. The same words from a larger sample will appear less frequently by virtue of the new unique words in the larger sample. This is counter to the usual rule of statistics that a larger sample gives more accuracy, and it means that comparisons between samples of different sizes have to be treated with care (see [1] for extensive detail).

It is also observed that by taking samples of a specific size within a fixed corpus there is considerable variation in the sampled word frequencies [1]. This variation is more than can be explained by random chance alone and points to a style variation imposed by the author as part of the creative process. It is an interesting question to ask whether the variation itself is different for different authors but is preserved between different books written by the same author.

As a first step to answering this question, this chapter illustrates this variation for sequential fixed-size windows within a document and fits the Zipf-Mandelbrot distribution to each as a way of summarizing the differences. Comparison is also made to random samples of the same size to illustrate that the sequential windows vary from a random distribution. By observing how the differences vary for different authors, some evidence is seen that authors have a variation of style that is different from other authors but which is preserved for different works by the same author.

The chapter makes extensive use of RapidMiner version 6.1 with sufficient detail to allow the processes to be reused by others.

2.2 Structure of This Chapter

The rest of this chapter is structured as follows. Related works and various aspects of rank–frequency distributions are considered in Section 2.3 and Section 2.4. RapidMiner processes are described in Section 2.5. These processes implement various aspects of the overall process to generate rank–frequency distributions and fit Zipf-Mandelbrot distributions to the data. Section 2.6 describes the results, Section 2.7 provides discussion, and Section 2.8 summarises.

2.3 Rank–Frequency Distributions

A rank–frequency distribution is constructed by identifying each word in a document and counting the number of times it occurs. The resulting list of unique words is sorted with the most common word being given the rank of one, the second the rank of two and so on. By normalizing the frequencies so they sum to 1, each frequency becomes a probability that the word appears in the document.

There are various empirical laws and curves that can be fitted to typical rank–frequency distributions and to the total number of words and unique words. Among the most important are Heaps' Law, Zipf's law and the Zipf-Mandelbrot distribution. These are all described in the following sections.

It is important to state the definition of what defines a word to ensure repeatability so that the same words are used for fairer comparisons between different documents. Throughout this chapter, words are defined as sequences of one or more letters separated by non letters. All words are converted to lowercase, and no filtering to remove any tokens is performed.

2.3.1 Heaps' Law

Heaps' law [4] is an empirical law that relates the number of unique words in a document to the count of all the words with the following formula:

$$M = KN^{\alpha} \qquad (2.1)$$

where M is the number of unique words, K is a constant generally between 10 and 100, N is the total number of words in the document, and α is a constant generally between 0.4 and 0.6.

The formula for this empirical law matches the observation that, as a document increases in size, the number of unique words increases. This means the ever increasing number of unique words must reduce the probability of preexisting words which is what is observed in real texts.

2.3.2 Zipf's Law

The empirical law described in 1932 by G.K. Zipf ([5], [6]) applies to rank–frequency distributions and states that the rank of a word multiplied by its frequency is a constant. For example, in a document containing 1,000 words, of which 50 are the most common word (usually "the" in English), the law predicts that the next most common word should appear 25 times and the third most common 17 times. The rule is that the frequency multiplied by the rank is a constant, so in this case $50 \times 1 = 25 \times 2 = 17 \times 3$. Indeed, Heaps' law and Zipf's law express the same conclusion, and it is possible to relate them [7], [8]. The law is empirical and in practice, all texts exhibit divergences from it.

Mathematically, the law can be expressed as follows:

$$f_r r = C \qquad (2.2)$$

where the frequency of the word of rank r is f_r, and C is a constant.

This can be recast into the following formula (for details see [9]):

$$p_r = [rH(N, \alpha)]^{-1} \tag{2.3}$$

where p_r is the probability of the word of rank r, r is the rank of the word, $H(N, \alpha)$ is the harmonic number, N is the total number of unique words, and α is the order of the exponent. For Zipf's law this exponent is set to 1. The harmonic number of order N, α is shown as follows:

$$H(N, \alpha) = \sum_{i=1}^{N} r^{-\alpha} \tag{2.4}$$

In the limit for large N the harmonic number in the Zipf case simplifies to

$$H(N) \approx ln(N) + \gamma \tag{2.5}$$

where γ is the Euler-Mascheroni constant with approximate value 0.57721. The value of $\exp^\gamma \approx 1.78$, allows Equation 2.3 to become Equation 2.6 for large N:

$$p_r \approx [rln(1.78N)]^{-1} \tag{2.6}$$

This shows an important point that the probability of a given ranked word depends on the total number of words in a document and the larger the document the lower the probability of finding that word. This has the consequence that comparing documents of different sizes must lead to different values for the probabilities of words.

For example, if a 5,000-word sample is taken from a larger book, Heaps' law with parameter values of $\alpha = 0.5$ and $K = 20$ in Equation 2.1 would give an estimate for the number of unique words as 1,414. Using this number with Zipf's law from Equation 2.6 would give an estimate that the most common word would appear with a probability of 0.128. Increasing the document to be 100,000 words reduces the probability for the most common word to 0.107. Taking this further, if the author has written 100 books each 100,000 words in length the total corpus for that author would consist of 10,000,000 words and the estimated probability for the most common word would reduce to 0.0860.

Aside from the variation that arises from different sample sizes, the law itself never fits precisely to real data. These variations can be exploited to reveal differences between authors, and there exist many authorship attribution techniques that partially use rank or frequency data (see [10], [11], [3], [12], and [13]).

The law is extremely simple, and various attempts have been made to create a better fit.

2.3.3   Zipf-Mandelbrot

Mandelbrot proposed a modification to Zipf's law [14] to enable it to fit more closely rank–frequency distributions, particularly at both ends of the distribution. The mathematical equation is given in Equation 2.7.

$$p_r = C(r + A)^{-B} \tag{2.7}$$

where p_r is the probability of a word of rank r, and A, B, C are constants that must be fitted to the data. The equation is more complex than Zipf's law, and this affords the possibility that fitting it to different distributions will yield different values for the constants that could reveal something about the style being adopted by the author.

Additional discussion about this will be given towards the end of Section 2.4 after consideration of sampling from a fixed corpus in general.

2.4 Sampling

As stated in the introduction, a sliding window is to be moved through a document. When sampling randomly from a population, it is possible to place statistical limits on the characteristics of the sample and in this way, the assumption of randomness can be tested.

As a worked example, in a document containing 100,000 words with the most common word appearing with a probability of 0.1 then a truly random sample of 5,000 words should still contain the same proportion of this word. With an observed sample probability and sample size it is possible to assess how well the assumption holds up against the population probability if this is already known.

Equation 2.8 is the approximate standard error of the sample proportion

$$standard\_error \approx \sqrt{(P(1-P)/n)} \qquad (2.8)$$

where P is the known population probability, and n is the sample size. For the worked example, if 5,000 words are sampled and P is known to be 0.1, Equation 2.8 gives 0.00424. If the observed sample probability is 0.095 this means the observed probability is $(0.095 - 0.1)/0.00424 = -1.18$ standard deviations from the expected value. Statistically, given the assumption of randomness, this z-score means the observation is likely to be observed. If the observed probability was 0.05 the observation would have a z-score of -11.8 and would therefore be extremely unlikely to be observed.

An assessment of the sample probability of words in a sliding window through a document gives the possibility to assess whether the words written by an author are random or have been arranged to meet some unconcious style. As an illustration, Table 2.1 contains data from the novel *Moby Dick* by Herman Melville [15].

TABLE 2.1: Variation of z-score for the most common words in sequential 5,000-word windows for the novel *Moby Dick*.

Window	the	of	and	a
0-4,999	−0.707	3.028	−0.102	3.159
5,000-9,999	−1.617	−0.192	0.651	7.431
10,000-14,999	−5.489	−2.833	2.157	6.072
15,000-19,999	−0.422	1.129	−0.270	3.936
20,000-24,999	−2.642	−2.338	2.408	−0.336

This table was produced by moving a 5,000-word window through the document and calculating the observed probability for words. The known probabilities for the whole document were also calculated and this allowed the standard error to be calculated using Equation 2.8. Subtracting the population mean and dividing by the sample error gives a z-score which is shown in the table. The table shows that there are some large z-scores which it would be extremely unlikely to observe from a purely random sample. Plotting all the z-scores as a histogram shows that these sequential windows exhibit significant variations for all words. For example Figure 2.1 shows this z-score variation for the word "the" within the novel *Moby Dick* [15]. This novel contains more than 210,000 words and the figure shows the observed probability for the 42 sequential windows each of 5,000 words. The results show that there is considerable variation that cannot be explained using the assumption that the words are randomly arranged within the sequential windows. Other words are also observed to have similar large variations, and it would be possible to create a summary

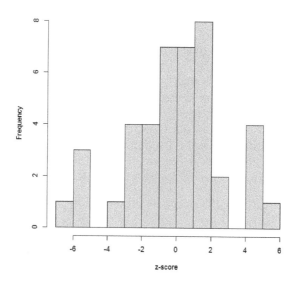

FIGURE 2.1: Observed variation for the word "the" for consecutive 5,000-word windows within the novel *Moby Dick*.

statistic that captured these. This summary could then be used as a feature vector for an author to determine if the author exhibited a variation that was unique.

Returning to the Zipf-Mandelbrot distribution from Section 2.3.3, one possibility is to use this as a way to fit the distribution to the observed probabilities and use the values of the parameters A, B, C of Equation 2.7 as a proxy for the deviation from randomness. This makes sense because the rank–frequency distribution is known from the entire book and the sample provides different probabilities. By keeping the window sizes fixed and by using probabilities from the entire book, variations relating to different sample sizes can be minimised.

One final step is to restrict to the most common words. These are typically function words that by themselves do not convey meaning and which all authors use. This affords the possibility that the approach may allow different authors to be compared. For this chapter, the most frequent 100 words are used. To be clear, this means that when a document is analysed, the most frequent 100 words are selected. When sequential or random windows are chosen, the presence of the 100 words from the main document is used to determine the rank–frequency distribution. This means that when comparing books there is a possibility that different 100 words will be chosen.

2.5   RapidMiner

This section shows the use of RapidMiner [16] to create processes for the key steps to calculate rank–frequency distributions for documents and sequential windows within the documents as well as fitting the Zipf-Mandelbrot distribution to these windows using an evolutionary or genetic algorithm approach. Three processes are provided and are described in Table 2.2; the processes are advanced and the key features are described in the referred sections. All the processes are available from the website for this book.

TABLE 2.2: RapidMiner processes and sections where they are described.

Process name	Details in Section
generateWindowedWordFrequencies	2.5.1
iterateAndExecuteZipfMandelbrotFit	2.5.2
fitZipfMandelbrot	2.5.3

2.5.1 Creating Rank–Frequency Distributions

The high-level process is shown in Figure 2.2. There are four main process sections in this, labelled A to D, and more detail for each of these is given in Figures 2.3, 2.4, 2.5, and 2.6, respectively. Table 2.3 summarises these and refers to the sections where the detail of each is given.

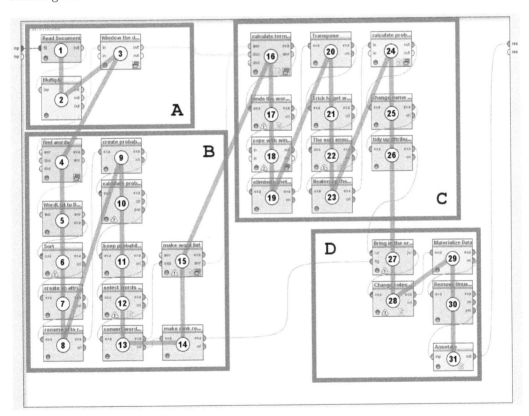

FIGURE 2.2: RapidMiner process to calculate word frequencies.

2.5.1.1 Read Document and Create Sequential Windows

This process section (A) reads the document to be processed. This is passed from the process context to the operator *Read Document*. The process context reads documents from a repository. To place documents in a repository it is necessary to use the operator *Open*

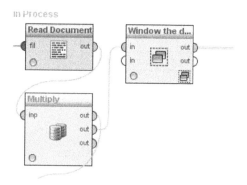

FIGURE 2.3: Process Section A within Figure 2.2.

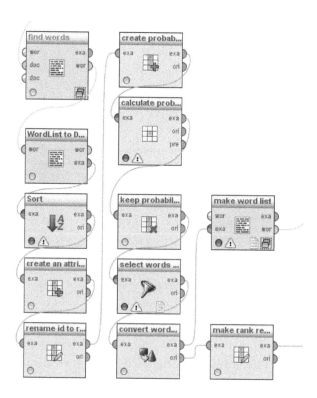

FIGURE 2.4: Process Section B within Figure 2.2.

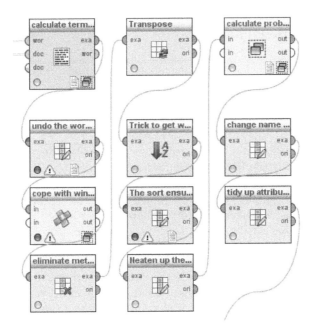

FIGURE 2.5: Process Section C within Figure 2.2.

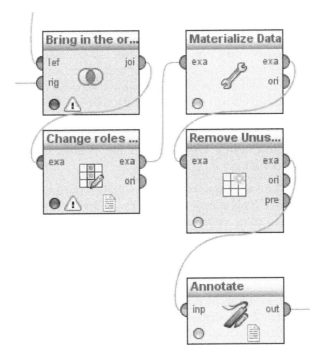

FIGURE 2.6: Process Section D within Figure 2.2.

TABLE 2.3: Process sections for RapidMiner process to calculate rank–frequency distributions.

Process Section	Description	Section
A	Read document and create sequential windows	Section 2.5.1.1
B	Calculate rank–frequency probability distribution for entire document and create word list for most common words	Section 2.5.1.2
C	Calculate rank–frequency probability distributions for windows within document	Section 2.5.1.3
D	Combine whole document and window rank–frequency probability distributions	Section 2.5.1.4

File followed by the *Store* operator. This is not shown in the process as it is straightforward to implement. The process section multiplies the document into two copies. One copy is sent to process section B and the other is sent to a *Sub-process* operator where it is split into sequential windows. The size and offset between windows is defined by the macros *windowStepSize* and *windowLength* defined in the process context (in this chapter these are both 5,000). The operator *Window Document* uses these macros to create the windows. It is important to get the input to this operator correct. To do this requires tokenizing the input document. As mentioned in Section 2.3 the document is tokenized using the *Tokenize* operator with parameter set to *non letters* and all tokens are converted to lower case. There is one work around that is needed to cater for the addition of the window meta data attribute added by the *Window Document* operator. This involves replacing any token with the value *window* with another value that does not occur in the text. Later on, within process section C, this will be reversed. It should be noted that the latest versions of RapidMiner (version 6.1 as at the time of writing: early 2015) cope better with this, but the workaround presented here will work with older versions of RapidMiner.

2.5.1.2   Create Rank–Frequency Distribution for Whole Document and Most Common Word List

This process section (B) finds all the words in the original document and makes a rank–frequency distribution from it. This is done by using the operator *Process Documents* which contains the same tokenizing rules as described in Section 2.5.1.1. The *Process Documents* operator creates a vector based on term occurrences; the count of the number of times each word appears in the document. The word list output from this operator is converted to an example set and various manipulations are performed to sort the result so the most common word is given the rank of 1. By using the *Normalize* operator set to *proportion transformation*, the counts are transformed into probabilities. The process section also outputs a word list of selected words. Section 2.4 describes using the most common words and this is controlled by the macros *firstExample* and *lastExample* defined in the process context. For this chapter these macros are set to 1 and 100, respectively. To create a word list, the process section takes the example set corresponding to these words and uses *Process Documents from Data* to create the list.

2.5.1.3 Calculate Rank–Frequency Distributions for Most Common Words within Sequential Windows

Process section C takes the windowed input document and word list of the words of interest and creates an example set containing an example for each word and an observed probability for the occurrence of the word in each of the windows within the entire document. The example set that is created contains as many examples as there are words of interest with one attribute called *word* describing the word and attributes called *window_n* where n is a number denoting the starting point for the number of characters through the document where the window starts. The process section uses some advanced techniques. Firstly, the workaround for the window meta-data attribute introduced by the *Window Document* operator is reversed. This is done by renaming the meta data attribute called *window* to be *0_window* (this is important later on when transposing) and if there is an attribute corresponding to the occurrence of the word window in the original text, this is also renamed. This is done inside a *Branch* operator because it is entirely possible that a text and the windows within it do not contain the word *window*. Secondly, the *Transpose* operator is used. This swaps rows and columns with the important point that an id attribute is created containing the original names of the attributes. By sorting this and knowing that the window attribute is called *0_window* it is possible by sorting to ensure that this is the first example of the transposed example set. This allows the operator *Rename By Example Values* to be used so the name of the attributes of the transposed example set are meaningful. Certain other renaming and manipulation operations are performed to get to the desired end result.

2.5.1.4 Combine Whole Document with Sequential Windows

The final part of this process (D) is to combine the rank–frequency distribution of the words of interest of the whole document with the sampled probabilities from each window. This is done using the *Join* operator. This process section also uses the *Remove Unused Values* operator to remove unused nominal values in the example set and in addition uses the *Materialize Data* operator. This last operator should not be needed, but there are times when it is invaluable as it seems to clear transient memory issues brought about by complex preprocessing.

2.5.2 Fitting Zipf-Mandelbrot to a Distribution: Iterate

Two RapidMiner processes are provided to calculate the optimum fit of the Zipf-Mandelbrot distribution to the observed rank–frequency measurements. The first contains various looping operations to iterate over all the sequential windows and call the second using the *Execute Process* operator. The first process is described in this section, and the second is described in Section 2.5.3.

The process to iterate over all the windows requires an input example set containing an attribute named *rank*, which must be a nonregular attribute and at least one regular attribute named *window_n* where n is a number. The location of the example set is defined in the process context. Figure 2.7 shows the top-level process. This takes the input example set, selects only those with the required names and then loops through all the attributes called *window_n* using the *Loop Attributes* operator. The inner operators of the loop perform more processing and execute the RapidMiner process to fit the Zipf-Mandelbrot distribution. The output of the loop is a collection of example sets. Each example set contains the window name and the optimum values of the parameters A, B, C for it. The collection is combined into a single example set using the *Append* operator, and the *Guess Types* operator is used to convert numbers to numeric types to make graphical plotting possible. Returning to

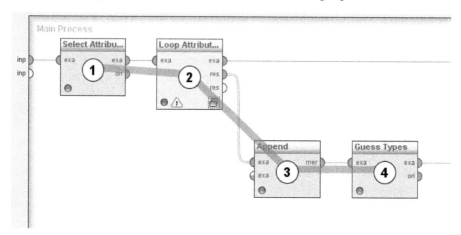

FIGURE 2.7: RapidMiner process to execute process for all attributes to fit Zipf-Mandelbrot distribution.

the inner operators of the *Loop Attribute* operator, Figure 2.8 shows these. These work

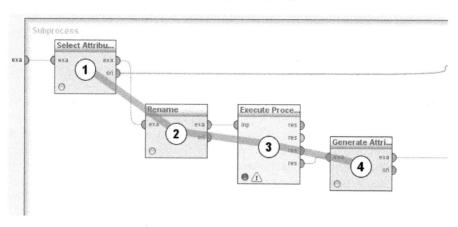

FIGURE 2.8: Detail of RapidMiner process to execute Zipf-Mandelbrot distribution fit.

as follows. The *Loop Attributes* operator provides a macro corresponding to the current attribute, which is used to select only this attribute (note the important point that the original example set must be passed to the first output of the *Loop Attributes* operator to make it work properly). The rank attribute will also be selected by virtue of it not being a regular attribute. The selected attribute is then renamed to *probability* since the process to fit to the Zipf-Mandelbrot distribution requires this and then *Execute Process* is called. The output from this is the optimum values fitted to the observed data, and an extra attribute is created corresponding to the current window.

2.5.3   Fitting Zipf-Mandelbrot to a Distribution: Fitting

The top-level process that fits a rank–frequency distribution is shown in Figure 2.9. Referring to this figure, the operators labelled 1, 2, and 3 ensure there is an example set passed to the rest of the process. The operator labelled 1 is a *Branch* operator that detects if no example set has been passed and will read from the repository in this case. This allows the whole process to be tested and used in a stand alone fashion. This is an important technique when developing and debugging processes. The operator labelled 4 contains the heart of the

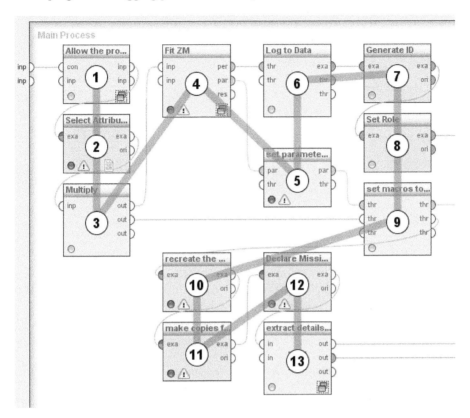

FIGURE 2.9: RapidMiner process to fit Zipf-Mandelbrot distribution.

process and is a *Loop Parameters (Evolutionary)* operator. This will be considered in more detail shortly. The output from this operator is a performance vector corresponding to the optimum parameters to fit the distribution and log entries containing the parameters and total error calculated as the looping operation proceeds. The log entries are converted to an example set using the *Log to Data* operator (the operator labelled 6 in Figure 2.9) and an id attribute is added to ensure the order in which the entries were produced can be retained. The parameter set output is used to set the parameter values of certain operators (operator 5), and various macros are then set based on these so they can be used to recreate how the parameters recreate the optimum fit (operator 9).

Returning to the *Optimize Parameters* operator, Figure 2.10 shows the configuration of the parameter settings for this operator. This shows that three parameters are defined and these correspond to the Zipf-Mandelbrot parameters from Equation 2.7. The *Optimize Parameters (Evolutionary)* operator uses a genetic algorithm approach to find the smallest error for a performance vector as these parameters are used in a function to fit to the known result. The operator repeats the fitting process with different parameter values and the genetic algorithm approach ensures an efficient convergence to a good solution. Figure 2.11 shows the inner operators within this operator. The operators numbered 1, 2, and 3 in this operator are there to receive the parameters defined by the optimizing operator itself. Closer inspection of these reveals that these are in fact *Generate Data* operators. The only reason these are used is to work around a restriction exhibited by the *Optimize Parameters*

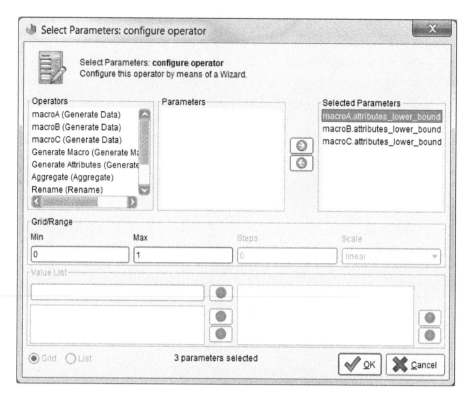

FIGURE 2.10: Configuration for *Optimize Parameters (Evolutionary)* operator.

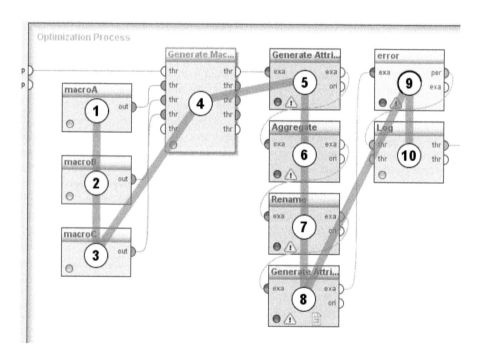

FIGURE 2.11: Details for *Optimize Parameters (Evolutionary)* operator.

(Evolutionary) operator that prevents it from setting numerical parameters directly into macros. By using an intermediate operator that is able to take a numeric parameter, numeric values can be set up and then read by a *Generate Macros* operator (labelled 4 in Figure 2.11). The *Generate Macros* operator uses the built in function *param()* to do this and sets the values of macros A, B, and C. Figure 2.12 shows the detail for this operator.

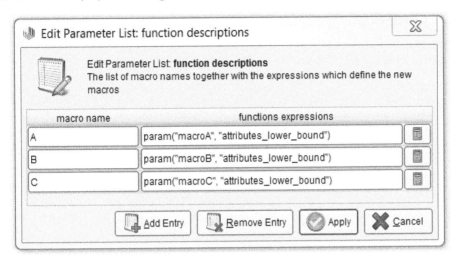

FIGURE 2.12: Details for macro-generation workaround to pass numerical parameters to Optimize Parameters operator.

Once the macros A, B, and C have been populated, they can be used with the formula in Equation 2.7 and the example set containing rank and probability values. This is operator 5 from Figure 2.11, and the parameters to this are shown in Figure 2.13. This shows the calculation of an estimated probability as well as a difference between the estimate and the known probability from the sample. The error is the absolute value of the difference, but other error calculations could be used here such as the square. Having calculated the

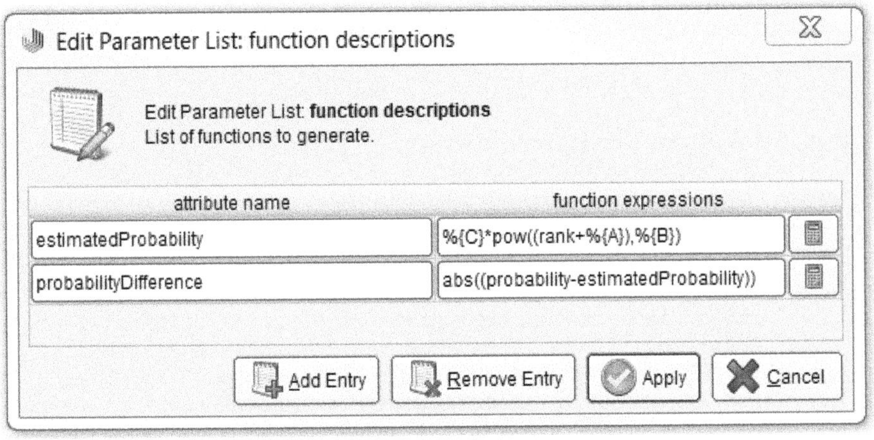

FIGURE 2.13: Calculation of Zipf-Mandelbrot probability and error from known probability.

error for each example, these are aggregrated using the *Aggregate* operator (labelled 6), which simply sums all the individual errors. The next operator allows more calculations to be performed on the aggregated result if desired. For the results in this chapter, it simply raises the aggregate error to the first power (i.e., no change). This could be changed to find the square root of the aggregate if desired. The operator is left in as a placeholder only.

The final part of the operator chain calculates a custom performance (operator 9). It does by using the data value of the single aggregated error calculated in the preceding operators. By this method, the sum of the errors for each example is reduced to a single error value and this is the performance for the values of the macros A, B, and C when calculating the Zipf-Mandelbrot fit. The last operator (labelled 10) writes log entries for the macros and errors. The *Optimize Parameters (Evolutionary)* operator has a configuration setting to minimize or maximize errors; in this case, it is set to minimize.

2.6   Results

2.6.1   Data

Various novels are used in this chapter. These are freely available public domain texts available from the Project Gutenberg site [15]. Table 2.4 itemizes the ones used in this chapter.

TABLE 2.4: Details of texts used in this chapter.

Author	Title	Number of words
Jane Austen	*Pride and Prejudice*	122,815
Jane Austen	*Sense and Sensibility*	120,718
Jane Austen	*Mansfield Park*	161,429
Arthur Conan Doyle	*The Return of Sherlock Holmes*	114,407
Arthur Conan Doyle	*The Adventures of Sherlock Holmes*	105,900
Herman Melville	*Moby Dick*	218,378
Herman Melville	*The Piazza Tales*	81,089

In all cases, light editing was performed to remove the Project Gutenberg specific preamble and license agreements at the start and end of each document.

2.6.2   Starting Values for Parameters

Consideration of Equation 2.7 leads to some limits on the possible values for the parameters A, B, C. It is important to apply limits for practical reasons since it reduces the amount of time taken to find optimum solutions. More importantly, however, by limiting the search to meaningful regions of the search space, solutions can be found that make sense. With this in mind, the following ranges were used for the parameters.

TABLE 2.5: Details of parameter ranges used in this chapter.

Parameter	Range
A	0 to 1
B	−2 to 0
C	0 to 0.2

2.6.3   Variation of Zipf-Mandelbrot Parameters by Distance through Documents

As an illustration of what the processes do, Figure 2.14 shows a comparison between the observed rank–frequency data for an entire document and for a 5,000-word window within the document. In addition the optimum Zipf-Mandelbrot fit to the observed values is shown on the same graph. The optimum parameter values for A, B, C are included in the caption. The processes were run against the books described in Section 2.6.1 to determine the optimum Zipf-Mandelbrot parameters for all the windows within the documents. In addition to the 5,000-word sequential windows, 200 random selections of 5,000 words were also chosen from each of the books and the Zipf-Mandelbrot distribution was fitted to these (The creation of random samples is straightforward to implement within RapidMiner but the process is not described in this chapter for reasons of space.)

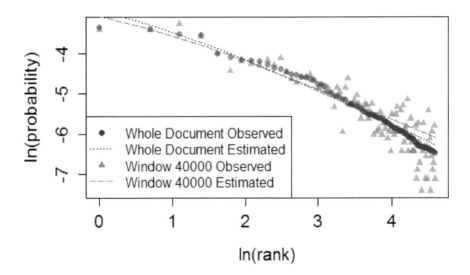

FIGURE 2.14 (See color insert.): Log of probability and estimated probability as a function of log rank for the 100 most common words within all of *Pride and Prejudice* and for the sequential window from 40,000 to 45,000 words. The values of the parameters from Equation 2.7 are for the whole document: A = 0.958, B = −0.846, C = 0.094 and for the window: A=0.888, B=-0.761, C=0.076. This graph was produced using R with the basic plot, points and lines functions used to overlay additional information on a base plot.

Starting with the random samples, examination of the results showed that even for these there was variation in the fitted parameters. However, it was observed that the variations seemed to form clusters when 2- or 3-dimensional plots were examined. This showed up most clearly with the two parameters A and C. There was some similarity between books by the same author and differences between authors. When the sequential windows were included, some were observed to coincide with the random clusters. As an illustration, Figure 2.15 shows the results for the book *Moby Dick* where the Zipf-Mandelbrot parameters A and C are plotted for each of the 200 random samples and 15 sequential windows.

The random points are observed to form clusters, and some of the sequential points

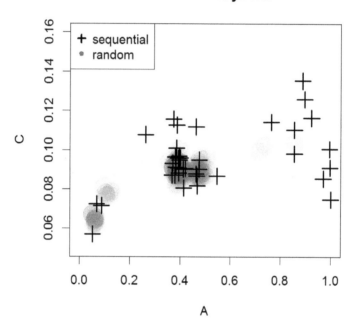

FIGURE 2.15: Zipf-Mandelbrot scatter plot for A and C parameters for random samples and sequential windows within *Moby Dick*. Each window contains 5,000 words; results for 50 random and 42 sequential windows are shown. This graphic and the others in this style were all produced using R. The basic plot function was used to create the initial graph with the points function being used to add additional points in a different style on top of the initial plot.

coincide with them. This gives some confidence that the process to fit the Zipf-Mandelbrot distribution is indeed finding correct distributions. The sequential windows are often signifi-cantly far from the clusters formed from random samples. The same graphical representation for the collection of short stories *The Piazza Tales* also by Herman Melville is shown in Fig-ure 2.16. It is noticeable that the main clustering corresponding to the random samples

Melville: PiazzaTales

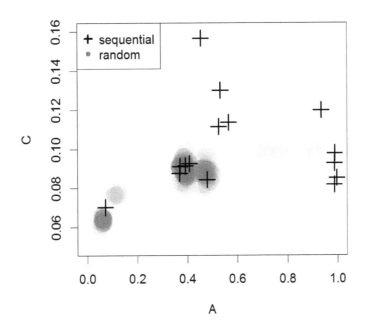

FIGURE 2.16: Zipf-Mandelbrot scatter plot for A and C parameters for random samples and sequential windows within *The Piazza Tales*. Each window contains 5,000 words; results for 50 random and 15 sequential windows are shown.

is similar to that of Figure 2.15. It is also noticeable that the sequential windows are also outliers from the main cluster with some similarities in their distribution. As was shown in Figure 2.1 sequential samples of words exhibit more variation than can be explained from the assumption that the words are randomly arranged within the windows and so it is not surprising that the sequential window points diverge from the random points. It is, however, noteworthy to see that it is the variation in Zipf-Mandelbrot parameters that is showing this.

However, the differences are not so clear-cut for the other books. Firstly, the two Jane Austen novels *Sense and Sensibility* and *Mansfield Park* are shown in Figures 2.17 and 2.18, respectively. The general shape of the clustering is different from the novels by Melville (the limits for the axes have been arranged to be the same to aid comparison) but there does seem to be some empirical similarity between the books. The sequential samples seem to show some evidence that they are outliers from the random samples.

Secondly, the two Sherlock Holmes books are compared in Figures 2.19 and 2.20, respec-tively. The two books show similarities and there is some slight evidence that the points for the sequential windows are outliers. A more significant number of the random and sequen-tial points have a value for the A parameter near 1. This suggests that the range for this parameter during the fitting process could be extended.

It is interesting to note that novels written by the same author seem to show similarites

Austen: SenseAndSensibility

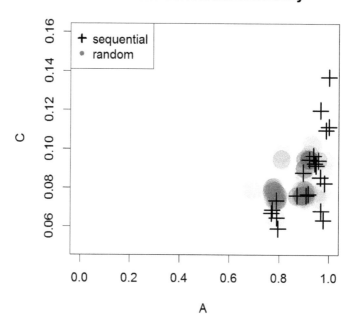

FIGURE 2.17: Zipf-Mandelbrot scatter plot for A and C parameters for random samples and sequential windows within *Sense and Sensibility*. Each window contains 5,000 words; results for 50 random and 23 sequential windows are shown.

Austen: MansfieldPark

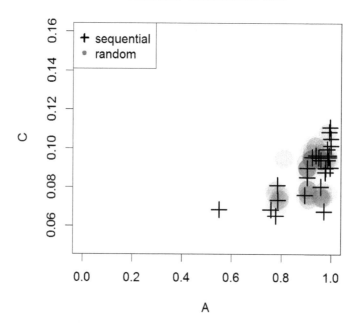

FIGURE 2.18: Zipf-Mandelbrot scatter plot for A and C parameters for random samples and sequential windows within *Mansfield Park*. Each window contains 5,000 words; results for 50 random and 31 sequential windows are shown.

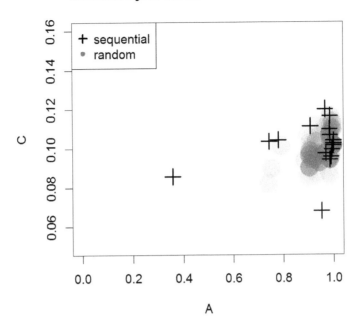

ConanDoyle: ReturnOfSherlockHolmes

FIGURE 2.19: Zipf-Mandelbrot scatter plot for A and C parameters for random samples and sequential windows within *The Return of Sherlock Holmes*. Each window contains 5,000 words; results for 50 random and 21 sequential windows are shown.

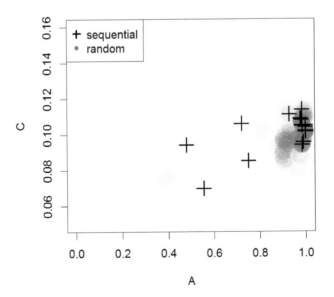

ConanDoyle: AdventuresOfSherlockHolmes

FIGURE 2.20: Zipf-Mandelbrot scatter plot for A and C parameters for random samples and sequential windows within *The Adventures of Sherlock Holmes*. Each window contains 5,000 words; results for 50 random and 20 sequential windows are shown.

when the random sample are considered, although the sample size is too small to draw firm conclusions. It is also interesting to note that the sequential windows show some divergences from random, but more work would be needed to determine if there is a consistent pattern to this. This is discussed more in Section 2.7.

2.7   Discussion

The results show evidence that fitting the Zipf-Mandelbrot distribution to randomly selected 5,000-word samples from an author's work leads to similarities between books by the same author. Given the small number of books considered, this result would need a larger sample to allow firmer conclusions to be drawn.

There is some evidence that sequential windows fitted to the Zipf-Mandelbrot distribution show variations that differ from what would be expected from a purely random sample. This shows up particularly for the two novels by Herman Melville. There are some questions to be resolved however.

Firstly, the genetic algorithm approach can sometimes fail to converge on a global solution. The results from the random sample fitting and the sequential window coincidence with these show evidence that reasonable solutions are being found but it is by no means certain. This can often be resolved using more iterations although this inevitably would require more processing time. As mentioned in Section 2.6.2, increasing the parameter ranges would widen the search space and may allow better global solutions to be found or it might worsen the situation. The only way to determine this is by further investigation. It may be wise to use an alternative method to fit the distribution to the observed data to check the algorithm is finding the best solution.

Secondly, the genetic algorithm itself may also repay more analysis. The RapidMiner environment treats operators as black boxes and detailed knowledge of how they work is not needed, but there could be some hidden feature of the evolutionary algorithm that causes it to behave in a way that causes global solutions to be missed. The evolutionary operator has many parameters, and it would certainly be valuable to explore how these vary the solution finding ability of the algorithm. The RapidMiner product does have an open-source version (5.3), and consequently it is possible to examine its source code. The version of the code used in this chapter is 6.1 so there is a slight possibility that the code has been modified since the open-source version was released.

Thirdly, the sequential variations are observed empirically by visual inspection to be different from the random ones, but more statistical rigour is needed to confirm this to eliminate any wishful thinking.

Lastly, as discussed in Section 2.3.2, probabilities for words are dependent on the size of the text from which they are taken. This makes comparing works even by the same author difficult and calls into question the value of the absolute parameters derived from the fitting process. This means that any summary statistic that captures variation should endeavour to be independent of sample size to allow comparisons between works to be made more easily. The Zipf-Mandelbrot parameter set may be a good candidate given the empirical law that they are derived from, and it is on this basis that they may be a good starting point for more detailed investigation.

2.8   Summary

This chapter has shown detailed and advanced RapidMiner processes that determine the optimum fit of the Zipf-Mandelbrot distribution for sequential windows and random samples within documents. The distribution of the fitted parameters for all the windows within a document were compared by the author. Some evidence, with caveats, that the variation of the fitted parameters is an author-specific trait was observed for the random samples, and divergences exhibited by the sequential windows was also observed. Future investigation may be valuable to determine if the caveats can be addressed and whether there is a genuine style variation that could be exploited to identify authorship.

Bibliography

[1] R.H. Baayen. *Word frequency distributions*, volume 18. Springer, 2001.

[2] F. Mosteller and D.L. Wallace. Inference in an authorship problem. *Journal of the American Statistical Association*, 7:275–309, 1963.

[3] J. Burrows. delta: A measure of stylistic difference and a guide to likely authorship. *Literary and Linguistic Computing*, 17(3):267–287, 2002.

[4] H.S. Heaps. *Information retrieval: Computational and theoretical aspects*. Academic Press, Inc., 1978.

[5] G.K. Zipf. *Selected studies of the principle of relative frequency in language*. Harvard Univ. Press, 1932.

[6] G. Zipf. *Human behaviour and the principle of least-effort*. Addison-Wesley, Cambridge, MA, 1949.

[7] D.C. van Leijenhorst and T.P. Van der Weide. A formal derivation of Heaps' Law. *Information Sciences*, 170(2):263–272, 2005.

[8] L. Lü, Z.K. Zhang, and T. Zhou. Zipf's law leads to Heaps' law: analyzing their relation in finite-size systems. *PloS one*, 5(12):e14139, 2010.

[9] A.W. Chisholm. An investigation into Zipf's law and the extent of its use in author attribution. Master's thesis, Institute of Technology Blanchardstown, IE, 2012.

[10] P. Juola. Authorship attribution. *Foundations and Trends in Information Retrieval*, 1(3):233–334, 2006.

[11] M. Popescu and L.P. Dinu. Comparing statistical similarity measures for stylistic multivariate analysis. *Proceedings RANLP 2009*, 2009.

[12] J. Rybicki and M. Eder. Deeper delta across genres and languages: do we really need the most frequent words? *Literary and Linguistic Computing*, 26(3):315–321, 2011.

[13] S. Argamon and S. Levitan. Measuring the usefulness of function words for authorship attribution. In *Proceedings of ACH/ALLC*, volume 5. Citeseer, 2005.

[14] B. Mandelbrot. An informational theory of the statistical structure of language. *Communication Theory*, pages 486–502, 1953.

[15] Project Gutenberg. [Last Accessed: July 2015, Available at: http://www.gutenberg.org].

[16] I. Mierswa, M. Wurst, R. Klinkenberg, M. Scholz, and T. Euler. Yale: Rapid prototyping for complex data mining tasks. In *Proceedings of the 12th ACM SIGKDD international conference on Knowledge discovery and data mining*, pages 935–940. ACM, 2006.

Part II

KNIME

Chapter 3

Introduction to the KNIME Text Processing Extension

Kilian Thiel

KNIME.com, Berlin, Germany

3.1 Introduction

The Konstanz Information Miner (KNIME) [1] is a modular and open data analytics platform that enables easy visual assembly and interactive execution of data workflows. Its visual workbench combines data access, data transformation, initial investigation, predictive analytics, and visualization. The KNIME Analytics Platform is open-source and available under GPL license.

KNIME workflows are assembled of modules or nodes. Each node is a single processing unit that processes the input data and/or model(s) and produces results on its outputs. An example workflow can be seen in Figure 3.1. Individual settings that affect the node's execution can be configured in the dialog of each node. Data are passed from node to node via data tables that consist of data cells, encapsulating primitive as well as complex data types, such as textual documents, networks, images and more.

The KNIME Text Processing extension is an extension of the open-source KNIME Analytics Platform. It is designed to read, enrich, manipulate, and extract textual data, and to transform it into numerical representations, such as document or term vectors. Once numerical vectors are created, regular KNIME nodes can be applied, for example, for predictive modeling, clustering analysis, or visualization.

The extension allows for reading and parsing of texts in various formats. It provides nodes and models for part-of-speech (POS) tagging as well as named entity recognition. Texts can be filtered, stemmed, and preprocessed in many ways. Different frequencies and scores for terms in documents can be computed, keywords and topics can be extracted, and documents can be visualized by tag clouds.

This chapter is organized as follows: installation of the Text Processing extension is explained first. In section 3.2, philosophy and usage is described, meaning which nodes can be applied in which order, what needs to be done, and what can be done and during which step. Section 3.3 describes two new data types storing documents and terms. In section 3.4 different structures of KNIME data tables are explained, which are required as inputs by certain nodes. Section 3.5 demonstrates most of the theory about the usage of Text Processing nodes, the data types and tables by an example application. This section describes how a classification model can be built on textual data to predict sentiment labels of movies reviews. The last section concludes this chapter.

3.1.1   Installation

Installing KNIME Analytics Platform and the Text Processing feature is easy. KNIME is open-source and the latest version can be downloaded from `www.knime.org`. Versions for Windows, Linux and MacOS are available as zip archives or installer executables. For an easy and straight forward installation it is recommended to download and execute these installers.

Additional extensions, such as the Text Processing extension can be installed conveniently via the KNIME update mechanism. An installation wizard can be started in KNIME under "File → Install KNIME Extensions". All the available extension categories are shown, e.g., KNIME Extensions, KNIME Labs Extensions, or various Community Extensions. The Text Processing extension can be found in the KNIME Labs Extensions category. Many more extensions are available for installation, such as extensions for network analysis, XML processing, image processing, or computational chemistry. For more details about installing KNIME extensions see `http://www.knime.org/downloads/update`.

3.2   Philosophy

The order in which Text Processing nodes are organized in a workflow is important. On the one hand, the nodes require specific structural specification of the input data tables, on the other hand, the order of certain nodes affects the result of the analysis. For example, before a filter node—filtering nouns verbs or adjectives—can be used on a set of documents, a POS Tagger Node has to be applied in advance. This assigns POS tags to all terms of the documents. Creating a bag-of-words with the *BoW Creator* node from a set of documents requires a data table with one column containing documents (document cells) as input. This node can only be configured and executed properly with an input data table, which consists of a column of documents. The output data table of this node is a bag-of-words. The *BoW Creator* node, and all other nodes of the Text Processing extension require input data tables of specific structure and create output data tables of a specific structure. Consequently, certain types of nodes can be used only in a certain order. This order or configuration is the basic philosophy behind the KNIME Text Processing extension.

To process and analyze textual data with the KNIME Text Processing feature, usually five important steps have to be accomplished, although not all of them are mandatory:

1. Reading textual data

2. Semantic enrichment by named entity recognition and POS tagging

3. Preprocessing

4. Frequency computation

5. Transformation

The Text Processing node repository contains a category folder for each of these steps. An example workflow including the nodes for all of the steps is shown in Figure 3.1.

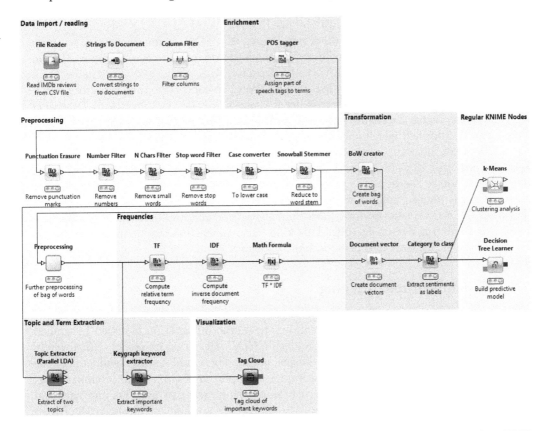

FIGURE 3.1: An example workflow illustrating the basic philosophy and order of KNIME text processing nodes.

In this example workflow textual data are loaded from a CSV file and converted into KNIME document cells. Then POS tags are assigned, followed by a cascade of preprocessing nodes, such as filters, case converters and stemmers. Then a bag-of-words is created, term frequencies are computed, and document vectors are created. These vectors are then used for predictive model building and clustering analysis, both with regular KNIME nodes. In addition, topics and keywords are also extracted from the preprocessed documents. In the following sections each of the five steps will be described in detail.

3.2.1 Reading Textual Data

In the first step, textual data have to be loaded into KNIME and converted to document cells. Document cells are a specific KNIME data type that can be handled by all nodes of the Text Processing extension. These cells contain documents represented in a complex data structure, which allows storage of and access to text at a word and sentence level and also to meta information such as authors, category, or source. More details about these data types can be found in section 3.3.

There are two possible approaches to creating document cells. The first option is to read text from document format files, for example, PDF. The Text Processing extension provides a set of nodes that parse document format files, extract the textual data, and create a document cell for each file. These parser nodes are contained in the folder */KNIME labs/Text Processing/IO* of the KNIME node repository. Nodes to parse Microsoft Word, PDF, flat text files, and more are available.

However, texts are not always available as PDF or Word files. The second approach therefore involves converting textual data, represented as KNIME string cells, into document cells. KNIME Analytics Platform provides many nodes to do so. Data can be imported from files of various formats e.g., CSV and CSV-like formats, XLS, XML, and many more. Data can be selected from databases or loaded from the Web. To convert textual data from string cells into document cells the Text Processing extension provides the *Strings to Document* node. The node creates a document cell for each row of the input data table. In the node dialog it can be specified which columns contain the data for which field of the document, such as title, text, authors, or category.

All parser nodes, as well as the *Strings to Document* node, apply word tokenization and sentence detection to the texts to create the document cells. The output of these nodes is a data table consisting of a column with document cells. An example data table is illustrated in Figure 3.2. The icon, shown in the header of the second column, indicates that the data type of this column is document cells. This kind of document list can be used as input by all nodes of the enrichment and preprocessing category.

3.2.2 Enrichment and Tagging

The second step consists of enriching and tagging terms in the documents. This step is not mandatory for all text mining applications. Semantic information is added by named entity recognition and POS tagging. The folder */KNIME labs/Text Processing/Enrichment* in the node repository contains so called *Tagger* nodes. These nodes scan documents of the input data table and recognize named entities, for example, names of persons, organizations, or locations, biomedical-named entities, such as names of genes or proteins and chemical compounds. Terms that have been recognized as entities are labeled by tags. All *Tagger* nodes require an input data table containing exactly one column of document cells. The output data table consists again of exactly one column of documents with tagged recognized named entities.

A tag value is assigned to each term recognized as a named entity, e.g., "person" and a tag type e.g., "NE" for named entity. The tag type represents the domain or type of a

| Table "default" - Rows: 594 | Spec - Column: 1 | Properties | Flow Variables |

Row ID	📄 Document
Row...	"Italian With Pizzazz"
Row...	"Who Doesn't like Italian?"
Row...	"Great Italian Food Served by Italian People"
Row...	"Fantastic Italian"
Row...	"Outstanding Italian!"
Row...	"Super good thin crust pizza"
Row...	"Great pasta, pizza and service!"
Row...	"Great Italian dinner"
Row...	"Fantastic experience, delicious meal!!"
Row...	"What a delight!!"
Row...	"Authentic italian food, worth waiting for."
Row...	"True Italian"
Row...	"Great pizza and attentive service"

FIGURE 3.2: A data table with a column containing document cells. The documents are reviews of Italian restaurants in San Francisco.

tagger (e.g., biomedical named entities or chemical named entities). The value represents a particular characteristic in that domain, e.g., "gene" in the biomedical field.

The *POS Tagger* node, for example, assigns English POS tags. The assigned tag type is "POS", and the values are those of the Penn Treebank tag set [2]. The node applies the POS model of the Apache openNLP project[3].

The *Stanford Tagger* node uses the models of the Stanford Natural Language Processing Group [4] to assign POS tags. The node can be applied to English, German, and French texts. The corresponding models can be selected in the node dialog. The STTS Stuttgart Tübingen tag set [5] is used for German texts, and the French Treeblank tag set [6] for French texts.

Each tagger assigns tags of its own domain and thus uses its own tag type and set of values. Based on these tag types and values, filtering can be applied subsequently and in such a way as to extract and visualize the named entities.

Figure 3.3 shows a column that contains terms (term cells). In addition to the word of the term, the assigned tags are also listed. For example the POS tag "NNS" has been assigned to the term "People", indicating a noun plural. The term "Italian" has the tag "JJ" assigned, indicating an adjective.

To identify and tag standard named entities (e.g., names of persons) the *OpenNLP NE Tagger* node can be applied, which uses models from the Apache openNLP project [3]. For biomedical entities (e.g., names of genes) the *Abner Tagger* node is applied, which uses the ABNER [7] model. Chemical compounds can be recognized and tagged by the *Oscar Tagger* node based on the model of the OSCAR chemical named entity recognizer framework [8].

The KNIME Text Processing extension also features the *Dictionary Tagger* node and the *Wildcard Tagger* node. These nodes allow for the specification of a dictionary of named entities to identify. The dictionary of the *Wildcard Tagger* may contain wild cards and regular expressions that are used to search for specific terms. These two nodes require a second input data table. This table must consist of at least one column that contains string cells, which represent the dictionary entries. The dictionary data table can be created using existing KNIME nodes, such as the *File Reader*, or the *Database Reader*.

T Term
Served[VBN(POS)]
People[NNS(POS)]
sign[NN(POS)]
authentic[JJ(POS)]
Italian[JJ(POS)]
food[NN(POS)]
restaurant[NN(POS)]
run[VBP(POS)]
happy[JJ(POS)]
people[NNS(POS)]

FIGURE 3.3: A column of a data table containing term cells. The terms have been assigned POS tags (tag values and tag types).

Due to the open nature of KNIME, additional tagger nodes as well as custom tag sets can also be integrated.

3.2.2.1   Unmodifiabililty

Recognized and tagged named entities can be set as *unmodifiable* in order to prevent them from being separated, manipulated, or filtered by subsequent nodes of the preprocessing category. Usually recognized named entities should not be filtered or manipulated by subsequent nodes in the workflow. It does not make much sense to stem e.g., a first or last name of a person. To avoid their manipulation of preprocessing nodes, these terms are flagged *unmodifiable* by the corresponding tagger node by default, except for POS tagger nodes. In the dialog of each tagger node it can be specified whether recognized named entities are flagged *unmodifiable* or not.

Figure 3.4 shows the dialog of the *OpenNLP NE Tagger* node. The first checkbox in the Tagger options tab of the dialog specifies whether named entities are flagged *unmodifiable* or not.

3.2.2.2   Concurrency

Tagging can be computationally expensive, depending on the used method and model. To make use of all CPU cores all tagger nodes are parallelized. The data of the input data table are split up into chunks. The data chunks are then processed in parallel.

In the dialogs of all tagger nodes it is possible to specify the number of parallel threads, as can be seen in Figure 3.5. Each thread loads a separate tagging model into main memory to process its data chunk. Note that some models (e.g., from the Stanford Natural Language Processing Group) do require some hundred megabytes of memory.

3.2.2.3   Tagger Conflicts

If two tagger nodes are applied one after the other, the latter will overwrite the tagging of the former in the event of conflicts. For example, if, first of all, the *OpenNLP NE Tagger* node recognizes the term "Megan Fox" as the name of a person, and then the *Dictionary Tagger* nodes recognizes "Megan" as the name of a product (automobile), based on a product list as a dictionary, the previously recognized term "Megan Fox" is split up and "Megan" (without "Fox") is tagged as a product name.

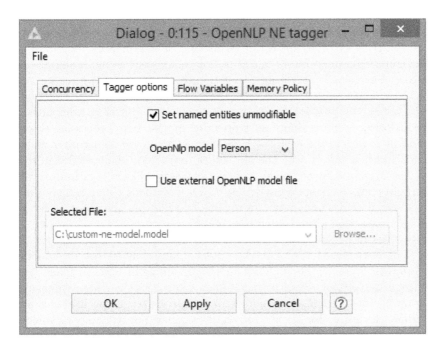

FIGURE 3.4: Dialog of the *OpenNLP NE Tagger* node. The first checkbox allows for specification as to whether or not the named entities should be flagged *unmodifiable*.

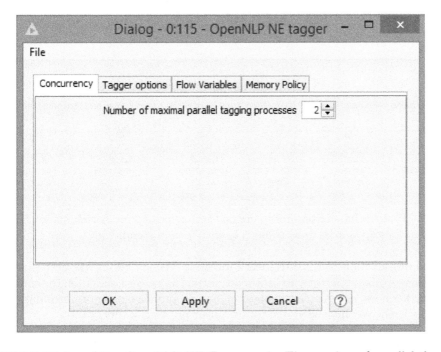

FIGURE 3.5: Dialog of the *OpenNLP NE Tagger* node. The number of parallel threads to use for tagging can be specified here.

3.2.3　Preprocessing

The third step is the preprocessing step in which terms are filtered and manipulated. Filtering is necessary in order to get rid of terms that do not contain very much content or information considered undesirable as features of document vectors. Manipulation (e.g., stemming or case conversion) is performed to normalize terms. All preprocessing nodes are contained in the */KNIME labs/Text Processing/Preprocessing* folder of the node repository.

Besides the regular preprocessing nodes such as stemming or stop word filtering, etc. there are various other preprocessing nodes provided by the Text Processing extension to manipulate and filter terms. For each tag type there is a corresponding filter node, which filters terms with certain tag values. The tag values to filter can be specified in the dialog of the nodes. The *Stanford Tagger* node, for example, assigns POS tags from the "STTS" tag set to German texts. Correspondingly, the *STTS filter* node filters terms have certain "STTS" tags assigned. This combination of tagging and filtering allows for a very powerful identification and extraction of named entities of different types.

Other very powerful preprocessing nodes are the *RegEx Filter* node and the *Replacer* node, which both work based on regular expressions and can be specified in the node dialog. The *Snowball Stemmer* node allows for the stemming of texts in many languages, for example, English, German, Spanish, and Italian. Internally, the node uses the Snowball stemming library [9]. The *Dict Replacer* node replaces certain terms specified in a dictionary with other terms, which are also specified in the dictionary. For example, this node allows terms to be replaced by their synonyms.

Figure 3.6 shows a typical chain of preprocessing nodes used in many text mining applications. First punctuation marks are removed. Note that information indicating the beginning and ending of sentences is not lost when punctuation marks are removed. It is only the punctuation characters that are erased from the terms. Next, terms consisting of digits only are filtered, as well as those terms composed of fewer than three characters. Finally terms are converted to lowercase, and stemming is applied.

Preprocessing

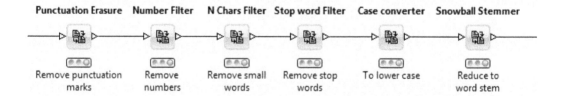

FIGURE 3.6: Typical chain of preprocessing nodes to remove punctuation marks, numbers, very small words, stop words, conversion to lowercase, and stemming.

Since the introduction of KNIME Text Processing Version 2.9, it has been possible to apply preprocessing nodes directly to lists of documents as tagger nodes from the enrichment category. Furthermore, preprocessing nodes can be also applied on bag-of-words data tables. However, this is not recommended due to the longer processing time.

3.2.3.1　Preprocessing Dialog

The dialogs of all preprocessing nodes contain a "Preprocessing" tab, shown in Figure 3.6. Three settings can be specified in this tab:

1. Deep preprocessing: this option is selected by default. It specifies whether the preprocessing step (e.g., stop word filtering) is applied to the terms contained in each document. This option needs to be checked if the node is applied to a list of documents, otherwise the terms in the documents are not filtered or manipulated. It only makes sense to uncheck this option if the input data table of the nodes is a bag-of-words. In this case only the terms in the term column of the bag-of-words are processed but not in the documents themselves.

2. Appending unchanged documents: if deep preprocessing is applied, terms inside the documents are preprocessed. Sometimes it can be useful to keep the original documents. This option is checked by default. The original, unchanged documents are appended in an additional column in either a bag-of-words or a document list data table.

3. Ignore unmodifiable flag: by default all preprocessing nodes do not apply preprocessing on terms that have been flagged *unmodifiable* beforehand by any tagger node of the enrichment category. This unmodifiable flag can be ignored and filtering or manipulation be applied to *unmodifiable* terms as well. By default this option is unchecked.

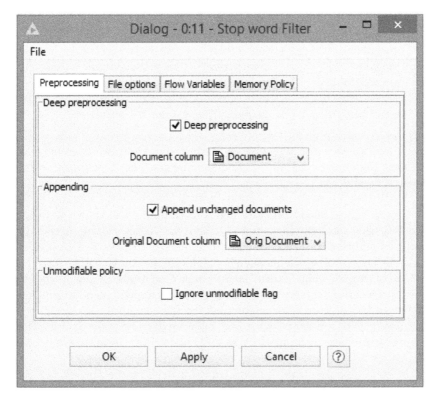

FIGURE 3.7: The Preprocessing tab of the *Stop word Filter* node. Deep preprocessing is applied, original documents are appended, and *unmodifiable* terms are not filtered.

3.2.4 Frequencies

After preprocessing is finished, frequencies of terms in documents and the whole corpus can be computed. All nodes that compute frequencies are contained in the */KNIME labs/Text Processing/Frequencies* folder of the node repository.

Nodes of the frequency category require a bag-of-words data table as input table. Thus the data table containing the list of documents has to be transformed into a bag-of-words, which can be done using the *BoW Creator* node.

Figure 3.8 illustrates a bag-of-words data table with one term column and two document columns. The original documents are stored in the column, "Orig Documents". The "Document" column contains the preprocessed documents. It can be seen that the words "italian" and "pizzazz" are converted to lowercase. Furthermore, the stop word "with" has been filtered. The data table structure is explained in more detail in Section 3.4.

T Term	📄 Document	📄 Orig Document
italian[JJ(POS)]	"italian pizzazz"	"Italian With Pizzazz"
pizzazz[NNP(POS)]	"italian pizzazz"	"Italian With Pizzazz"
particular[JJ(POS)]	"italian pizzazz"	"Italian With Pizzazz"
eater[RB(POS)]	"italian pizzazz"	"Italian With Pizzazz"
tried[VBN(POS)]	"italian pizzazz"	"Italian With Pizzazz"
reviews[NNS(POS)]	"italian pizzazz"	"Italian With Pizzazz"
disappointed[JJ(POS)]	"italian pizzazz"	"Italian With Pizzazz"
food[NN(POS)]	"italian pizzazz"	"Italian With Pizzazz"
literally[RB(POS)]	"italian pizzazz"	"Italian With Pizzazz"
melted[VBN(POS)]	"italian pizzazz"	"Italian With Pizzazz"
mouth[NN(POS)]	"italian pizzazz"	"Italian With Pizzazz"

FIGURE 3.8: Bag-of-words data table with one term column and two documents columns. The column, "Orig Document" contains original documents. The "Document" column contains preprocessed documents.

The Text Processing extension provides nodes to compute well-known frequency measures (i.e. the *TF* node for term frequency, tf, and the *IDF* node for inverse document frequency , idf). In addition to inverse document frequency, there is also an the *ICF* node which computes inverse category frequency , icf. This frequency is analog to idf, however the number of documents in which a term occurs is not used as the divisor; rather the number of documents of a certain category is used. These nodes append an additional numerical column to the input bag-of-words, which contains the frequency values.

Figure 3.9 shows a bag-of-words with one additional numerical column. The values are absolute term frequencies computed by the *TF* node. Each term in each document is assigned a frequency.

Based on the computed frequencies, terms can be filtered by the *Frequency Filter* node. There are more nodes available in this category to create n-grams and count their frequencies as well as to extract co-occurring terms and their number of co-occurrences.

3.2.5 Transformation

At a certain point the textual data have to be transformed into numerical vectors. A vector has to be created for each document. This is usually performed by the *Document Vector* node. The node creates a binary or numerical representation for each document based on the filtered bag-of-words input data table. The vector representation can then be used

T Term	📄 Document	📄 Orig Document	↓ TF abs
italian[JJ(POS)]	"italian pizza...	"Italian With Pizza...	2
pizzazz[NNP(POS)]	"italian pizza...	"Italian With Pizza...	1
particular[JJ(POS)]	"italian pizza...	"Italian With Pizza...	1
eater[RB(POS)]	"italian pizza...	"Italian With Pizza...	1
tried[VBN(POS)]	"italian pizza...	"Italian With Pizza...	1
reviews[NNS(POS)]	"italian pizza...	"Italian With Pizza...	1
disappointed[JJ(POS)]	"italian pizza...	"Italian With Pizza...	1
food[NN(POS)]	"italian pizza...	"Italian With Pizza...	1
literally[RB(POS)]	"italian pizza...	"Italian With Pizza...	1
melted[VBN(POS)]	"italian pizza...	"Italian With Pizza...	1
mouth[NN(POS)]	"italian pizza...	"Italian With Pizza...	1

FIGURE 3.9: Bag-of-words data table with an additional column with absolute term frequencies.

by standard data mining methods, such as clustering or classification nodes. Usually the transformation into numerical vectors is the final step to be handled by the Text Processing nodes.

The */KNIME labs/Text Processing/Transformation* folder of the node repository contains all nodes that transform structures of data tables or that convert types of columns into different types. The *BoW Creator* node can also be found in the transformation category. The node requires a list of documents as the input table and creates a bag-of-words for these documents. Furthermore, there are other transformation nodes, which allow for the conversion of tags to strings, terms to strings, vice versa, and more.

3.3 Data Types

As already mentioned in previous sections, the KNIME Text Processing extension provides two KNIME data types: the document cell, which stores complex documents, and the term cell, which stores terms. Both types can be handled and are required by nodes of the Text Processing extension.

3.3.1 Document Cell

Document cells store documents in a complex data structure. The structure allows storage of and access to the text at a word and sentence level and also to meta information such as authors, category, publication date, and more. A data table containing document cells can be seen in Figure 3.2. The icon shown in the column header of the "Document" column indicates that this column contains cells of the document type. Each cell in the data table contains one complex textual document.

Table views that display document cells only show the title, as can be seen in Figure 3.2. The full text is usually too long to be visualized reasonably in a table cell. However, documents can of course consist of more text than just a title. The *Document Viewer* node can be used to view the full document text, including all meta information.

When a new document cell is created (e.g., by parser nodes or by using the *Strings to*

Document node), word tokenization and sentence detection is applied automatically. Here, word and sentence tokenizers are used from Apache's openNLP project. Words are the finest level of granularity in a document. Each word token, created by the word tokenizer, is stored separately. Each word consists exactly of one string. Words can be transformed and combined to terms by tagger nodes. A named entity tagger, for example, can combine the two words "Megan" and "Fox" to the term "Megan Fox". Thus, a single term can contain one or more words. In addition, terms can have tags assigned. Terms, again, are combined to sentences. Each sentence consists at least of one term.

Meta information, such as category, authors, publication date, and source are stored in additional fields. Furthermore, generic meta information can be stored in documents as key value pairs.

3.3.2   Term Cell

For the representation of terms, the term cell type is provided by the Text Processing extension. A term can contain one or more words and none, one or multiple tags. After creation of a document, each single word represents a term with no tags assigned. Tagger nodes can change the granularity of terms and combine multiple words to a term.

Figure 3.3 illustrates a column containing term cells. The term cell icon can be seen in the column heading. The string representation of a term, shown in table views, is assembled by its words first, followed by the attached tags in brackets. The name of the tag is depicted first (e.g., "NNS") followed by the tag type (e.g., "POS").

3.4   Data Table Structures

Certain nodes require a certain structure of the input data table in order to configure and execute properly. There are three different kinds of structures:

1. Document list: one or more document columns, as shown in Figure 3.2.

2. Bag-of-words: at least one document and one term column, as shown in Figure 3.9.

3. Vectors (document or term): one document column and one or more numerical columns representing terms or documents, illustrated in Figure 3.10.

Document lists are created by parser nodes or the *Strings to Document* node. Tagger nodes as well as preprocessing nodes require a list of documents as the input data table. These nodes can append an additional column containing the original unchanged document right after the column with the processed documents.

A bag-of-words data table consists of tuples of terms and documents. Each row of a bag-of-words represents the occurrence of a particular term in a document. This means that for each unique term contained in a document, one row is created in the corresponding bag-of-words data table. Depending on the number of documents and the number of unique words in documents, bags of words can become huge.

The basic bag-of-words data table can be extended by numerical columns that contain frequencies or the original unchanged documents, which is useful when deep preprocessing is activated, as shown in Figure 3.9. It can be seen that the document titles of the column in the middle differ from those of the right column. The original documents on the right still have the original titles, whereas the titles of the documents in the middle column, affected by deep preprocessing, have been changed by preprocessing nodes (i.e. stop word filtering and conversion to lowercase).

Document vectors are numerical representations of textual documents. The features of a vector are all unique terms that occur in the whole set of documents. A value in the vector greater than 0 indicates that the corresponding term occurs in a document, 0 indicates that the term does not occur in the document. Alternatively to the *Document Vector* node the *Pivoting* node can be used on the bag-of-words to create the vectors. As parameters of the *Pivoting* node, the document column needs to be specified as group column and the term column as pivot column.

Figure 3.10 illustrates a data table with document vectors of 10 documents. The documents are reviews about dim sum restaurants in San Francisco. It can be seen that all documents contain the terms "dim" and "sum". Furthermore, in some documents the terms "wife", "city", or "restaurant" occur.

📄 Document	D ▼ dim	D ▼ sum	D wife	D city	D view	D restaur...	D lunch
""Dim Sum No Mor...	1	1	1	1	1	1	1
"APPALLED By DE...	1	1	1	0	0	0	0
"Alleyway disapp...	1	1	0	0	0	0	0
"Authentic Dim Su...	1	1	0	0	0	1	0
"Bar none, the be...	1	1	0	0	0	0	0
"Best Dim Sum"	1	1	0	0	0	1	0
"Best Dim Sum EV...	1	1	0	0	0	1	0
"Best Dim Sum an...	1	1	0	0	0	0	0
"Best Dim Sum ev...	1	1	0	0	0	0	0
"Best Dim Sum in ...	1	1	0	0	0	1	0

FIGURE 3.10: Document vectors of 10 documents. The documents are stored in the left-most column. The other columns represent the terms of the whole set of documents, one for each unique term.

Analogous to the document vectors, term vectors can be created as well. A term vector is a numerical representation of a term. The features of the vector are all unique documents. The term vector matrix is the transposed document vector matrix. Term vectors can be created with the *Term Vector* node, or alternatively again with the *Pivoting* node.

3.5   Example Application: Sentiment Classification

Sentiment analysis of free-text documents is a common task in the field of text mining. In sentiment analysis predefined sentiment labels, such as "positive" or "negative" are assigned to documents. This section demonstrates how a predictive model can be built in order to assign sentiment labels to documents with the KNIME Text Processing extension in combination with traditional KNIME learner and predictor nodes.

The data set used in this example is a set of 2,000 documents sampled from the training set of the Large Movie Review Dataset v1.0 [10]. The Large Movie Review Dataset v1.0 contains 50,000 English movie reviews along with their associated sentiment labels "positive" and "negative". For details about the data set see [10]. 1,000 documents of the positive group and 1,000 documents of the negative group have been sampled. The goal is to assign the right sentiment label to each document.

Figure 3.11 illustrates the workflow used in this example. The textual data are imported from a csv file and converted to documents. The documents are preprocessed and document vectors are created. The class labels are extracted and colors assigned based on these labels. Finally the data set is split up into a training and a test set, and a decision tree model is built on the training set and scored on the test set. The nodes used for the creation of documents and the preprocessing nodes collapse in two meta nodes.

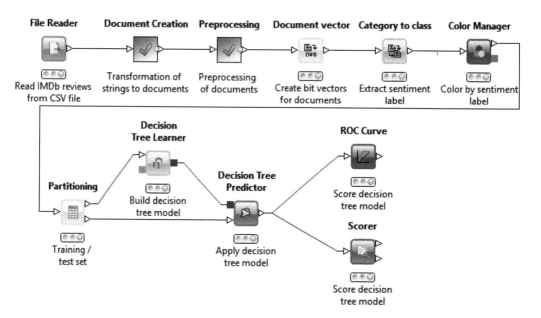

FIGURE 3.11: Chain of preprocessing nodes of the *Preprocessing* meta node.

3.5.1   Reading Textual Data

The workflow starts with a *File Reader*. The node reads a csv file, which contains the review texts, the associated sentiment labels, the IMDb URL of the corresponding movie, and its index in the Large Movie Review Dataset v1.0. In addition to the sentiment column, the text column is also important here. In the first meta node *Document Creation* document cells are created from string cells, using the *Strings to Document* node. The sentiment labels are stored in the category field of each document in order to extract the category afterwards. All columns are filtered with the exception of the column that contains the document cells. The output of the first meta node is a document list data table.

3.5.2   Preprocessing

The tagging step is skipped here since it is not necessary to recognize named entities or assign POS tags. All preprocessing nodes are contained in the *Preprocessing* meta node, shown in Figure 3.11.

First, punctuation marks are removed, numbers and stop words are filtered, and all terms are converted to lowercase. Then the word stem is extracted for each term.

In the lower part of the meta node all those terms are filtered from the bag-of-words that

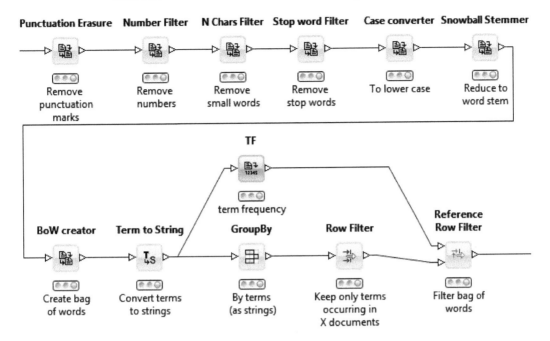

FIGURE 3.12: Chain of preprocessing nodes inside the *Preprocessing* meta node.

occur in fewer than 20 documents. This is done by grouping by the terms, counting all the unique documents that contain these terms, filtering this list of terms, and finally filtering the bag-of-words with the *Reference Row Filter* node. Thereby we reduce the feature space from 22,105 distinct terms to 1,500.

The minimum number of documents is set to 20 since we assume that a term has to occur in at least 1% of all documents in order to represent a useful feature for classification. This is a rule of thumb and of course can be changed individually.

3.5.3 Transformation

Based on these extracted terms document vectors are then created and used in the following for classification by a decision tree classifier. In this example bit vectors were created by the *Document vector* node. The values of bit vectors are 1 or 0 depending on the presence of a term in a document. However, the previously computed tf values or any other scores or frequencies computed beforehand could be used as vector values as well.

3.5.4 Classification

Any of the traditional mining algorithms available in KNIME can be used for classification (e.g., decision trees, ensembles, support vector machines). As in all supervised learning algorithms a target variable is required (see, e.g., [11]). In this example the target is the sentiment label, which is stored as category in the documents. The target or class column is extracted from the documents and appended, as string column, using the *Category to class* node. This category can then be used as the target class for the classification procedure. Based on the category a color is assigned to each document by the Color Manager node. Documents labeled "positive" are colored green; documents labeled "negative" are colored red.

The data set is then split up into a training (70%) and test set (30%). A decision tree is trained on the training set and scored on the test set. The accuracy of the decision tree model is 93.667%. Figure 3.13 shows the confusion matrix of the *scorer* node. The

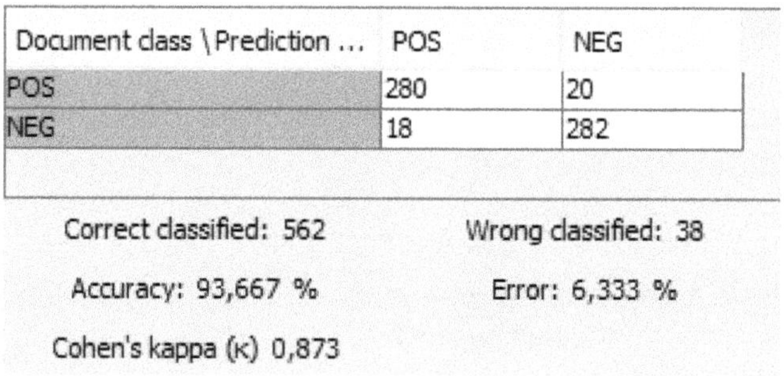

Document class \ Prediction ...	POS	NEG
POS	280	20
NEG	18	282

Correct classified: 562   Wrong classified: 38

Accuracy: 93,667 %   Error: 6,333 %

Cohen's kappa (κ) 0,873

FIGURE 3.13: Confusion matrix and accuracy scores of the sentiment decision tree model.

corresponding receiver operating characteristics curve can be seen in Figure 3.14.

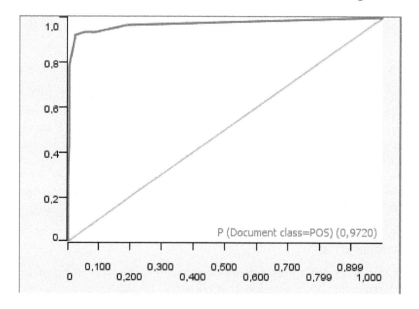

FIGURE 3.14: ROC curve of the sentiment decision tree model.

The aim of this example application is to clarify and demonstrate the usage of the KNIME Text Processing extension rather than achieve the best accuracy. Other learner nodes, such as support vector machines, or decision tree ensembles can be applied easily in KNIME in order to build better models. Furthermore, scores, such as $tf - idf$ could be used instead of bit vectors. In addition to features that represent single words, n-gram features representing multiple consecutive words can be used as well. Cross validation could be applied to achieve a more precise estimation of accuracy.

3.6   Summary

In this chapter the KNIME Text Processing extension has been introduced. The functionality as well as the philosophy and usage of the extension have been described. It has been shown which nodes need to be applied and in what order to read textual data, add semantic information by named entity recognition, preprocess the documents, and finally transform them into numerical vectors which can be used by regular KNIME nodes for clustering or classification. The KNIME data types provided by the Text Processing feature, as well as the document cell and the term cell have also been explained. These techniques were demonstrated as an application example, building a sentiment classification of movie reviews.

More information and example workflows for clustering and classification of documents, usage of tag clouds, and other visualizations can be found at `http://tech.knime.org/examples`.

All results were generated with the open-source KNIME Analytics Platform. KNIME workflows and data are provided with this chapter. The required KNIME extension is the Text Processing extension.

Bibliography

[1] M. R. Berthold, N. Cebron, F. Dill, T. R. Gabriel, T. Kötter, T. Meinl, P. Ohl, C. Sieb, K. Thiel, and B. Wiswedel. KNIME: The Konstanz Information Miner. In *Studies in Classification, Data Analysis, and Knowledge Organization (GfKL 2007)*. Springer, 2007.

[2] Mitchell M., G. Kim, M. A. Marcinkiewicz, R. MacIntyre, A. Bies, M. Ferguson, K. Katz, and B. Schasberger. The penn treebank: Annotating predicate argument structure. In *Proceedings of the Workshop on Human Language Technology*, HLT '94, pages 114–119, Stroudsburg, PA, 1994. Association for Computational Linguistics.

[3] Apache opennlp, 2014. http://opennlp.apache.org.

[4] C. D. Manning, M. Surdeanu, J. Bauer, J. Finkel, S. J. Bethard, and D. McClosky. The Stanford CoreNLP natural language processing toolkit. In *Proceedings of 52nd Annual Meeting of the Association for Computational Linguistics: System Demonstrations*, pages 55–60, 2014.

[5] Stts stuttgart tübingen tag set, 2014. http://www.isocat.org/rest/dcs/376.

[6] A. Abeillé, L. Clément, and booktitle=Treebanks pages=165–187 year=2003 publisher=Springer Toussenel, F. Building a treebank for french.

[7] B. Settles. ABNER: An open source tool for automatically tagging genes, proteins and other entity names in text. *Bioinformatics*, 21(14):3191–3192, 2005.

[8] L. Hawizy, D. M. Jessop, N. Adams, and P. Murray-Rust. Chemicaltagger: A tool for semantic text-mining in chemistry. *Journal of cheminformatics*, 3(1):17, 2011.

[9] Snowball stemming library, 2014. http://snowball.tartarus.org.

[10] A. L. Maas, R. E. Daly, P. T. Pham, D. Huang, A. Y. Ng, and C. Potts. Learning word vectors for sentiment analysis. In *Proceedings of the 49th Annual Meeting of the Association for Computational Linguistics: Human Language Technologies*, pages 142–150, Portland, Oregon, USA, June 2011. Association for Computational Linguistics.

[11] M. R. Berthold, C. Borgelt, F. Hoeppner, and F. Klawonn. *Guide to Intelligent Data Analysis: How to Intelligently Make Sense of Real Data*, volume 42 of *Texts in Computer Science*. Springer-Verlag, 2010.

Chapter 4

Social Media Analysis — Text Mining Meets Network Mining

Kilian Thiel

KNIME.com, Berlin, Germany

Tobias Kötter

KNIME.com, Berlin, Germany

Rosaria Silipo

KNIME.com, Zurich, Switzerland

Phil Winters

KNIME.com, Zurich, Switzerland

4.1 Introduction

Social media channels have become more and more important for many organizations in order to reach targeted groups of individuals as well as understand the needs and behaviors of their users and customers. Huge amounts of social media data are already available and growing rapidly from day to day. The challenge comes in accessing that data and creating usable and actionable insights from it. So far, there are three major approaches that are typically used to analyze social media data: channel reporting tools, overview score-carding systems, and predictive analytics with focus on sentiment analysis. Each has its useful aspects but also its limitations. In this chapter we will discuss a new approach that combines text mining and network analysis to overcome some of the limitations of the standard approaches and create actionable and fact based insights.

Sentiment analysis on the one hand is a common approach in text mining to estimate and predict the attitude of users with respect to products, services or certain topics in general. On the other hand centrality measures are used in the field of network analysis to identify important nodes (users), so-called influencers. In our approach we combine these two techniques in order to analyze the sentiments of influencers of a social media platform, as well as the impact of users with certain sentiments. We show that participants who are very negative in their sentiment are actually not highly regarded as thought leaders by the rest of the community. This result goes against the popular marketing adage that negative users have a very high effect on the community at large. To explain and demonstrate the approach we used the publicly available Slashdot data set. The results have been created with the open-source KNIME Analytics Platform, the Text Processing extensions, and the Network Mining extension.

This chapter is organized as follows. First, an introduction to the Slashdot data set is given. Section 4.3 explains the sentiment analysis approach used to determine the attitude of each user. In section 4.4 we show how the user network was created and influencers are identified. Section 4.5 describes how the two techniques are combined and new insights have been generated. Section 4.6 concludes this chapter.

4.2   The Slashdot Data Set

Slashdot[1] is a popular website, which was created in 1997. It publishes frequent short news posts mostly about technological questions and allows its readers to comment on them. The user community is quite active with more than 200 responses to a thread tending to be the rule rather than the exception. Most of the users are registered and leave comments by their nickname, although some participate anonymously. The data we used are a subset of the Slashdot homepage provided by Fundación Barcelona Media4.[2] The subset contains about 140,000 comments to 495 articles about politics from a total of about 24,000 users.

4.3   Text Mining the Slashdot Data

In a first step our goal is to identify negative and positive users, that is, to determine whether the known (not anonymous) users express predominantly positive or negative opinions, attitudes, feelings, or sentiments in their comments and articles.

In order to measure the sentiment of a user a level of attitude is determined, which measures whether a user writes his or her comments and articles mainly negatively or positively. The level of attitude can also be used to categorize the users afterwards. To categorize sentiments a lexicon containing words (clues) uses their polarity values. The polarity of a word specifies whether the word seems to evoke something positive or something negative. Possible polarity values are: positive, negative, both, and neutral. Naturally, the lexicon is incredibly important as not only the language but the contextual usage of the language for the given audience is significant. With KNIME, the lexicon that is most appropriate for your text data can be chosen freely, or alternately, KNIME can be used to build or modify an available lexicon to suit your tasks.

Due to the lack of labeled training data a model that predicts sentiment labels, as shown in Chapter 3 cannot be trained and used here. The predictive model described in Chapter 3 was trained on movie reviews. These reviews differ compared with Slashdot articles and comments in terms of spelling type, vocabulary, topics, and domain. For this reason the predictive model of the previous chapter cannot be used on the Slashdot data set.

---

[1]http://slashdot.org/
[2]http://www.knime.org/files/slashdot.zip

For the Slashdot data, the sentiment analysis of the user comments and articles is based on the MPQA subjectivity lexicon [1, 2], a publicly available lexicon. In this lexicon, the words as well as their polarity have been identified and collected manually and automatically from annotated and nonannotated data.

Before applying text mining, it is important to understand the structure of the Slashdot data and how it is read into KNIME and transformed. An article is an initial contribution. A comment is a note or a reply to an article or to another comment. Each article with all its following comments and notes represents a document. Users write their comments and notes on many documents. To quantify the user attitude, we then need to navigate through all the documents and measure the amount of negativity and positivity the person has been expressing.

As we have seen, a word can be seen as positive or negative just by itself or can vary depending on the context. The frequency of negative and positive words throughout a document defines the attitude of the document. Similarly the frequency of negative and positive words, among all words used by specific users across all documents, defines the attitude of the user. The more negative words used by a user, the more negatively the user attitude is perceived. In contrast, the more positive words a user uses, the more positively the user attitude is perceived.

We excluded the "anonymous" user from the analysis, since this represents a collection of many different users rather than a single user and therefore carries no interesting information.

For each nonanonymous user, the frequencies of positive and negative words, respectively, $f_{pos}(u)$ and $f_{neg}(u)$, are calculated over his or her contributions across all documents. The difference between such frequencies defines the user attitude as $\lambda(u) = f_{pos}(u) - f_{neg}(u)$. Positive λ define positive users, and negative λ define negative users.

In the first part of the workflow built to text mine the Slashdot data in Section 4.2, a *Table Reader* node and a few traditional data manipulation nodes read the data, remove the anonymous user and isolate the posts. Each post is then converted into a document cell to allow further text analysis operations. At the same time, another branch of the same workflow reads data from the MPQA corpus, extracts the polarity associated with each term, and creates two separate sets of words: the set of positive words and the set of negative words. Finally, the *Dictionary Tagger* node associates a sentiment tag to each word of the Document column.

Now that all words in the posts are tagged as positive or negative, we can proceed with the calculation of the level of attitude for each post and for each user. Therefore, a bag of words is created and absolute term frequencies are computed. Negative and positive term frequencies are then aggregated over user IDs to obtain the total frequency of negative and positive words for each user. The level of attitude of each user is then measured as the difference between the two term frequencies. A picture of the text mining workflow used to compute the sentiment score for each user can be seen in Figure 4.1.

We would like to categorize the users using only three categories "positive", "neutral", and "negative" based on their level of attitude. We assume that the user level of attitude is Gaussian distributed (Figure 4.2) around a mean value μ_λ with a variance σ_λ and that most users around μ_λ are neutral. Therefore, we assume that users with a level of attitude λ inside $\mu_\lambda \pm \sigma_\lambda$ are neutral, while users with λ in the left queue of the Gaussian ($\lambda \leq \mu_\lambda - \sigma_\lambda$) are negative users and users with λ in the right queue of the Gaussian ($\lambda \leq \mu_\lambda + \sigma_\lambda$) are positive users.

Based on the calculated values for μ_λ and σ_λ, the binning process results in 67 negative users, 18,685 neutral, and 1,131 positive users. Figure 4.3 shows a scatter plot of all known users. The x axis represents the frequency of positive words, and the y axis represents the

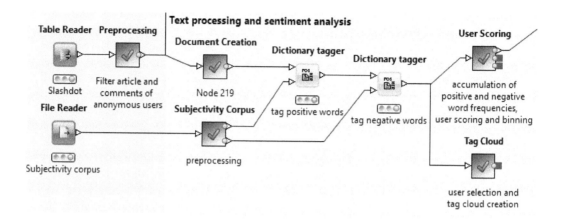

FIGURE 4.1: The text mining workflow used to compute the sentiment score for each user.

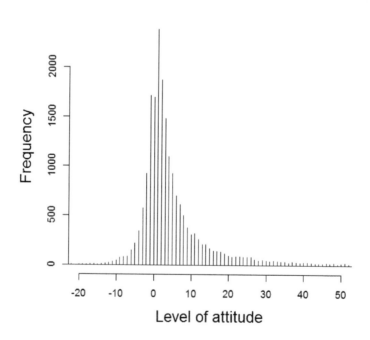

FIGURE 4.2: Distribution of the level of attitude λ by user, with -20 as minimum attitude and 50 as maximum attitude.

frequency of negative words used by a user. Negative users are colored red, positive users green, and neutral users are gray.

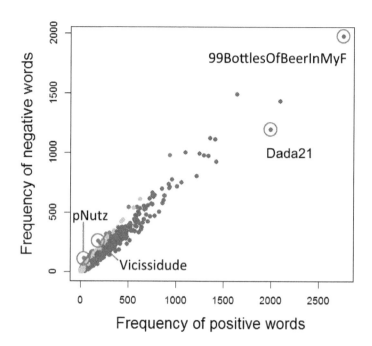

FIGURE 4.3 (See color insert.): Scatter plot of frequency of negative words vs. frequency of positive words for all users.

The most prolific users — that is, those that have written the most (positive and negative words) — are positive or neutral users. The user with the highest number of words (positive and negative) is "99BottlesOfBeerInMyF", which can be seen in the right top corner of Figure 4.3. However, he or she is not the user with the highest level of attitude.

The most positive user is "dada21" with over 1,992 positive words and only about 1,196 negative words. He or she is a frequent writer as well. A tag cloud of the 500 most frequent nouns and adjectives of "dada21" can be seen in Figure 4.4. Stop words have been removed, positive words are colored green, negative words are colored red, and neutral words are colored gray. The most frequent word is "government" followed by "money" and "people". It is clear that there are more positive than negative words.

In contrast, the user with the lowest level of attitude is "pNutz", with only 43 positive words and 109 negative. This user is not a frequent writer. It seems that this user simply wished to vent his anger once but did not want to participate in a reasonable conversation. A tag cloud of the 500 most frequent nouns and adjectives of "pNutz" can be seen in Figure 4.5. Stop-words have been removed, positive words are colored green, negative words are colored red, and neutral words are colored gray. Here, the most frequent word is "stupid" and the negative words outnumber the positive words.

The average word frequency (positive and negative) of positive users is at 327, much more than that of negative users with 192. Thus, negative users do not write frequently.

FIGURE 4.4 (See color insert.): Tag cloud of user "dada21".

FIGURE 4.5 (See color insert.): Tag cloud of user "pNutz".

4.4 Network Mining the Slashdot Data

Network analysis of social media data focuses on the relationships between individuals using their communication on particular topics as the connectors between them. These networks can become incredibly complex, but advanced networking techniques not only identify the network, but can translate it into either graphical representations or solid numeric features, which can be used for analytics.

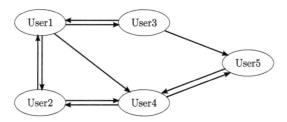

FIGURE 4.6: Example of a network extracted from Slashdot where vertices represent users, and edges comments.

The main goal of this network analysis is to detect leaders and followers based on their activity in the Slashdot forum. In order to do so we create a network $G(V, E)$ that reflects the posts of the Slashdot forum users. In the network each vertex $v \in V$ represents a user. Comments in the forum are represented by directed edges $e = (u, v) \in E$ with the source vertex u representing the user who has commented on an article and the target vertex v representing the user who has written the initial article. For example the connection between "User1" and "User4" in Figure 4.6 indicates that "User1" has commented on an article in the forum written by "User4". After filtering all articles and comments submitted by anonymous users, the created network consists of 20,912 vertices representing users and 76,437 edges representing comments.

In order to detect the main leaders and followers, we borrowed the Hyperlink Induced Topic Search algorithm [3] from web analytics. This centrality index was mainly developed to improve the results of web searches by discovering the most authoritative web pages for a broad search topic. It is an iterative algorithm that assigns each vertex $v \in V$ two different nonnegative weights, called authority weight $x^{\langle v \rangle}$ and hub weight $y^{\langle v \rangle}$. Starting with an initial value of 1 for the authority and hub weight of each vertex the authority weight is computed as

$$x^{\langle v \rangle} = \sum_{u:(u,v)\in E} y^{\langle u \rangle}$$

and the hub weight as

$$y^{\langle u \rangle} = \sum_{v:(u,v)\in E} x^{\langle v \rangle}.$$

After each iteration the weights are normalized to maintain the invariant.

A vertex v is assigned a high hub weight $y^{\langle v \rangle}$ if it refers to many vertices with a high authority weight. A vertex v is assigned a high authority weight $x^{\langle v \rangle}$ if it is referenced by many vertices with a high hub weight. Therefore, a high hub weight is assigned to users who frequently react to articles posted by others; in contrast, a high authority weight describes those users whose articles generate a lot of comments.

Figure 4.7 shows a scatter plot of the leader vs. follower score for all users in the net-

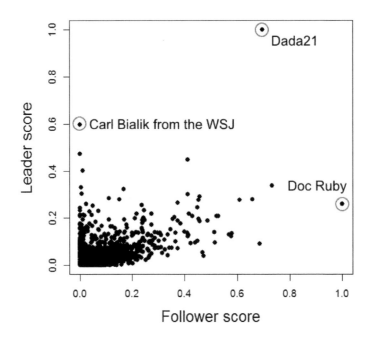

FIGURE 4.7: Scatter plot of leader vs. follower score for all users.

work. The x axis represents the follower score based on the hub weight, whereas the y axis represents the leader score based on the authority weight.

The user that attracts immediate attention is "dada21", who has the highest authority weight of 1 and a very high hub weight of 0.7. This user thus receives a lot of comments from other users in his or her posts (high leader score) and at the same time comments often on other users' articles and comments. When inspecting the posts one can see that this user is indeed one of the most active users with regard to the political topics in Slashdot.

Another user that might be of interest is the user with synonym "Carl Bialik from the WSJ". This user has a very high authority weight of 0.6 but a very low hub weight of 0, implying that he is followed by a very high number of people, but never responds to anyone elses entries.

On the opposite side of the scatter plot, we find the user "Doc Ruby". "Doc Ruby" has the highest hub weight of 1 and only a moderate authority weight of 0.3, meaning that he leaves a lot of comments on other users posts but rarely writes a post of his own, and, if he/she does, rarely receives a comment. This makes him one of the top followers.

4.5   Combining Text and Network Mining

Text mining and network are now widely used as analytic approaches for revealing new insights in social media data. However, each technique follows its own very specific goal.

In text mining, the emphasis is on translating the textual data into sentiment in a carefully controlled process, which places the emphasis on words and expressions within a given context. However, the information about the actual creator of the text, the sentiment expressed in it, and the counts and numbers of readers and responders cannot reveal the relevance of that person with respect to all others in that community, nor can it reveal the relative interactions between that person and other people and how they relate to each other.

Network mining, on the other hand, does a very good job of identifying how individuals interact with each other. It does not rely on a categorical captured "thumbs up" or "star rating" of individuals to rate the importance of a person, but rather identifies those people of influence and those that are followers through physical nodes and connectors. Network mining is also very good at identifying anomalies, such as "I will vote for you and you will vote for me", which is a classic challenge for text mining used in sentiment analysis. And yet powerful, networking analysis alone cannot provide us with any information about the context.

Taking advantage of having both network mining and text processing available within the KNIME environment, we combined the results from the sentiment analysis with the results from the network analysis in order to better position each user inside his or her community in terms of influence (leaders vs. followers) and sentiment (positive, neutral, and negative users).

The workflow that integrates the text mining results with the network analysis results can be seen in Figure 4.8.

In general the goal of marketing is to identify negative and neutral users and, by means of dedicated operations, to convince them to become positive users. However, working on all possible users might be impractical and expensive. Thus, from time to time a new marketing trend emerges trying to identify only the top influencers and to act on them. An even better strategy, in terms of saved resources, would be to identify only the top negative and/or neutral influencers. Indeed, it might not be as effective to try to influence an already positive user, since he or she is already writing mostly positive comments and an excessive marketing action might push him/her train of thoughts in an unwanted direction.

The real power of predictive analytics and visualization comes when we combine both scatter plots, as shown in Figure 4.9. The x axis represents the follower score, and the y axis represents the leader score. In addition, users are colored by their attitude: red for negative users; green for positive users; and gray for neutral users.

The top influencers are the users with the highest leader score. These users are most likely to have a high impact on other users, since their articles and comments are widely read and used as reference by other users. What first becomes clear is that very few negative users have a high leader score. One such user who clearly requires further investigation is "Vicissidude", the top negative attitude leader. Virtually all other negative attitude users are only occasionally followers and have almost no leader influence. This goes against the popular marketing adage that says that all negative attitude users are relevant.

Positive users such as "dada21" or "Doc Ruby" would also not be relevant for marketing actions since they are positive anyway, even though they have a high leader score.

On the other hand, we can clearly identify users like "Carl Bialik from the WSJ" who would be top targets for a marketing campaign. They are neutral or negative and are followed by many other users.

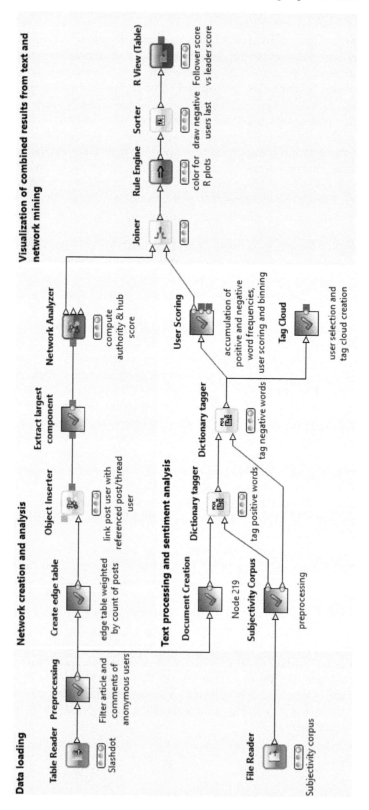

FIGURE 4.8: KNIME workflow that combines text and network mining.

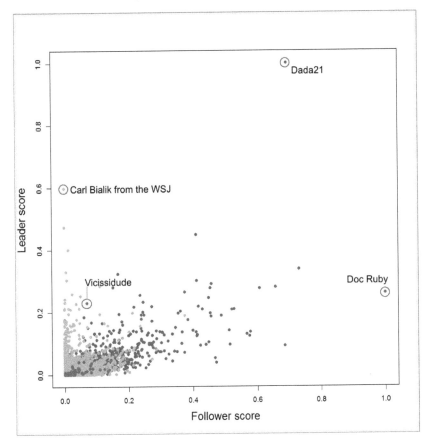

FIGURE 4.9 (See color insert.): Leader vs. follower score colored by attitude for all users. Users with a positive attitude are marked green, users with a negative attitude red.

4.6 Summary

In this chapter we explained and demonstrated a new approach to analyze social media data. The approach combines text mining and network analysis techniques in order to create fact-based, heterogeneous, and actionable insights into social media user behavior. This would not have been possible by using just one analytic technique.

Combining sentiment analysis from online forum posts together with reference structures from the quotation network has allowed us to position negative and positive users in context with their relative weight as influencers or followers in the underlying discussion forum. The approach was demonstrated on the publicly available Slashdot data set. It can be applied to other data sets that contain both text and networking relationship data.

The approach can be improved by applying a predictive model for sentiment classification that has been trained on labeled data of the used social media platform. Further enhancements are the integration of additional relevant data sources, such as company and product names, political parties known users of products, and so on. The additional data would enhance the method capability of identifying, segmenting, and drilling down to interesting user groups.

All results have been created with the open-source KNIME Analytics Platform. KNIME workflows and data are provided with this chapter. The required KNIME extensions are Text Processing, Network Mining, and R Integration.

Bibliography

[1] T. Wilson, J. Wiebe, and P. Hoffmann. Recognizing contextual polarity in phrase-level sentiment analysis. In *Proceedings of the conference on human language technology and empirical methods in natural language processing*, pages 347–354. Association for Computational Linguistics, 2005.

[2] MPQA subjectivity lexicon, 2014. http://mpqa.cs.pitt.edu/lexicons/subj_lexicon.

[3] J.M. Kleinberg. Authoritative sources in a hyperlinked environment. *Journal of the ACM*, 46(5):604–632, 1999.

Part III

Python

Chapter 5

Mining Unstructured User Reviews with Python

Brian Carter

IBM Analytics, Dublin, Ireland

5.1   Introduction

Pillreports.net is an online database of reviews of Ecstasy pills. The site states its aim as providing qualified information to consumers of Ecstasy about the quality of the pill in terms of its effects, contents, and the possible presence of adulterants that may induce unwanted or unexpected effects for the consumer.

In consumer theory, illicit drugs are experience goods, in that the contents are not known until the time of consumption. As such, sites like Pillreports.net may be viewed as an attempt to bridge that gap and to potentially flag instances where a particular *identifiable* pill is producing undesirable effects.

Yellow SR

Date Submitted:	April 9, 2006, 6:59 am GMT
Submitted By:	veruca salt (member since October 7, 2005)
Name:	Yellow SR
State/Province:	Melbourne
Logo:	SR
Colour:	yellow
Shape:	large round, thick pill
Height:	6.0 mm
Width:	8.0 mm
Texture:	smooth and well pressed
Edges:	sharp, no bevels either side
Report Quality Rating:	★ ★ ★ ★ ★ (5 stars, 1 vote)
Description:	-logo quite deep and well defined. So is the score on the back which has even thickness, bout half mm wide and stops just short of the edge of the pill -pill isn't bright yellow, more like a baby yellow :) -colour is pretty uniform, tiny tiny darker yellow specks -thick pill! 4.5mm width not including the dome rise of bout 1mm each side of the pill. Tried to include side view but but can't make the pic small enough argh -doesn't seem crubmly, edges are intact but there is powder/residue sitting in the grooves on the pill so yeh powdery? -pill has slight aniseed smell (nice), hardly got to taste it as i swallowed but was that bitter taste.
Suspected Contents:	MDMA
Rating:	MDxx High
Warning:	no
Tested:	no
Consumed:	yes
User Report:	(btw I'm a hmm moderate user? ~2 times/month, pretty good tolerance) In short, this was an awesome pill, was very impressed. Dropped full one last nite n by T+30mins PEAKING. Felt awesome, rushes, massive pupils. Went to this DnB thing which wasn't that suitable coz couldn't dance my ass off n not my thing anyway but since I was so chopped enjoyed it/the feeling n was crazy, chatty n energetic.Euphoria n empathy associated with MDMA felt.Didn't heat up, wasn't that thirsty.Minor eye wobbles I think but neva really get that n the jaw clenching. Chewed the hell out of a fair bit of gum tho :p Was peaking I'd say for 2hrs but kept coming bak for 2hrs after that. Fact that my friends piked it n we had to go home affected/dampened it I think but even chilling out up to 5 n 6 hours after the drop I was still feeling it! So impressed. "Makes my head feel good" I'd commented at the time.I jus sorta drifted into this lovely content spaced out/sleepy state n was ready for bed. Slept no probs. Clean comedown n feeling fine today, not scattered really.I didn't bother taking the second one given how the nite panned out, can't wait to have it at a club. Best pill I've eva had, gonna try n stock up on these n you should too if given the chance. Sposed to be imports from Europe. My mate who's a long time user sampled half n reckons its the shit- 'a proper MD pill' party crazy hard pple :p

FIGURE 5.1: Pillreports.net standard report.

Each entry/record contains a set of nominal (*Color, Logo, Rating ...*), binary (*Consumed, Tested, Warning*), numeric (*Height, Width*), temporal, and geographic attributes. There are two free text entries (*Description, User Report*). In addition, a series of *Comments* can be associated with each report. Figure 5.1 displays a screen shot of a typical entry.

Table 5.1 presents descriptions and some summary statistics for each column, indicating the original name as found on the Pillreports.net site and the name as stored in the database.

The mixture of data types in the presence of the free text entries presents an ideal opportunity to examine if there are underlying patterns in the free text fields that can be linked back to the data in the binary/nominal columns. This chapter will exploit this and work through the following examples:

- A classification problem using the free text field *Description:* as the input variables and the *Warning: = Yes/No* field as the class label.

- A cluster analysis of the *User Report:* field to determine if there are underlying identifiable patterns.

5.1.1   Workflow of the Chapter

The chapter presents a sequence of processes required to set the stage in order that the text mining objectives can proceed:

- Scraping the data from Pillreports.net - `2.Web Scraping`

- Data shaping and cleansing - `3.Data Cleansing`

- Data visualization and exploration - `4.Data Visualization`

- Classification - `5.Classification`

- Clustering - `6.Clustering`

The emphasized text refers to an `iPython Notebook` associated with each chunk of the overall process. Each notebook presents a series of steps for each process, the Python libraries used, and the actual code. The coding was completed using Python (Version 2.7.8).

In addition to Python, a MongoDB database was used to store the data as they were being scraped from Pillreports.net. Links are provided to instructions for installing and setting up MongoDB on your machine. A CSV file of the cleansed data is also provided. It is possible to jump straight to the visualization and exploration processes using the CSV file if desired.

`iPython Notebook` is a browser-based computation environment. A notebook is a JSON document that can be converted to Python script using the iPython terminal. As the code is stored in a JSON document, there are methods provided to convert it to other formats including HTML, Latex, and PDFs, providing very flexible sharing and documentation possibilities.

5.1.2   Scope of Instructions

The information and discussion provided in this chapter will focus on the technical aspects of implementing the previously outlined project workflow solely using Python and iPython

TABLE 5.1: Column descriptions and statistics.

Pillreports.net Name	DB Name	Data Type	Description	Unique Entries	Blank Cells	min value	max value	average
ID:	ID:	ID	Incremental ID for referencing webpages	5001	0	26940	34120	
.id	mongo.id:	ID	System generated key	5001	0			
Description:	Description:	text	Free text field, focuses on describing what an ecstasy pill looks like, but may vary.	4975	0			
User Report:	User Report:	text	Free text field, documents user experiences of consuming ecstasy pill.	3225	1762			
	UR Length:	continuous	Generated: string length of User Report:	1809	0	0	9336	702
	Desc Length:	continuous	Generated: string length of Description:	1131	0	1	5406	369
	Language:	nominal	Generated: Language of User Report: free text field.	8	0			
Language Percentage:	Language Percentage:	continuous	Generated: Confidence level of the prediction of Language: label	3021	1981	0.571	0.999	0.998
Texture:	Texture:	text		1743	1238			
Color:	Color:	text		1259	6			
Edges:	Edges:	text		1092	2080			
Logo:	Logo:	text	Series of columns detailing various attributes of the ecstasy pill under review.	2556	20			
Name:	Name:	text		3496	1			
Shape:	Shape:	text		989	7			
Height:	Height:	continuous		67	3184	0.2	99.9	5.19
Width:	Width:	continuous		64	3169	0.4	99.9	7.74
State/Province:	State/Province:	text	Geographic location of where report was submitted from, user entered.	1629	1			
Country:	Country:	nominal	Generated: based on State\Province: column	56	0	USA (2051), Australia (969), Netherlands (364)		
Date Submitted:	Date Submitted:	date	Date of report submission.	4988	0	2011-08-11	2014-11-14	
Last Updated:	Last Updated:	date	Date report was last updated or revised.	3374	1600	2011-08-11	2014-11-14	
Member Since:	Member Since:	date	Generated: Date owner of report is member of the site based on Submitted by: column	1386	205	2005-09-05	2014-11-14	
Submitted By:	Member Name:	text	Name and joining date of a member / Generated: Member name taken from Submitted By: column	2546	0			
	User Admin:	binary	Generated: Boolean value indicating if member is a site Administrator\Moderator	2	0	TRUE (205), FALSE (4796)		
	Total Comments:	continuous	Generated: Total comments per report	51	84	1	55	10.7
Report Quality Rating:	Report Stars:	continuous	Review of report with stars (1-5) and number of voters / Generated: Number of stars given to a report based on Report Quality Rating:	44	1252	0	4.8	3.97
	Report Votes:	continuous	Generated: Number of votes given to a report based on Report Quality Rating:	22	1252	1	23	3.04
Tested:	Tested:	binary	Binary value Yes\No indicating if ecstasy pill has been tested.	2	0	yes(2746), no (2255)		
Mandelin Reagent:	Mandelin Reagent:	nominal		7	4014			
Marquis Reagent:	Marquis Reagent:	nominal	Series of different types of testing kits and input of the value (typically a color)	11	2525	Black (1375), Other (272), Purple (269)		
Mecke Reagent:	Mecke Reagent:	nominal		7	3667			
Robadope Reagent:	Robadope Reagent:	nominal		4	4794			
Simons Reagent:	Simons Reagent:	nominal		4	3972			
Rating:	Rating:	nominal	Rating of the pill in terms of believed active ingredients	7	0	Tested Only (1445), MDxx High (875), MDxx Medium (948), Adulterated (821)		
Suspected Contents:	Suspected Contents:	nominal	User opinion on the active ingredients in the pill	31	0	MDMA (1821), MDxx (897), Unknown (828)		
SC Category:	Suspected Contents:	nominal	Generated: Refined grouping of Suspected Contents:	5	0	mdxx (2859), unknown (1038), amphet (504)		
Warning:	Warning:	binary	Binary value Yes\No indicating if pill has unwanted effects.	2	0	no (3184), yes (1817)		
Consumed:	Consumed:	binary	Binary value Yes\No indicating if user consumed the pill.	2	0	yes (3244), no (1757)		

Notebook. The rationale behind choosing Python is discussed, and the pros/cons of using Python in the context of various steps in the data mining project are highlighted.

At various points throughout, an overview of some of the more thorny issues that a user may experience with various Python libraries and coding conventions is presented.

By focusing on the technical aspects, there is light treatment given to the theoretical aspects of text mining and/or data mining algorithms. [1] provides a very good overview of the data mining process and many of the most often used algorithms. For a more mathematical and statistical focus to the data mining methods see [2].

The remainder of this section outlines the following:

- Setting up the technical stack

- A discussion on the support for sparse matrices support in Python

- A discussion on character encoding with ASCII and UTF-8 in Python

5.1.3 Technical Stack Setup

5.1.3.1 Python

Download Python and `Python Notebook` from the Anaconda distribution available at `https://store.continuum.io/cshop/anaconda/`.

Anaconda will download most of the popular Python packages with its distribution. To start with `Python Notebook` simply open a `Command Prompt/Terminal` window and type `ipython notebook`. This will open up a browser window. Create a new notebook and you can enter the commands shown in Figure 5.2. The second command will output the Python version that you are running.

```
In [1]: print ("Hello World")

Hello World

In [2]: import sys
        print sys.version

2.7.8 |Anaconda 1.9.2 (x86_64)| (default, Aug 21 2014, 15:21:46)
[GCC 4.2.1 (Apple Inc. build 5577)]
```

FIGURE 5.2: Code: Check Python setup.

As stated many of the libraries used in the chapter install with the Anaconda distribution. Anaconda provides a package manager `"conda"`. It installs libraries from its own package repository and as such not all libraries are available, especially more experimental libraries. The standard Python package manager is `pip`. This is used to download the additional libraries.

There are five additional libraries used in the project that are not part of the Anaconda distribution. The installation instructions are listed below. Open a new `Command Prompt/Terminal` and enter each command separately. Your machine must be connected to the internet and it will grab each library and install it.

- `pip install pymongo`

- `pip install beautifulsoup4`

- `pip install langdetect`

- `pip install seaborn`

- `pip install git+git://github.com/amueller/word_cloud.git`

5.1.3.2   MongoDB

MongoDB is an open-source database. It is a NoSQL database, sometimes referred to as a document store. NoSQL stands for *Not only* SQL. In the context of this chapter NoSQL is a nonrelational database. This has beneficial properties, in that it is very flexible with regard to specifying the column names of the data being scraped.

This is important when doing a large Web scrape, where each webpage may contain different/new data. The structure of the webpage may be the same but the content differs. This is the case for Pillreports.net.

In this chapter, 5,001 records were scraped, resulting in 26 columns, of which 15 were present for each page. Some of the columns only appeared in the middle of the scrape and could not be determined in advance. Using a NoSQL DB as the initial repository for the data meant this was not an issue. To understand it, think of when you fill out a form on a website: only some of the entries are mandatory, these are the 15 columns.

Installing MongDB is relatively straightforward. It can be downloaded from `http://mongodb.org/downloads`. Setting up the initial instance can be a bit more tricky. There are very good instructions for all the major operating systems at `docs.mongodb.org/manual/`. The main thing to remember when initially setting up is that you need to create a *data directory* called `data/db` where all the databases will be stored.

After the setup, apart from making sure the MongoDB server is running, all interaction with the MongoDB will be done via the `pymongo` library.

5.1.4   Python for Text Mining

Before setting off into the coding for the chapter, it is worth taking a few minutes reading over the next two sections. The first explains what sparse matrices are. In any text mining project the ability to handle sparse table entries (lots of zeros) is crucial. The second contains a discussion on character encoding. This is within the context of Python but may be applicable in other languages. Understanding how Python handles text will save you a lot of frustration in the long run.

5.1.4.1   Sparse Matrices

Most text mining tasks require that the data are represented in a matrix or vector form. This is referred to as a *document-term-matrix (DTM)* or the *transpose term-document matrix (TDM)*.

A collection of documents is referred to as a **corpus**. For example, take the Roald Dahl poem, *Hey Diddle Diddle*, shown at the start of Figure 5.3.

Taking each line of the poem as its own individual document, the poem represents a corpus of six documents. The corpus can be represented by a matrix as presented in Table 5.2.

A 6×25 matrix is created representing 6 documents and 25 unique words. This is not very efficient as many of the entries are zero. In fact only 30 cells contain nonzero entries. (Note the information about the order of the words is lost in the matrix representation.

TABLE 5.2: Example dense matrix.

Line/Word	all	and	are	by	carefully	cash		take	the	until	up	we	which	work
Line 1	0	0	0	0	0	0	...	0	0	0	0	0	0	0
Line 2	1	0	1	0	0	0	...	0	1	0	0	1	0	0
Line 3	0	1	0	0	0	0	...	0	0	1	1	0	0	0
Line 4	0	0	0	0	0	1	...	1	0	0	0	1	0	0
Line 5	0	0	0	0	1	0	...	0	0	0	0	1	1	0
Line 6	0	1	0	1	0	0	...	0	2	0	0	1	0	1

Using ngrams of words can preserve some of the word order.)

A sparse matrix provides a more efficient way to store the information. Sparse matrix store references to the nonzero elements only. There are a number of different methods of implementing sparse matrices; dictionary of keys (DOK), list of list (LL) and co-ordinate list (COO). The sklearn machine library in Python uses the latter method. COO stores the information in {row, column, value} form where; row is a vector of row indexes indicating the row location of the nonzero values, column is a vector of the column indexes indicating the column location of the nonzero values and **value** are the nonzero values in the matrix.

The entries are sorted by row index and column index to enable faster search and retrieval. A representation of the poem in COO format is shown in Table 5.3. There are 30 entries to represent the poem, compared with 150 when the zeros are included.

TABLE 5.3: Example sparse matrix.

Line	Word	Count	row,col,value
Line 2	all	1	2,1,1
Line 3	and	1	3,2,1
Line 6	and	1	6,2,1
Line 2	are	1	2,3,1
...	...	...	...
Line 5	we	1	5,23,1
Line 6	we	1	6,23,1
Line 5	which	1	5,24,1
Line 6	work	1	6,25,1

The Python **sklearn.feature_extraction.text** method can be used to convert a corpus of documents to a sparse matrix representation (COO) of word counts.

The Python code for creating the representation of the *Hey Diddle Diddle* poem is shown in Figure 5.3. From this small toy example, the memory used is reduced by 1,448 - 464 = 784 bytes or 2/3. This memory saving scales exponentially as the size of the corpus grows.

A key advantage of using Python is that a sparse matrix can be passed to many of the machine learning methods in the **sklearn** library and they will work, (a notable exception being tree based algorithms including Random Forests). The ease and flexibility of this

```
In [1]: import pandas as pd

        poem="""Hey diddle diddle,
                We are all on the fiddle,
                And never get up until noon.
                We only take cash,
                Which we carefully stash,
                And we work by the light of the moon."""

        #Split poem by "," or ".". and save in dataFrame df
        #Use 're' package - regular expressions
        #Include newline \n splitting as will remove
        import re
        lines=re.split(',\n|.\n',poem)
        df=pd.DataFrame({"Lines":lines})


In [3]: #Create Sparse and Dense Matrix
        from sklearn.feature_extraction.text import CountVectorizer
        countVec = CountVectorizer()
        poemSparse=countVec.fit_transform(df['Lines'])
        poemDense=pd.DataFrame(poemSparse.todense(),
                               columns=countVec.get_feature_names())


In [4]: print "Dense matrix non-zero values:",((poemDense!=0).sum()).sum()
        print "Sparse matrix entries:",len(poemSparse.data)

Dense matrix non-zero values: 30
Sparse matrix entries: 30


In [9]: #Size of the data frame in memory is
        #values + index + column names
        print "Dense matrix size:",poemDense.values.nbytes + \
              poemDense.index.nbytes + poemDense.columns.nbytes, "bytes."
        print "Sparse matrix size:",poemSparse.data.nbytes + \
              poemSparse.indptr.nbytes + poemSparse.indices.nbytes, "bytes."

Dense matrix size: 1448 bytes.
Sparse matrix size: 464 bytes.
```

FIGURE 5.3: Code: Creating a sparse matrix in Python.

representation can significantly speed a project's development time and reduce computation overheads.

5.1.4.2 Text Representation in Python

The data used in this project is scraped off the Web. As such it is impossible to control what types of text will be returned. The text may contain accented characters { être — to be in French, köszönöm — thank you in Hungarian } or indeed characters outside that of the Latin alphabet; Cyrillic, Chinese Mandarin, and Arabic. Python 2.7 can produce some confusing output when working with text.

```
In [8]:  eng="thank you"
         hun="köszönöm"
         print ("String Length:",len(eng),"Type:",type(eng))
         print(hun, "String Length:",len(hun),"Type:",type(hun))
         #k,s,z,n,m print correctly


('String Length:', 9, 'Type:', <type 'str'>)
('k\xc3\xb6sz\xc3\xb6n\xc3\xb6m', 'String Length:', 11, 'Type:', <type 'str'>)


In [9]:  eng="thank you"
         hun=u"köszönöm"
         print(eng, "String Length:",len(eng),"Type:",type(eng))
         print(hun.encode('ascii','replace'), "String Length:",len(hun),
             "Type:",type(hun))

         #Type has changed. String Length of hun reduced 11 to 8.


('thank you', 'String Length:', 9, 'Type:', <type 'str'>)
('k?sz?n?m', 'String Length:', 8, 'Type:', <type 'unicode'>)
```

FIGURE 5.4: Code: Confusing output with text in Python.

These types of output may also occur when reading files in. The cause of this is *character encoding*. When computers were in their infancy, characters were encoded using ASCII (American Code Standard Information Interchange). ASCII, created in 1963, original contained 128 bytes. The original ASCII coverage is shown in Figure 5.5.

Computers converse in bits and bytes. An ASCII *encode* is quite simply a lookup table. Given the byte \x4D a program can look up the table and know to print out a capital M and so on. The encoding standard was extended further with *Latin-1* and *Windows 1252* giving a range of 256 bytes on a lookup table. These include the original subset of ASCII byte lookups.

Clearly 256 bytes is not enough to represent the full set of characters of all the languages in existence. A proliferation of encodings ensued to address these shortcomings. *Unicode* was and is the solution. Unicode is a catalog of over 1 million integers. Every possible character in the world has its own unique integer. (Currently about 10% of the possible spaces are used).

The Unicode-integer or code point is encoded according to a selected encoding standard that translates it to bytes. These bytes can then be sent from computer to computer. Once received they can be decoded to get the relevant code point and its character. The misuse and interchange of the terms (encode, encoding, Unicode) can cause significant confusion. Figure 5.6 illustrates the paradigm.

	0	1	2	3	4	5	6	7	8	9	A	B	C	D	E	F
0x	NUL	SOH	STX	ETC	EOT	ENQ	ACK	BEL	BS	TAB	LF	VT	FF	CR	SO	SI
1x	DLE	DC1	DC2	DC3	DC4	NAK	SYN	ETB	CAN	EM	SUB	ESC	FS	GS	RS	US
2x		!	"	#	$	%	&	'	(	)	*	+	,	-	.	/
3x	0	1	2	3	4	5	6	7	8	9	:	;	<	=	>	?
4x	@	A	B	C	D	E	F	G	H	I	J	K	L	M	N	O
5x	P	Q	R	S	T	U	V	W	X	Y	Z	[	\	]	^	_
6x	`	a	b	c	d	e	f	g	h	i	j	k	l	m	n	o
7x	p	q	r	s	t	u	v	w	x	y	z	{	|	}	~	DEL
8x	€		,	ƒ	„	…	†	‡	^	‰	Š	‹	Œ		Ž	
9x		'	'	"	"	•	–	—	~	™	š	›	œ		ž	Ÿ
Ax		¡	¢	£	¤	¥	¦	§	¨	©	ª	«	¬		®	¯
Bx	°	±	²	³	´	µ	¶	·	¸	¹	º	»	¼	½	¾	¿
Cx	À	Á	Â	Ã	Ä	Å	Æ	Ç	È	É	Ê	Ë	Ì	Í	Î	Ï
Dx	Ð	Ñ	Ò	Ó	Ô	Õ	Ö	×	Ø	Ù	Ú	Û	Ü	Ý	Þ	ß
Ex	à	á	â	ã	ä	å	æ	ç	è	é	ê	ë	ì	í	î	ï
Fx	ð	ñ	ò	ó	ô	õ	ö	÷	ø	ù	ú	û	ü	ý	þ	ÿ

ASCII:
Created 1960's.
128 characters
33 special,
95 printable.

Windows-1252:
Created 1990
for Windows
3.0

ISO 8859-1:
or
Latin-1:
Created 1987

UTF-8 includes all 3 encodings as a subset.

FIGURE 5.5: Original byte encoding — 256 characters.

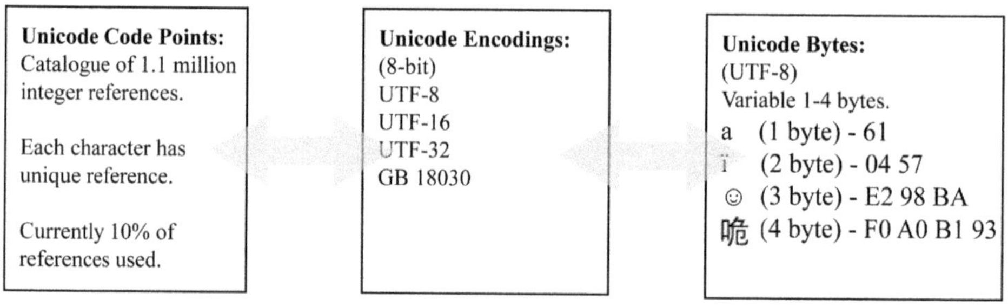

Unicode Code Points:
Catalogue of 1.1 million integer references.

Each character has unique reference.

Currently 10% of references used.

Unicode Encodings:
(8-bit)
UTF-8
UTF-16
UTF-32
GB 18030

Unicode Bytes:
(UTF-8)
Variable 1-4 bytes.
a   (1 byte) - 61
ï   (2 byte) - 04 57
☺   (3 byte) - E2 98 BA
呩   (4 byte) - F0 A0 B1 93

FIGURE 5.6: Unicode encoding paradigm.

pillreports										
p	i	l	l	r	e	p	o	r	t	s
70	69	6c	6c	72	65	70	6f	72	74	73

ASCII Byte

pïℓℛёℙ☺ℝтＳ									
p	ï	ℓ	ℛ	ё	ℙ	☺	ℝ	т	Ｓ
0070	0457	2113	211B	0451	2119	263A	211D	0442	0024
70	D1 97	E2 84 93	E2 84 9B	D1 91	E2 84 99	E2 98 BA	E2 84 9D	D1 82	24

Unicode Hex Code Point

UTF-8 Byte(s)

FIGURE 5.7: Character bytes and code points.

UTF-8 is one such encoding standard. In fact it is the de facto standard with over 90% of all webpages now encoded as such. Figure 5.7 shows the word *pillreports* and a mocked up version of the same word using strange but recognizable characters from other alphabets. The mapping between the characters and the original ASCII byte is shown. In the mocked up version, the layer of hex code points between the character and the subsequent byte(s) is displayed. The original ASCII characters have a code point that maps to the same byte as back in 1963.

5.1.4.3   Character Encoding in Python

The previous section detailed the accepted Unicode Standard. This section outlines its implementation in Python. There are some data type conventions that require explanation and the reader should be aware that these differ significantly between Python 2.7.x and Python 3.x.

Python 2.7 has two <basestring> types; <str> and <unicode>. <str> are **bytes** whereas <unicode> is composed of unicode **code points**. The differences between the <str> and <unicode> are illustrated in Figure 5.8. The code is entered in an Python Notebook.

The unicode symbol for a *smiley face* is entered and printed. The corresponding code point and byte length (of the code point) are printed. Note that the encoded has defaulted to UTF encoding.

The <str> byte representation of the *smiley face* symbol is then printed out, 3 bytes long. Finally an attempt is made to encode the symbol using ascii which throws an error as ascii does not have a representation for a *smiley face*.

```
In [11]:  #Create unicode symbol for a smiley face
          #u\u263a - unicode code point
          smiley=u"\u263A"
          print(smiley)


In []:  ord(smiley) # = 9786 decimal value of code point = 263A in Hex.


In []:  len(smiley) # = 1 This is a <unicode>. Length in code-points


In []:  # prints '\xe2\x98\xba' the bytes - it is <str>
        # its length = 3 - 3 bytes
        smiley.encode('utf8')


In []:  #Encode unicode point with ascii
        #Error no coverage in ascii for this code-point
        print u"\u263A".encode('ascii')
```

FIGURE 5.8: Code: Python encoding for text correct use.

In the above example a **u** is prefixed before the string entered. This tells the Python 2.7 interpreter that this is a <unicode> type. If this was not included the interpreter would assume it was <str> type. In Python 3.0 this is reversed, the default *without* a prefix is <unicode> and a prefix **b** must be specified to get a <str> type.

Relating this back to text mining, a firm understanding of the difference between getting an error message with \xe2\x98\xba relating to a <str> of bytes and similarly \u263A relating to <unicode> will help debugging if they should arise.

In order to avoid these errors, explicitly encode files with the correct encoding, *('UTF-8',ASCII)*, when reading a file at the start of a project and similar encoding a file when writing it out after processing has completed.

The encoding must be known when reading in a file. However, it is reasonable to assume that it is *UTF+8* unless otherwise stated. You will see this convention used in all the code accompanying this chapter. (Note if you open up the accompanying CSV files in Excel and examine the free text columns, especially for non–English-language entries, you will see strange symbols. Excel is using its default *ANSI* encoding for reading the file in, not *UTF+8* that the file was explicitly encoded with.)

For a very informative video on everything discussed in this section [3] provides an excellent overview.

5.2   Web Scraping

There are three parts involved in Web scraping part of the chapter. Firstly we need to be able to navigate to the correct location, the webpage. Secondly we need to be able to traverse that webpage and select the parts that are of interest and finally we need somewhere to store that data. The Python library `urllib2` is used to navigate to the correct landing page. The `BeautifulSoup` library traverses the webpage and the `pymongo` library is used to save the data to a *collection* in a database located on the local MongoDB server.

`urllib2` is a Python module that can be used for fetching URLs. The most basic way to use the library is to send a request to a server (pillreports.net) and providing a successful connection has been made, read in the data as a string.

`BeautifulSoup` takes advantage of the nested tree structure of HTML documents. It automatically converts a document to unicode and parses the document. It is then possible to traverse the document tree to find any relevant parts of the document. A little bit of knowledge of HTML tags is required to supply the correct arguments. Figure 5.9 displays an example of using both libraries.

Note the use of the `.text` method to extract the content from within a HTML tag. In the example, the text is extracted from a string bounded by HTML tags in the form *<td >This is HTML in side tags <td >*. In fact `BeautifulSoup` is using regular expressions to achieve this. Note in the code proper, a regular expression is used instead of `.text` method, in order to remove white space and extra HTML tags that may be within the text. See the discussion in Section 5.2.1.

Once the information has been extracted from the webpage, it must be stored. A MongoDB is used as the database. The reasons for choosing MongoDB were outlined in Section 5.1.3.2.

The `pymongo` package is used to connect to a *running* MongoDB server. A new database is created with two collections, one for the reports and the other for the associated comments. For each webpage, a Python dictionary is created with the relevant data extracted. The dictionary is then saved to the relevant collection, recursively (similar to inserting a row into a table). Figure 5.10 illustrates these conventions.

```
In [39]: from bs4 import BeautifulSoup
         import urllib2
         #Open webpage and scrape it.
         web_path = ("http://www.pillreports.net/index.php?"
                        "page=display_pill&id=34087")
         web_page = urllib2.urlopen(web_path).read().decode('utf-8')
         #Convert to Beautiful soup object.
         soup=BeautifulSoup(web_page)


In [40]: #Find all the tables in soup - findChildren
         #Returns all <table> tags
         no_tables = len(soup.findChildren('table'))
         print "Total Tables: "+str(no_tables)
         #Find all the rows - find_all
         #Returns all <tr> tags in <table>
         no_rows = len(soup.find_all('table')[0]('tr'))
         print "Rows in first Table: "+str(no_rows)
         #Find the cells - find_next
         #Returns the next HTML tag. Should be <td> for table cell
         #but may not be.
         first_cell=(soup.find_all('table')[0]('tr')[3]).find_next()
         second_cell=first_cell.find_next()
         print "Text of First Cell in Row 4: "+first_cell.text
         print "Text of Second Cell in Row 4: "+second_cell.text


Total Tables: 3
Rows in first Table: 21
Text of First Cell in Row 4: Date Submitted:
Text of Second Cell in Row 4: November 10, 2014, 4:28 pm GMT
```

FIGURE 5.9: Code: Scraping webpages.

```
In [ ]: #Python Dictionary
        post={"Data Submitted:":"December 24, 2014",
            "Rating:" : "Adulterated",
            "Warning:" : "yes"}

        import pymongo
        #Connect to MongoDB server with default settings.
        conn=pymongo.MongoClient()
        db = conn[myfirstdatabase] #Create the database
        reports = db.reports #Create collection in database
        reports.insert(post) #Insert dictionary into collection
        conn.close() #Close the connection
```

FIGURE 5.10: Code: Connecting to a database in MongoDB.

5.2.1   Regular Expression in Python

Regular expressions (prefixed with *r* in Python) are a text pattern that can be used to match content in a string. This can be for replacement, verification, splitting, etc. They are very powerful in simplifying many text processing tasks. However they need to be used with skill. Err on the side of simplicity when creating them.

Regular expressions use a wide array of special characters (and combinations) that cause different behaviors. In Python these characters are (. ^ $ * + ? { } [ ] \ — ( ) -). In addition the letters (A,b,B,d,D,s,S,w,W,z) when prefixed with \ also have special behaviors.

It is beyond the scope of this chapter to go into a huge amount of detail. In the accompanying notebooks regular expressions are used at a number of points. Figure 5.11 provides an overview of the main ways that they are employed.

The sub() function of the Python re module performs a search and replace across a whole string. All matches are replaced with the specified string. It is possible to limit the number of replacements by setting the count parameter to a nonnegative integer.

The findall() function returns all matches to a whole string. It is possible to set a starting and ending position to begin/finish searching the string. The returned result will be in a *list*.

Both methods make a call to compile() method; therefore, it is possible to create an instance of this method with the parameters pre-set.

Placing parentheses () around a regular expression string, causes a regular expression to find *groups* or pairs of matching strings returned in *tuples*. The tuples can then be indexed.

You may notice many similarities between the functions for the re module and the BeautifulSoup library. BeautifulSoup is in part a very neat wrapper around regular expression targeted towards HTML code. For a comprehensive overview of regular expressions [4] covers every possible aspect that you will ever need in many programming languages including Python.

5.2.2   PillReports.net Web Scrape

This section describes the Web scraping of the pillreports.net site itself. A quick look at any of the reports on the site, indicates that the data is very neatly structured inside sets of HTML tables. Using a trial and error process, similar to the methods shown in Figure 5.9, it is relatively easy to work out that there are three tables. The first contains the report and third contains the associated comments.

The address of the website is an incremental ID for each report. It is straightforward to setup a loop to run through a number of iterations increasing the ID to move through reports. In this chapter the most recent report was selected; at the time of the scrape, 17/11/2014, this was www.pillreports.net/index.php?page=display_pill&id=34120. The id was decremented (34120, 34119,...) until 5,001 pages had been captured. Note this required 7,180 iterations, as over 2,000 webpages did not return a result.

The pseudo code for the process is outlined in Algorithm 5.2.2. The full code for the scraping of pillreports.net is provided in **iPython Notebook:** 2.Web Scraping.

In addition to the logical checks in place to ensure the structure for each webpage is as expected, there are also checks to ensure that the encoding is correct and has worked. The incremental reference system may have reports that are deleted or that are not published. This will not affect the webscrape as these are simply discarded and an error message is printed. The code can be used straight away provided there is a MongoDB server running on your machine.

The two parameters that need to be changed are a) the number of reports to download and b) the starting place. These parameters are shown in Figure 5.12. The data will

```
In [118]:  import re
           text="""Hey diddle diddle, We are all on the fiddle,
           And never get up until noon. We only take cash,"""

In [119]:  #1. Sub
           print (re.sub('We', 'They', text))
```

Hey diddle diddle, They are all on the fiddle,
And never get up until noon. They only take cash,

```
In [120]:  #2. Findall

             #{4,6} 4 to 6 in a row.
             print (re.findall(r"[a-zA-Z]{4,6}", text))
             #+ = 1 or more * = 0 or more repetitions.
             print re.findall(r'n[o|e][a-z]*',text)
             #()Indicates grouping \w and letter
             print re.findall(r'([\w]+)dd([\w]+)',text)
```

['diddle', 'diddle', 'fiddle', 'never', 'until', 'noon', 'only', 'take', 'cash']
['never', 'noon']
[('di', 'le'), ('di', 'le'), ('fi', 'le')]

```
In [121]:  #3. Search
             #Returns first match only in groups.
             a=re.search(r'([\w]+)dd([\w]+)',text)
             print a.group(0),a.group(1),a.group(2)
```

diddle di le

```
In [122]:  #4. Using Compile
           re_1=re.compile(r'We')
           re_2=re.compile(r'n[o|e][a-z]*')

           print re_1.sub('They',text)
           print re_2.findall(text)
```

Hey diddle diddle, They are all on the fiddle,
And never get up until noon. They only take cash,
['never', 'noon']
diddle

FIGURE 5.11: Code: Regular expressions.

Algorithm Looping through pillreports.net webpages.

Require: target = positive integer *(number of pages to collect)*
Require: top_index = positive integer *(starting index of website*
Require: connection to MongoDB database; collection created *(reports)*
Ensure: MongoDB Server Running
  for count < target **do**
    Pass the index to web_scrape() for downloading the page
    if number of table **not** 3 **then**
      return false
    else
      return soup
    end if
    if soup **not false then**
      Pass (soup,index, db connection, db collection) to parse_tables()
Require: pill_reports_dict - *empty python dictionary*
      for row in table **do**
        col1=row.findnext()
        col2 = col1.findnext()
        python_report_dict[col1] = col2
      end for
      insert python_report_dict into MongoDB collection *reports*
    end if
  end for

---

be saved into a new MongoDB database named with the current date in the form pillreports_DDMonYY.

```
In []: #Scrape x number of pages starting at the most recent.
        target=50
        top_index=34120


In []: #Introduce time delay to stop overloading sites.
        from time import sleep

        while download_count <= target:
            sleep (0.25)
            soup=web_scrape(top_index)
```

FIGURE 5.12: Code: Setting scraping parameters.

A final word of caution, if you hit a server with too many requests at once you may be blocked from accessing it. If that is the case it may be worthwhile encapsulating your requests within a time delay as shown in Figure 5.12.

5.3 Data Cleansing

The previous section outlined the scraping of the data from the Web. As part of that process, regular expression were applied to the pillreports.net landing page, to extract the relevant features. In effect this was the start of the data cleansing, stripping away the HTML tags.

This section briefly outlines more aspects of data cleansing namely data tidying and data enrichment. Cleansing or shaping of the textual fields *(Warning:* and *User Report:)* continue throughout the project and are discussed further in the sections detailing the classification (5.5) and clustering (5.6) objectives.

Data tidying is relatively straightforward. In this chapter the tasks are defined as

(a) Renaming the columns (5.2)

(b) Cleaning up the date format (5.3)

(c) Remove trailing *mm* to get integer millimeter (5.7)

(d) Splitting column *Report Quality Rating:* (5.8)

(e) Categorize *Suspected Contents:* column (5.9)

(f) Splitting the *Submitted By:* column (5.10)

(g) Reorder the columns (5.11)

(h) Stripping out white space on binary labels (5.12)

These steps are well outlined in the accompanying **iPython Notebook:** 3.Data Cleansing. The numbers in brackets refer to the actual code chunk in the notebook. Many of the steps use regular expression methods as described in Section 5.2.1.

The data is read from the MongoDB into the ubiquitous pandas data frame. pandas is a library for data analysis in Python. A data frame is a tabular structure of rows and columns similar to a database table or a spreadsheet.

In addition to regular expression, a few Pythonic constructs (lambda, apply) and the datetime library are utilized in the data cleansing.

The lambda construct allows for the creation of functions without specifying a name for the function or even a return value. They are sometimes referred to as anonymous, throwaway or mini functions. Figure 5.13 concisely illustrates the concept.

The input to the function in the above case *(x)* is specified on the left of the colon and the operation on *(x)* on the right.

Apply is a method of the pandas library. It applies an operation to a column of a pandas data frame using the row index. (In the example presented in Figure 5.14 the operator is an unnamed lambda function, applied to every row.)

The datetime module is utilized to recode columns containing date information. The datetime module supplies a number of classes for manipulating dates and times. In the example presented in Figure 5.14 the strptime() method creates a datetime object from a string.

The string is represented with a series of defined characters *(for example %B is the full length English word for a month)*. Once a string has been converted to a datetime object it is then possible to apply a number of defined operations to work out time differences (called time deltas), days of the week, etc. It is good practice to set all dates to one unified

```
In [8]:  #Defined Function
         def square_func (x) :
             return x*x

         #Using Lambda
         square_lamb = lambda x: x*x

         print(square_func(5))
         print(square_lamb(5))


25
25
```

FIGURE 5.13: Code: Lambda method.

```
In [51]:  import pandas as pd
          data=[u'January  3, 2014, 3:19 pm GMT',
                u'March  17, 2014, 1:02 am GMT',
                u'November 14, 2014, 5:19 pm GMT']
          df = pd.DataFrame(data,columns=["Date"])

In [52]:  from datetime import datetime
          #use strptime to represent dates  as Timestamp('2014-11-09 14:05:00')

          df['Date2'] = df['Date'].apply(lambda d:
                                 datetime.strptime(d, "%B %d, %Y, %I:%M %p GMT"))
          #Standard format
          print df['Date2'][2]
          print "The first day is "+(df['Date2'][0]).strftime("%A")

          #Create a time delta
          days=(df['Date2'][2]-df['Date2'][0]).days
          print str(days)+" days between dates."


2014-11-14 17:19:00
The first day is Friday
315 days between dates.
```

FIGURE 5.14: Code: **DateTime** library, **Apply & Lambda** methods.

format, as it allows for much quicker development later on.

The data enrichment consists of three steps

(a) Recode the *State/Province:* column to *Country* (5.4)

(b) Calculate the number of comments per report (5.5)

(c) Determine the language of entries in *User Report:* using the `langdetect` library (5.6)

Recoding of the *State/Province* column was the most laborious part in the cleaning process. The column is free text and could be filled with a multitude of values. The original column had 1,629 different entries. The `Google Refine` application was used to cluster these based on similarity, resulting in 1,158 unique entries. These were then hand coded by sight in `Excel` to their respective countries. This is far from ideal and not recommended for large datasets, but in this case was acceptable. Table 5.4 illustrates some example cases. Note the value *So-Cal* an abbreviated version of South California coded to the United States. A lot of granularity is lost with this methodology.

TABLE 5.4: Geo-coding *State/Province:* column.

Geo Coding		
Refine Cluster	**Row Count**	**Country**
MELBOURNE	107	Australia
Chicago	93	USA
CALIFORNIA	91	USA
NSW-Sydney	60	Australia
So-Cal	57	USA

The comments associated with each report were also saved to the MongoDB during the webscrape. A reference to the corresponding reports was included, the report *ID:* The comments collection is extracted from the MongoDB, the number of *ID:*s summed and this is merged with the data frame. See step 5.5 in the accompanying notebook.

The final part of data enrichment involves the Google developed `langdetect` library. `langdetect` is a Python port of a Google created Java library for language detection. The library was developed using machine learning. It was supplied with a volume of Wikipedia articles from different languages and trained using Naïve Bayes. The library is the resultant Naïve Bayes ruleset or filter. It can detect 49 languages using the created ruleset with 99% accuracy, requiring a minimum 10–12 words depending on the language.

The `langdetect` methods were applied to the *User Report:* column. This was chosen over *Description:* column as it had more empty entries. The machine learning in this chapter is limited to English only and the labels determined by `langdetect` are used to filter the rows. If *Description:* column is used, it is possible to get a label indicating English but a blank entry in the *User Report:* field. The choice of *User Report:* therefore has an effect on the number of rows used in the Classification and Clustering processes. This is discussed further in Section 5.5.

A synopsis of the results from applying `langdetect` to the data is shown in Table 5.5. The determined language is shown with the generated *Country:* column. The *Unknown* are predominately empty or very short entries for *User Report:* field.

TABLE 5.5: Summary of *Country:* and *Language:* columns.

Country of Report	Total Rows	Language							Lang. not determined
		en	nl	tr	pl	ru	af	no	
USA	2051	1065							986
Australia	969	591							378
Netherlands	364	208	29						127
England	324	223							101
Unknown	282	160		1			1		119
Ireland	217	122							95
49 other countries	794	593	3	19	2	2		1	175
	5001	2962	32	20	2	2	1	1	1981

(en=English, nl=Dutch, tr=Turkish, pl=Polish, ru=Russian, af=Afrikaans, no=Norwegian)

Table 5.6 displays a summary of the prediction confidence as generated by the `langdetect` ruleset.

TABLE 5.6: Summary of language prediction confidence.

Lang-uage	Total Rows	Prediction Confidence			
		min	max	avg.	std.
en	2962	0.571	1	0.999	0.014
nl	32	0.714	1	0.92	0.108
tr	20	0.571	1	0.943	0.126
pl	2	0.857	1	0.929	0.101
ru	2	1	1	1	
af	1	0.571	0.571	0.571	
no	1	1	1	1	

(1,981 rows have no language determined, 1,762 rows have no text, remainder typically too short)

5.4   Data Visualization and Exploration

The success of data mining and by extension text mining projects lie in part with the visualization and exploration of the data.

In Section 5.1.4.1 the power of Python's implementation of sparse matrices and the tight integration with the `sklearn` library was extolled as a driver in choosing Python as the data mining tool for text mining. A downside to choosing Python is that there currently does not exist an easy to use and mature library for data visualization, certainly not comparable to the ease of use of the *ggplot2* package [5] in the R statistical programming language.

Up until very recently the `Matplotlib` library was really the only option for visualization in Python. In the last few years, a number of new libraries have emerged, some built upon the foundations of `Matplotlib`.

Some of these (*Bokeh, Chaco, Plotly, Vincent*) are orientated towards interactive visualizations either locally or hosted. Others (*Seaborn, ggplot*) aim to emulate the ease of use of *ggplot2* for R. For a good treatment of their various strengths and weaknesses see [6].

All of the above libraries are in nascent stages of development. Therefore currently the best option is to use `Matplotlib` as the base tool and the other tools where appropriate. For this chapter the `Seaborn` library was used at different points. It is built on top of Matplotlib and aims to remove much of the time consuming coding burden of creating nice plots in Matplotlib, more of which in the next section (5.4.1).

5.4.1 Python:Matplotlib

A quick search of questions on *stackoverflow.com* tagged with Matplotlib reveals $\approx$ 10,250 tags. The next nearest of the libraries listed in the previous section is *Bokeh* $\approx$ 130 and *Seaborn* $\approx$ 100 (as of 1 Feb, 2015), reflecting Matplotlib's popularity, perpetuity, and pain!

Matplotlib has a low-level API. The amount of code required to create only moderately complex statistical visualizations can be onerous, certainly compared to that of *ggplot2*.

`Seaborn` is built on-top of Matplotlib and and provides nice wrappers for creating nicely formatted visualizations without the coding and time overhead. It also works well with `pandas` data frames. However, it is relatively new and therefore it does not have the full suite of functions or controls as are often required.

The best way to learn these libraries is through repeated use. Section 5.4.2 presents the results of data exploration with a mixture of visualizations and tables. It provides links to the accompanying notebooks. The focus of the code explanations is on *rolling up data* to the point where a visualization with `Matplotlib` is possible.

Before presenting the results, Figure 5.15 shows a simple Matplotlib `subplot` containing a line chart and bar graph. Figure 5.16 presents the associated code with 3 alternate ways of achieving this plot with Matplotlib. This goes some way to explaining why it can be difficult to get going with Matplotlib. It is an extensive library with a huge amount of open-source development and thus has a lot of cross over functionality.

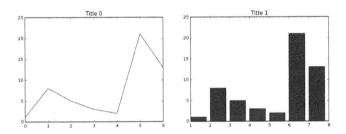

FIGURE 5.15: Simple matplotlib subplot example.

In Matplotlib, there is the concept of the current plot or often referred to as an **axes** (not axis). Until a new plot is generated, all commands entered are targeted at the most recently generated graphic. Alternatively a handle to the individual plot object *(ax1,ax2)* can be used to pass commands to a particular graphic. For a good introduction to Matplotlib refer to [7].

5.4.2 Pillreports.net Data Exploration

This section focuses on describing the downloaded data. The code for the actual plots can be found in **iPython Notebook:** `4:Visualization.ipynb`. Where code is presented it is to illustrate how rows are aggregated before passing to the Matplotlib method.

```
In []: %matplotlib inline
        import numpy as np
        import matplotlib.pyplot as plt

        fib = (1, 8, 5, 3, 2,21,13)
        x = np.linspace(1,len(fib),num=len(fib))


In []: plt.figure(1,figsize=(12,4))  #1. Using Subplots

        plt.subplot(121)
        plt.plot(fib),plt.title("Title A")

        plt.subplot(122)
        plt.bar(x,fib),plt.ylabel("Y Label: B")


In []: #2. Using figure and axes
        fig, ((ax1,ax2)) = plt.subplots(1,2,figsize=(12, 4))

        ax1.plot(fib),ax1.set_title("Title A")
        ax2.bar(x,fib),ax2.set_ylabel("Y Label: B")


In []: #3. Using ravel()
        fig, axs = plt.subplots(1,2, figsize=(12, 4))

        axs = axs.ravel()
        for i in range(2):
            if i==0:
                axs[i].plot(fib)
            if i==1:
                axs[i].bar(x,fib)
            axs[i].set_title(('Title '+str(i)))
```

FIGURE 5.16: Code: matplotlib subplots.

A total of 5,001 reports were downloaded. The `User:` and `Description:` columns represent the corpus of documents in the usual sense of text mining. The earliest report submitted report was on 08/08/2011 and the most recent on 17/11/2014. On average there were 29 reports being submitted per week for this time period. Figure 5.17 displays graphs of the weekly count of reports submitted both by year and over the whole time period.

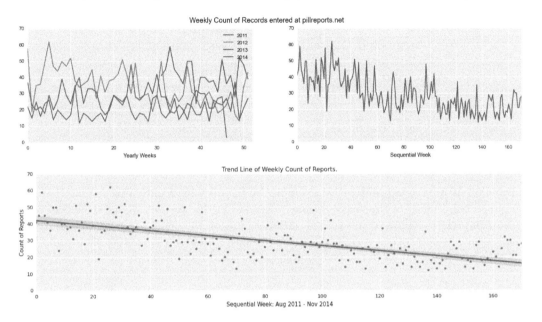

FIGURE 5.17 (See color insert.): Weekly count of reports.

There is an obvious decline in number of reports being submitted over the time period. In 21 weeks' worth of data from 2011 there averaged 41 reports per week. This drops to 20 reports by 2014. The causes of this are not known. Interestingly the number of reports with the value *Warning=No* increases over this time period from 50% to 70% as shown in Figure 5.18.

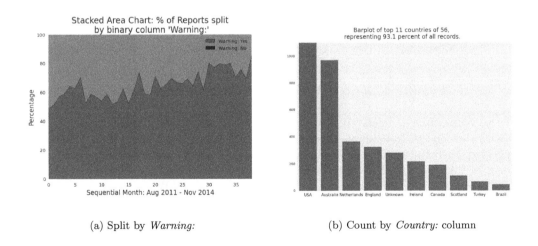

(a) Split by *Warning:*

(b) Count by *Country:* column

FIGURE 5.18: *Warning:* Column cross-tabulated with *Country:* column.

It could be that there is an increased usage of testing kits to determine the presence of adulterants in ecstasy pills over this period of time. The breakdown of the suspected contents of a pill is shown in Table 5.7.

TABLE 5.7: Suspected contents *(SC Category:)* and *Warning:* label.

Suspected Contents Category	Warning: no	yes	percent yes
amphet (Amphetamines)	107	397	79
MDxx	2809	50	2
Other	34	287	89
pip (Piperzines)	3	276	99
Unknown	231	807	78

Table 5.7 is used as an illustrative example for the data aggregation or *roll up* that is required to build much of the visualizations presented in this section. Many visualizations rely on comparison counts of categorical variables and/or the comparison of quantitative variables split by categorical variables. Three alternative methods to achieve the results in the Table 5.7 are presented in the code snippet shown in Figure 5.19.

```
In [83]: import pandas as pd
         import numpy as np
         df=pd.read_csv("Data/prReports.csv",encoding='utf-8')


In []: #Pivot Table
        df.pivot_table(index='SC Category:', columns='Warning:',values="ID:",
               aggfunc=len)

        #Cross Tabulation
        pd.crosstab(df['SC Category:'],df['Warning:'],margins=False)

        bySCCategory=df.groupby(['SC Category:'])
        bySCCategory['Warning:'].value_counts().unstack()


In []: #len=number of rows, mean, max of UR Length, by w
        bySCCategory['UR Length:'].agg([len,np.mean,np.max])
```

FIGURE 5.19: Code: Weekly count of reports submitted.

The `pivot_table` is relatively straight forward to understand if you have any familiarity with the concept from spreadsheets. The categorical variables for rows and columns are specified, then the value that is under observation and the summation measures are provided. In this case the *ID:* column is passed and its `len` or number of rows counted.

Passing the *ID:* is bit of a workaround in the above example. When counts of rows are required `pandas` provides a much simpler `crosstab` function to achieved this.

The final method shown is `groupby` which is arguably the most powerful and flexible of the above methods. Using `groupby` allows for multiple variables and multiple aggregation functions to be computed simultaneously as required.

Much of the rolling up processes presented here are hard coded into the new visualization libraries discussed. It is beneficial to expose these calculations, as it can aid better understanding if you have an appreciation of what is going on under the hood. [8] provides a comprehensive overview of aggregating data using the `pandas` library. The focus of the data mining objectives set out, is to build supervised and unsupervised models based on the textual data using the *Description:* and *User Report:* columns. An analysis of these columns is required. String lengths is a useful way of examining textual data to understand if key differences exist for certain groupings.

Table 5.8 displays the string lengths of *User Report:* grouped by *Country:* and *Warning:* columns. Only the top 7 countries are displayed.

TABLE 5.8: *User Report:* string length grouped by *Country:* and *Warning:*.

Country	All Rows	Warning=Yes			Warning=No		
		Rows	Mean Len.	std.	Rows	Mean Len.	std.
USA	1131	505	1297	1261	626	1481	1228
Australia	631	186	929	745	445	973	738
Netherlands	258	21	719	642	237	849	944
England	229	47	872	579	182	1079	875
Unknown	184	66	836	892	118	1062	960
Canada	163	148	810	1016	15	1357	805
Ireland	126	34	885	894	92	977	717
Scotland	91	18	1178	1183	73	1158	804

There are differences in length based on the country of origin, with the USA, Scotland and Australia having longer responses. When looking at the *mean* of the string length split by *Warning:* value, there is slight increase in the length where *Warning:=no*. It should be noted that the string length of *Description:* entries have a log normal distribution. This has long been observed in language composition [9].

A visualization of the string lengths transformed by the natural logarithm ($log_e x$) is shown in 5.4.2. In addition a `boxplot` and `violin` plot are presented using the plotting functions from the `Seaborn` library (see step 4.9 of the accompanying notebook).

The `violin` plot shows the distribution for *Warning:=Yes* has a less dense mean peak. This may indicate that people give either sharper/shorter responses or longer/detailed responses in this instance.

The next section presents an outline of taking the textual data in *Description:* column and manipulating it to a format where its features (the words) can be used as the input variables of a classification model.

5.5 Classification

The *Warning:* field is populated from a drop-down list with a binary option *Y*es/No, indicating whether a pill being considered is believed to be adulterated i.e. contains ingredients not comparable to 3,4-methylenedioxy-methamphetamine, commonly referred to as MDMA, the key active ingredient of ecstasy.

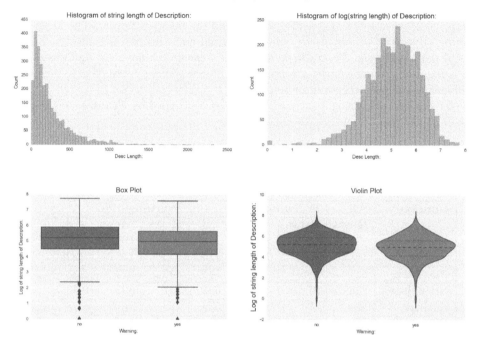

FIGURE 5.20: String length of *Description:* column.

This provides a good target label to build a prediction on. The *Description:* field was chosen as the text field to generate input features for the prediction model. The *Description:* free text field was chosen over *User Report:* as it is mandatory and the latter optional. In addition it was believed that a label *Warning:=Yes* may preclude an entry into *User Report:* field. (Would a person consume a pill if they believed it to be adulterated?)

The distribution between the labels is No (N=3,184, 64%) and Yes (N=1,817, 36%). There is no significant skew in the label distributions, therefore the measure of *Accuracy* is suitable for reporting model results.

$$Accuracy = \frac{TP + TN}{TP + FP + TN + FN} \qquad (5.1)$$

where TP is true positive, TN is true negative, FP is false positive and FN is false negative.

The next section moves through the process of setting up a classification model with the `sklearn` library. The full code is presented in accompanying **iPython Notebook:** `5.Classification`.

5.5.1   Classification with sklearn

The `sklearn` package allows for the development of classification models in straightforward and intuitive steps. This allows for manageable creation of very complex models.

The first step after reading in the data is to set up the methods for vectorizing the text data into a sparse matrix as outlined in Section 5.1.4.1. A basic outline of this is shown in Figure 5.21

The `CountVectorizer` tokenizes text into individual words, creating the *bag of words*

```
In [1]:  import pandas as pd
         df=pd.read_csv("Data/prReports.csv",encoding='utf-8')


In [2]:  #Set up data transformation and model parameters
         from sklearn.feature_extraction.text import CountVectorizer
         from sklearn.feature_extraction.text import TfidfTransformer
         vec = CountVectorizer(min_df=0.001,max_df=0.95)

         from sklearn.naive_bayes import MultinomialNB
         clf = MultinomialNB()
```

FIGURE 5.21: Code: Setting up vectorizer and models for classification.

representation. In the presented example, the default parameters are used, that is uni-ngram and frequency count. It is possible to change the parameters for multi-ngrams and/or binary occurrence. The `min_df` and the `max_df` parameters are set to (0.001 , 0.95) respectively.

`min_df` determines how infrequent words are handled. In this example any word that appears in fewer than 0.1% of documents (or five documents with 5,000 documents) should be discarded. Similarly `max_df` determines how very frequent words should be treated. Frequent words may, but not be, limited to *english stopwords*. In this domain it is conceivable that the word *drug* may be frequent.

The `TfidfTransformer` can be used to create a *term-frequency inverse document frequency* or *tf-idf* representation of the corpus. The calculation of the *tf-idf* for a term t is:

$$TF(t) = \frac{\text{Count of } \mathbf{t} \text{ in document}}{\text{Total number of terms in document}} \tag{5.2}$$

$$IDF(t) = log_e\left(\frac{\text{Count of documents}}{\text{Count of documents containing } \mathbf{t}}\right) \tag{5.3}$$

$$\text{tf-idf(t)} = TF(t) * IDF(t) \tag{5.4}$$

The effect of *tf-idf* is to increase the importance of a word according to the number of times it occurs in a document and offset it by the frequency with which it occurs across all the documents, in effect filtering for domain specific common words.

```
In [7]:  #Split the data. Recode text label as numeric (TRUE/FALSE)
         X=df['Description:'].values
         y=(df['Warning:']=='no').values.astype(int)

         from sklearn import cross_validation
         X_train, X_test, y_train, y_test = cross_validation.train_test_split(
                                  X,y,test_size=0.4,random_state=79)
```

FIGURE 5.22: Code: Splitting into train and test sets.

Figure 5.22 illustrates the `cross_validation.train_test_split` method to split the data into training and test sets. Note the use of the `random_state`. This controls how the random number generator of the splitting method is created, so as to allow the comparison of various models. If this was not held constant a different subset of rows would be selected each time the method was called. This could potentially obscure any improvements or degradation of the score of *accuracy* when altering model parameters. This would be typically removed once the model is finalized.

Figure 5.23 introduces the sklearn `Pipeline` class. `Pipeline` is a very powerful feature of the `sklearn` library, allowing the chaining or serialization of data transformations before applying the data to the model. In essence it builds a data stream. A lot of the heavy lifting in machine learning are the transformations and adjusting of parameters for generating the input feature set. Using `pipeline` facilitates this especially when passing user defined function or wrapping it in a loop and altering the parameters (see step 5.4 of the accompanying notebook).

```
In []: #Set up a pipeline, transformations and
       #model will be serialized.
       from sklearn import pipeline
       pipe = pipeline.Pipeline([('vectorizer', vec),
       ('tfidf',TfidfTransformer()),
       ('classifier', clf)])
       pipe.fit(X_train, y_train)
```

FIGURE 5.23: Code: **sklearn pipeline**.

The final part in classification is reporting the model results. Figure 5.24 presents the `metrics` class with a number of different methods for outputting relevant results.

```
In []: #Use metrics methods to print get results.
       from sklearn import metrics

       print (metrics.accuracy_score(pipe.predict(X_test), y_test))
       print (metrics.classification_report(pipe.predict(X_test), y_test))
       print (metrics.confusion_matrix(pipe.predict(X_test), y_test))
```

FIGURE 5.24: Code: Model metrics.

5.5.2   Classification Results

In the code for this chapter, a series of vector representations of the text in the *Description:* column, with different settings were created. Two classifiers were used: Naïve Bayes and Stochastic Gradient Descent. A sklearn `pipeline` was wrapped inside a loop and the vector representation and model were interchanged. This resulted in a matrix of (2 models $\times$ 6 vector representations $\times$ 2 term counting schemes) 24 combinations. The top 5 results based on training accuracy are presented in Table 5.9.

From a baseline accuracy of 0.710 in the first model (as outlined in Figure 5.22) the accuracy only increases slightly to 0.72 using Naïve Bayes and relatively straightforward vector representation with words containing alpha character only. Stochastic Gradient Boosting with tf-idf weighting, stemming and 1-3 ngrams achieves only a modest improvement.

The number of features is quite large, 2,785 and 16,847, respectively. [10] have cited that a significantly reduced feature set can improve accuracy in text classification. The next step therefore is to reduce the feature set.

Taking the best results for both the model types (Naïve Bayes and Stochastic Gradient Descent) feature selection is applied. `sklearn` provides simple methods for feature selection, presented in Figure 5.25.

TABLE 5.9: Top 5 models: binary classification on *Warning:* column.

Rank	Model	Number Features	Train Acc.	Train std.	Test Score	Count	Ngrams	Stemmed
							Vectorization	
1	NV	2,785	0.722	0.014	0.726	freq	1 gram	
2	SGD	1,6,847	0.722	0.024	0.705	tfidf	1-3 grams	✓
3	NB	2,905	0.72	0.016	0.733	freq	1-3 grams	
4	SGD	1,1,819	0.715	0.024	0.7	tfidf	1-2 grams	
5	SGD	167,136	0.711	0.021	0.706	tfidf	1-3 grams	

Minimum and maximum document frequency held at constant percentages (0.001, 0.95), respectively.

```
In []: from sklearn.feature_selection import SelectKBest, chi2

        for sel in [150,300,450,600]:

            #Feature selection based on select k number of features
            fs = SelectKBest(chi2, k=sel)
            X_train_reduced = fs.fit_transform(X_train, y_train)
            X_test_reduced = fs.transform(X_test)
            pipe.fit(X_train_reduced, y_train)
```

FIGURE 5.25: Code: Feature selection.

Currently the implementation of `sklearn.feature_selection` is limited to the *chi-squared* measure. This allows selection of features using the `SelectPercentile` where the top % predictive words are selected based on the chi-square measure. It is possible to write a user defined function to determine other measures such as *information gain*, etc. and pass these into the `feature_selection` method. The results from applying feature selection are shown in Table 5.10.

TABLE 5.10: Classification accuracy using feature selection.

Model	Select Feat.	% Feat.	Train Acc.	Train std.	Test Acc.
Naïve Bayes; word frequency count, alpha characters only, 1 gram **(2,785 features)**	417	0.15	0.779	0.021	0.722
	557	0.2	0.793	0.022	0.722
	450	0.162	0.782	0.022	0.722
SGD; tf-idf weighting, alpha characters only, 1-3 grams **(16,487 features)**	600	0.036	0.779	0.019	0.723
	300	0.018	0.755	0.014	0.723
	450	0.027	0.765	0.015	0.712

While feature selection improves the training accuracy it appears to overfit the data as there is only a modest increase, if any, in the test score. Not withstanding this, feature selection provides an interesting way to examine the predictive power of individual words. Using many of the code methods outlined above and combining with the process for generating plots outlined in Section 5.4.1, a scatter plot of the top 250 predictive uni-gram words was created based on the *chi-square* measure. The code for this is contained in step 5.6 of **iPython Notebook:** `5.Classification`.

The coding process is very similar to classification, with one key difference. Rather than counting the words using term frequency (TF) or TF-IDF, the binary occurrence is used. Binary occurrence gives a term a value of one it occurs in a document, regardless of the number of times its occurs in that document, zero otherwise. A zoomed in version of the plot is shown in Figure 5.26.

The effect of the using binary occurrence is the plot shows the count of documents that a particular term occurs in across the whole corpus. The count is split by the class label *Warning:=yes/no* of each document. They size of the bubbles represents the *chi-square* value of that term.

It is interesting to note that words like *(sour, stay, away, warning, speed)* are associated with *Warning:=yes*. "Stay away" probably has more predictive power as a bi-gram. Contrast this with the words for *Warning:=no* such as *amazing, instantly, tolerance* and words associated with testing kits *mecke, mandeline, reagent*. There is a significantly lower probability of a *Warning=Yes* if the pill has been tested, as illustrated in Table 5.7. The examination of the individual words predictive power, motivates examination of the *User Report:* entries detailed in the next section.

5.6 Clustering & PCA

The previous section outlined a supervised learning exercise. This section explores unsupervised learning using two methods Clustering and Principal Component Analysis (PCA).

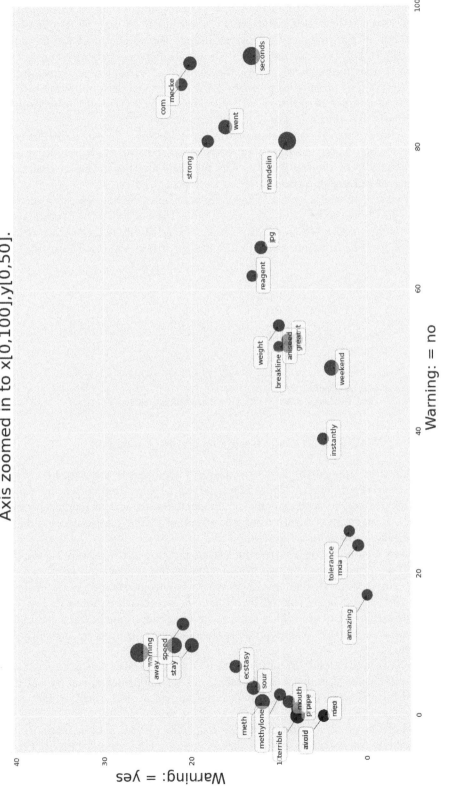

FIGURE 5.26: Scatter plot of top predictive features.

These are applied to the *User Report:* column. Performing unsupervised learning on textual data may be considered as data exploration [11] depending on the context of the project.

It is assumed that the user is familiar with Clustering. PCA may be less familiar. In structured data, one of the challenges is understanding the interaction between multiple variables. Many times, pairwise calculations of correlation between two variables are used. Sometimes there is a requirement to reduce the number of variables, while retaining as much as the information as possible as possible. PCA is one such data reduction technique to transform a large number of variables to a smaller set. It is beyond the scope of this chapter to sufficiently explain PCA. For a good treatment see [12].

The processes for setting up vector representation of the *User Report:* is similar to that detailed in Section 5.5.1. Note that binary occurrence is used and Tf-idf weighting is used to control for documents of varying lengths. The full code for this section is contained in the accompanying **iPython Notebook:** 6. Clustering & PCA.

Setting up a cluster model is exactly the same as outlined for classification models in Figure 5.22. To run PCA, the `sparse matrix` that is the output of the vectorization of the words, must be first converted to a `dense matrix` as the PCA method of `sklearn` currently does not handle sparse matrices. Example code is presented in Figure 5.27

```
In []: from sklearn import cluster
       from sklearn.decomposition import PCA

       #Clustering
       k = 3, kmeans = cluster.KMeans(n_clusters=k)
       kmeans.fit(data)

       #PCA convert the sparse matrix to dense() representations
       pca = PCA(n_components=2)
       UR_PCA = pca.fit(data.todense()).transform(data.todense())
```

FIGURE 5.27: Code: Clustering and PCA models.

After PCA has been applied the first two principal components are added to the data frame. These are a series of numeric values and thus can be visualized on a scatter plot. A exploratory question arises, do these principal components represent a particular phenomena of the data set? An attempt at interpreting the meaning of the principal components is provided using available categorical variables.

The components are plotted on a scatter plot using `matplotlib`. In addition the points are colored based on a particular nominal field, including the membership label as a result of the clustering (three clusters). Figure 5.28 presents the output. Here a matrix of six plots is created, each plot's point being colored by a different categorical variable.

Moving through the graph, plot (1) is colored by the cluster membership created with k-means. Compare it to plot (3). This represents the documents colored by the value of the *Warning:* column.

There is a definite split in plot (3) and this seems to be replicated to some extent in the cluster membership displayed in plot (1). Therefore, the second principal component (along the y axis) could be said to be exposing the variation in words used based on the value of *Warning:=yes/no* and the k-means clustering algorithm finds this also.

Plot (2) is colored by creating a binning of the *User Description:* field based on its string length, with equal numbers of points per bin (low, medium, high - string lengths). The split here also shows some relation to the clustering of the documents in plot (1). Moreover it could be said the first principal component (along the x axis) is capturing the length of the documents.

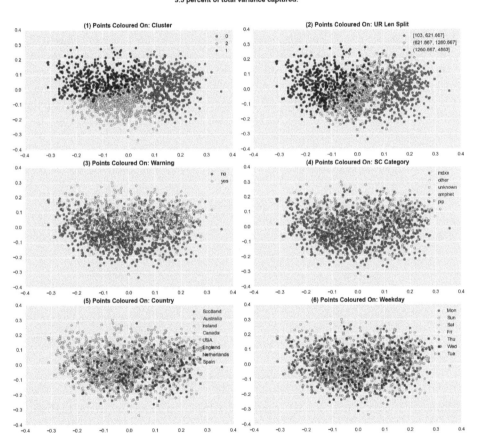

FIGURE 5.28 (See color insert.): Principal components scatter plot.

Plot (4) represents the points colored by the *SC Category:* column. Note the points where *SC Category: = mdxx* appear to follow the same pattern as the points where *Warning: = no*, show in plot (3). This is not surprising as Table 5.7 illustrated significant differences in distribution of the *Warning:* values based on the suspected contents.

Plot (5) is colored by the country of origin of the report. There appears to be the outline of a pattern here, perhaps indicating differing english vocabularies based on the origin of the report. The final plot (6) is based on the day of the week a report was posted. It was hypothesized that reports filled in or around the weekend would vary somewhat. This is not supported here.

5.6.1   Word Cloud

Taking the observations reviewed already, it might be interesting to visualize the differences in language use of the *User Experience:* field based on the *Warning:* label. The *SC Category:* label appears to mimic the *Warning:* value and could be used as a proxy. As it is multinominal it can provide more granularity than a binary variable.

A wordcloud of the *User Experience:* field split the value of *SC Category:* provides a very accessible way of visualizing this. Using all the words can overwhelm such a visualization type. It is often better to focus on descriptive or rich words. To achieve this the words can be filtered by their type (e.g., noun, adjective, adverb).

The first step is to tag each word in the column with their relevant tag using the `nltk` library. The words can then be filtered based on their type. The code for this is shown in Figure 5.29.

```
In []:  #Using nltk tag all words with their part of speech.
        #Returns tuples (word,pos).
        from nltk import pos_tag
        clusterDF['Tagged']=(clusterDF['User Report']).map(
                            lambda x: pos_tag(word_tokenize(x)))

        #Select only those words that are common adjectives and common nouns
        clusterDF['Rich_words']=(clusterDF['Tagged']).map(
                            lambda x: ' '.join([y[0].lower() for y in x
                                    if y[1] in ['JJ','NN']]))
```

FIGURE 5.29: Code: Tagging words using **nltk** library.

Wordclouds are based on frequency counts of words. The word with the highest count receives the largest relevant plotting space (or font size). Sometimes if *stopwords* are left in or a particular word has very high frequency it dominates the the wordcloud. In order to control for this, the top words can be filtered out.

The `collections` module provides an extremely fast counter for achieving this. In the example shown in Figure 5.30, each row of the data frame is joined to form one very large string. This is then tokenized. The `defaultdict` loops through and adds any unseen words as a key and for seen words increments a counter or value.

The top words can then be viewed and added to a list of stopwords as necessary. The final step involves using the `wordcloud` library developed by [13]. Using a set of controls within a for loop, allowing for the increment of the number of stopwords, a matrix of plots is created, shown in Figure 5.31.

This yields some very interesting differences between the language used in the text column *User Report:* based on the associated value in *Suspected Contents:*. Users who take *MDMA* substances focus more of adjectives/nouns associated with empathy. Contrast that

```
In []:  #Join all words into a long string
        words = ' '.join(clusterDF['Rich_words']

        from collections import defaultdict
        word_counts = defaultdict(int)

        #Tokenize each word loop over and created count
        for w in word_tokenize(words):
                word_counts[w] += 1
```

FIGURE 5.30: Code: Counting word frequency with the collections module.

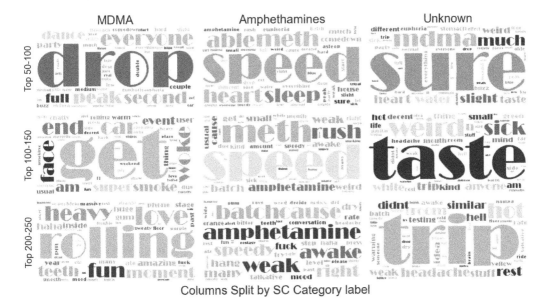

FIGURE 5.31: *User report:* Word cloud.

with users who take *Amphetamine* type substances where the focus is on adjectives/nouns related to trajectory or energy. The last column are those where the user does not know what the substance being consumed is. These are dominated by the words associated with the physical body.

5.7 Summary

This chapter outlined the processes for working through a text mining project using Python. The binary classification model based on the *Description:* field achieved a modest 1.9 point increase from the baseline model (.714) to (.733).

The application of clustering was validated visually using principal components projection and available labels. While the clustering was not entirely successful, the subsequent scatter plot visualizations led to a new avenue of investigation. This is often the case in data mining.

Numerical validation of clusters was not completed. There are a wide variety of numerical measures to validate clusters; see [14] for a comprehensive list. However cluster validation is currently an area of open research. Methods for selecting the correct number of clusters is more a matter of usability and interpretation rather than a defined measurement. For more information about the mathematical underpinnings of clustering see [15].

(Clustering in the context presented in this chapter may not be the best data mining technique to expose underlying patterns. Topic modeling may be a more suitable approach.)

The word cloud, while relatively elementary in their creation, was powerful and could certainly be a convincing visualization to aid understanding of Ecstasy drug culture. For the reader that wishes to do more experimentation using the aforementioned data sets there a wealth of possible questions that could be posed.

The classification section focused on modeling the *Description:* free text column. The *Description:* column contains significantly less information than the *User Report:* column. These could be swapped and or combined and differences in the model accuracy appraised.

The classification model focused on the binary label *Warning:*. It is possible to use a different column for multinominal classification (*SC Category:*) or indeed use a real number for a regression model with either of the (*Report Stars:, Report Votes:, Total Comments:*) columns.

The collection of associated comments for each report is completely unexplored (it is provided unprocessed in a CSV file). At a simple exploration level, which reports generate the most comments? Which users post comments regularly? Can comments be clustered? What are the characteristics of a comment discussion that generate an Admin/Moderator user intervention? These are just a few possible ideas.

From a programming perspective there are lots of avenues of further investigation. Many of the processes shown, especially in the classification section could be parallelised to speed up the computation time. The `pipelining` method outlined, is only briefly utilized. It can be extended to build very complex chains of data transformations.

One the best resources for learning about Python and data/text mining is through iPython notebooks and *PyCon* conferences that occur regular. Many of these are recorded and posted on YouTube with links to the accompanying notebooks.

Python for text mining can be very rewarding. There is a very vibrant community with lots of people who are willing to share their knowledge and experience. All the libraries detailed here are continually being developed and improved. Finally by using the iPython environment it is very easy for you to become part of this community and share your knowledge and insights in your domain.

Bibliography

[1] P-N Tan, M. Steinbach, V. Kumar, et al. *Introduction to data mining*, volume 1. Pearson Addison Wesley, 2006.

[2] K. P. Murphy. *Machine learning: a probabilistic perspective.* MIT press, 2012.

[3] N. Batchelder. *How Do I Stop the Pain.* (https://www.youtube.com/watch?v= sgHbC6udIq), 2012.

[4] J. Goyvaerts and S. Levithan. *Regular expressions cookbook.* O'reilly, 2009.

[5] H. Wickham. *ggplot2: elegant graphics for data analysis.* Springer, 2009.

[6] C. Moffitt. *Overview of Python Visualization Tools.* (http://pbpython.com/ visualization-tools-1.html), 2015.

[7] A. Devert. *matplotlib Plotting Cookbook.* Packt Publishing Ltd, 2014.

[8] W. McKinney. *Python for data analysis: Data wrangling with Pandas, NumPy, and IPython.* O'Reilly Media, Inc., 2012.

[9] W. C. Wake. Sentence-length distributions of Greek authors. *Journal of the Royal Statistical Society. Series A (General)*, pages 331–346, 1957.

[10] Y. Liu, H. Tong Loh, and A. Sun. Imbalanced text classification: A term weighting approach. *Expert Systems with Applications*, 36(1):690–701, 2009.

[11] S. M Weiss, N. Indurkhya, and T. Zhang. *Fundamentals of predictive text mining.* Springer Science & Business Media, 2010.

[12] I. Jolliffe. *Principal component analysis.* Wiley Online Library, 2002.

[13] A. Mueller. *Python word cloud.* (https://github.com/amueller/word_cloud), 12 2014.

[14] M. Charrad, N. Ghazzali, V. Boiteau, and A. Niknafs. Nbclust: An r package for determining the relevant number of clusters in a data set. *Journal of Statistical Software*, 61(6):1–36, 2014.

[15] R. Xu and D. Wunsch. *Clustering*, volume 10. John Wiley & Sons, 2008.

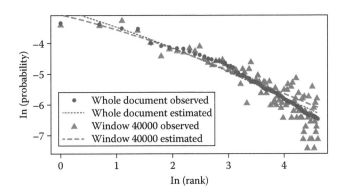

FIGURE 2.14: Log of probability and estimated probability as a function of log rank for the 100 most common words within all of *Pride and Prejudice*.

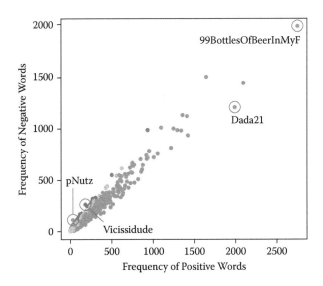

FIGURE 4.3: Scatter plot of frequency of negative words vs. frequency of positive words for all users.

FIGURE 4.4: Tag cloud of user "dada21".

FIGURE 4.5: Tag cloud of user "pNutz".

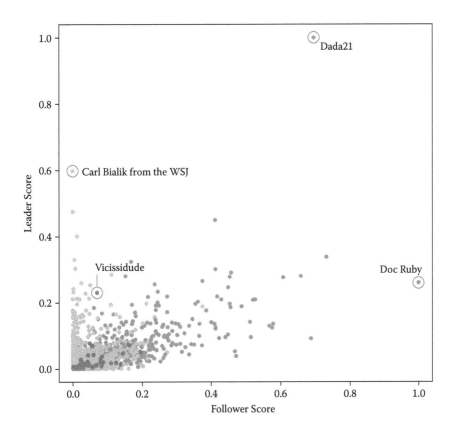

FIGURE 4.9: Leader vs. follower score colored by attitude for all users. Users with a positive attitude are marked green, users with a negative attitude red.

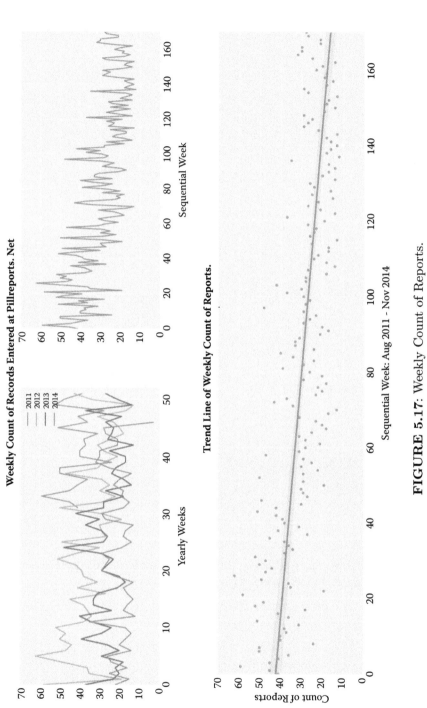

FIGURE 5.17: Weekly Count of Reports.

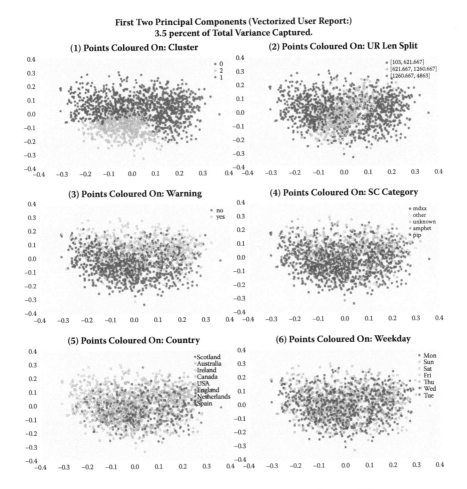

FIGURE 5.28: Principal Components Scatter Plot.

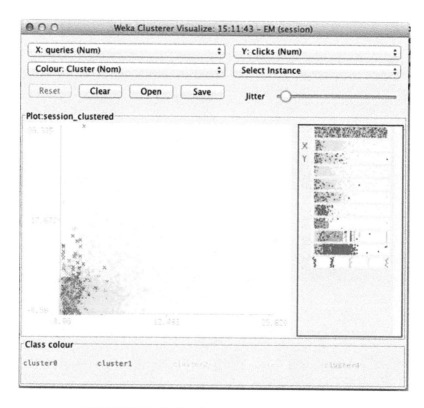

FIGURE 7.7: Configuring the visualization.

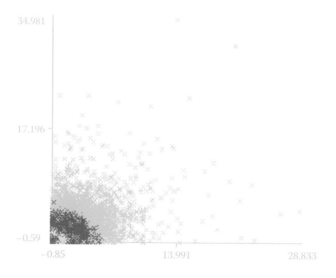

FIGURE 7.8: 100,000 AOL sessions, plotted as queries vs. clicks.

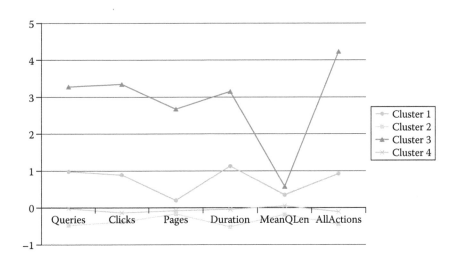

FIGURE 7.9: Four clusters based on six features.

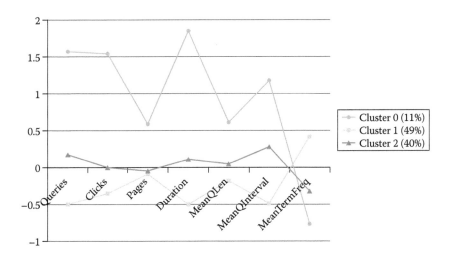

FIGURE 7.10: Three clusters based on seven features.

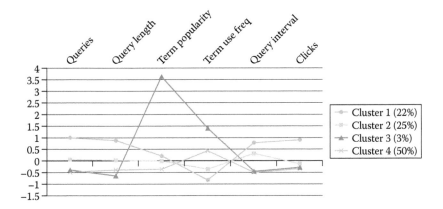

FIGURE 7.11: Applying EM using Wolfram et al.'s 6 features to 10,000 sessions from AOL.

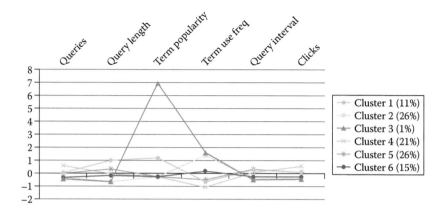

FIGURE 7.12: Applying EM using Wolfram et al.'s 6 features to 100,000 sessions from AOL.

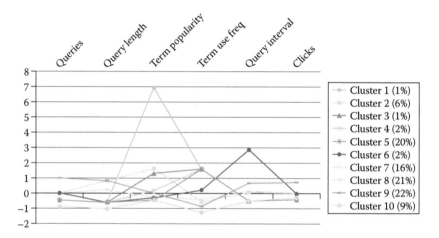

FIGURE 7.13: Applying XMeans ($k <= 10$) and Wolfram et al.'s 6 features to 100,000 sessions from AOL.

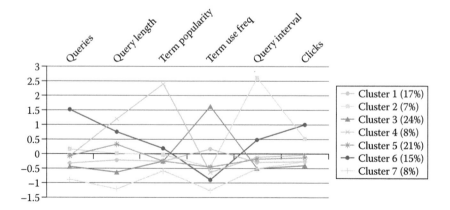

FIGURE 7.14: Applying EM and Wolfram et al.'s 6 features to 100,000 filtered sessions from AOL.

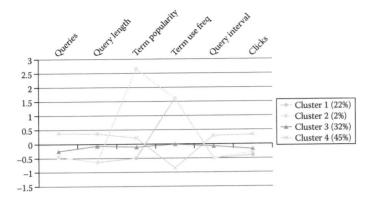

FIGURE 7.16: Applying kMeans ($k = 4$) and Wolfram et al.'s 6 features to 100,000 sessions from AOL.

China Takes On Big Risks in Its Push for Shale Gas

By KEITH BRADSHERAPRIL 11, 2014

JIAOSHIZHEN, China — Residents of this isolated mountain valley of terraced cornfields were just going to sleep last April when they were jolted by an enormous roar, followed by a tower of flames. A shock wave rolled across the valley, rattling windows in farmhouses and village shops, and a mysterious, pungent gas swiftly pervaded homes. "It was so scary — everyone who had a car fled the village and the rest of us without cars just stayed and waited to die," said Zhang Mengsu, a hardware store owner. All too quickly, residents realized the source of the midnight fireball: a shale gas drilling rig in their tiny rural hamlet. This verdant valley represents the latest frontier in the worldwide hunt for shale gas retrievable by the technology of hydraulic fracturing, or fracking. It is a drilling boom that has upended the energy industry and spurred billions of dollars of investment.

Like the United States and Europe, China wants to wean itself from its dependence on energy imports — and in Jiaoshizhen, the Chinese energy giant Sinopec says it has made the country's first commercially viable shale gas discovery. Its efforts could also help address another urgent issue, as Beijing looks to curb an overwhelming reliance on coal that has blackened skies and made China the largest contributor to global warming.

But the path to energy independence and a cleaner fossil fuel is fraught with potential pitfalls. Threats to workplace safety, public health and the environment all loom large in the shale gas debate — and the question is whether those short-term risks threaten to undermine China's long-term goal. The energy industry around the world has faced criticism about the economic viability of vast shale projects and the environmental impact of the fracking process. But interviews with residents of six hamlets here where drilling is being done, as well as with executives and experts in Beijing, the United States and Europe, suggest that China's search poses even greater challenges.

Topics (multinomials over words)
gas, shale, drilling, fracturing,fracking, coal, energy, fuel, fossil, flames

china, united states, europe, beijing, jiaoshizen, country, worldwide

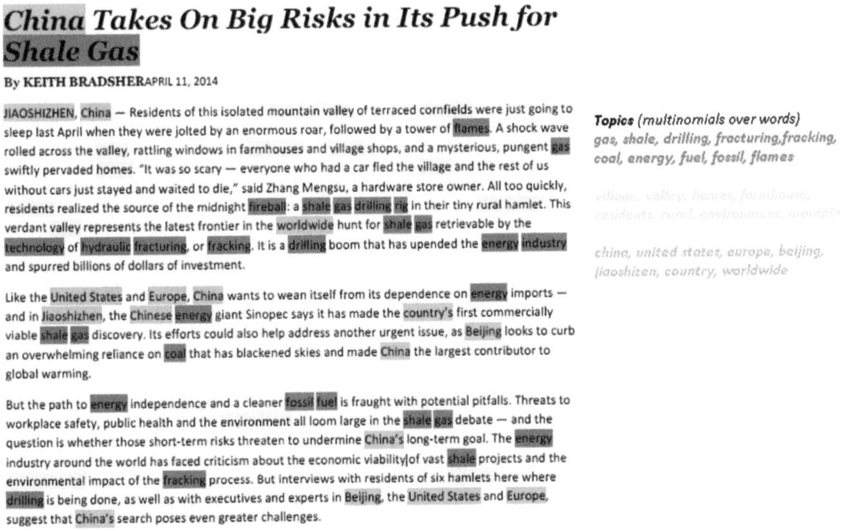

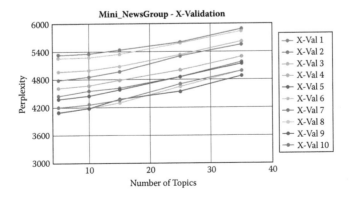

FIGURE 11.1: News extract topics.

FIGURE 11.3: Cross-validation — optimum number of topics.

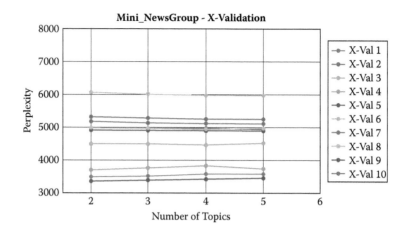

FIGURE 11.4: Cross-validation — optimum number of topics (2 to 5).

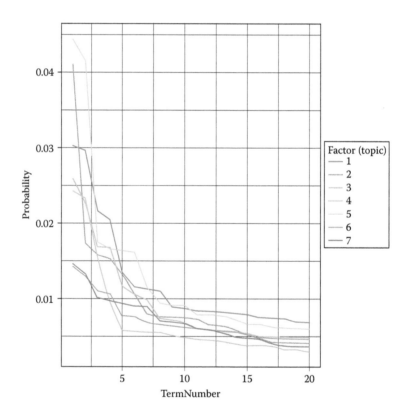

FIGURE 11.5: Term distribution.

Chapter 6

Sentiment Classification and Visualization of Product Review Data

Alexander Piazza
Institute of Information Systems, Friedrich-Alexander-University Erlangen-Nuremberg, Germany

Pavlina Davcheva
Institute of Information Systems, Friedrich-Alexander-University Erlangen-Nuremberg, Germany

Abstract

The chapter presents a process for sentiment classification of product review data. Our data set consists of reviews on six categories of products from Amazon.com. We use the star review system to determine whether the review is positive or negative. Emoticons substitution, tokenization, stopwords removal, and text normalization are applied, features are generated, which then are used for training the classifier. The resulting classifier is evaluated based on a k-fold stratified cross-validation strategy using the accuracy and a confusion matrix as measure for determining the quality of the prediction. As a final step, we demonstrate two visualization techniques to reveal the context behind the sentiment.

6.1   Introduction

As human beings, it is only natural for us to express our opinion on different topics, products, companies, and anything else that is part of our daily lives. The task of sentiment analysis, also known as opinion mining, is detecting the polarity of these opinions. The term opinion in itself has many definitions in the literature. However, the focus of sentiment analysis are mainly the opinions, which express or imply positive or negative statements [1].

Sentiment analysis has gained an increasing importance in the last years, especially due to the rising of social media. Sharing our opinions on products and services, and companies mining these opinions has become the rule rather than the exception. This is a reason why so many advancements in the field of natural language processing are being made.

The content that we as users generate on a daily basis (also known as user-generated content, or UGC) is of great value for companies because of several reasons: they have an easy access to what their customers think about their products and services, what they like or dislike, as well as suggestions for improvement. Companies can also respond in real time to the demands and complaints of the customers.

In spite of such major advantages, the UGC poses its challenges for the data analyst — data volume is increasing rapidly, and since it is mostly text and thus, unstructured data, it is increasingly difficult for a company to process such data. Other issues are related to the way users tend to express themselves by using mostly colloquial language and abbreviations. For a machine to understand language in a way human does, it is necessary to have large amounts of training data. Even in such case, however, the machine cannot detect the fine line between sarcasm and literal meaning.

There are quite a few tools for analysing text data, including sentiment classification. The advanced commercial tools (Sysomos, Radian6) that major companies are using, do a good job in extracting data from the web based on user-defined queries, as well as diverse visualization techniques for text data (e.g., buzz graphs, word clouds) so that the user can immediately get a glimpse of the main topics in large amounts of articles. Nevertheless, even these expensive tools cannot provide a high accuracy of the sentiment. On articles from newspapers and magazines, the sentiment tends to be of the highest accuracy due to the precise and correct language. From our practical experience, even in such cases the accuracy is around 80 to 85%, depending on the language (e.g., English, German). When social media content like tweets, forum data and other user reviews are considered, the sentiment is often of a very low accuracy. For this reason, some companies for which analysis of UGC is of high value develop their own in-house solutions, which are combining the strengths of commercial and open-source tools for data analysis, such as R and Python.

In this chapter, we present a method for sentiment classification of product reviews from amazon.com. The goal of this chapter is less to provide an optimized process for predicting the sentiment of the given data set, but more to provide a first framework which enables the reader to conduct his or her own experiments and optimizations within the code. The reviews are not manually labelled as positive or negative. We chose such data intentionally since in a real-world scenario it would be a very time-consuming task to do so. We present a different option by using the 5-star user ratings system (also used by [2]). We also present visualization techniques that assist in revealing the context behind the sentiment. This is important because a company would like to know not only the sentiment but also the product features to which the sentiment refers. For example, the information that there is an 80% negative statement on a query related to a newly released product, is valuable only to a very low extent. It is very important to detect the exact reason for the negative reaction of the customers towards the product (e.g., shape or text and image labels are often such reasons, with the latest example of retailer Zara removing a T-shirt due to its resemblance to an attire worn by Jewish people during the Holocaust).[1]

In the rest of the chapter we present and explain the process for sentiment classification and visualization following the steps presented in Figure 6.1.

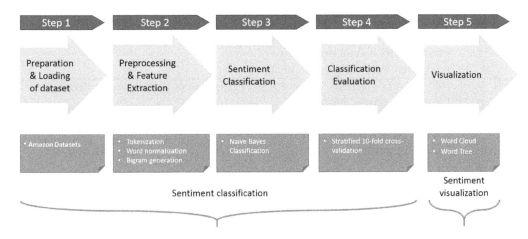

FIGURE 6.1: Sentiment classification and visualization process.

We start with an overview of the libraries we used for the classification and description of the data set. In step 1, we explain how to load and parse the data set. In step 2, we explain the preprocessing and extraction of features required for training the classifier. In step 3, the classification of the sentiment is demonstrated followed by evaluation of the sentiment accuracy in step 4. Finally, in step 5 we show some options for visualizing the data with the open-source tools Wordle and Jigsaw. The chapter concludes with a brief summary.

Used Libraries

Table 6.1 gives an overview of the libraries we used for the sentiment classification part of this chapter along with the link where the libraries can be downloaded. The algorithms demonstrated were implemented and tested on a computer running on Windows 8. Nevertheless the implementation should be platform agnostic. Because of stability issues it is recommended to use only 32-bit versions of Python and the used modules.

Data Set Description

For this project, we chose a data set that consists of reviews for six product categories: camera, mobile phone, TV, laptop, tablet, and video surveillance system. [3] collected the data set from www.amazon.com.[2] The reviews are organized in separate folders according to the product category and are in JSON (JavaScript Object Notation) format. JSON is an open data interchange format that stores data in attribute-value pairs. Table 6.2 shows the number of reviews in each category and the number of positive and negative reviews, excluding multiple postings of the same review. The total number of reviews is 20,821, which is sufficient for meaningful analysis. Moreover, for our purpose, it is useful to have different types of products reviewed by customers based on diverse characteristics, mainly for the visualization part of this chapter. Since some of the reviews do not have text content (i.e.,

---

[1]For more information, see: http://www.ibtimes.co.uk/zara-removes-childs-holocaust-pyjamas-sale-following-complaints-1462767

[2]The data set can be downloaded from: http://sifaka.cs.uiuc.edu/ wang296/Data/.

Software	Description	Link
Python 3.4.1 for Windows (32 Bit)	Python installer for Windows	https://www.python.org/downloads/
NumPy 1.8.1 Superpack win32	NumPy is a general-purpose array-processing package designed to efficiently manipulate large multi-dimensional arrays of arbitrary records (python.org).	https://pypi.python.org/pypi/numpy/
NLTK 3.0.0b1.win32	A Python package for natural language processing	https://pypi.python.org/pypi/nltk/
Scipy 0.14.0-win32-superpack-python 3.2	A Python package containing algorithms for numeric and scientific computing	https://pypi.python.org/pypi/scipy/

TABLE 6.1: Table of used libraries.

they contain only a star review) we consider just reviews with text content. Sometimes the same review is posted multiple times. In such case, we kept only one entry of the review.

Product Category	Number of reviews	Number of unique positive comments (4 & 5 stars)	Number of unique negative comments (1 & 2 stars)
Video Surveillance	2,790	672	223
TVs	2,365	1,507	180
Tablets	1,049	523	120
Mobile Phone	4,471	2,707	678
Laptops	2,473	1,615	269
Cameras	7,673	4,041	695
Total:	20,821	11,065	2,165

TABLE 6.2: Number of reviews per product category.

Each product and review have certain attributes as follows:

- Product attributes: product ID (unique), name, product features, listing price, and image URL.

- Review attributes: review ID (unique), author, title, content, overall rating, and date.

For sentiment analysis, we need only the review attributes *content* and *overall rating*.

6.2   Process

In the following, a program code for conducting sentiment analysis with Python and NLTK is introduced. In each subsection, parts of the code are explained. For reproducing the example conducted in this chapter, the following source fragments should be stored in one file like *sentiment_analysis.py*.

In the beginning of the source file, the necessary modules shown in Listing 6.1 have to be imported. The *json* and the *glob* modules are built-in modules in Python, the first for accessing data in the JSON format, the latter for navigating and accessing the file system with Unix-style pattern (refer to lines 1 – 2). From the *NLTK* library we load modules for preprocessing and feature creation (lines 4 – 9), which are used in the preprocessing in Section 6.2.2 step 2 and modules for the classification (lines 11 – 12) in Section 6.2.3, step 3, which are described more in detail in the following pages. The last two imports are related to the classifier evaluation in step 4, where we use the arrays from the *numpy* module for the data preparation, and the cross validation function from the *scikit-learn* module for conducting the evaluation.

```
 1  import json
 2  import glob
 3
 4  from nltk.tokenize import word_tokenize
 5  from nltk.corpus import stopwords
 6  from nltk.stem.snowball import SnowballStemmer
 7  from nltk.collocations import BigramCollocationFinder
 8  from nltk.metrics import BigramAssocMeasures
 9  from nltk.util import bigrams
10
11  import nltk.classify.util
12  from nltk.classify import NaiveBayesClassifier
13
14  import numpy as np
15  from sklearn import cross_validation
```

Listing 6.1: Imported modules.

6.2.1   Step 1: Preparation and Loading of Data Set

In the first step we describe how we read the data from the *JSON* files, parse these data and filter out flawed review entries.

We have bundled all necessary steps for loading and filtering the review data from the JSON files in the function *readJSONdata()*, which is shown in Listing 6.2. The argument *opinionData* of the function indicates the path to the directory containing the JSON files (e.g., "c:\projects\AmazonReviews\mobilephone*") and returns two lists of strings having all positive and negative reviews (pos_reviews or neg_reviews).

Within the function, first all files in a directory are read within the *opinionData* folder by using the glob module, which offers file system access possibilities similar to unix-environments. This means Unix shell wildcards like *.zip and relative pathnames like "..\TVs*" can be used. First, we read the names of all JSON files in the directory opinion-Data (line 2), and then read iteratively all JSON files (line 6) into *json_data*. In lines 9-10 we check if the JSON file has a "content" and "overall" entry. The "content" entry holds the text of the review and the "overall" entry the star rating. If the review entry has an overall rating of 4 or 5 stars it is classified as positive, and if it has 1 or 2 stars as negative. The review is added to the *pos_reviews* or *neg_reviews* list if it contains a review text (line 13 or 18, third condition). Since reviews with 3 stars are considered as being neither positive nor negative, they are omitted.

For the later sentiment classification, it is important to consider only comments consisting of natural text and to avoid text not belonging to the review like code fragments, which could appear during an imperfect Web crawling. In our Amazon data set there are

139 reviews containing only code or markup fragments. These are filtered out by the fourth condition in lines 12 and 17 by not considering review texts starting with "<!--", which indicates a comment in HTML.

As a last step we want to ensure that each comment is loaded only once for the later analysis to avoid noise in the classification. Therefore, we filter out multiple occurrences of the same comments in lines 14 – 15 for positive reviews and lines 19 – 20 for negative ones.

```
 1  def readJSONdata(opinionData):
 2      allfiles = glob.glob(opinionData)
 3      pos_reviews = []
 4      neg_reviews = []
 5      for elem in allfiles:
 6          with open(elem) as json_file:
 7              json_data = json.load(json_file)
 8              if json_data.get("Reviews"):
 9                  if "Content" in json_data["Reviews"][0].keys():
10                      if "Overall" in json_data["Reviews"][0].keys():
11                          if (json_data["Reviews"][0]["Overall"] == "5.0" or json_data[
                                "Reviews"][0]["Overall"] == "4.0") and \
12                              json_data["Reviews"][0]["Content"] and not str(json_data["
                                Reviews"][0]["Content"]).startswith("<!--"):
13                              tmp = str(json_data["Reviews"][0]["Content"])
14                              if not tmp in pos_reviews:
15                                  pos_reviews.append(tmp)
16                          if (json_data["Reviews"][0]["Overall"] == "1.0" or json_data[
                                "Reviews"][0]["Overall"] == "2.0") and \
17                              json_data["Reviews"][0]["Content"] and not str(json_data["
                                Reviews"][0]["Content"]).startswith("<!--"):
18                              tmp = str(json_data["Reviews"][0]["Content"])
19                              if not tmp in neg_reviews:
20                                  neg_reviews.append(tmp)
21      return(pos_reviews, neg_reviews)
```

Listing 6.2: Load review data.

6.2.2 Step 2: Preprocessing and Feature Extraction

After loading the data, the reviews have to be preprocessed and the features extracted so they can be provided to the classification algorithm. The demonstrated preprocessing steps may differ depending on the data set used. For instance, if the sentiment analysis is performed on Twitter data, URLs have to be removed as they normally do not have an influence towards the sentiment of the tweet. In sentiment analysis a string of characters, whole words, and word combinations (so-called n-grams) are considered as features. In this chapter we use a combination of single words (unigrams) and two-word combinations (bigrams).

We grouped all preprocessing and feature extraction steps in a function called *preprocessing()*, which is illustrated in Listing 6.3. As an argument the function takes a list of strings each holding a text review, and the polarity of these comments, which might be positive or negative. This function is later called two times: once for preprocessing the positive comments, and once for preprocessing the negative ones. During the next steps, the preprocessing is demonstrated with the following example sentence:

Example: *One which is smaller, but large enough to hold the camera but not large enough to hold the charger, and your lunch. :-)*

```
1   def preprocessing(allReviews, polarity):
2       stemmer = SnowballStemmer("english")
3       stops = set(stopwords.words('english') + ['.',',','!','?',';',':','[',
            ']']) - set(['not'])
4       smiley_happy = [' :-)',' :)',' (:',' (-:',' =)',' (=']
5       smiley_sad = [' :-(',' :(',' ):',' )-:',' =(',' )=']
6       smiley_wink = [' ;-)',' ;)',' (;',' (-;']
7       pos_reviews_tok = []
8       reviewsPreprocessed_unigram = []
9       reviewsPreprocessed_bigram = []
10      reviewsPreprocessed = []
11
12      for review in allReviews:
13          tmp = str(review).lower()
14          for smiley in smiley_happy:
15              tmp.replace(smiley, 'SMILEY_HAPPY')
16          for smiley in smiley_sad:
17              tmp.replace(smiley, 'SMILEY_SAD')
18          for smiley in smiley_wink:
19              tmp.replace(smiley, 'SMILEY_WINK')
20          tmp = nltk.word_tokenize(tmp)
21          tmp = [word for word in tmp if word not in stops]
22          tmp = [stemmer.stem(word) for word in tmp]
23          reviewsPreprocessed_unigram.append(list(set(tmp)))
24
25          bigramFinder = BigramCollocationFinder.from_words(tmp)
26          tmpBi = bigramFinder.nbest(BigramAssocMeasures.chi_sq,1000)
27          reviewsPreprocessed_bigram.append(list(set(tmpBi)))
28
29      def labeling(features):
30          return dict([(feature, True) for feature in features])
31
32      finalFeatures = [(labeling(features), str(polarity)) for features in
            reviewsPreprocessed_bigram]
33      finalFeatures += [(labeling(features), str(polarity)) for features in
            reviewsPreprocessed_unigram]
34      return(finalFeatures)
```

Listing 6.3: Preprocessing and feature extraction.

Substitution of Emoticons

In general emoticons can play a significant role during sentiment classification [4]. From a sentiment classification point of view, one challenge is that different emoticons exist having a similar meaning. For instance, ":-)" and "=)" both indicate a feeling of happiness. To bring such emoticons to a canonical form we substitute them to a unique symbolic representation in form of a specific string. In lines 4 – 6 smilies are grouped into happy, sad, and wink ones. Then in lines 14 – 19 all these smilies are replaced by the strings SMILEY_HAPPY, SMILEY_SAD or SMILEY_WINK. By this, the classifier treats different smilies with a similar meaning in the same way. It is recommended to apply this step before the tokenization process, as depending on the tokenization approach the symbols relating to one emoticons can be grouped to one token [:-)] or each symbol to an individual one [:,-,)]. The used list of emoticons is covering only three classes of common emoticons. By further defining more classes with more emoticons it is expected to have a positive influence to the classification performance.

Example: *One which is smaller, but large enough to hold the camera but not large enough to hold the charger, and your lunch. SMILEY_HAPPY*

Tokenization

In simple terms, tokenization means dividing a given text into smaller and meaningful elements like sentences and words. For example, let us assume we have the following review on a phone:

The battery of the Nokia phone is crap and the display as well.

After tokenization, the sentence could take the following form as illustrated in Table 6.3.

| The | battery | of | the | Nokia | phone | is | crap | and | the | display | as | well | . |

TABLE 6.3: Tokenization example.

The final output depends on the tokenizer applied. It could also be the case that "well" appears together with full stop next to it (e.g., "well") or the full stop might not be present at all. Similarly, when we have "don't" in the sentence, possible tokens could be "don't" or "do" and "n't" . In our case we use the default tokenization function *nltk.word_tokenize()*, which first splits up a given text into its sentences by using the so-called *Punkt-Sentence-Tokenizer* followed by splitting up the sentences in words by applying the *Treebank-word-tokenizer* (line 20).

Example: *['one', 'which', 'is', 'smaller', ',', 'but', 'large', 'enough', 'to', 'hold', 'the', 'camera', 'but', 'not', 'large', 'enough', 'to', 'hold', 'the', 'charger', ',', 'and', 'your', 'lunch', '.', 'SMILEY_HAPPY']*

Stopwords and Punctuation Marks Removal

Stopwords are words that occur frequently in text documents and possess only low characteristics from a text classification point of view [5] [6]. Within Python there is a defined corpora of stopwords for the English language in the module *nltk.corpus* called *stopwords*, and it includes words like *a, or, am, I*, and *as*. In addition, we remove punctuation marks like the full stop, comma or exclamation mark — in Listing 6.3 they are defined in the variable *stops* in line 3 and removed in line 21. As illustrated in line 3 along with the predefined words we add additional symbols like brackets to the stopwords list, as we expect they do not have a significant impact on the sentiment classification. Moreover, we remove the word "not" from the predefined stopword list, as it can have a significant impact on the classification. In the last step of the tokenization process punctuation marks are removed.

Example: *['one', 'smaller', 'large', 'enough', 'hold', 'camera', 'large', 'enough', 'hold', 'charger', 'lunch', 'SMILEY_HAPPY']*

Text-normalization

In natural languages, words are modified according to their grammatical context. For text classification in general, and also specifically for sentiment classification it is beneficial to have a canonical and generalized form of the words. Therefore, as a first step, all characters of the text are set to lowercase (see line 13), so words like "camera" and "Camera" are treated case insensitively as the same word. Afterwards, stemming is applied to derive a generic form of a word independent of its inflections.

As it is the case with tokenization, there are different stemmers that could be used for this purpose, and the right choice will depend on our goal [7]. NLTK in version 3 provides various implementations of stemming supporting languages like English, German, and Spanish. In addition, lemmatization is available. Lemmatization is a more advanced form of stemming, which uses the contextual and grammatical information related to the word to determine the lemma (i.e., the root of the word) [8] but at the same time is computationally more expensive. In general, there is a trade-off between the benefits of bringing words into their canonical form by stemming and losing valuable information. An example for information loss is "defense" and "defensive", which by stemming will be reduced to "defens". The former word has a more positive connotation, whereas the latter a more negative; however, both are treated after the stemming as the same. From our experience with product information, stemming has a slightly positive influence on the sentiment classification, but we advise to conduct experiments with and without stemming based on the own data and context the reader is intending to apply sentiment classification. We have used the Snowball stemmer (see line 22) which is initialized for the English language in line 2.

Example: *['one', 'smaller', 'larg', 'enough', 'hold', 'camera', 'larg', 'enough', 'hold', 'charger', 'lunch', 'smiley_happi']*

Feature Extraction

The features for the classifier consist of a combination of uni- and bigrams. *Unigrams* are individual words resulting from the tokenization process. *Bigrams* are a version of n-grams consisting of two words. Studies have shown that bigrams are effective features for classifying text, especially in the context of sentiment analysis. Since bigrams are less common than individual words, they help the classifier to make better decisions [9].

In general, n-grams in sentiment classification can be regarded in two ways. One is to consider them as so-called presence features, which means it is only considered whether a word appears or not in a text, and the other way is to consider them according to the frequency they appear in a given text. In the latter case the frequency takes the role of a weight of the feature. In sentiment classification experimental results show that the appearance based approach seems to be more effective, as the frequency of words are not related to their degree of sentiment indication [10]. Therefore, we check only if a word appears in the review but not its frequency. This is done in Listing 6.3 in line 23 by adding the preprocessed words which are stored in the variable *tmp* by adding it to a list called *reviewsPreprocessed_unigram*. We eliminate multiple occurrences of words by converting the list of preprocessed words into a set data type. As in the mathematical concept of sets, this data type holds only one instance of each element. Then this set is casted again into a list data type for the later processing.

In the context of the classification of sentiment polarization, the individually extracted features consisting out of unigrams and bigrams have different predictive performance. From these features only those having a larger predictive performance should be selected. Normally features mainly occurring only in one of the two classes (positive or negative reviews) are considered to have a greater predictive power than features occurring in a similar frequency in both classes. The latter case can be considered as noise, as it does not provide clear and meaningful information to the classifier. To quantify such relationships between classes and features, measures like the information gain or the chi-square measure are used [5]. For that NLTK provides so-called n-gram association measures within the *NLTK.metrics.association* module. Within this chapter we limit the demonstration at bigram features and the selection based on the chi-square measure. Therefore in line 25 first we are creating bigrams from the preprocessed words in variable *tmp* by creating an instance of the *BigramCollocationFinder* class by using the method *from_words()*. In the following line the 1,000 most significant bigrams based on the *chi-square* independence test are returned. The value of 1,000 is based on our experience with the given data set, but varying this parameter is in general a good idea for conducting further experiments to improve the classifier. To illustrate this, in the following example we show unigrams and bigrams based on the previous example sentence.

Example bigrams: *[('charger', 'lunch'), ('enough', 'hold'), ('larg', 'enough'), ('lunch',* 'smiley_happi'), ('one', 'smaller'), ('camera', 'larg'), ('hold', 'camera'), ('hold', 'charger'), ('smaller', 'larg')]

Example unigram: *[['one', 'smaller', 'larg', 'enough', 'hold', 'camera', 'larg', 'enough', 'hold', 'charger', 'lunch', 'smiley_happi']]*

As a last step during the preprocessing and feature creation the derived unigrams and bigrams have to be labeled depending on whether they appear in a positive or negative review. Therefore, we define a function labeling in line 29, which transforms the processed data into a dictionary data type with annotated label, which is held into the variable polarity and contains in our case the string "pos" for positive and "neg" for negative reviews.

Example: results of labeling the data with a "pos" label:

[({ 'enough': True, 'smiley_happi': True, 'smaller': True, 'camera': True, 'charger': True, 'not': True, 'lunch': True, 'larg': True, 'hold': True, 'one': True}, 'pos'), ({'not': True, 'camera': True}, 'pos'), ({'charger': True, 'lunch': True}, 'pos'), ({'enough': True, 'hold': True}, 'pos'), ({'enough': True, 'larg': True}, 'pos'), ({'lunch': True, 'smiley_happi': True}, 'pos'), ({'one': True, 'smaller': True}, 'pos'), ({'hold': True, 'camera': True}, 'pos'), ({'charger': True, 'hold': True}, 'pos'), ({'larg': True, 'not': True}, 'pos'), ({'larg': True, 'smaller': True}, 'pos')]

6.2.3   Step 3: Sentiment Classification

Following the feature extraction explained in the previous subsection, in a next step we continue with the sentiment classification process by training our classifier. This will allow us to automatically classify new reviews into positive or negative. Within the context of sentiment analysis the most applied classifiers are Naïve Bayes, Maximum Entropy and Support Vector Machines. The first two are implemented within the NLTK library, the latter is provided in the the the scikit-learn module. In this chapter we are focusing on the Naïve Bayes approach which provides good accuracy and performance in sentiment classification. Nevertheless, the readers are encouraged to try the other two classifiers as well.

Simply put, the Naïve Bayes classifier makes observations from the training data and estimates the probability of a negative or positive sentiment based on the presence of certain features. It is especially useful for classification tasks with a large number of attributes or dimensions that need to be taken into consideration to calculate the probability of an event to occur (or in this case a sentiment to be positive or negative). It treats all features as independent, which leads to a simple yet effective classifier [11][3].

We encapsulated all needed functionalities within the function *sentiment_classification* in Listing 6.4, which takes as argument a list of training features and a list of test features. After we initialized the variables for the later determination of a confusion matrix in line 5, an instance of the Naïve Bayes classifier is created and trained with the training data (line 7). Afterwards we iterate through all test samples (line 8-20), applying one review per iteration at the classifier (line 9), and determine the type of classification error (line 11-20). We determine the features with the most informative values according to the classifier in line 22 (this is commented out in the listing). An example result of the most informative features for the product category mobilephone can be seen in Table 6.4. In the end the function returns the four values of the determined confusion matrix.

---

[3]For more information on the Naïve Bayes we refer you to [12] and [13]

Feature	Information degree regarding sentiment
('return', 'item') = True	neg : pos = 22.6 : 1.0
('money', 'back') = True	neg : pos = 22.2 : 1.0
('sent', 'back') = True	neg : pos = 21.6 : 1.0
('high', 'recommend') = True	pos : neg = 19.5 : 1.0
('took', 'phone') = True	neg : pos = 17.3 : 1.0
('not', 'return') = True	neg : pos = 17.3 : 1.0
crisp = True	pos : neg = 17.3 : 1.0
('worst', 'phone') = True	neg : pos = 16.8 : 1.0
shot = True	pos : neg = 16.6 : 1.0
('not', 'unlock') = True	neg : pos = 16.5 : 1.0
refund = True	neg : pos = 15.6 : 1.0

TABLE 6.4: Example results for information degree per feature.

```
1  def sentiment_classification(trainfeats, testfeats):
2    #initialize confusion matrix variables
3    #TN = true negative; TN = true positive
4    #FN = false negative; FP = false positive
5    (TN, TP, FN, FP) = (0, 0, 0, 0)
6
7    classifier = NaiveBayesClassifier.train(trainfeats)
8    for (testReview, polarity) in testfeats:
9      predictedSentiment = classifier.classify(testReview)
10     #count resulting prediction classes
11     if predictedSentiment == polarity:
12       if predictedSentiment == "neg":
13         TN += 1
14       else:
15         TP += 1
16     else:
17       if predictedSentiment == "neg":
18         FN += 1
19       else:
20         FP += 1
21   #uncommen the following line to show the most informative features
22   #classifier.show_most_informative_features(30)
23   return((TN, TP, FN, FP))
```

Listing 6.4: Sentiment classification.

6.2.4   Step 4: Evaluation of the Trained Classifier

In general the accuracy of classifiers is measured by dividing a given data set into a training and testing sample. This process is known as *validation* and it is used to assess the ability of our classifier to accurately classify new unlabeled reviews. One of the most used strategies for evaluating classifier is the *k-fold cross-validation* approach. In this approach the given data set is divided into k mutual-exclusive subsets. During the evaluation phase, k-1 subsets are used for training the classifier and one subset for testing its accuracy. The average accuracy is then estimated by iterating k-times through all possible subset combinations until all subsets are used once as test set. In practice, a 10-fold cross-validation has shown good results for estimating the overall classification accuracy [14]. In this chapter we apply the so-called stratified version of the 10-fold-cross validation. Stratification means that the frequency of all class representations in the k-1 subsets are similar to the one of

		Actual Sentiment	
		Positive	Negative
Predicted Sentiment	Positive	*TruePositive*	*FalsePositive*
	Negative	*FalseNegative*	*TrueNegative*

TABLE 6.5: Structure of confusion matrices in case of binary classification.

the original data set. In a sentiment classification task, this will ensure that the ratio of positive and negative opinions appear in each of the k subsets in equal frequency.

To assess the quality of the sentiment classifications we calculate the general accuracy measure as well as the contingency matrix. The accuracy is calculated by the following formula: $accuracy = \frac{numberOfCorrectPredictions}{NumberOfAllPredictions}$. To get a more detailed quality assessment of the classifier's prediction, besides the overall accuracy, we determine the so-called confusion matrix. The confusion matrix indicates the frequency of correct and incorrect classifications for both positive and negative sentiments. Table 6.5 illustrates the structure of such a matrix. Expecially in cases where the classes are immoderately unbalanced, as it is with the data set used in this chapter, this is an important aspect to consider. For instance in the mobile phone category there are approx. four times more positive than negative reviews. In the extreme case that a classifier just predicts every review to be positive, without considering any features of the review, we get an accuracy of 79%. By this each positive review is classified correctly, and each negative one incorrectly. In our case of predicting the sentiment of reviews for marketing decision, we rather need both classes to be predicted in a similarly good quality, in order to get an accurate view on the customers' opinion, and not having one class beeing very accurate, and one beeing too inaccurate. To evaluate the quality of the prediction of the classes occuring with minor frequency, an overall confusion matrix is calculated. The matrix concists out of four entries: *True Positive* (TP) and *True Negative* (TN) entries, indicating the correct classification of positive and negative opinions; and *False Positive* (FP) and *False Negative* (FN) entries, indicating the incorrect classification.

In Listing 6.5 we first initialize three variables holding statistics about the maximal, minimal and average accuracy determined during the k-folds. In line 11 the number of folds are defined. As mentioned already, in practice often 10 folds are used. Then we get the positive and negative comments by loading the data specified in variable *opinionDataset* with the function *readJSONdata()*, which is explained in Section 6.2.2 step 2. Afterwards we preprocess these data in lines 9 and 10 by the function defined in Section 6.2.3 step 3. For the evaluation we use the *cross_validation* module from the scikit-learn library (line 25). Therefore, we have to prepare an array storing the labels for review data, which we store in the variable *data* in line 19. The cross-validation function is expecting a numpy array. One special feature of these arrays is the possibility to index the field with a list of indices, which is used by the cross validation function. We define the array in line 22 by labeling the positive reviews with a 1 and the negative reviews with a −1. Then we instantiate a cross_validation object by giving the labeled list and the review data as an argument. In the for-loop in line 28 we iterate through all the k test- and training-set combinations (in our case 10-times). As the NLTK classifier expects standard python arrays, not numpy arrays, we reconvert them in lines 29 and 30.

Finally, we call our classifier function *sentiment_classification()* by passing the training and *test_dataset* created in previous steps. In the following lines, we store statistics like the minimal and maximal accuracies during the loops, calculate, and print the total average accuracy in lines 42 and 45.

In Table 6.6 the average accuracies based on a stratified 10-fold cross-validation are illustrated as well as the minimal and maximal accuracies of the 10 training and test iterations.

Product Category	Average Accuracy	Minimal Accuracy	Maximal Accuracy
Video Surveillance	0.73	0.54	0.87
TVs	0.63	0.31	0.91
Tablets	0.76	0.55	0.83
Mobile Phone	0.84	0.80	0.89
Laptops	0.72	0.46	0.91
Cameras	0.85	0.82	0.90

TABLE 6.6: Sentiment classification accuracies per product category.

		Actual Sentiment	
		Positive	Negative
Predicted Sentiment	Positive	519.4	82.3
	Negative	21.8	53.3

TABLE 6.7: Resulting average confusion matrix for the mobile phone category.

The average consistancy table resulting from the cross-validation process is demonstrated in Table 6.7. This table is built by summing all entries of the consistency table per cross-validation iteration, and by dividing this sum by the number of folds (10 in our case). This table shows that positive reviews are classified with an accuracy of 96%, and the negative ones with an accuracy of 61%. This accuracy is calculated by the following formula:

$$accuracy_{positive} = \frac{TP}{TP+FP}, \text{ and } accuracy_{negative} = \frac{TN}{TN+FN}.$$

For increasing the accuracy of the negative classifications, we suggest to experiment with resampling techniques of the data set such as oversampling or undersampling to reduce the inbalance of the classes. The idea of oversampling is to randomly duplicate entries of the minority class, whereas in undersampling entries of the majority class are randomly removed [15].

6.2.5 Step 5: Visualization of Review Data

In the first four steps of the process, we trained a classifier and managed to achieve an overall accuracy of approximately 75%. We now know that the category mobile phone has approximately 80% positive and 20% negative sentiment. Therefore, we are interested to gain more insight and understand the context behind such sentiment. What do the customers like or dislike about the phones we sell? To achieve this, commercial tools as Sysomos are using different text visualization options:

- Word clouds: representation of most frequent words occurring within a text

- Buzz graphs: not only the keywords, but also the relationships between them – how often words are mentioned in relation to each other

- Popular phrases within the text

- Entities: categorization of words (e.g., name, place, organization, person) [16]1

```
1  #initialize statistics variables
2  maxAccuracy = 0
3  minAccuracy = 1
4  averageAccuracy = 0
5  average_TP = 0
6  average_TN = 0
7  average_FP = 0
8  average_FN = 0
9
10 #number of folds used in cross validation
11 kFold = 10
12
13 opinionDataset = r"C:\project\AmazonReviews\mobilephone\*"
14
15 pos_reviews, neg_reviews = readJSONdata(opinionDataset)
16 posfeats = preprocessing(pos_reviews,'pos')
17 negfeats = preprocessing(neg_reviews,'neg')
18
19 data = posfeats + negfeats
20
21 #prepare label array indicating positive reviews with 1, negative with -1
22 label = np.array([1]*len(posfeats) + [-1]*len(negfeats))
23
24 #create indices for k cross validation combinations
25 crossValidationIter = cross_validation.StratifiedKFold(label, n_folds=
      kFold)
26
27 #perform stratisfied k-fold cross-validation
28 for train_index, test_index in crossValidationIter:
29   trainingData = [data[i] for i in train_index]
30   testData = [data[i] for i in test_index]
31   (TN, TP, FN, FP) = sentiment_classification(trainingData, testData)
32   accuracy = (TP + TN)/(TN + TP + FN + FP)
33   average_TP += TP
34   average_TN += TN
35   average_FN += FN
36   average_FP += FP
37   if accuracy > maxAccuracy: maxAccuracy = accuracy
38   if accuracy < minAccuracy: minAccuracy = accuracy
39   averageAccuracy += accuracy
40
41 #print average classification accuracy
42 print("Average Accuracy: " + str((averageAccuracy/kFold)) + "\nMinimal
      Accuracy: "+ \
43 str(minAccuracy) + "\nMaximum Accuracy: " + str(maxAccuracy))
44 #print average confusion matrix
45 print("\nAverage Confusion Matrix\nTP: " + str(average_TP/kFold) + " FP:
      " + str(average_FP/kFold) + \
46       "\nFN: " + str(average_FN/kFold) + " TN: " + str(average_TN/kFold))
```

Listing 6.5: Evaluation of the classifier.

Although these techniques might differ slightly in terms of the way they are named, in most cases they work on the same principle. A word cloud will only show the frequency of the words appearing in the reviews, which is not enough to understand the context behind the sentiment. Similarly, the buzz graphs show the relationship between words, but not the sentiment context. Therefore, it is more useful when different visualizations are used in combination rather than independently. There are currently some freely available tools for text visualization like Wordle,[4] Voyant Cirrus, and[5] Jigsaw.[6] They are easy and

---

[4]http://www.wordle.net.
[5]http://voyant-tools.org/tool/Cirrus.
[6]http://www.cc.gatech.edu/gvu/ii/jigsaw/index.html.

straightforward to use, mainly requiring a simple copy and paste of your data to display the visualization.

```
 1  import json
 2  import glob
 3  import io
 4  import re
 5
 6  opinionData = r"E:\test-data\AmazonReviews\laptops\*"
 7  posCommentsFile = r"E:\test-data\AmazonReviews\_only_comments_\
        laptops_pos.txt"
 8  negCommentsFile = r"E:\test-data\AmazonReviews\_only_comments_\
        laptops_neg.txt"
 9
10  allfiles = glob.glob(opinionData)
11  pos_reviews = []
12  neg_reviews = []
13
14  f_pos = io.open(posCommentsFile,'w', encoding="utf8")
15  f_neg = io.open(negCommentsFile,'w', encoding="utf8")
16
17  for elem in allfiles:
18      with open(elem) as json_file:
19          json_data = json.load(json_file)
20          if json_data.get("Reviews"):
21              if "Content" in json_data["Reviews"][0].keys():
22                  if "Overall" in json_data["Reviews"][0].keys():
23                      if (json_data["Reviews"][0]["Overall"] == "5.0" or json_data["
                            Reviews"][0]["Overall"] == "4.0") and json_data["Reviews"
                            ][0]["Content"] and not str(json_data["Reviews"][0]["
                            Content"]).startswith("<!--"):
24                          tmp = str(json_data["Reviews"][0]["Content"])
25                          if not tmp in pos_reviews:
26                              f_pos.write((tmp+str('\n\n')))
27                          pos_reviews.append(tmp)
28                      if (json_data["Reviews"][0]["Overall"] == "1.0" or json_data["
                            Reviews"][0]["Overall"] == "2.0") and json_data["Reviews"
                            ][0]["Content"] and not str(json_data["Reviews"][0]["
                            Content"]).startswith("<!--"):
29                          tmp = str(json_data["Reviews"][0]["Content"])
30                          if not tmp in neg_reviews:
31                              f_neg.write((tmp+str('\n\n')))
32                          neg_reviews.append(tmp)
```

Listing 6.6: Data extractor.

To demonstrate some of the visualization techniques, we decided to use the category mobile phones and the open-source visualization tools Wordle (for word cloud) and Jigsaw (for word tree).

In a first step, however, it is necessary to extract the content of the reviews. As seen in the data set description, each review file contains not only the content but also other attributes like ID and author. To achieve good results, we need to remove all other attributes and keep the relevant text content only. With the help of a small script (see Listing 6.6), we extracted all positive and all negative reviews per category and saved them in separate text files accordingly by using the following scheme: product category neg.txt and product category pos.txt, where product category is replaced by laptops or cameras, for example.

On the Wordle homepage, just click "Create your own" link, and you will see a screen where you can paste your text. We pasted the clean data from both the negative and positive reviews from this category.[7] Click on the "Go" button. Wordle will generate a word cloud

---

[7] Use files mobilephone_neg.txt and mobilephone_pos.txt

that can be customized to a certain extent by changing the color, the layout, font, and, most importantly, excluding stopwords in several languages. The initial word cloud will show that the word "phone" was used most often. This is understandable and not really useful for the analysis. Wordle allows the exclusion of any word from the generated word cloud. Right click on the word "phone" and choose "Remove phone". You should now see a word cloud as in Figure 6.2.

FIGURE 6.2: Word cloud for the positive and negative reviews of the mobilephone category.

From Figure 6.2 it becomes clear that users have mostly discussed the words "screen", "battery", and "camera". This is a valuable and interesting information, but it is unfortunately not detailed enough since we cannot understand the context behind those words.

To achieve this, we would benefit from a visualization technique called word tree. In the following, we generate a word tree and explain the insights it brings to the analyst.

The word tree visualization is a more complex visualization than a word cloud, and gives the best context overview of any word or phrase you want to search for and that is mentioned in the reviews. To demonstrate this, we will use Jigsaw, a tool for visual exploration of text data. It is available as a free download.

After you start the tool, you see the welcome screen, as shown in Figure 6.3. To import

FIGURE 6.3: Jigsaw's welcome screen.

the data, click on "File" in the upper menu and then "Import". You will see a screen as in Figure 6.4.

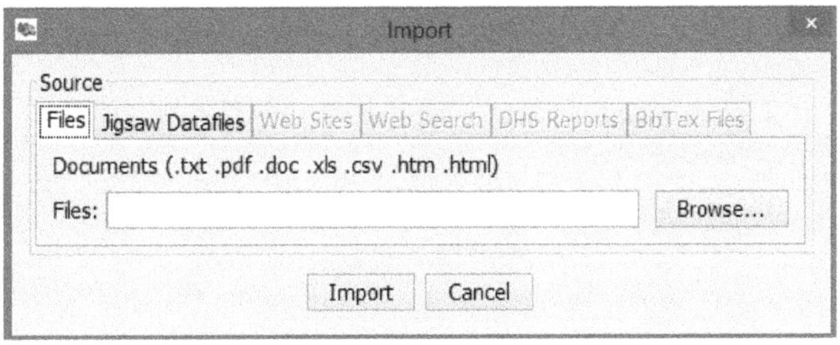

FIGURE 6.4: Import screen in Jigsaw.

Click "Browse" and locate the folder _only_comments_ where we stored the cleaned product data. You can choose to import one or more TXT files to import in a single step. We chose to import the product reviews for the category mobile phone with both positive and negative sentiment. These are the files mobilephone_pos.txt and mobilephone_neg.txt. Click "Import". You will see a screen as in Figure 6.5.

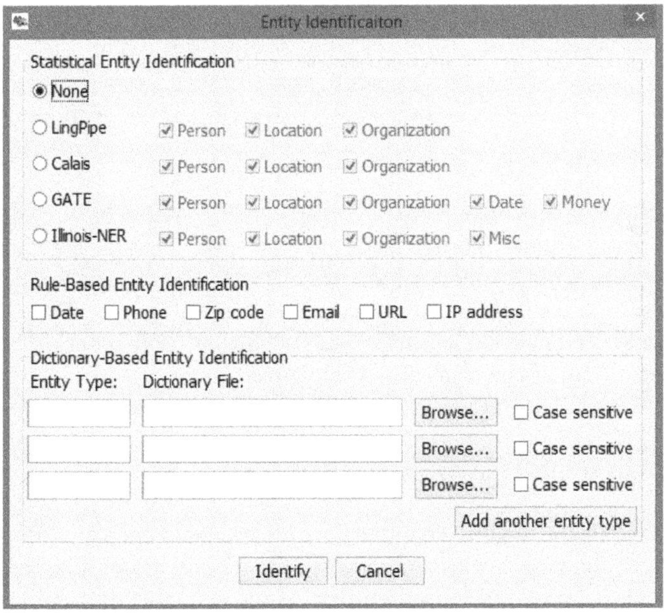

FIGURE 6.5: Entity identification screen in Jigsaw.

Since for this visualization it is not necessary to identify entities, select "None", and click "Identify". After the data import is finished, the welcome screen appears with a short confirmation that there are two documents in the project. To create a word tree, click on "Views", and select "Word Tree".

Initially, you see a relatively blank screen, containing a menu and a search bar. This is because the visualization works only when the user enters a word or a phrase. From the generated word cloud we now know which words are mentioned more often in the reviews. The word tree can reveal the reason and perhaps the sentiment behind this. If we enter "screen" in the search box, we get a branch like structure as in Figure 6.6, where *screen* is the root of the tree and the branches are the different contexts in which this word appears in the text.

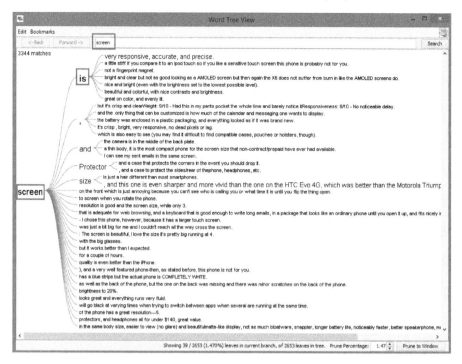

FIGURE 6.6: Word tree view for "screen".

Some of the words in Figure 6.6 are in larger font size. This means that they appear more frequently in the reviews. To investigate more closely the branch "is", we can click on it. The screen zooms in and displays only that branch, as in Figure 6.7.

From the word tree visualization it can be concluded that users mention "screen" mostly in a positive context. Some of the sentences that appear are:

"screen is very responsive."

"screen is bright and clear."

"screen is small but everything comes out in great detail.".

To inspect specifically the negative context in which screen is mentioned, if any, it would be easier to import the file with negative reviews only and investigate further. Furthermore, Jigsaw initially displays a word tree based on part of the available data for the chosen word or phrase. You can change this setting in the prunning section at the bottom of the word tree view window (See Figure 6.7).

This type of visualizations can contribute significantly to understanding the reason behind the sentiment. It is certainly much easier to use a professional tool, which offers diverse text visualizations. However, these tools are usually quite expensive and a perfect solution is yet to be developed because of the many disadvantages of text data. It is difficult for computers to understand language the way humans do. On the other hand, due to social media, text data are growing exponentially and the need to develop more sophisticated tools and techniques for text analytics is still present. The main disadvantage of relying on open-source tools is that one may need to use several tools to get the desired results.

FIGURE 6.7: Word tree view for "screen is".

6.3   Summary

In this chapter, we presented a framework approach for training a sentiment classifier on product review data. It uses a preexisting overall rating score as a proxy for positive or negative sentiment and is able show some relationship between this and the text contained within the review. We also demonstrated an approach for determining the context behind the sentiment by applying different visualization techniques. We now give recommendations for further improvement of our classifier. Depending on the data set, it is advisable to perform several experiments by changing and applying different variables and settings:

- Emoticons: by further defining more classes with more emoticons it is expected to have a positive influence to the classification performance.

- Tokenizer: via the NLTK other tokenizers can be employed. For sentiment analysis the reader can try the Regexp Tokenizer where individualized rules for the token creation can be defined. Another option is the Stanford tokenizer.

- Classifier: we used the Naïve Bayes classifier because of its good accuracy and performance in the context of sentiment classification. Nevertheless, the reader in encouraged to try further classification algorithms like the maximum-entropy or support vector machines, which are provided in the NLTK and scikit-learn module.

- Data sampling: because of the unbalanced nature of the used data set the prediction accuracy of the class of a smaller sample size is lower than the predictions of the class which has a larger sample size. By applying oversampling or undersampling techniques, the prediction quality of the smaller class may be increased (see Section 6.2.4).

Bibliography

[1] B. Liu. *Sentiment analysis and opinion mining*, volume lecture #16 of *Synthesis lectures on human language technologies*. Morgan & Claypool, San Rafael, CA, 2012.

[2] Q. E. McCallum. *Bad data handbook.* O'Reilly Media, Sebastopol, CA, 2012.

[3] H. Wang, Y. Lu, and C. X. Zhai, editors. *Latent aspect rating analysis without aspect keyword supervision.* ACM, 2011.

[4] A. Hogenboom, D. Bal, F. Frasincar, N. Bal, F. de Jong, and U. Kaymak. Exploiting emoticons in polarity classification of text. *J. Web Eng.*, 14(1&2):22–40, 2015.

[5] R. Feldman and J. Sanger. *Text mining handbook: advanced approaches in analyzing unstructured data.* Cambridge University Press, 2006.

[6] S. M. Weiss, N. Indurkhya, and T. Zhang. *Fundamentals of predictive text mining.* Springer-Verlag, 2010.

[7] G. S. Ingersoll, T. S. Morton, and A. L. Farris. *Taming text: How to find, organise, and manipulate it.* Manning and Pearson Education [distributor], 2013.

[8] G. Miner. *Practical text mining and statistical analysis for non-structured text data applications.* Academic Press, 2012.

[9] J. Perkins. *Python 3 text processing with NLTK 3 cookbook: Over 80 practical recipes on natural language processing techniques using Python's NLTK 3.0.* Packt Pub., 2014.

[10] B. Pang and L. Lee. Opinion mining and sentiment analysis. *Found. Trends Inf. Retr.*, 2(1-2):1–135, January 2008.

[11] M. J. Zaki and W. Meira. *Data mining and analysis: Fundamental concepts and algorithms.* Cambridge University Press, 2014.

[12] B. Lantz. *Machine Learning with R: Learn how to use R to apply powerful machine learning methods and gain an insight into real-world applications.* Packt, 2013.

[13] S. Bird, E. Klein, and E. Loper. *Natural language processing with Python.* O'Reilly, 2009.

[14] J. Han and M. Kamber. *Data mining: concepts and techniques.* Morgan Kaufmann, 2006.

[15] B. W. Yap, K. A. Rani, H. A. A. Rahman, S. Fong, Z. Khairudin, and N. N. Abdullah. An application of oversampling, undersampling, bagging and boosting in handling imbalanced datasets. In *Proceedings of the First International Conference on Advanced Data and Information Engineering (DaEng-2013)*, pages 13–22. Springer, 2014.

[16] Nilesh Bansal. Sysomos Text Analytics Roundup: Making Sense of Data [ONLINE] Available at `http://blog.sysomos.com/2011/04/18/sysomos-text-analytics-roundup-making-sense-of-data/`. Accessed 01 August, 2015.

Chapter 7

Mining Search Logs for Usage Patterns

Tony Russell-Rose

UXLabs, UK

Paul Clough

Information School, University of Sheffield, UK

7.1 Introduction

One of the greatest opportunities and challenges of the 21st century is the ever-increasing significance of data. Data underpin our businesses and our economy, providing awareness and insight into every sphere of life, from politics to the environment, arts, and society. The everyday interactions between people and devices can be harnessed to power a new generation of products and services, allowing us to better understand human needs, aspirations, and behaviour.

One particular area that has received considerable interest in recent years is search or transaction log mining [1]. Valuable insights can be gained from analysing the traces people leave when they *search* for digital information. In browsing the Web, people reveal something about their behaviour and habits but little about their *intent*. By contrast, when people *search* for information, they express in their own words their explicit needs and goals. This data represent a unique resource that offers extraordinary potential for delivering insights that can drive the next generation of digital services and applications.

Various studies have been undertaken to understand how and why people interact with search engines. Such studies have led to the creation of frameworks that describe distinct patterns of use, ranging from individual queries to entire information seeking episodes.[1] These patterns may focus on information-seeking behaviour [3], the types of search tasks that users perform [4], their goals and missions [5], their task-switching behaviour [6], or the tasks, needs, and goals that they are trying to address when using search systems [4, 7]. In this article we use search logs to analyse search patterns: the actions (sometimes referred to

---

[1]A search *episode* is defined as "the activity in between the initiation and termination of interacting with a particular external information resource" [2] (p. 394).

as *moves*) taken in conducting a search. The search patterns are behavioural manifestations of users' search strategies: the approaches people take in searching for information [8].

It is, however, important to recognise that the logs only capture *what* people do (i.e., their search patterns), not *why* they do it (i.e., their search strategies or mental models). As Jansen [9] clearly points out, " [Query log data] cannot account for the underlying situational, cognitive or affective elements of the searching process". This is a known limitation of relying on evidence from search logs alone to characterise and establish search behaviour where additional techniques, such as interviews, can be used to capture more subjective and in-depth data [10, 11].

Indeed, the academic community is not alone in showing an interest in mining search logs. Two highly influential commercial organisations, ElasticSearch and LucidWorks, have both recently released independent log file analysis platforms (Kibana[2] and SiLK[3], respectively). What unites all of these efforts is the belief that finding distinct, repeatable patterns of behaviour can lead to a better understanding of user needs and ultimately a more effective search experience.

In this chapter, we explore the use of data mining techniques to find patterns in search logs, focusing on the application of open source tools and publicly available log data. To start with we outline the fundamentals of search log analysis, examining the basic anatomy of search logs, search sessions and the features that characterise them (Section 7.2). We then explore the use of clustering to find patterns in search logs, and describe a number of experiments in which the Weka platform [12] was used to analyse sessions from a publicly available query log (Section 7.3). We then discuss role of validation and the extent to which different approaches can reveal different patterns in the data, and consider what this might mean for the replication of previous published studies (Section 7.4). Finally, we draw these threads together and reflect on the outputs from the analysis and our conclusions regarding the methodology itself (Section 7.5).

7.2   Getting Started

Search logs are created when a search engine records its interactions with other agents. Typically, such agents are people interacting with the search engine via a Web browser or other type of client application. However, automated agents such as bots, spiders, and indexing agents can also interact with a search engine, and their activity may be recorded in the logs. Each interaction results in the addition of one or more records to the log, so these files can eventually grow to several gigabytes in size.

Since there are many different types of search application, serving different audiences with different content for different needs, the type of information that gets stored in search logs also varies. Some logs can be relatively simple, storing just minimal information, whereas others can be highly detailed, with extensive metadata describing each interaction. No standard format exists for what should be recorded in a search log, or indeed how it should be formatted. But as a minimum a search log should store the content of the query strings submitted by the user and the items that they click on in response. Jansen [9] provides a useful conceptual model for a typical search transaction log consisting of queries and page views that can be realised as a relational database.

Since logs can vary so widely, it is prudent to start with one that is well-known and

---

[2]http://www.elasticsearch.org/overview/kibana/
[3]http://www.lucidworks.com/lucidworks-silk/

publicly accessible. One such example is the AOL search log.[4] released in 2006 [13]. It consists of a compressed text file containing 21,011,340 queries by 657,426 users over a 3-month period. This log has a somewhat infamous history, due to concerns that users could potentially be identified by their searches.[5] However, it is useful as it is relatively large and the records contain a variety of fields that offer a range of data mining possibilities. A sample from the log is shown in Figure 7.1.

```
1326    cascadefamilymedical        2006-03-14 11:36:57
1326    cascadefamilymedical.com    2006-03-14 11:39:49
1326    milaniwheel.com        2006-03-14 12:37:30
1326    www.ameicaneaglewheel.com  2006-03-14 18:53:20
1326    www.ameicaneaglewheel.com  2006-03-15 12:27:48
1326    pop up adds    2006-03-15 20:07:38
1326    pop up adds    2006-03-15 20:08:29
1326    the childs wonderland company      2006-03-21 11:50:10
1326    the child's wonderland company     2006-03-21 11:59:03 6
        http://www.wonderlandtheatre.com
1326    the child's wonderland company     2006-03-21 12:00:55
1326    the child's wonderland company grand rapids michigan 2006-03-21 12:01:24
1326    the child's wonderland company grand rapids michigan 2006-03-21 12:01:59
1326    the childs wonderland co.  2006-03-21 21:20:42
1326    the child's wonderland co. 2006-03-21 21:22:16
```

FIGURE 7.1: A sample of records from the AOL log.

The data include the following fields (AnonID, Query, QueryTime, ItemRank, Click-URL):

- **AnonID**: an anonymous user ID number.

- **Query**: the query issued by the user, case shifted with most punctuation removed.

- **QueryTime**: the time at which the query was submitted for search.

- **ItemRank**: if the user clicked on a search result, the rank of the item on which they clicked is listed.

- **ClickURL**: if the user clicked on a search result, the domain portion of the URL in the clicked result is listed.

The search log in Figure 7.1 represents users' actions with the search engine (either a query or clicked search result) using a customised format. However, it is common that the starting point is the raw web server log that will contain all request/responses between the web browser and server resulting in more lines in the log. This requires filtering to identify only those lines in the log that reflect user actions rather than system requests, such as elements to create a web page (e.g., requests for images and CSS files). In addition, non-human requests (e.g., from bots) must be excluded from the dataset for analysis as the focus in search log analysis is the user–system interactions. In his book on Web Data Mining, Bing Liu [14] (pp. 527–594) provides a comprehensive discussion of methods that can be used to pre-process (also known as *data preparation*) and analyse transactional data, including search logs.

---

[4]The AOL log can be downloaded from: http://www.gregsadetsky.com/aol-data/. Other logs can be found at http://jeffhuang.com/search_query_logs.html and http://faculty.ist.psu.edu/jjansen/academic/transaction_logs.html.

[5]http://en.wikipedia.org/wiki/AOL_search_data_leak.

When analysing search logs it is helpful to think of them in terms of user *sessions*: periods of continued interaction between a specific user and a search application during one visit to the site [9, 15, 16, 17]. A session typically begins with a query and ends with a webpage or some arbitrary time-based cut off, such as 30 minutes of inactivity, and contains a continuous sequence of user actions with the system [18].

By convention, a session captures the interactions between a specific IP address and search system. The IP address can be used as a proxy for *user* to identify repeating patterns across multiple sessions (anonymised user ID in the log described in Figure 7.1). However, this can be problematic for a number of reasons. For example, Internet Service Providers may assign different IP addresses to the same user as they browse the web, and multiple users may share a single IP address (e.g., the users of a library catalogue situated in a publicly accessible location). More reliable methods include using client-side cookies or user authentication if available; alternatively if using IP address then additional information, such as user agent and referrer, can also be used to identify users more reliably.

Various methods exist for segmenting the search logs into sessions (commonly referred to as *sessionisation*) [15]. The simplest methods are *time-based* and rely on timstamping each user action (typically starting with the initial query). One approach assumes that sessions do not exceed some pre-defined length (e.g., no longer than one hour); another approach involves computing the times between consecutive lines in the log from a single user and segmenting sessions based on a maximal time gap (e.g., 30 minutes). The assumption behind this is that long periods of inactivity will signal the start and end of different sessions. Of course these assumptions can be broken: users may engage in very long sessions beyond some pre-defined maximum and users may re-convene sessions following a break. Other, more sophisticated methods make use of referrer information, site structure and semantic information derived from queries to infer session breaks [15].

By way of example, taking a simple time-based approach based on segmenting sessions if the time difference between lines from the same user exceeds 30 mins (a commonly used time-out period), in the previous sample we might infer that there are seven individual sessions, as illustrated in Figure 7.2.

```
SESSION1: 1326        cascadefamilymedical        2006-03-14 11:36:57
SESSION1: 1326        cascadefamilymedical.com    2006-03-14 11:39:49
SESSION2: 1326        milaniwheel.com       2006-03-14 12:37:30
SESSION3: 1326        www.ameicaneaglewheel.com 2006-03-14 18:53:20
SESSION4: 1326        www.ameicaneaglewheel.com 2006-03-15 12:27:48
SESSION5: 1326        pop up adds   2006-03-15 20:07:38
SESSION5: 1326        pop up adds   2006-03-15 20:08:29
SESSION6: 1326        the childs wonderland company      2006-03-21 11:50:10
SESSION6: 1326        the child's wonderland company     2006-03-21 11:59:03 6
          http://www.wonderlandtheatre.com
SESSION6: 1326        the child's wonderland company     2006-03-21 12:00:55
SESSION6: 1326        the child's wonderland company grand rapids michigan 2006-03-21
12:01:24
SESSION6: 1326        the child's wonderland company grand rapids michigan 2006-03-21
12:01:59
SESSION7: 1326        the childs wonderland co. 2006-03-21 21:20:42
SESSION7: 1326        the child's wonderland co. 2006-03-21 21:22:16
```

FIGURE 7.2: A sample from the AOL log divided into sessions.

Evidently, the 30-minute cut off is only a heuristic, as it can indicate two sessions where one would perhaps be more reasonable (e.g., sessions 3 and 4), and vice versa. During a given session a user may work on multiple tasks (often referred to in the literature as *episodes* — a subset of semantically or functionally related consecutive actions [14] (p. 537)), such as researching holiday destinations whilst simultaneously comparing alternative weather forecasts. Likewise, a given task may be performed across multiple sessions [5, 6] or across multiple channels such as desktop and mobile [19].

To characterise search patterns, we need to identify and quantify suitable *features*. These features could capture aspects of the user's query formulation and reformulation strategies, resources selected and viewed and specific features of the search system that are used during the session. These features can be used to investigate aspects of users' search strategies. Common approaches to analysing search patterns include using information mined from the logs to answer specific questions or hypotheses; alternatively a more inductive approach could be used based on exploratory analyses. Search patterns mined from logs can be used (with care) to predict search behaviour. For example, researchers have used evidence gathered from search logs (e.g., the rank position of clicked items, number of query reformulations and length of session) to predict whether a search was likely to have been successful or not [20]. Patterns of users' click behaviour (e.g., the time spent viewing a page — *dwell time* — and subsequent actions) have also been shown to be good predictors of document relevance [21].

Measures based on quantifying feature occurrences can be computed for the session (e.g., total number of queries issued, total number of items selected, the ratio of queries to clicks) offering a *descriptive* summary. Analysis can also be carried out on *sequences* of actions, for example by computing a *transition matrix* that computes the probability of moving from one action to another (e.g., the likelihood of a click following a query is typically very high). Analysis may also be carried out to study patterns of query reformulation that may also suggest common strategies for refining a search [22, 23, 24, 25].

In analysing users' search strategies, Vakkari [26] gathers information about three aspects of a search session: (i) the search terms used (e.g., variety in vocabulary, length of queries and specificity of search terms); (ii) the search tactics used (e.g., how users start a session, patterns of query reformulation, use of operators including Boolean, use of advanced search features), and (iii) how users make relevance judgments (e.g., what items are selected as relevant). It is obviously easier to capture some of these features from a log file than others (e.g., search terms used vs. items judged as relevant). Although there is no agreed list of features that can be used to characterise search patterns and any features could be selected, it is worth asking whether a feature can be explained and how the feature can be captured from a search log and quantified. Not all features identified may be suitable at characterising search patterns and some element of feature selection could be applied.

To find patterns in the AOL log, we identified a number of descriptive features that had been used in previous work when clustering search patterns into distinct behavioural patterns:

1. **Query length** [17, 27]: the mean number of terms per query

2. **Session duration** [16, 27, 28]: the time from first action to session end

3. **Number of queries** [16, 17, 27, 28]: the number of keyword strings entered by the user

4. **Number of viewed hits / items retrieved** [16, 27, 28]: the number of links clicked by the user

5. **Number of requested result pages** [27]: the number of explicit page requests

6. **Number of activities** [27]: the sum of all the interactions with the system

These features are all reasonably straightforward to extract from a log such as AOL using Python or any other scripting language, and the output can be represented as a set of *feature vectors* for each session, as shown in Figure 7.3.

```
1.00,172,2,0,0,2
1.00,0,1,0,0,1
1.00,0,1,0,0,1
0.00,0,0,0,1,1
3.00,51,1,0,1,2
5.00,709,3,1,2,6
4.00,94,2,0,0,2
```

FIGURE 7.3: A set of feature vectors from the AOL log.

There are of course a great many other features we could extract or derive from this log, and the process of feature selection is something to which careful thought should be given. But for now let us consider another key question: What are the most effective techniques for revealing common patterns in such data? One such approach is to use an unsupervised learning technique, such as *clustering* [16, 17, 27]. Categorising search patterns across users into groups is useful in identifying common and distinct manifestations of search strategies and behaviours. These strategies might help to improve search systems. For example, if a common reoccurring pattern was a mis-spelt query followed by users correcting the query then adopting automated spell-checking detection and correction might improve the search experience. It is also commonplace for search providers to run online tests where search patterns are analysed both with and without a new search feature and differences in behaviours captured and investigated to establish whether the new feature is likely to benefit users or not.

7.3   Using Clustering to Find Patterns

In unsupervised learning there is no right answer in the sense that different outputs can be obtained and no single output is necessarily more correct than the others (although the patterns should be shown to be stable and repeatable, as discussed later). The outputs should also make sense and be explainable in the light of what is known from previous literature about search strategies and behaviours.

Instead, the utility of a particular clustering depends on the extent to which it provides useful insight into the phenomenon of interest (e.g., user behaviour). Consequently, it is prudent to adopt an exploratory strategy at the outset and try a range of approaches. A machine learning platform such as Weka[6] [12] provides a useful starting point as it offers an extensive range of algorithms for unsupervised learning and a helpful (but somewhat less polished) set of routines for result visualisation.

Let us start by taking a random sample of 100,000 sessions from the AOL log and then applying feature scaling so that values are normalised over a given range (e.g., a standard deviation of 1 and mean of zero). This ensures that features with particularly wide ranges in the raw data do not disproportionately influence the clustering process [29] (pp. 321-352). We can then use Weka to apply a clustering algorithm such as expectation maximization —[7]

---

[6]http://www.cs.waikato.ac.nz/ml/weka/.
[7]http://en.wikipedia.org/wiki/Expectation\%E2\%80\%93maximization_algorithm.

and then visualise the results. The steps to perform this are as follows, with sample code to perform these operations available from the website that accompanies this book.

7.3.1   Step 1: Prepare the Data

1. Extract the feature vectors (note that it may be prudent to experiment with a subset of the AOL log to begin with, e.g., the first million lines or so):

```
> python parse14.py -v fullcollection.1000000
```

2. Select a sample from the output:

```
> python selectRandomVectors.py output.log -s 100000 >
100000.sample1
```

3. Prepend this with the Weka ARFF header[8] :

```
> cat ARFFheader 100000.sample1 > 100000.sample1.arff
```

4. Apply feature scaling:

```
> python normalise_sessions.py 100000.sample1.arff >
100000.sample1.norm.arff
```

7.3.2   Step 2: Cluster Using Weka

1. Start Weka and choose the *Experimenter* interface (Figure 7.4)

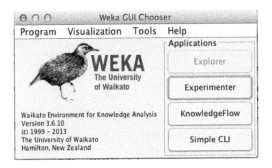

FIGURE 7.4: The Weka GUI chooser.

2. Select the Preprocess tab and open the output of Step 1 in Weka (Figure 7.5)

3. Select the Cluster tab and choose the Expectation Maximization (EM) algorithm (Figure 7.6)

4. Select the Ignore attributes button and make sure that any attributes other than the six above are ignored.

5. Select the option to Store clusters for visualisation, and then run the EM algorithm by selecting the *Start* button.

---

[8]http://www.cs.waikato.ac.nz/ml/weka/arff.html

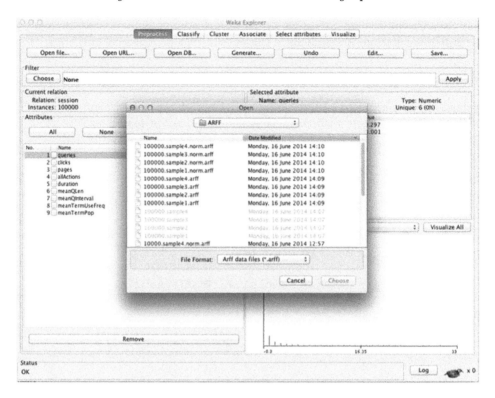

FIGURE 7.5: Loading the data into Weka.

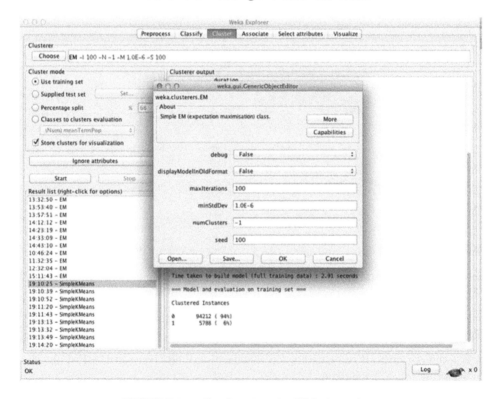

FIGURE 7.6: Configuring the EM algorithm.

7.3.3 Step 3: Visualise the Output

1. Right click on the last item in the Results list, and select the option to Visualize cluster assignments.

2. In the pop-up window, set the x axis to queries and the y axis to clicks, and apply a little jitter to smooth out the points (Figure 7.7). The output should be a chart similar to that shown in Figure 7.8.

FIGURE 7.7 (See color insert.): Configuring the visualization.

Figure 7.8 reveals four clusters (shown by the different coloured points), projected onto a two-dimensional space defined by the number of queries and the number of clicks. Note that there is nothing special about the number four; if you take a different log or use different features you will almost certainly get a different result. So it is important to perform multiple iterations, to ensure that the patterns are stable (i.e. replicable across different samples from the same population).

Let us focus for a moment on the image in Figure 7.8. What does it tell us? Well, not a lot so far: the presence of 4 clusters may be significant, but the projection does not deliver much insight into that. Instead, we need a visualisation that reveals the difference in feature values between clusters. If we take the output of Step 2 above (which is stored in the Clusterer Output window) and enter it into a suitable charting tool, we obtain an output similar to that of Figure 7.9.

This shows how the mean values for the four clusters vary across the six features. But now it is the data that are somewhat underwhelming: it suggests that we have a group of users who are relatively active (i.e., demonstrate a lot of interactions), a group who do relatively little, and two other groups in between. This is hardly the kind of insight that will have market research professionals fearing for their jobs.

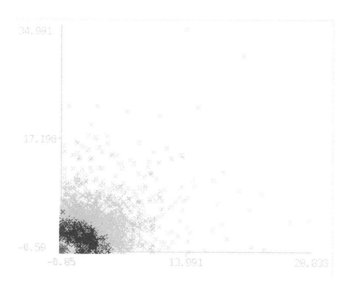

FIGURE 7.8 (See color insert.): 100,000 AOL sessions, plotted as queries vs. clicks.

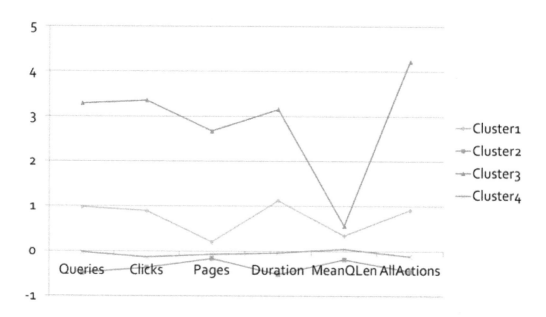

FIGURE 7.9 (See color insert.): Four clusters based on six features.

So at this point it may be prudent to review our choice of features; after all we have just six so far that were selected in a relatively informal manner. To be maximally useful (e.g., indicative of a latent variable such as behaviour type), we would want them to be relatively independent, i.e. uncorrelated with each other. But if we run a Pearson correlation across the ones above we find the opposite: most of them are actually highly correlated, particularly pairs such as All Actions and Duration. In this instance, these features may be "drowning out" interesting patterns that we might otherwise see. Therefore, we can try dropping the 'All Actions' feature and adding in two new features, which are less likely to be correlated with overall activity levels:

- **Term use frequency** [17]: the mean frequency of usage of each query term within the session

- **Query interval** [17]: the mean time between query submissions within a session

To do this we simply repeat Steps 1-3, selecting the appropriate seven attributes in Step 2.4. Now the results seem a bit more interesting (Figure 7.10). We could interpret these features as follows:

- **Cluster 0**: seems to be a relatively small group users who are highly engaged, in long sessions but issuing queries that are diverse/heterogeneous (possibly changing topic repeatedly)

- **Cluster 1**: seems to be a large group of users who engage in short sessions but often repeat their query terms and do more paging than querying

- **Cluster 2**: seems to be a middle or general group, whose defining characteristics we'll know more about when we've extracted more features.

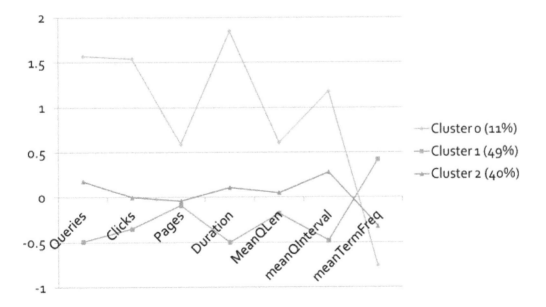

FIGURE 7.10 (See color insert.): Three clusters based on seven features.

7.4   Replication and Validation

From this point there is evidently a number of different ways we could extend the analysis. But instead of just adding more features and applying ever more exotic visualisations to new data sources, it is perhaps more prudent to take a moment to reflect on the process itself and confirm that what we are doing really is valid and repeatable. One way to do this is to replicate other published studies and compare the results. For example, Wolfram et al. [17] used the following features:

1. **Session size**: the number of queries submitted during the session

2. **Terms used per query**: the average number of terms used per query over the session

3. **Term popularity**: the average frequency of usage of each query term within the session when measured across all users over the dataset

4. **Term use frequency**: the average frequency of usage of each query term within the session

5. **Query interval**: the average time between query submissions within a session

6. **Pages viewed per query**: the average number of page requests per query within a session

Wolfram et al. [17] applied these to a number of search logs and showed (among other things) evidence of four distinct behavioural patterns in a sample of approximately 65,000 Web search sessions from the Excite 2001 data set [30]. If we can replicate their results, then we not only vindicate the specific conclusions they reached, but more importantly, provide evidence that our approach is valid and scalable to new data sources and research questions.

Note, however, that to calculate term popularity we need first to compute the mean frequency of usage of each term across the entire data set. The steps to perform this are as follows, with sample code to perform these operations available from the website that accompanies this book.

1. Split all the query terms onto their own line:

   ```
   > awk '{ for (i=1; i<=NF; i++) print $i }' aolquerylist.txt >
   temp
   ```

2. Sort the output, merge and count the lines, then sort again in descending order:

   ```
   > sort temp | uniq -c | sort rn > temp2
   ```

3. Reformat as csv to make subsequent processing easier:

   ```
   > awk -f format_as_csv.awk temp2 > aolquerylist.csv
   ```

Once this is complete, we can repeat Steps 1-3 in Section 7.3, selecting the appropriate six attributes in Step 2.4. Note that running the EM algorithm on large data samples can take some time to complete, so it may be prudent to experiment with smaller samples first (e.g., by selecting a sample of 10,000 lines in Step 1.2. The output is shown in Figure 7.11. This time, we find four clusters as Wolfram et al. [17], but the patterns are very different. (Note that display order of the features is changed here to facilitate comparison with Wolfram et al.'s results, and their labels have been simplified). But crucially, the results are not even replicable within themselves: a further three samples of 10,000 sessions produces widely different outcomes (5, 6, and 7 clusters, respectively). Even increasing the sample size to 100,000 seems to make little difference, with 7, 13, 6, and 6 clusters produced on each iteration (despite the suggestion in Wolfram et al.'s paper that subsets of 50k to 64k sessions should produce stable clusters).

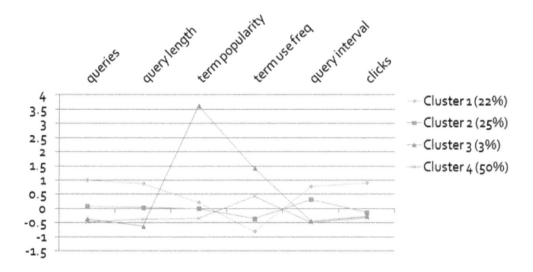

FIGURE 7.11 (See color insert.): Applying EM using Wolfram et al.'s 6 features to 10,000 sessions from AOL.

So why are we seeing such different results? One interpretation may be of course that these insights are indeed an authentic reflection of changes in user behaviour due to differences in context (e.g., a different search engine, time period, demographic)

But let's pause for a moment and examine the pattern in more detail. There is something very odd happening with term popularity now: we see a small cluster (just 3% of the sessions) where this feature seems to be something of an outlier, compressing the remaining traces into a narrow band. Indeed, the phenomenon becomes even more pronounced when we take a sample of 100,000 sessions. (To do this, we simply repeat Steps 1-3, passing 100,000 as a parameter to the sampling process in Step 1.2). The output is shown in Figure 7.12.

Perhaps this is an artifact of the clustering algorithm? We could try XMeans[9] in Step 2.3 instead (which is a variant of kMeans,[10] where the value for k is determined automatically). For our data sample, XMeans finds a local optimum at $k = 10$, so the number of clusters is now different. But the overall pattern, with a small cluster (1% of sessions) representing outlier values for term popularity, is again clearly visible (Figure 7.13).

So something else must be at play. It turns out that there is indeed an artifact of the data which is causing this: there is a small number of sessions that contains just a single query, consisting solely of the character '-'. Precisely why they are present in the log is a matter for speculation: they may have been the default query in some popular search application, or a side-effect of some automated service or API. But sessions like these, along

[9]http://weka.sourceforge.net/doc.packages/XMeans/weka/clusterers/XMeans.html.
[10]http://en.wikipedia.org/wiki/K-means_clustering.

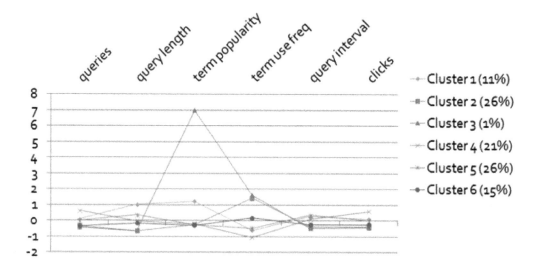

FIGURE 7.12 (See color insert.): Applying EM using Wolfram et al.'s 6 features to 100,000 sessions from AOL.

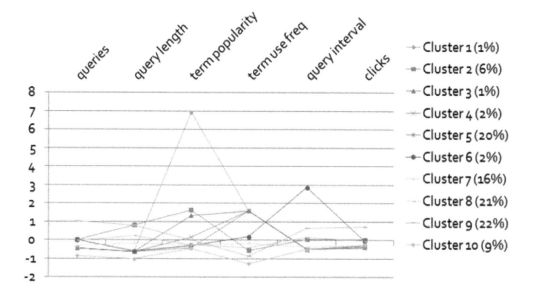

FIGURE 7.13 (See color insert.): Applying XMeans ($k <= 10$) and Wolfram et al.'s 6 features to 100,000 sessions from AOL.

with other robot-generated sessions, are not generally helpful when trying to understand human behavioural patterns. Instead, they are best removed prior to analysis. Of course, there are no 100% reliable criteria for differentiating robot traffic from human, and what should be removed is a matter for judgement, often on a case-by-case basis [31]. In this case, including these single-character queries appears to be counter productive. A simple shell script or single line of Awk can do this for us:

```
> awk '!/\t-\t/' fullcollection.1000000 >
fullcollection.1000000.filtered
```

With a new sample of 100,000 sessions excluding these outlier queries, we see Steps 1-3 using EM produce a very different output (Figure 7.14).

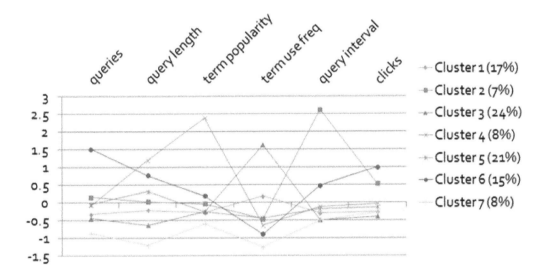

FIGURE 7.14 (See color insert.): Applying EM and Wolfram et al.'s 6 features to 100,000 filtered sessions from AOL.

This pattern is much more stable, with four iterations producing 7, 7, 7, and 9 clusters respectively. At this point we can start to speculate on what these patterns may be telling us. For example:

- **Cluster 6**: appears to be a group of users that engage in longer sessions, with many queries and many page views (clicks) but few repeating terms

- **Cluster 4**: appears to be a smaller group who seem to specialise in relatively long but popular queries, also with few repeating terms

- **Cluster 3**: appears to be a relatively large group who make greater use of repeated terms but are otherwise relatively unengaged (with shorter sessions and fewer page views)

And so on. Evidently, the previous patterns are somewhat hard to interpret due to the larger number of clusters and lines on the chart. What would happen if we tried to determine the optimum number ourselves, rather than letting XMeans find one for us? One way of investigating this is to specify different values for k *a priori*, and see how the within-cluster sum of squared errors (which is calculated by Weka as part of its output) varies on each iteration. To do this, simply repeat Step 2 nine times, selecting XMeans in Step 2.3 and varying k from 2 to 10 on each iteration. When we plot the output as a chart, we see a function similar to that shown in Figure 7.15.

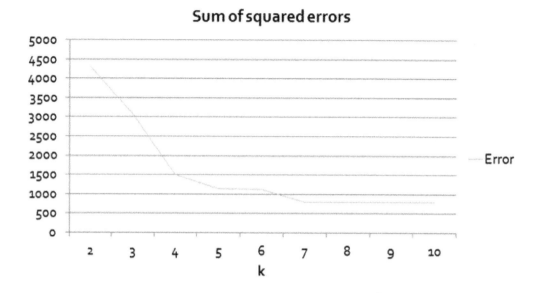

FIGURE 7.15: Sum of squared errors by k for 100,000 filtered sessions from AOL.

As we can see, there is an elbow around $k = 4$ and another around $k = 7$. This implies that either of these two values may be good choices for a local optimum. We have already seen the output for $k = 7$ (which is the optimum that XMeans found), so now we repeat Step 2 with kMeans and $k = 4$. The output is shown in Figure 7.16.

This time the groups are somewhat easier to differentiate. For example, we might suggest that:

- **Cluster 3**: represents a baseline or generic cluster of users who hover around the average for all measures

- **Cluster 4**: represents a relatively large group of users who engage in longer sessions (with more queries and page views) but are diverse in their interests, with few repeated terms

- **Cluster 1**: represents a smaller group who are the converse to cluster 4, engaging in shorter sessions but with more repeated terms

- **Cluster 2**: represents a tiny group (2%) of users who are similar to cluster 1 but focus on highly popular queries

7.5   Summary

Evidently, there are other ways we could analyse these data, and there are other ways we could interpret the output. What has been presented is really just a starting point for

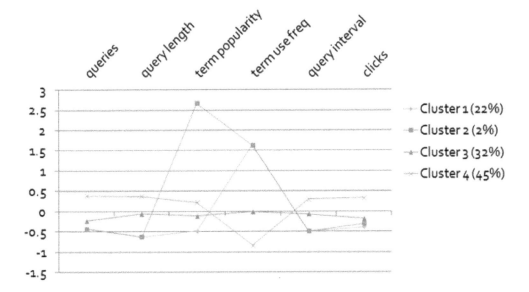

FIGURE 7.16 (See color insert.): Applying kMeans ($k = 4$) and Wolfram et al.'s 6 features to 100,000 sessions from AOL.

exploration. So for now, let us draw some of the threads together and review what has been covered.

- **Start with the end in mind**: Mining search logs for usage patterns is inherently an exploratory activity, so it makes sense to consider a number of different approaches. In each case, the utility of the results should be judged by the extent to which they provide useful insight into the phenomenon of interest (e.g., user behaviour).

- **Results may not generalise**: it is possible that the insights gained from one search log may not generalise to logs from other systems as users' patterns of interaction will be influenced by many factors including differences in system content, functionalities, interfaces, and user groups [11]. However, analysis of search logs can highlight key aspects of user–system interaction, thereby potentially "enlighten[ing] interface development, and devising the information architecture for content collections" [9] (p. 407).

- **There is no right answer**: As in many investigations of naturalistic phenomena, there is a tendency to look for patterns that align with our expectations. However, those expectations themselves are a subjective, social construct. The fact that we can produce multiple interpretations of the same data underlines the need for a common perspective when comparing patterns in search logs and to apply recognised models of information-seeking behaviour when interpreting the outputs.

- **Look for orthogonal features**: The hypothesis underlying much search log analysis of this type is that behaviour type is a latent variable whose influence can be measured indirectly via features such as those above. To be maximally useful these features should be highly correlated with the behaviours we wish to observe but relatively independent of each other.

- **Apply Occam's razor**: It is tempting to select features based on whatever a particular data source offers and to include as many as possible in the learning process. But not all are equally useful, and some can indeed drown out the influence of more important signals. So rather than starting from what the data can offer, identify the information-seeking behaviours you'd like to explore, and try to find the features that most closely align with them.

- **Replicate to validate**: As researchers, our instincts are to explore the unknown, to solve the unsolvable, and to favour novelty over repetition. But sometimes it benefits us to focus on the replication: by applying new techniques to old data, we validate our methodology and build a more reliable baseline for future experimental work.

Acknowledgments. Work partially funded by a Google Research Award project: "Developing a Taxonomy of Search Sessions".

Bibliography

[1] F. Silvestri. Mining query logs: Turning search usage data into knowledge. *Found. Trends Inf. Retr.*, 4(1–2):1–174, January 2010.

[2] S.J Lin and N. Belkin. Validation of a model of information seeking over multiple search sessions. *J. Am. Soc. Inf. Sci. Technol.*, 56(4):393–415, February 2005.

[3] M. Kellar, C. Watters, and M. Shepherd. A field study characterizing web-based information-seeking tasks. *J. Am. Soc. Inf. Sci. Technol.*, 58(7):999–1018, May 2007.

[4] Y. Li and N. J. Belkin. A faceted approach to conceptualizing tasks in information seeking. *Inf. Process. Manage.*, 44(6):1822–1837, November 2008.

[5] R. Jones and K. L. Klinkner. Beyond the session timeout: Automatic hierarchical segmentation of search topics in query logs. In *Proceedings of the 17th ACM Conference on Information and Knowledge Management*, CIKM '08, pages 699–708, New York, NY, USA, 2008. ACM.

[6] A. Spink, M. Park, B. J. Jansen, and J. Pedersen. Multitasking during Web search sessions. *Inf. Process. Manage.*, 42(1):264–275, January 2006.

[7] A. Broder. A taxonomy of web search. *SIGIR Forum*, 36(2):3–10, September 2002.

[8] G. Marchionini. Information-seeking strategies of novices using a full-text electronic encyclopedia. *J. Am. Soc. Inf. Sci.*, 40(1):54–66, January 1989.

[9] B. J. Jansen. Search log analysis: What it is, what's been done, how to do it. *Library & Information Science Research*, 28(3):407 – 432, 2006.

[10] C. Grimes, D. Tang, and D. M. Russell. Query logs alone are not enough. In *Proceedings of the WWW 2007 Workshop on Query Logs Analysis: Social and Technological Challenges*, 2007.

[11] M. Agosti, F. Crivellari, and G.M. Di Nunzio. Web log analysis: a review of a decade of studies about information acquisition, inspection and interpretation of user interaction. *Data Mining and Knowledge Discovery*, 24(3):663–696, 2012.

[12] M. Hall, Eibe F., G. Holmes, B. Pfahringer, P. Reutemann, and I.H. Witten. The weka data mining software: An update. *SIGKDD Explor. Newsl.*, 11(1):10–18, November 2009.

[13] G. Pass, A. Chowdhury, and C. Torgeson. A picture of search. In *Proceedings of the 1st International Conference on Scalable Information Systems*, InfoScale '06, New York, NY, USA, 2006. ACM.

[14] B. Liu. *Web data mining exploring hyperlinks, contents, and usage data*. Springer-Verlag New York, Inc., Secaucus, NJ, USA, 2011.

[15] D. Gayo-Avello. A survey on session detection methods in query logs and a proposal for future evaluation. *Inf. Sci.*, 179(12):1822–1843, May 2009.

[16] I. Weber and A. Jaimes. Who uses Web search for what: and how. In *Proceedings of the Fourth ACM International Conference on Web Search and Data Mining*, WSDM '11, pages 15–24, New York, NY, 2011. ACM.

[17] D. Wolfram, P. Wang, and J. Zhang. Identifying web search session patterns using cluster analysis: A comparison of three search environments. *Journal of the American Society for Information Science and Technology*, 60(5):896–910, 2009.

[18] D. He and A. Göker. Detecting session boundaries from web user logs. In *Proceedings of the BCS-IRSG 22nd annual colloquium on information retrieval research*, pages 57–66, 2000.

[19] Y. Wang, X. Huang, and R. W. White. Characterizing and supporting cross-device search tasks. In *Proceedings of the Sixth ACM International Conference on Web Search and Data Mining*, WSDM '13, pages 707–716, New York, NY, 2013. ACM.

[20] H. Wang, Y. Song, M.-W. Chang, X. He, A. Hassan, and Ryen W. White. Modeling action-level satisfaction for search task satisfaction prediction. In *Proceedings of the 37th International ACM SIGIR Conference on Research & Development in Information Retrieval*, SIGIR '14, pages 123–132, New York, NY, 2014. ACM.

[21] G. Dupret and C. Liao. A model to estimate intrinsic document relevance from the clickthrough logs of a web search engine. In *Proceedings of the Third ACM International Conference on Web Search and Data Mining*, WSDM '10, pages 181–190, New York, NY, 2010. ACM.

[22] M. Whittle, B. Eaglestone, N. Ford, V. J. Gillet, and A. Madden. Data mining of search engine logs. *J. Am. Soc. Inf. Sci. Technol.*, 58(14):2382–2400, December 2007.

[23] J. Huang and E. N. Efthimiadis. Analyzing and evaluating query reformulation strategies in web search logs. In *Proceedings of the 18th ACM Conference on Information and Knowledge Management*, CIKM '09, pages 77–86, New York, NY, USA, 2009. ACM.

[24] B. J. Jansen, M. Zhang, and A. Spink. Patterns and transitions of query reformulation during web searching. *International Journal of Web Information Systems*, 3(4):328–340, 2007.

[25] S. Y. Rieh and H. Xie. Analysis of multiple query reformulations on the web: the interactive information retrieval context. *Inf. Process. Manage.*, 42(3):751–768, May 2006.

[26] P. Vakkari. A theory of the task-based information retrieval process: a summary and generalisation of a longitudinal study. *Journal of Documentation*, 57(1):44–60, 2001.

[27] D. Stenmark. Identifying clusters of user behavior in intranet search engine log files. *Journal of the American Society for Information Science and Technology*, 59(14):2232–2243, 2008.

[28] H.-M. Chen and M. D. Cooper. Using clustering techniques to detect usage patterns in a web-based information system. *Journal of the American Society for Information Science and Technology*, 52(11):888–904, 2001.

[29] O. Maimon and L. Rokach. *Data Mining and Knowledge Discovery Handbook*. Series in Solid-State Sciences. Springer, 2010.

[30] A. Spink, B. J. Jansen, D. Wolfram, and T. Saracevic. From e-sex to e-commerce: Web search changes. *Computer*, 35(3):107–109, March 2002.

[31] Y. Zhang and A. Moffat. Some observations on user search behavior. In *Proceedings of the 11th Australasian Document Computing Symposium*. Brisbane, Australia, 2006.

Chapter 8

Temporally Aware Online News Mining and Visualization with Python

Kyle Goslin

Department of Computer Science, College of Computing Technology, Dublin, Ireland

8.1   Introduction

The quantity of information rich data on the Web has been increasing year on year providing a further burden on users to decipher what is relevant to them. The use of aggregation services to define what is considered relevant and useful have become the norm during the Web browsing process. A good example of an aggregation service pulling content from a wide number of sources is Google News.

However, the quantity of information being presented to the user is still quite vast and also time sensitive, for instance, news stories changing every few minutes on Google News. The quantity of data creates the need for further processing of aggregated data to present the content to the user in a easily consumable format.

News stories that have been aggregated often come clearly marked with title text, description text, date, and timestamps as standard fields during the publication process. One of the most useful fields is the timestamp associated with data, which, although simple, can be an effective measure of document relevance at the current moment in time.

This chapter aims to provide a detailed overview of the development of a temporally aware news mining tool with visualization using free and open-source software. By providing a temporal window on the data an additional level of depth can be achieved during the selection process allowing a quick decision-making process before retaining resources for further processing.

The process of deciding text value is not described in this chapter but can be found in other chapters of this book. All of the code samples in this chapter can be downloaded from the official text mining book webpage at `http://www.text-mining-book.com`.

8.1.1   Section Outline

The aim of this chapter is to provide an example of the scraping and selection process needed for extracting data from a news aggregation website. Once these data have been extracted, they can then be assessed for relevance and visualized using free and open-source visualization tools.

Section 8.1 provides a brief introduction to the area of scraping a visualization. Section 8.2 outlines the tools that are needed for this work. Section 8.3 outlines the difference between crawling and scraping. Section 8.4 outlines the concept of time and issues that can arise. Section 8.5 outlines the process of analyzing input sources. Section 8.6 outlines the process of scraping a webpage. Section 8.7 outlines the process of generating a visual representation with JSON. Section 8.8 outlines the viewing process using SigmaJS. Section 8.9 outlines additional concerns during the scraping process. Section 8.10 concludes this chapter with a summary of what was covered in this chapter.

8.1.2   Conventions

In this chapter, commands that should be typed out in the operating system command line or terminal will be proceeded with the following syntax:

>>

The command that must be typed will follow these two characters do not type the two
>>   characters.

8.2 What You Need

Before starting, this section outlines each of the tools that are needed to develop the application outlined in this chapter. The examples outlined in this chapter are performed on a Microsoft Windows-based operating system. However, due to the cross-platform nature of Python [1] and JavaScript, each of the steps outlined here can be easily ported to the operating system of your choice.

To get the most out of this chapter, having a basic knowledge of the Python programming language and how to develop applications locally will help. If you do not have a knowledge about the Python programming language, a wealth of knowledge is available at Python.org.

8.2.1 Local HTTP Host

For the visualization process we will be using a JavaScript library for rendering. To avoid any issues during this process, we first need to download a local HTTP server where we can locally host our visualization code. During this tutorial we will be using XAMPP [2] as it provides all of the functionality that we need with a simple user control panel.

You can download XAMPP from `https://www.apachefriends.org/index.html` and clicking on the download link. This installer is rather large and may take some time to download. During the visualization steps, we will be looking into the details of using this tool. XAMPP by default will attempt to run the Web server on port 80. Ensure that you do not have any other services running on this port. If you are experiencing any issues during this process whereby the service will not start, ensure that the firewall on your system is turned off and that you are running the sever in administrator mode. This can be done by right click on the control panel icon and clicking *Run as Administrator*. If issues with port 80 persist, you can easily change the port number of the HTTP server to an alternative port using the XAMPP control panel.

8.2.2 Python Interpreter

The most important tool we will be using is the Python interpreter. The Python interpreter allows you to run Python program files with a .py extension. This interpreter can be downloaded from Python.org. Although a number of different versions of the interpreter exist such as the later version 3.0, to aid backwards compatibility we will be working with the stable Python 2.7 for this project chapter.

It is important that we can access our Python interpreter and *Scripts* folder from anywhere on our system. To do this we must add Python into our system *path* variable. On Microsoft Windows-based systems, this is done by editing the environment variables on our system to include the path to where Python was installed. This can done by:

1. Entering into the Windows control panel

2. Clicking on the System icon

3. Once the system menu has opened, on the left-hand side we can then enter into the *Advanced System Settings*. The system properties menu will then open for us.

4. From here we can click the *Environment Variables* button.

5. In the collection of *System Variables* that are available, locate the PATH variable and click the Edit button.

6. Insert a new entry at the end of the value for this variable (not replacing the current string!); The values that must be appended to this string are:

   ;C:\Python27;C:\Python27\Scripts This should reflect the path where your Python installation is located on your system. You may need to alter this to reflect the drive on your system where Python is installed.

7. To finish click Ok on each of the three open windows.

It is important to ensure that this string is proceeded by a semicolon, if this is omitted then your path variable will not be updated correctly.

If you are working in a Linux environment, Python is often installed as a default as part of your installation. To check what version is installed on your installation, from the command line type the following command:

>> python -V

It is important to remember that Python is space sensitive. Correct indentation must be added to your code to ensure it will run correctly. This can be difficult to users who have no experience with Python code as their code may look correct but will not correctly be interpreted.

8.2.3 PIP Installer

When working with a number of different libraries, the process of downloading each individual library and keeping track of where they are located can become a monotonous task. As a solution to this process, a tool was developed called PIP [3], which is used for downloading and installing different Python libraries quickly and easily on your system.

To install PIP, we first need to download the *get-pip.py* script from `https://bootstrap.pypa.io/get-pip.py`. This can be done by opening the file in a Web browser and then right-clicking the file in the Web browser and clicking *Save As*. This file should be saved to your desktop for easy access in later steps.

Once you have download the file, you need to run the PIP installer script. This is done by opening up the Windows command line for your machine. To do this click the *Start* button and then type the command *cmd* into the search box and hit the enter key. The command line will open at your home directory shown in Figure 8.1.

FIGURE 8.1: Windows command prompt.

Once the command line has been opened, we need to navigate to the desktop by typing in the following command:

>>   cd Desktop

After you have moved to the desktop, we use the following command to run the *get-pip.py* installer script.

>>   python get-pip.py

This will then begin the installation process for the PIP installer tool. A message will appear in the console telling you the current progress of your download and installation. At the end of this process a message will be presented telling you if your installation succeeded or failed. If you get a message saying that Python cannot be found, this may be an indication that you have not installed Python or have not updated the *path* variable. If this happens check to see if you have installed Python and added the Python directory to your *path* variable by reviewing the steps in Section 8.2.2.

8.2.4   lxml and Scrapy

Scrapy [4] is a Python-based application that allows us to develop a Web scraping application without the need to focus on the finer details of the scraping process. We will use PIP which we have previously installed to install Scrapy. However, to use Scrapy, we must first download and install the lxml [5] parser.

To use the PIP that we previously installed, we must navigate into the folder where PIP is located on your local machine. PIP can be found inside the *Scripts* folder inside of the directory where Python has been installed. To navigate into this folder, type the following command into the command line:

>>   cd C:\Python27\Scripts

Once we are inside the *Scripts* folder, we can the run the following command to install lxml using PIP:

>>   pip install lxml

Like the previous process, a message will be printed to the console telling you if your installation process was successful or not. After we have installed lxml, we can then begin the process of installing Scrapy. From the directory we are in type the following command into the command line:

>>   pip install scrapy

After this process has completed you should have both lxml and Scrapy successfully installed on your local machine.

8.2.5   SigmaJS Visualization

The application that we are building will contain visualizations of the data we collect. To do this we will need to use an additional visualization package. Although Python is used for a variety of different text scraping and processing tasks, we will not be using Python for the visualization of the data. We will opt for a Web-based visualization tool called SigmaJS [6] which is a light-weight open-source JavaScript based visualization library. To get started:

1. Downloaded SigmaJS from http://sigmajs.org by clicking on the download button. You will then be directed to the download page.

2. On this page, under the release section, click and download the .zip file containing SigmaJS source code. This will begin a download of a single .zip file.

3. Once this file has downloaded, you must then right-click and extract the contents of the .zip file to your Desktop.

4. Open the extracted folder and view the contents.

Figure 8.2 shows the contents of this folder. Right-click this folder and rename this folder *sigma.* In the rest of this chapter, we will treat the *sigma* folder as the entire visualization application.

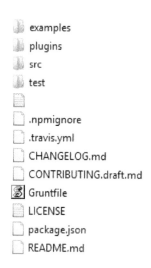

FIGURE 8.2: Contents of the SigmaJS folder.

Inside this folder you will see an *examples* folder. It contains a number of different samples of SigmaJS in action. The one we are most interested in is the *load-external-json.html* file. This gives a fully working sample of SigmaJS pulling in the JSON content of a file for visualization. The file which it is pulling in will later be generated by our application.

8.2.6 News Source

The focus of this chapter is temporally aware news mining and visualization, we will need to have a site of interest to us that we will perform this mining process on. For this chapter, we will be working with the Google News aggregation service. Each story comes with the attributes we are interested in for this chapter such as the date, time, title, and description text for each story.

The process followed in this chapter is not specific to Google News and can be altered to work with any other online news source.

8.2.7 Python Code Text Editor

Although it can be tempting to get involved in using an integrated development environment, for this project it is not needed. Windows Notepad can provide all of the features you need. However, if you would like some additional features, a simple lightweight editor such as Notepad++ (`https://notepad-plus-plus.org`) can offer syntax highlighting to make the code editing process a little bit easier.

If you are working in a Linux environment, gedit or vi will perform just as well for each of the tasks.

8.3　Crawling and Scraping — What Is the Difference?

Although the terms crawling and scraping are often found together, they are two different processes. The process of crawling is identifying links on a website and following through each webpage looking for subsequent links to crawl. The tools that perform this task are often called spiders, due to their crawling nature. Scraping, however, is performed when a page of interest has been found. The content on the page is scraped and stored in a local repository for further processing.

When a website of interest has been found it may contain a collection of additional links. It is possible, due to a combination of links on the website that the crawling tool may unintentionally revisit the same link a number of times causing additional wasted resources, or loop on a collection of pages. An example of this is a naïve crawler that may keep revisiting the home link on a website, starting the same crawling process over and over again. To prevent this from happening, it is often the case that a log of visited pages is retained and utilised. Before any pages are scraped the list of links that have previously been scraped is assessed for similarity.

The concept of depth is often cited that refers to how many links should be followed on a webpage. A max depth MD is often set for a given webpage, P. When considering a webpage as a tree-like structure with the *index* page as the root of the tree, each link followed is considered an additional level deep or $D + 1$. The value for D should always remain $\leq$ than MD.

Scrapy by default does not follow or gather any links. As we will be scraping the index page of Google News, we do not need to set up any additional settings for crawling or following links.

8.4　What Is Time?

When working with data, having a timestamp attached provides a great insight during the relevancy decision-making process. Time, however, is a complex concept when considering a worldwide audience and variations can exist. Depending on the country of origin the layout of the timestamp can also cause confusion. An example of this is the American-style datestamp that places the month first, followed by the day and year in comparison to the European timestamp, which places the day first followed by the month and year. A number of other variations of these timestamps exist, such as spelling out the month (e.g., October-2014) compared with using numeric form (e.g., 10-2014). Other variations can exist in the format such as the use of hyphens, slashes, or dots to break each component of the timestamp.

As a solution to date-related problems, typically the time reference Epoch is often used in the Unix world. Epoch is the 1st of January, 1970. From this date the number of seconds that have lapsed since then can easily be calculated and stored e.g. 1408975329. This allows all timestamps to be saved in a unambiguous format without complex formatting issues. These seconds based timestamps can then be easily converted into the desired format before presenting the timestamp to the user.

An important element of working with time-sensitive data is the process of specifying a time window where data can be considered relevant. We will logically break down *time windows* into discrete individual periods of time. Each individual window is then given a unique ID. An example of these windows are shown in Table 8.1.

TABLE 8.1: Time windows.

Window	Days	Hours
1	Today	All posts in the last 12 hours
2	Last 2 Days	All posts in the last 48 hours
3	Last 3 Days	All posts in the last 72 hours
4	Last 7 Days	All posts in the last 168 hours

We are using hours as the metric for time as breaking news is related in terms of hours since the story was published. Older news stories (greater than 1 day old) do not come with an *hours* based stamp but are given in terms of a traditional time/date stamp. An example of this is when a news story on the front page of a news website becomes older than 24 hours it reverts to the complete date format (e.g., 1/11/14). We will need to apply further transformations to convert the date stamp into a useable format for future processing. This process is described in later sections.

8.5   Analyzing Input Sources

To get the best quality results from your scraping process it is important that the data sources which you use are of high quality. Individual news sources can be used to gather content such as CNN.com or a news aggregator such as Google News. Using a single news source can have advantages as a single format of webpage is known so all implementations can follow strict scraping rules.

We will be looking at the webpage as a single entity for this project. When viewing a HTML page, we can note that a common structure is always followed:

```
1 <html>
2  <head>
3     <title> </title>
4  </head>
5
6  <body>
7  </body>
8 </html>
```

HTML documents can contain a mixture of HTML and CSS. The page that we will be looking at is the Google News home page. This page consists of a standard HTML structure, but also inside of the simple HTML document a main parent div titled *content-pane-container* is found. The structure of this div is as follows:

```
1 <div class="content-pane-container">
2 </div>
```

Inside this div, a number of child divs are added for each news story. Each of these contain a title describing the news story, description text for the story, a timestamp outlining when the story was published, and a URL address pointing to the news story. What follows is a sample child div added to the container div:

```
1 <div class="blended-wrapper esc-wrapper">
2 </div>
```

The high-level view of the logical structure of a Google news page would look like the following after news stories have been added:

```
1 <html>
2 <head>
3    <title> </title>
4 </head>
5
6 <body>
7    <div class="content-pane-container">
8       <div class="blended-wrapper esc-wrapper"> </div>
9       <div class="blended-wrapper esc-wrapper"> </div>
10      <div class="blended-wrapper esc-wrapper"> </div>
11   </div>
12 </body>
13 </html>
```

In this example you can see that inside the body a single *content-pane-container* exists, and inside this multiple different divs with the class attribute set to *blended-wrapper esc-wrapper* can be seen. For each additional news story on the page, an additional *blended-wrapper esc-wrapper* is then added to this parent div. Inside the div with class type *blended-wrapper esc-wrapper*, the four elements are added that are of interest to us are described as follows:

1. The div with class type *esc-lead-snippet-wrapper* contains information describing the news story.

2. The Span of class type *titletext* is a short title for the news story.

3. A link, shown here as a <a target=_blank .. is the link element which contains the URL to the actual news story being shown.

4. A final span tag with class type *al-attribution-timestamp* contains a text based timestamp outlining how long ago the news story had been published. This can contain either the number of minute(s) or hour(s).

A complete example of the contents of a *blended-wrapper esc-wrapper* for an individual news story is shown as follows with header and trailing HTML removed:

```
1 <span class="titletext">2014 World Series Game 6 Preview: Jake
2 Peavy vs. Yordano Ventura</span>
3 ...
4
```

```
5 <a target="_blank" class="article usg-AFQjCNHszuSN7CVG9y5hIa7zlQvEU3t-aQ
    sig2-5Vjs9uBMiqZO9p3HXLiX7Q did--2408506129546916749 _tracked" href="
    http://news.google.com/news/url?sr=1&amp;ct2=us%2F0_0_s_3_1_a&amp;sa=
    t&amp;usg=AFQ......" url="http://www.cbssports.com/mlb/eye-on-
    baseball/24772127/world-series-game-6-preview-jake-peavy-vs-yordano-
    ventura" rel="noreferrer" id="MAA4AEgDUABgAWoCdXM" ssid="s"
    saprocessedanchor="true" originalhref="http://www.cbssports.com/mlb/
    eye-on-baseball/24772127/world-series-game-6-preview-jake-peavy-vs-
    yordano-ventura"><span class="titletext">2014 World Series Game 6
    Preview: Jake Peavy vs. Yordano Ventura</span></a>
6
7
8 ...
9 <span class="al-attribution-timestamp">18 minutes ago</span>
10
11 ...
12 <div class="esc-lead-snippet-wrapper">The Giants and Royals are set to
    resume the World Series in Kansas City's Kauffman Stadium on Tuesday
    night. San Francisco leads the series three games to two and is one
    win away from their third title in the last five seasons.</div>
13
14 ...
```

8.5.1   Parameters for Webpages

Most websites offer the ability generally to add additional parameters in the URL. This allows additional user specific changes to be made to the request, such as the language, geographic region of interest or number of different resources to be returned to the caller. An example of this for the Google News website is a parameter for setting the Edition (shown as *ned* parameter).

In the following snippet, the *ned* parameter is being set to *en_ie*. If we wanted to get the American edition of Google News this parameter could be changed to *us*.

```
1 ned=en_ie
```

This parameter is passed in via the request URL:

```
1 https://news.google.com/?edchanged=1&ned=us
```

When crawling through webpages it is often the case that not all of the pages are directly linked to but can be accessed by passing the correct parameter through a URL variable. Crawlers often create variations of these parameters (e.g., where a story ID is set to the numbers between 1 and 1,000 with the chance of discovering a webpage that has not been directly linked to).

8.5.2   Processing Sections of Webpages vs. Processing Full Webpages

Webpages have a number of different elements such as HTML, CSS and JavaScript which are not useful to us during our processing as we are only interested in the text content. In addition to this, content may be added to the pages such as advertisements which are large sections of text that are not relevant to the current task. Before any further processing is done, we must be sure to remove these from the document.

To help us remove elements of content that are not useful to us, we can use the *Selector* class which comes with Scrapy. The Selector allows us to select a div inside the HTML document we are currently working with. This is done by identifying the class name of the div we would like to select using XPath notation. If you are comfortable with other selection tools such as BeautifulSoup or lxml, you can use this instead of the Selector class offered by Scrapy.

In this particular example, we know the name of the class that we would like to remove from the document. Generally large companies such as Google AdWords or other advertisement networks use a similar set of IDs for the divs where their advertisements are shown, allowing easy identification and removal.

After we have selected the div we would like to remove, we can then use the Python function shown here as *body.replace*, to remove the content that we have just selected from the main document. In the following example, a sample selection by div name and removal using *body.replace* is being performed on a sample HTML document.

After we have removed the content, we are then printing out the cleaned document out using the Python *print* function.

```
1  from scrapy.selector import HtmlXPathSelector
2  from scrapy.selector import Selector
3
4  body = '<html><body><div class="advert">This is an advert!</div><span>
      good</span></body></html>'
5  selectElement = Selector(text=body).xpath('//div[@class="advert"]').
      extract()
6
7  str = ''.join(selectElement)
8
9  print str
10 cleaned = body.replace(str, '')
11
12 print cleaned
```

In addition to removing the advertisements, we may also want to filter out other pieces of data that are not relevant from the document (e.g., repeated copyright notices and header information). Depending on the website that you are working with, you may manually identify the elements that you would like to remove from the document and remove these sections before automating the task of content removal from the document.

8.6 Scraping the Web

The process of scraping content from the Web can be performed in two different ways. The first of these is developing a custom Web scraping utility which makes a direct connection using a Python library such as *urllib*. After the connection has been made the webpage is then downloaded and parsed manually. The second of these approaches is to use an existing library for processing. There are a number of benefits to using a predefined library, such as handling of errors, authentication, session data management, and other smaller aspects of the scraping process that can become time-consuming when a custom scraping tool has been developed. For these time saving benefits, we will be working with the premade Python-based Web scraping tool Scrapy.

8.6.1   Pseudocode for the Crawler

Because the process of scraping, filtering, and processing data is complex, before we begin creating any code we will first step back and consider what the pseudocode for this process will look like. Now we outline a rough guide to what steps are involved in our initial scraping process:

```
1   Using Scrapy Connect to the URL and access the page HTML
2   Search the document we receive for blended-wrapper esc-wrapper div tags
        using XPath notation
3   Process each individual news story div
4   For each story div tag block search for the timestamp and titletext
5   Analyze the timestamps to see if the text is within our current range
        of interest
6       IF timestamp in our time window THEN
7           Store timestamp, title text, unique id for story as a new
                NewStory object
8           Add story object to local storage list
```

8.6.2   Creating a Basic Scraping Tool

In the following sections we will begin the process of creating our custom scraping tool. To begin, we will start the process of creating a new Python script file and placing it inside the Python27\Scripts folder on your local machine. Using your favourite text editor, save a blank file titled *simplecrawler.py* inside of your Scripts folder. From this point on, we will assume your default directory for Python is in the C: drive of your machine. The folder where we will place our code can be found at

C: \Python27\Scripts

After creating the empty *simplecrawler.py* file, we will then begin by putting in the class for the following SimpleCrawler script:

```
1   class SimpleCrawler(Spider):
2       name, start_urls = 'googlenews', ['http://news.google.com']
3
4       def parse(self, response):
5           print 'Inside parse function'
```

The *start_url* shown in the example is the website address where we will begin the scraping process. This is not a recursive process and the scraper will only scrape the current page that we have provided and not follow any of the links.

The *parse* function that can be seen in the previous example receives a *response* object which contains the content from the webpage that we have just scraped. All of our processing will be done on this response object. When the scraper runs it will trigger the *parse* function to perform some tasks on the content that has been scraped. When you are finished making the changes, save the file.

8.6.3   Running a Scraping Tool

Now that we have created a sample script, we then then begin the process of running the utility. To do this, open up a command line and using the *cd* command move into the Scripts folder:

>>   cd C:\Python27\Scripts

Once inside the Python27\Scripts folder where our scraping tool is located, we then need to call Scrapy and pass the source code file we just created as an argument by issuing the following command:

>> scrapy runspider simplecrawler.py

If all goes to plan, your scraping tool will make a connection to the Google News website and trigger the *parse* function. As we have not added any implementation specific functions into the *parse* function, no actions will be performed.

8.6.4　News Story Object

As we will be working with individual news stories, to make the process a little easier we will need to make a *News Story* object template. At the top of your *simplecrawler.py* file, add the following code:

```
1 class NewsStory:
2     wordList = list()
3     timestamp = 0;
4     storyid = 0;
5     weight = 0;
```

Inside this class definition, you will see four different variables that each of the news stories will have. A *wordList* is used for storing each of the words in the title, a *timestamp* variable for storing the timestamp of the story, a *storyid* variable for storing the unique story ID, and a *weight* variable for storing the weight of the story.

As we encounter different news stories, we will create a new *NewsStory* object for each and store them locally for later processing. After you have finished save your *simplecrawler.py* file.

8.6.5　Custom Parsing Function

The following example shows the alterations that we have made to the parsing function. The *response* object is the name given to the content currently being processed by Scrapy. In this example, we have used the *HTMLXPathSelector* class on the response object that we have just received. This class allows us to use XPath notation for identifying the elements that we are interested in selecting. In this example, we are selecting the HTML div tags in the response object that have a class name of *blended-wrapper esc-wrapper*.

The XPath notation is passed into the select function. This is telling the selector to search for a div where the class is equal to *blended-wrapper esc-wrapper*. Once it has selected the div tags, it then uses the text to collect the content. To aid the process of identification, a storyid variable was created that increases incrementally every time a new story has been encountered.

Update your parsing function to include the following code to do this:

```
1 def parse(self, response):
2     hxs = HtmlXPathSelector(response)
3     namesubs = hxs.select('//div[@class="blended-wrapper esc-wrapper"]/
           *').extract()
4     storyid = 0;
5
6     for namesub in namesubs:
7         self.processNewsStory(namesub, storyid);
8         storyid = storyid+1;
```

After we have selected each of these divs, we begin the looping process over the list of divs using a for-loop and passing each individual div to a custom function along with a unique story id. This custom function titled *processNewsStory* is where the processing for each individual news story will be performed.

8.6.6   Processing an Individual News Story

In this section we will review each of the sections of code that go into our custom *processNewsStory* function. Each individual news story is passed to the *processNewsStory* function in the form of a namesub variable and a storyid variable. Once the complete namesub variable has been received, processing is then started to extract the key information from the story.

In the code sample below you can see that we are using XPath notation to select the span with a class title of *al-attribution-timestamp*. Once we have selected this, we are then extracting the text. After this has been done, the replace function is being used to strip out some unwanted characters by replacing them with nothing.

Once the timestamp has been extracted, the focus is then placed upon the title text of the news story. Again, XPath notation is used to select the span where the class attribute is set up *titletext*. This value is then extracted. A small amount of cleaning is also performed on this string to strip out unwanted characters. Update the *processNewsStory* function (shown below) to include the following code and then save the file.

```
1   def processNewsStory(self, namesub, storyid):
2       print 'processing'
3       timestamp = Selector(text=namesub).xpath('//span[@class="al-
            attribution-timestamp"]/text()').extract()
4
5       cleaned_string= str(timestamp).replace("[u'\u200e",'')
6       cleaned_string2 = str(cleaned_string).replace("\u200e']", '')
7
8       titletext = Selector(text=namesub).xpath('//span[@class="titletext"
            ]/text()').extract()
9       title_string= str(titletext).replace("[u'\u200e",'')
10      cleaned_title = str(title_string).replace("\u200e']", '')
```

After the initial selection of the data has been performed, processing is then started on the timestamp to analyze which of the stories are of interest to us. The format of the timestamp however is in a human readable format such as 1 hour ago or 1 minutes ago.

To work with these timestamps in a machine readable format, depending on the timestamp that was entered, a different block in a nest of if statements is executed to correctly convert the timestamp. Inside each of these blocks the original text in the timestamp is removed. The initial number which was provided is then multiplied by a factor of 60 to turn the timestamp into the number of seconds in total since the news story was published if it is in minutes format, or 60 * 60 if it is in hour format. This provides a common base for all timestamps to be compared. The code for processing timestamps is shown as follows:

A variable titled *number_of_seconds_old* is created to store the seconds that have lapsed since the story was published in seconds form.

```
1
2       number_of_seconds_old = 0;
3
4       if 'minutes' in str(cleaned_string2):
5           print 'contains minutes'
6           timestamp = str(cleaned_string2).replace('minutes','')
```

```
7       timestamp2 = str(timestamp).replace('ago','')
8       timestamp_trimmed = str(timestamp2).strip()
9
10      number_of_seconds_old = int(timestamp_trimmed) * 60
11
12  elif 'hours' in str(cleaned_string2):
13      print 'contains hours'
14
15      timestamp = str(cleaned_string2).replace('hours','')
16      timestamp2 = str(timestamp).replace('ago','')
17      timestamp_trimmed = str(timestamp2).strip()
18      number_of_seconds_old = int(timestamp_trimmed) * 60 * 60
19
20  elif 'hour' in str(cleaned_string2):
21      print 'contains hours'
22
23      timestamp = str(cleaned_string2).replace('hour','')
24      timestamp2 = str(timestamp).replace('ago','')
25      timestamp_trimmed = str(timestamp2).strip()
26
27      number_of_seconds_old = int(timestamp_trimmed) * 60 * 60
```

Insert this code into the end of your *processNewsStory* function. After information about the timestamp has been processed, we can then begin the process of deciding if we should keep the story or not. To do this, an if statement is created that checks to see if the variable *number_of_seconds_old*, which retains how old the current story is, is ≤ than the threshold of 3,000 seconds. If this is true, then we will begin the storage process of the following story:

```
1       ''' If the number of seconds old is greater
2           than our set time, then keep the story
3       '''
4       global Story_Object_Storage
5
6       if number_of_seconds_old > 3000:
7           print 'adding new story'
8           ns = NewsStory()
9
10          lower_case_title = [element.lower() for element in titletext]
11          ns.wordList = lower_case_title
12          ns.timestamp = number_of_seconds_old
13          ns.storyid = storyid
14          Story_Object_Storage.append(ns)
```

Insert the code above at the end of your processNewsStory function.

In this code, an instance of the *NewsStory* class is created, which is used for storing the story information (timestamp, story id, title content). Each of these fields are then added to the object, and then the object is appended onto the Story_Object_Storage list, which contains a list of each of the stories that we wish to keep for the visualization process. This list is a global variable stored at the top of our application, so it can be accessed by any subsequent sections of code.

8.6.7   Python Imports and Global Variables

At the very top of your *simplecrawler.py* file, some basic imports for the function of Scrapy are needed. Additional imports for working with JSON, random numbers and copying are also needed. The following code should be added to the top of your file:

```
1 from scrapy import Spider
2 from scrapy.selector import HtmlXPathSelector
3 from scrapy.selector import Selector
4 import json
5 from random import randint
6 import random
7 import unicodedata
8 import copy
```

Just below this code, a collection of global variables need to be added. These include the *counter* variable, which is used to count the number of nodes added; the *edge_counter* for counting the number of edges (connection between first story and all other stories); and the *Story_Object_Storage*, list which is used for holding each of the *NewsStories* in memory in an easily accessible format. The *addedEdgeId* is used for keeping track of the IDs associated to each edge created.

Add the following piece of code just below your imports in your *simplecrawler.py* file.

```
1 counter = 1
2
3 ''' Edge Counters '''
4 edge_counter = 0;
5 Story_Object_Storage = list()
6
7 addedEdgeId = 1;
```

8.7   Generating a Visual Representation

When creating a visualization of any data typically the data are first converted into a format that can be read by a visualization application. These formats are often XML, JSON, or CSV formatted files allowing for the easy manipulation of data. The data visualization package that we are using is the *SigmaJS* library, which takes JSON structured documents with defined nodes and edges.

The following sample shows an example of the structure of a JSON that is read in by SigmaJS.

```
1  {
2    "nodes": [
3      {
4        "id": "n0",
5        "label": "A node",
6        "x": 0,
7        "y": 0,
8        "size": 3
9      },
10     {
11       "id": "n1",
```

```
 2       "label": "Another node",
 3       "x": 3,
 4       "y": 1,
 5       "size": 2
 6     },
 7     {
 8       "id": "n2",
 9       "label": "And a last one",
 0       "x": 1,
 1       "y": 3,
 2       "size": 1
 3     }
 4   ],
 5   "edges": [
 6     {
 7       "id": "e0",
 8       "source": "n0",
 9       "target": "n1"
 0     },
 1     {
 2       "id": "e1",
 3       "source": "n1",
 4       "target": "n2"
 5     },
 6     {
 7       "id": "e2",
 8       "source": "n2",
 9       "target": "n0"
 0     }
 1   ]
 2 }
```

In the JSON document you can see that a number of different nodes are defined. Between each of these nodes a number of different edges can be seen. The *source* and *target* for each edge must correspond to one of the nodes that have been defined. In our application we will be representing each individual news stories as a single node. Edges between the nodes are the outlined as the strength of similarity between the first node and all of the other nodes in the application.

SigmaJS comes with a number of different visualization examples as part of the default code sample. The example that we are most interested in is the example that has the ability to read in JSON files directly from the local hard drive. This example can be found inside the *sigma/examples/load-external-json.html* file.

8.7.1 Generating JSON Data

After each of the news stories that we are interested in has been added to the *Story_Object_Storage class* during the parsing process, we now can begin the process of generating the JSON file using these data. A class titled *JSONMaker* is added which has two functions: one for creating *nodes* and one for creating *edges* between nodes in JSON format.

The following code should be added to the end of your *simplecrawler.py* file.

```
1 '''
2 JSON Output generator
3 '''
```

```
 4 class JSONMaker:
 5
 6    def createEdge(self, targetid, weight):
 7        global edge_counter
 8        global addedEdgeId
 9        global Story_Object_Storage
10
11        data = {}
12        data['id'] = '' +str(addedEdgeId)+''
13        data['source'] = ''+str(Story_Object_Storage[1].storyid)+''
14        data['target'] = ''+str(targetid)+''
15        data['color'] = '#ccc'
16        data['size'] = ''+str(weight+10)+''
17
18        addedEdgeId = addedEdgeId + 1
19        json_data = json.dumps(data, sort_keys=True,indent=4, separators=('
             ,', ': '))
20
21        if addedEdgeId == 2:
22            json_data +=str(',')
23
24        if edge_counter != len(Story_Object_Storage)-1 and addedEdgeId !=
             2:
25            json_data +=str(',')
26
27        edge_counter = edge_counter+1
28        return json_data
29
30
31    def createNode(self, id, value):
32        global counter
33
34        data = {}
35        data['id'] = ''+str(id)+''
36        data['label'] = ''+str(value)+''
37        data['x'] = randint(10,50) #Inclusive
38        data['y'] = randint(1,50) #Inclusive
39        data['size'] = 1
40        data['color'] = '#'+''.join([random.choice('0123456789ABCDEF') for
             x in range(6)])
41
42        json_data = json.dumps(data, sort_keys=True,indent=4, separators=('
             ,', ': '))
43
44        if counter != len(Story_Object_Storage):
45            json_data +=str(',')
46
47        counter = counter+1
48        return json_data
49
50 mk = JSONMaker()
```

As each of the stories must be plotted on an X and Y axis, for this example these values are generated using the *randint* random number generating function. A random color code generator is also used to give each of the nodes a unique color. Towards the end of this code, a check is performed to see if the current counter number is not the length of the

Story_Object_Store list. If it is, then no comma is added to the JSON that is being created as the last element does not include a trailing comma.

To finish, the *json_data* string containing the JSON for that particular node is returned back to the caller of the function to help build the final JSON output.

8.7.2   Writing a JSON File

To generate the final output, inside the original parse method of the crawler, a pipe is opened to create a *data.json* file that can be read into the SigmaJS example visualization.

For the JSON document to be fully valid, additional sections must be added such as the header of the JSON document and to the footer of the JSON document.

In the middle of this section of code, a loop is performed over the *Story_Object_Storage* list to pull down each of the *NewsStory* objects that have been stored. Each story is then passed to the *JSONMaker* outlined in the previous section to generate the JSON output for each story. This JSON output that is created is then embedded between the header and the footer of the JSON document to make a complete valid JSON document.

In the following sample you can see the file is being opened using the *open()* function, which is being passed the *w* flag to indicate to write to the file.

Just after the first for-loop inside the original *parse* function, the following code should be added:

```
1
2          ''' Loop over nodes '''
3
4          f = open('data.json', 'w')
5          header = '''
6          {
7            "nodes": [ '''
8
9          f.write(header)
10
11         footer = ''' ], '''
```

The following sample shows the process of looping over each of the stories stored inside of the *Story_Object_Store*. For each of the stories, the *createNode* function is being called to create a new node in the JSON file.

After the nodes have been created in JSON, they are then written to the *data.json* file using the *f.write* command. After generating the JSON for the nodes a JSON header for the edges is then output and then the first record from the object store is then pulled down and stored inside the *firstRecord* variable.

The first record will be treated as the single object that all other news stories will be compared against. We then loop over each of the news stories and call the *createNode* function to generate the associated JSON.

Add the following code to the end of your *parse* function:

```
1  global mk
2
3          for story in Story_Object_Storage:
4              f.write(mk.createNode(story.storyid, story.wordList))
5
6          f.write(footer)
7
8          edges = ''' "edges": [ '''
9          f.write(edges)
```

```
10
11        '''
12        Generate a list of edges between each of the nodes
13        if a similar words is found.
14        '''
15        firstRecord = str(Story_Object_Storage[0].wordList)
```

In the following code we check the text in the first news story word by word to the text in the rest of the news stories. The similarity strength between the first news story and all other stories is built up here by calculating how often the terms from the first story appeared in the other news stories.

For each time a term from the first record is found in record N, the *story.weight* integer is incremented by 1. To aid the readability the text *found a match!* is outputted to the console.

Add the following code to the end of your *parse* function:

```
1
2
3         '''
4         Calculate matches between the first record
5         and all the other records.
6         '''
7         for story in Story_Object_Storage:
8             for word in story.wordList:
9                 for term in firstRecord.split(' '):
10                    originalTerm = term.encode('ascii', 'ignore').decode('
                          ascii')
11                    sentence = word.encode('ascii', 'ignore').decode('ascii')
12                    if originalTerm in sentence:
13                        print 'found a match!'
14                        ''' Increment the weight of the story'''
15                        story.weight = story.weight+1
```

Once each of the weights indicating the strength between the first news story and all other stories is created, the final step is output the edge JSON. The following code outlines the process of skipping the first record and then calling the createEdge function to generate the associated JSON. This JSON is then written to a file using the *f.write* command.

Add the following code to the end of your *parse* function:

```
1         '''
2         Generate the edges
3         '''
4         for story in Story_Object_Storage:
5
6             if story.storyid != '0':
7                 print story.storyid
8                 print story.weight
9                 print '----'
10                f.write(mk.createEdge(story.storyid, story.weight))
```

To finish the end of the JSON file is output. Add the following code to the end of your *parse* function to complete the JSON document:

```
1         edges_footer = '''
2
3             ]
4         }'''
```

```
5
6        f.write(edges_footer)
7        f.close()
```

If at any stage of developing a JSON document you are getting an unexplained error, you can use one of the online JSON validation tools such as `http://jsonlint.com` to check that it is not stemming from a malformed JSON document.

You can now run this complete application by following the steps outlined in Section 8.6.3. This will output the *data.json* file for you. We will be using this *data.json* file in the next section.

8.8   Viewing the Visualization

The online nature of JavaScript applications often requires the code to be running in a Web browser from a Web address such as *localhost*. To prevent any issues arising with our code we will utilise a simple HTTP server on our local machine for testing.

Section 8.2.1 outlined the process of downloading XAMPP. After installing XAMPP, we need to start the Web server. This is done by first opening up the XAMPP control panel shown in Figure 8.3.

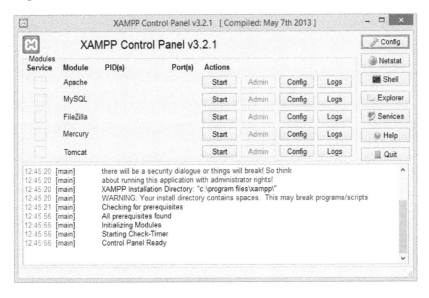

FIGURE 8.3: XAMPP control panel.

After starting XAMPP, click on the *Start* button beside Apache. Status messages will appear telling you if Apache has started and what port it is bound to. Next click on the *Explorer* button to open the root directory of the Web server. Place your *sigama* folder inside of the *htdocs* folder in the root of your XAMPP installation directory. By doing this we will sidestep the *XMLHttpRequest* error outlined earlier from appearing in the Web browser when running the code.

Before moving any further, we must move the *data.json* file that was output earlier into the *htdocs \sigma\examples\data* folder.

A slight alteration to the *load-external-json.html* file is made to allow the edge weights which have been added to be shown. The path to the file we have created is also changed to point to *data/data.json* that we output earlier.

```
1  ....
2  sigma.parsers.json('data/data.json', {
3
4  renderer: {
5    // IMPORTANT:
6    // This works only with the canvas renderer, so the
7    // renderer type set as "canvas" is necessary here.
8    container: document.getElementById('graph-container'),
9    type: 'canvas'
10   },
11   settings: {
12     minNodeSize: 1,
13     maxNodeSize: 10,
14     minEdgeSize: 0.1,
15     maxEdgeSize: 40,
16   }
17 });
18 CustomEdgeShapes.init(sigma);
19 sigma.refresh();
20 ....
```

After making the alterations and saving the file we can then open our Web browser and type the following path:

```
http://localhost/sigma/examples/load-external-json.html
```

Due to the quiet nature of JavaScript when something goes wrong it can be difficult to tell when an error has occurred. A great way to check what has error has occurred is by using the console that is available inside Google Chrome by right-clicking anywhere and then selecting Inspect Element from the menu that opens and then selecting Console. This will outline any of the errors on the page.

Figure 8.4 shows each of the nodes representing individual news stories. The edges between each of these nodes outlines the strength of the similarity between the first news story and each of the other news stories that have been saved. In some cases, as can be seen at the top of this figure, some news stories will have no connection to the first news story if no similarity is found. All stories not in the required time frame have been removed from the visualization before the JSON file has been generated.

Figure 8.5 shows a closer view of the news stories. Each of the labels attached to each of the nodes can be seen. In this view, the terms that make up the news story title can be inspected. This image outlines a view of the labels attached to each of the news stories when zoomed in closely.

8.9   Additional Concerns

Web content sources (although freely available to the user) may have a different policy when automated services are accessing their content. Generally most services offer a paid subscription to the service when any automatic processes are concerned due to the drain on resources often attributed to Web scraping utilities. Remember that a scraping utility

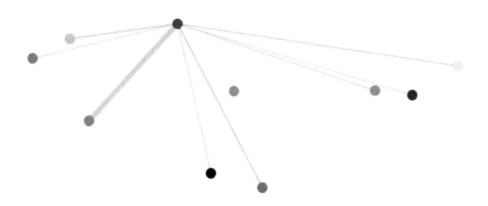

FIGURE 8.4: News stories.

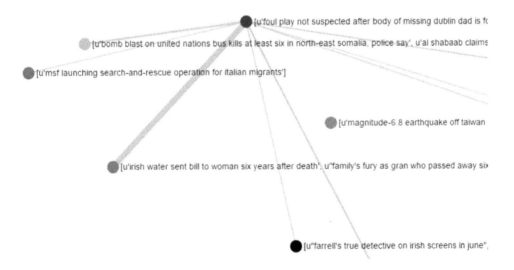

FIGURE 8.5: Closer view of news stories.

often has a one-track mind when retrieving content (e.g., keep scraping)! To prevent the misuse of a service, it is advised to read the terms and conditions of the site that you will be scraping to ensure they approve of the process.

To prevent any bad feeling between your scraping tool and the service, additional timeout periods can be established to allow the tool to automatically take a pause after a certain number of requests are made. The least desired result is for the content provider to blacklist your IP address due to overuse.

A plain text file added by the system administrator named *robots.txt* is often added to websites. The purpose of this file is to define how automated services should interact with the Web server and the content that it provides. Adhering to this policy is a responsibility given to the owner of the scraping utility. All applications that interact with Web services also have the ability to identify themselves to a server. This allows the Web server to allow or deny the scraper. It is often been the case that a user can access a webpage from their Web browser, but the Web crawler cannot access the page.

The fingerprint which is given by the Web browser may be accepted, (e.g., Internet Explorer or Google Chrome), but the fingerprint from a homebrew scraping utility may not be. This is often a quick way to gauge the reception of a content providers attitude towards automatic scraping utilities. To counteract this, scraping utilities often come with the ability to change the fingerprint they will leave to become a generic Web browser when they are asked to be identified by a Web server.

8.9.1   Authentication

When interacting with webpages, the views are often broken up into two main views. The first of these is the anonymous view whereby the user does not need to be logged into the system. This allows all of the content on the system to be available with ease. The second of these is the authenticated user. These user accounts require the user to have an account with the content provider to allow the content to be accessed. If the user does not have an account he or she is often just redirected to another page requesting the user to log into the page. The process of creating an account with a content provider is often designed so that a human user must authenticate with the service. This approach is used to help prevent the automatic creation of accounts and the spreading of spam.

When a tool is interacting with a content provider, a session is often created on the server side, and a token is stored on the client side. Each time a request is made, a token from the user is passed to the server so the server side session can be matched to the user again on subsequent requests.

8.9.2   Errors

Like most pieces of software, errors are not accepted very well when the constraints of real-time Web content processing is concerned. The large volumes of data that can quickly pass through the tool provide a one chance pass to ensure everything goes as planned without the need for reprocessing to occur. To maximize the uptime of the crawling tool, it is strongly encouraged that the native logging features of Python are utilized to create a comprehensive log of wherever errors have occurred during processing.

The concept of a graceful failure should always be kept in mind. If a website is currently offline or producing some undesirable output causing an error to be thrown, the error should simply be logged and the application should move onto the next website. This ensures that long, time-consuming Web crawls will not be in vain if worst does come to worst.

When interacting with Web servers, a number of different server response status codes [7] are often returned to the caller (e.g., the Web scraping utility), outlining what the status of the webpage or resource currently is. These status codes can be of vital importance as they give a quick summary of the webpage status, without the need for the entire website to be crawled. Two examples of status codes that can be an early warning of issues are the *307 Temporary Redirect* and *308 Permanent Redirect* codes. These outline that the page the crawler is looking for is not there and telling the crawler to move to a different page. If the crawler is a self-built tool then the tool may not have the capabilities required to follow to the new page. Other codes such as the *403 Forbidden, 404 Not Found* and *408 Request Timeout* are simple examples of status codes that can easily be found in everyday Web scraping and crawling.

8.10   Summary

With the ever-increasing amount of data on the Web competing for a user's viewing time, emphasis has been placed upon developers to create unique visualizations to find data most relevant to the current user. This chapter outlined the process of scraping data from the Web using the free and open-source Web scraping tool Scrapy. The HTML structure of the Google News aggregation webpage was described outlining fields that are of interest to us, mainly the timestamp and description text.

After the data had been scraped, a custom filtering process was created that applies time windows to the data and retaining and visualizing only the relevant information given a set time window. Additional filtering was described outlining how common features such as advertisement text and copyright notices can be removed from the data.

A custom JSON file was generated containing a unique node for each news story and edges identifying the similarity from the first news story to all the other news stories. The SimgaJS visualization library was used to show how a lightweight viewer can be created to visualise the complex connections between news stories.

Additional concerns such as authentication, server errors, and common scraping rules were outlined towards the end of the chapter. This chapter shows that creating a Web scraping and visualization utility can be quickly and easily developed with little overhead to the developer.

Bibliography

[1] Python. https://www.python.org/. Accessed: 2015-04-22.

[2] XAMPP. https://www.apachefriends.org/index.html. Accessed: 2015-04-22.

[3] PIP. https://pypi.python.org/pypi/pip. Accessed: 2015-04-22.

[4] Scrapy. http://scrapy.org/. Accessed: 2015-04-22.

[5] lxml. https://www.gephi.org/. Accessed: 2015-04-22.

[6] SigmaJS. http://sigmajs.org/. Accessed: 2015-04-22.

[7] Status Codes List of HTTP Status Codes. http://en.wikipedia.org/wiki/List_of_HTTP_status_codes. Accessed: 2015-09-30.

Chapter 9

Text Classification Using Python

David Colton

IBM, Dublin, Ireland

9.1 Introduction

This chapter will examine how Python, the Natural Language Toolkit (NLTK), scikit-learn, and Numpy can be used to classify text. Using a corpus of previously classified positive and negative movie reviews, a number of classification models will be developed to predict whether unseen movie reviews can be correctly identified as either positive or negative in nature.

This chapter is not a Python tutorial. It will cover just enough to let you run through the samples described. Nor does this chapter provide an in-depth analysis of the tools and packages described. There are many excellent books and online tutorials that can give you, the reader, a more thorough explanation of the concepts introduced here if required. What this chapter does provide, however, is an introduction to the packages mentioned and examples of how text can be classified.

9.1.1   Python

Python [1] is an open-source high-level programming language developed under an OSI approved open-source license. Although considered an excellent choice for the user who is only starting to learn how to program, Python offers enough features and functionality to meet the demands of the professional object-oriented programmer as well. It is highly scalable, portable, embeddable, and suitable for development projects of all sizes. Another great advantage of Python is a very active community that enthusiastically develops, releases, and supports commercial quality libraries, packages, tools, and platforms that enhance and extend the core Python capabilities. Two such packages, NLTK and scikit-learn, are extensively used in this chapter.

Python may already be installed on your machine. The simplest way to determine this to open a command prompt or terminal and type *'python'* or *'python3'*. If Python is already installed you should see something similar to the first two or three lines of Figure 9.1. If it is not, it can be downloaded from `https://www.python.org/downloads/`. Installation instructions will vary depending on your Operating System (OS), but there are many excellent references and tutorials available on the web. For this chapter Python version 3.4.1, 32 bit, was used. This is the version of Python recommended for use with NLTK version 3 at the time of writing.

9.1.2   The Natural Language Toolkit

The Natural Language Toolkit (NLTK) [2] is a leading platform for building Python programs to work with human language data. The NLTK provides a suite of libraries to handle text processing tasks such as corpora parsing, tokenisation, stemming, and classification.

The NLTK also provides libraries that support part-of-speech tagging, which converts a sentence into a list of word / tag tuples, and chunk extraction that can be used to extract a short phrase from a sentence that has previously been part-of-speech tagged. The NLTK provides easy access to WordNet, a large lexical database of English nouns, verbs, adjectives, and adverbs and over 50 text corpora.

Like Python, the NLTK is a free, open-source project. It is community driven and is available for Linux, Windows, and Mac OS machines. Instructions for installing NLTK on different operating systems is given at `http://www.nltk.org/install.html`. On this webpage an optional installation of the NumPy 1.8.1 package is suggested. Although NumPy is listed as optional, it, and SciPy, are both required by scikit-learn. It is suggested that both are installed at this point. NumPy and SciPy can be downloaded from the following locations:

- `http://sourceforge.net/projects/numpy/files/NumPy/`

- `http://sourceforge.net/projects/scipy/files/scipy/`

NLTK 3.0.0, NumPy 1.8.1 [3] and SciPy version 0.14.0 [4] were used in the Python scripts developed for this chapter.

9.1.3   scikit-learn

scikit-learn [5]is a simple and efficient tool for data mining, data analysis, and machine learning in Python. It utilises other Python libraries such as NumPy, SciPy, and Matplotlib. Like Python and NLTK, it is open-source available under a BSD license. scikit-learn includes many supervised learning algorithms including Naïve Bayes, Support Vector Machines, Random Forests and Decision Trees, as well as many unsupervised learning techniques, including clustering and hidden Markov models.

As well as supporting cross-validation and providing comprehensive grid search capabilities for parameter optimization, scikit-learn also provides extensive model evaluation metrics and scoring options including, for example, precision, recall, and accuracy as well as an easily accessible confusion matrix. Feature extraction including TF-IDF is also supported.

Like the NLTK, if you are using Mac or a flavour of Linux, scikit-learn can be installed using the Pip package install utility. If you are installing on a Windows machine an installer can be downloaded from `http://www.lfd.uci.edu/~gohlke/pythonlibs/` `#scikit-learn`

9.1.4 Verifying Your Environment

Python and the required third-party libraries and packages should now be installed and ready to use. To verify your environment, open the Python interpreter by typing *'python'* at your command or terminal prompt. Information about the version of Python installed on your machine will be displayed followed, on the next line, by three greater than signs >>>. Enter the following commands to verify the each required package is correctly installed. If each import command completes without throwing an error then you have successfully installed all required packages.

```
>>> import nltk
>>> import sklearn
>>> import numpy
>>> import scipy
```

The version of each package installed can also be displayed using the following commands. The expected output from running all commands is shown in Figure 9.1.

```
>>> nltk.__version__
>>> sklearn.__version__
>>> numpy.__version__
>>> scipy.__version__
```

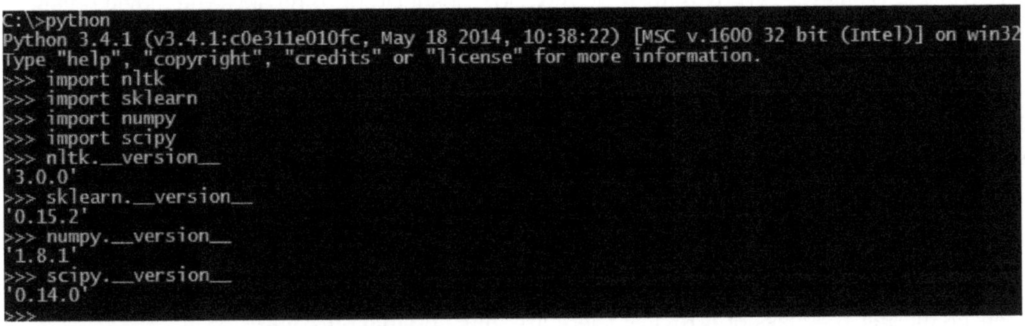

```
C:\>python
Python 3.4.1 (v3.4.1:c0e311e010fc, May 18 2014, 10:38:22) [MSC v.1600 32 bit (Intel)] on win32
Type "help", "copyright", "credits" or "license" for more information.
>>> import nltk
>>> import sklearn
>>> import numpy
>>> import scipy
>>> nltk.__version__
'3.0.0'
>>> sklearn.__version__
'0.15.2'
>>> numpy.__version__
'1.8.1'
>>> scipy.__version__
'0.14.0'
>>>
```

FIGURE 9.1: Verifying your Python environment on a Windows machine.

9.1.5 Movie Review Data Set

Now that the Python environment is correctly configured and ready to use, attention can be turned to getting the movie review data set. These data were first used in [6]. The movie review data set is one of the many corpora available with the NLTK. To install it, run the Python interpreter, and enter the following commands:

```
>>> import nltk
>>> nltk.download()
```

A new window should open, showing the *"NLTK Downloader"*. Click on the File menu, select Change Download Directory, and specify a central location, for example, c:\nltk_data. Select the Corpora tab, and then scroll down and highlight movie review data set. Click the download button to retrieve the corpus. Figure 9.2 shows the NLTK Downloader tool.

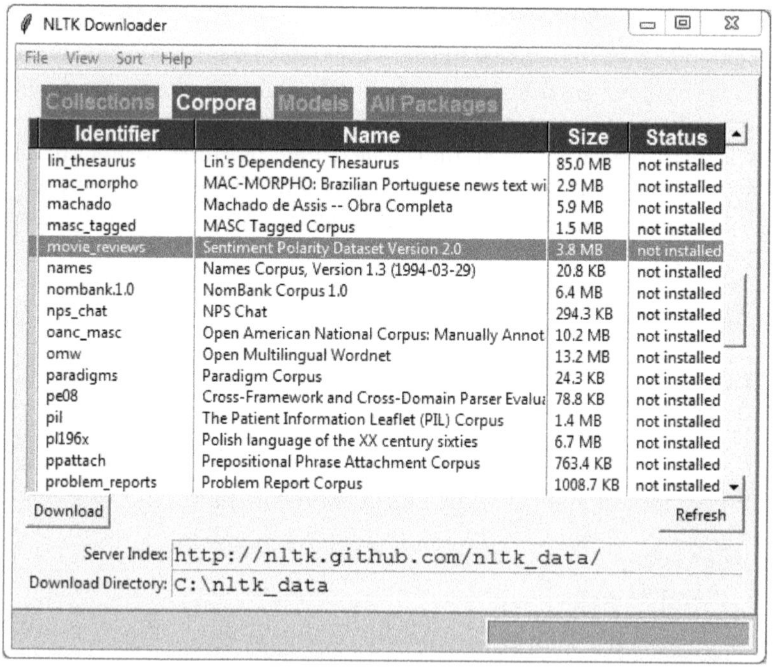

FIGURE 9.2: Using the NLTK built-in NLTK Downloader tool to retrieve the movie review corpus.

The data set contains 1,000 positive movie reviews and 1,000 negative movie reviews and will be examined in more detail later. Further background information about the corpus can be found in the read me file in the data set root folder.

9.1.6   Precision, Recall, and Accuracy

When evaluating the performance of a model precision, recall and accuracy will be used. When predicting the class of a review there are four possible outcomes:

1. **True Positive** (TP)
   A true positive is where a review is predicted as positive and was classified as positive

2. **False Positive** (FP)
   A false positive is where a review is predicted as positive but was classified as negative

3. **False Negative** (FN)
   A false negative is where a review is predicted as negative but was classified as positive

4. **True Negative** (TN)
   A true negative is where a review is predicted as negative and was classified as negative

The overall accuracy of a model is calculated as

$$\frac{Number of True Positives + Number of True Negatives}{Total Number of Examples} \tag{9.1}$$

Positive Class Precision is calculated as

$$\frac{Number of True Positives}{Number of True Positives + Number of False Positives} \tag{9.2}$$

Positive Class Recall is calculated as

$$\frac{Number of True Positives}{Number of True Positives + Number of False Negatives} \tag{9.3}$$

Negative Class Precision is calculated as

$$\frac{Number of True Negatives}{Number of True Negatives + Number of False Negatives} \tag{9.4}$$

Negative Class Recall is calculated as

$$\frac{Number of True Negatives}{Number of True Negatives + Number of False Positives} \tag{9.5}$$

Precision and recall are inversely related, which mean that as precision increases recall falls and inversely where recall rises precision decreases. The critical decision then is to develop a model that gives high precision and low recall or a model the delivers a low precision value but has high recall. A high precision value with a lower recall value implies that a high percentage of reviews that are predicted as positive will actually be positive. However, the downside of such a model is that a lot of positive reviews will not be correctly identified. High recall and low precision values obtained from a model would imply that a high percentage of positive reviews are correctly identified as such, but, as a consequence, a large number of negative reviews would be incorrectly identified as positive yielding a lower precision value. Usually a trade-off has to be made between precision and recall depending on the situation and the preferred outcomes.

9.1.7 G-Performance

In addition to standard classifier performance measures (e.g., accuracy, precision, recall), Kubat and Matwin [7] describe another measure that uses the geometric mean of the accuracies measured separately on each class. This measure they call the g-performance. The goal of this measure is to maximise the recall of both class but at the same time keeping them balanced such that a poor value for either the positive or negative class will give an overall poor performance for the classifier.

G-performance is calculated as

$$g = \sqrt{\frac{True Positives}{True Positives + False Positives} \times \frac{True Negatives}{True Negatives + False Positives}} \tag{9.6}$$

The g-performance of each model developed will be calculated and analysed to determine which models have performed the best.

9.2   Modelling with the Natural Language Toolkit

In this section you will develop several classifier models using the movie review corpus and the Natural Language Toolkit. Models will be developed with and without stops words and with unigrams, bigrams, and trigrams. However, before developing your first model it is important to understand the data set that you will be using.

9.2.1   Movie Review Corpus Data Review

Before starting any text mining exercise it is very important to first understand the data set that will be used. As you can see in Figure 9.3, beneath the top-level folder the movie reviews are separated into two folders: one for positive reviews, the *'pos'* folder; and one for negative reviews, the *'neg'* folder. As mentioned earlier a read me text file in the root folder gives the reader some background information on the history and use of the data set. There are 1,000 reviews in each folder.

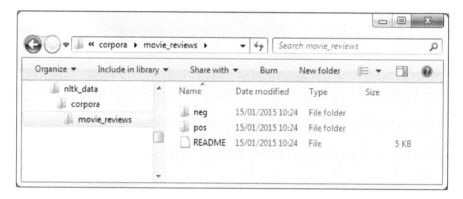

FIGURE 9.3: The structure of the movie review corpus.

Figure 9.4 shows a sample positive review. Examining the text it can be seen that all characters are lowercase. It can also be observed that punctuation marks such as full stops, commas, and brackets, are preceded and followed by a space. It also appears that there are no non-ASCII characters present in the files. This shows that a certain degree of preprocessing has already been performed on the text of the reviews. Standardising the case of all characters, removing non-ASCII characters, and separating the punctuation in this manner are all steps aimed at producing a standard set of tokens to be used in the development of the classification model. When seen by the learning algorithm, 'acting,' and 'acting' are two completely different tokens. So rather than having two occurrences of a single *"acting"* token, there are two different tokens that each occur only once.

Not all non-alphanumeric characters have been completely separated from words as highlighted in Figure 9.4. The author of the review has used a double dash, --, to isolate some of their thoughts from the rest of the review. These dashes could lead to the generation of unique tokens not seen elsewhere in the corpus. These tokens could then play an overemphasised role in the prediction of a positive or negative class, which is not what is wanted. On the other hand, the second highlighted token, father-and-son, is a concatenation of three words where it makes sense that they are treated as a single token.

```
cv280_8267.txt  cv754_7216.txt                                    ◁ ▷ ✕

kolya is one of the richest films i've seen in some time .
zdenek sverak plays a confirmed old bachelor ( who's likely to remain so )
, who finds his life as a czech cellist increasingly impacted by the
five-year old boy that he's taking care of .
though it ends rather abruptly-- and i'm whining , 'cause i wanted to spend
more time with these characters-- the acting , writing , and production
values are as high as , if not higher than , comparable american dramas .
this father-and-son delight-- sverak also wrote the script , while his son
, jan , directed-- won a golden globe for best foreign language film and ,
a couple days after i saw it , walked away an oscar .
in czech and russian , with english subtitles .
```

FIGURE 9.4: A sample positive review from the movie corpus.

9.2.2   Developing a NLTK Naïve Bayes Classifier

The first model we develop will use the Natural Language Toolkit utilising a Naïve Bayes learner and a feature-based bag-of-words approach. As seen, the data are stored in the NLTK corpus format where each review is written to a file in a folder that represents whether it was classified as a positive or negative review. The complete listing is available for download from the book website.

The development of a NLTK Naïve Bayes classifier is a relatively straight forward task. The first step is to create a categorised plain text corpus reader. The reader takes three parameters. The first parameter is the root folder for the corpus, the second is a regular expression used to identify the files in the corpus, the third is a regular expression used to determine the category types which are derived from the folder names within the corpus. In the code snippet shown in Listing 1, the corpus to be read is `movie_reviews` and all files with a `.txt` extension are included. Now that the reader is initialised the next step is to identify the file ids of each category type.

```
# Set the working folder to the nltk_data corpora folder
import os
from    nltk.corpus.reader import CategorizedPlaintextCorpusReader
os.chdir ('C:/nltk_data/corpora')
reader = CategorizedPlaintextCorpusReader('./movie_reviews',
                              r'.*\.txt',
                              cat_pattern=r'(\w+)/*')
```

Listing 1: Creating a categorised plain text corpus reader

Identifying the file ids of each category is an important step. The words in each file must be correctly labelled as either being positive or negative in nature. Achieving this is a simple matter of calling the `fileids` method of the reader object just created and manually passing the category name of the required file ids. The code snippet in Listing 2 returns two file lists. The first, `pos_ids` is a list of all the files, including each files relative path, in the positive review category while the `neg_ids` is the list of all files in the negative review category.

It's very simple to review a sample of the contents of each of these lists. Once you have successfully run the entire python script typing the following command into the interpreter will show you the first three elements of each list. You can also get the length, or number of elements, of each list using `len()`.

```
# The positive reviews
pos_ids = reader.fileids('pos')
# The negative reviews
neg_ids = reader.fileids('neg')
```

Listing 2: Identifying the file ids of each category

```
>>> pos_ids [:3]
['pos/cv000_29590.txt', 'pos/cv001_18431.txt', 'pos/cv002_15918.txt']
>>> neg_ids [:3]
['neg/cv000_29416.txt', 'neg/cv001_19502.txt', 'neg/cv002_17424.txt']
>>> len(pos_ids)
1000
>>> len(neg_ids)
1000
```

The NLTK uses the concept of a feature, in this case any word or token, and the presence of that token in a sample of text in order to predict which class the sample might belong to. The code in Listing 3 shows how a positive and negative feature dictionary is generated for each positive review file and for each negative review file. The `word_feats` function returns a dictionary, or hash, of key value pairs where each key is the individual word, or token, and the value is always true. The `pos_feat` and `neg_feat` objects are, in fact, a list of lists. Each element in the features list contains two elements. The first element is the dictionary returned by the `word_feats` function. The second element represents whether the category of the review is either positive or negative.

```
def word_feats(words):
    return dict([(word, True) for word in words])

pos_feat = [(word_feats(reader.words(fileids=[f])),
             'pos')
            for f in pos_ids]
neg_feat = [(word_feats(reader.words(fileids=[f])),
             'neg')
            for f in neg_ids]
```

Listing 3: Generation of the positive and negative feature dictionaries

It should be noted that all sentence word order has been lost when generating the feature dictionaries as would be expected when using a bag-of-words approach. A similar process is performed to create the negative features. To view the first element of the positive features list you can enter `pos_feat[0]` into the interpreter.

```
>>> pos_feat[0]
({'alan': True, 'crazy': True, 'won': True, 'menace': True,
  'manson': True, 'see': True, 'isn': True, 'carving': True
  ...
  'a': True, 'identity': True}, 'pos')
```

Next, the Naïve Bayes learner is trained. Unfortunately, NLTK does not natively support cross-validation so the samples were simply divided into a training set consisting of the first 800 samples and a testing set of the remaining 200. A Naïve Bayes classifier was then created using the training data set as shown in Listing 4. Also shown is the generation of a reference set and test set to be used later to calculate the performance of the classifier. To achieve this the actual classification of each of the test samples is loaded into the reference set and the value for the sample returned from the classifier, `observed = classifier.classify(feats)`, is loaded into the test set.

```python
# Create the test and train data sets
train = pos_feat[:800] + \
        neg_feat[:800]
test  = pos_feat[800:] + \
        neg_feat[800:]

# Create the classifier using the train data set
classifier = NaiveBayesClassifier.train(train)

# The NTLK metrics package uses sets to
# calculate performace metrics
# Create empty reference and test sets
refsets  = collections.defaultdict(set)
testsets = collections.defaultdict(set)

#Populate the metrics sets with values
for i, (feats, label) in enumerate(test):
    refsets[label].add(i)
    observed = classifier.classify(feats)
    testsets[observed].add(i)
```

Listing 4: Generation of the positive and negative feature dictionaries

The performance of the model can then be calculated using the NLTK Metrics package and the most informative features can also be displayed. Listing 5 shows how the performance of the model is calculated and the top five most informative features are displayed. The calculated performance values are then output to the screen as shown in Figure 9.5.

```
Most Informative Uni-gram Features
        outstanding = True     pos : neg  =    13.9 : 1.0
        insulting   = True     neg : pos  =    13.7 : 1.0
        vulnerable  = True     pos : neg  =    13.0 : 1.0
        ludicrous   = True     neg : pos  =    12.6 : 1.0
        uninvolving = True     neg : pos  =    12.3 : 1.0
pos precision:   0.6587837837837838
pos recall:      0.975
neg precision:   0.9519230769230769
neg recall:      0.495
model accuracy:  0.735
g-performance:   0.6947121706145647
execution time:  7.209441900253296
```

FIGURE 9.5: Performance values of the first NLTK model developed.

Considering the top five most informative features, it is clear to see how these tokens, real words in this example, could easily be included in a positive or negative review. Of the top five most informative features two are for postive reviews and three are for negative reviews. Taking `outstanding` as an example, where this token appears in a review it is 13.9 times more likely to appear in a positive review than in a negative review. The next token, `insulting`, is 13.7 times more likely to appear in a negative review than in a positive review.

```
# Calculate precision. recall, f-measure and accuracy
pos_pre  = nltk.metrics.precision(refsets['pos'], testsets['pos'])
pos_rec  = nltk.metrics.recall(refsets['pos'],    testsets['pos'])
neg_pre  = nltk.metrics.precision(refsets['neg'], testsets['neg'])
neg_rec  = nltk.metrics.recall(refsets['neg'],    testsets['neg'])
accuracy = nltk.classify.accuracy(classifier, test)
gperf    = math.sqrt(pos_rec * neg_rec)


# Show the top 5 most informative features
classifier.show_most_informative_features(5)


# Print out the overall performace measures
print ('pos precision:\t',  pos_pre)
print ('pos recall:\t',     pos_rec)
print ('neg precision:\t',  neg_pre)
print ('neg recall:\t',     neg_rec)
print ('model accuracy:\t', accuracy)
print ('g-performance:\t',  gperf)
```

Listing 5: Calculating the performance of the model and displaying output to screen

The overall accuracy of the model, 73.5%, could suggest that this was a very successful first attempt at developing a model to predict the class of these movie reviews. However, looking closely at the precision and the recall for the different classes, this is clearly not the case. The negative class precision, 95.1%, shows that nearly every sample classified as negative was an actual negative review sample. However, a negative class recall value of 49.5% shows that overall only half of all the negative samples, approximately 100 of the 200 samples, were identified as such. Examining the positive class next, a recall value of 97.5%, shows that nearly all of the positive reviews were correctly identified. However, a precision value of just 65.8% tells us that only approximately two-thirds of all the reviews predicted as positive were actually positive, that is approximately 300 of the test set samples were predicted as positive.. This tells us that this model is overpredicting test samples as positive and underpredicting negative samples.

9.2.3   N-Grams

Having developed the basic NLTK model, it is a simple matter to augment and hopefully enhance the performance of the model by using n-grams and stop word removal.

N-Grams are a contiguous sequence of n items from an extract of text or speech and in this occurrence the n-grams refer to words. Typical n-grams used in text mining are unigrams, bigrams, and trigrams. For example, given a sequence of words "The quick brown fox" the following trigrams, or sequences of three words, can be formed "The quick brown" and "quick brown fox". Modifying the script from Section 9.2.2 to use bigrams, for example, is a simple matter of importing the NLTK `ngrams` package and, instead of passing single words or tokens to the positive and negative feature generator, pass bigrams instead. This is shown for positive features in Listing 6.

Examining the performance metrics from the model using bigrams, Figure 9.6 shows that the introduction of bigrams has, in fact, positively impacted the overall accuracy of the model. Although the positive precision has fallen slightly all other measures have increased leading to a better model. Considering the top most informative feature, we understand

```
from nltk.util import ngrams
pos_feat = [(word_feats(ngrams(reader.words(fileids=[f]), 2)),
             'pos')
             for f in pos_ids]
```

Listing 6: Generation of the positive and negative feature dictionaries

that when the two words `not` and `funny` appear together we are 14.3 times more like to be looking at a negative movie review than a positive one.

```
        Most Informative Bi-gram Features
            ('not', 'funny') = True    neg : pos  =  14.3 : 1.0
            ('matt', 'damon') = True   pos : neg  =  13.7 : 1.0
            ('is', 'terrific') = True  pos : neg  =  13.7 : 1.0
            ('and', 'boring') = True   neg : pos  =  13.0 : 1.0
            ('perfect', 'for') = True  pos : neg  =  12.3 : 1.0
        pos precision:   0.6909090909090909
        pos recall:      0.95
        neg precision:   0.92
        neg recall:      0.575
        model accuracy:  0.7625
        g-performance:   0.739087274954724
        execution time: 39.54395389556885
```

FIGURE 9.6: Performance of NLTK model using bigrams.

Now that bigrams features have been modelled, using trigrams is as simple as changing the parameter passed to the `ngrams` function from 2 to 3 as shown in Listing 7.

```
pos_feat = [(word_feats(ngrams(reader.words(fileids=[f]), 3)),
             'pos')
             for f in pos_ids]
```

Listing 7: Generation of the positive and negative feature dictionaries

Looking at the performance of the model where trigrams were used, Figure 9.7, we can again see that there has been overall improvement when compared against the unigram and bigram models. Although there have been another very slight decrease in the positive class precision the values for positive recall and for negative precision and recall have all increased. A word of warning though. A look at the most informative features shows two trigrams which may suggest that the model may be over trained to the data. The trigrams 'work with ,' and 'well , and' are classified as being indicative of negative and positive reviews respectively. It is clear that neither n-gram is obviously positive or negative and it could be suggested that this model may not generalise well to the wider population of all movie reviews.

9.2.4 Stop Words

When processing natural language, stop words are words that are filtered out of the corpus, typically early on in the process. Stop words are usually what are called short function words or words with little or ambiguous meaning. Examples of English stop words include "the", "and", "at", and "which".

As we require that the stop words are removed before the n-grams are generated the only

```
Most Informative Tri-gram Features
    ('of', 'the', 'worst') = True    neg : pos = 15.8 : 1.0
    ('to', 'be', 'funny') = True     neg : pos = 12.3 : 1.0
    ('well', ',', 'and') = True      pos : neg = 11.7 : 1.0
  ('not', 'enough', 'to') = True     neg : pos = 11.0 : 1.0
    ('work', 'with', '.') = True     neg : pos = 11.0 : 1.0
pos precision:   0.7673469387755102
pos recall:      0.94
neg precision:   0.9225806451612903
neg recall:      0.715
model accuracy:  0.8275
g-performance:   0.819817052762383
execution time:  37.45374512672424
```

FIGURE 9.7: Performance of NLTK model using trigrams.

part of the code that needs to change to achieve this is in the call made to the `word_feats` function as shown in Listing 8.

```
pos_feat = [(word_feats(
            ngrams([word for word in reader.words(fileids=[f])
              if not word in stopwords.words('english')], 3)),
          'pos')
```

Listing 8: Generation of the positive and negative feature dictionaries

Analysing this code further, it is saying that for every word found in file `f`, if a word is not an English stop word pass it to the `ngrams` functions. The `ngrams` function then generates the required size n-gram, in this case three, and subsequently passes each n-gram to the `word_feats` function, which was previously described.

Running this model for unigram, bigrams, and trigrams with stop words removed returns the performance results summarised in Table 9.2.4. Comparing these results to those achieved earlier, when stop words were not excluded, shows that the performance of unigrams and trigrams has actually fallen. Only the performance of bigrams has improved. These performance results, coupled with a factor of 10 increase in the execution time of the script, would suggest that the removal of stop words was not beneficial. On closer inspection it was observed that the increase in execution time was solely caused by the stop word removal. The time taken to generate the model, and the classification of the unseen samples, was mostly unchanged. It was also seen that punctuation characters appear in the top-five most informative features for both bigrams and trigrams. For example:

- ('.', 'cameron')   = True   pos : neg = 11.7 : 1.0

- ('.', 'basically', ',') = True   neg : pos = 9.0 : 1.0

This could indicate that the removal of punctuation is another potential line of enquiry to improve the performance of the model.

9.2.5   Other Things to Consider

In the development of the initial model we considered n-grams and stop word removal as potential approaches to increase the performance of the model. Some other transformations we can apply to the text include:

- Removing punctuation

TABLE 9.1: Performance comparison of unigrams, bigrams, and trigrams when stop words have been removed.

Measurement	Uni-grams	Bi-grams	Tri-grams
pos precision	0.650	0.750	0.783
pos recall	0.975	0.930	0.795
neg precision	0.950	0.908	0.792
neg recall	0.475	0.690	0.780
model accuracy	0.725	0.810	0.788
g-performance	0.681	0.801	0.787
execution time	802.1	799.8	651.5

- Removing single characters or smaller tokens of a specific length

- Stemming

As previously seen, the format of the given review text has separated most punctuation characters from the rest of the text, for example `"sverak also wrote the script , while his son , jan , directed"`. These punctuation characters also appeared in some of the most informative bigram and trigram features. In this section we will examine how these characters can easily be removed. We will also develop a simple routine to remove tokens that are shorter than a specified characters length.

Stemming describes the process for reducing words to their word root, or stem. An English word stemmer might, for example, identify *"stemmer"*, *"stemming"*, and *"stemmed"* as all being based on "stem". Julie Beth Lovins first published a paper on stemming in 1968 [8]. Two stemmers provided by NLTK are called Porter and Snowball. In the sample provided the Snowball stemmer is used.

In the Python scripts developed to this point, the generation of the positive and negative features for use in the classifier was done in a single complex statement. To make it easier to understand the different steps taken during the processing of the text, a function was developed that separates each step out. The signature of this function is shown in Listing 9. The function takes 1 mandatory parameter, `file_ids` which holds the list of files to process, and six optional parameters. The optional parameters are:

- `removepunctuation`
  The remove punctuation parameter is used to signal if punctuation characters should be left in the text, `0`, or removed from the text `1`

- `minwordsize`
  This parameter defines the minimum size token allowed. For example, if set to 3 then only token of three characters are more are included. The default is 1 character which essentially includes all text.

- `removestopwords`
  The remove stop words parameter is used to signal if stop words should be left in the text, `0`, or removed from the text `1`

- `stemwords`
  The stem words parameter is used to signal if stemming should be applied to the words in the corpus. The default value, `0`, means words will not be stemmed, whereas `1` will cause all words to be stemmed.

- ngramsize
  The n-grams parameter is used to specify the size of n-grams to use. The default value is 1, which corresponds to using unigrams.

- reviewtype
  Specified whether the review is positive in nature, pos, or negative neg. The reviews are tagged as positive by default.

These parameters can be modified as required to turn on or off options and set the size for n-grams and minimum word size as required.

```
def prepare_review( file_ids,
                    removepunctuation=0,
                    minwordsize=1,
                    removestopwords=0,
                    stemwords=0,
                    ngramsize=1,
                    reviewtype='pos'):
```

Listing 9: The signature for the prepare review function

Listing 10 shows some of the details of the logic of how each of the text processing steps are implemented. Most of the processing steps simply treat the corpus text as a string. Regular expressions are used to remove punctuation characters. Minimum word size, stop words and word stemming is performed by testing each word in a review and, if it meets the specified criteria, it is re-included in the string for further processing. N-gram and feature generation is handled the same as before.

The new function can then be called to generate the positive and negative review feature as shown in Listing 11. This invocation of the script, using the default parameters, is the equivalent of the initial script described in Section 9.2.2. Unsurprisingly the performance results achieved and the most informative features obtained with this new script, and those obtained with the original script, are exactly the same.

An extreme example of how the prepare_review function could be called is shown in Listing 12. In this example punctuation characters are removed, the minimum allowed word size is four characters, stop words are removed, words are stemmed and an n-gram size 2 is used.

The results of this invocation of the script is actually quite promising with an over all g-performance measure of 0.801, see Figure 9.8. Although better results were achieved by some of the models explored earlier it is worth noting that the negative recall value of 0.73 achieved by this model was the best obtained using bigrams. There are endless potential combinations to explore using this simple function.

The complete listing for the prepare review function, including additional looping and variable definitions, is available for download from the book website.

9.3   Modelling with scikit-learn

The Natural Language Toolkit produced some promising models and was quite easy to use. It did not, however, offer much choice or scope for different lines of investigation during model development. Although additional functionality is made available to the developer

```
# Remove punctuation characters from the string
if removepunctuation:
  review = re.sub(r'[^\w\s]','',review)
# Remove words less than minwordsize length
if (minwordsize > 1):
  review = " ".join(
    word for word in review.split()
    if len(word) >= minwordsize
  )
# Remove stopwords if required
if removestopwords:
  review = " ".join(
    [word for word in review.split()
      if not word in stopwords.words('english')])
# Stemm words if required
if stemwords:
  review = " ".join(
    [stemmer.stem(word)
      for word in review.split()])
# Prepare ngrams and Generate Features
if (ngramsize > 1):
  # Bi-grams or Tri-grams are quired
  review = [word for word in ngrams(
    review.split(), ngramsize)]
  # Generate Features
  review = (word_feats(review), reviewtype)
else:
  # Just Generate Features
  review = (word_feats(review.split()), reviewtype)

reviews.append(list(review))
```

Listing 10: The details of the prepare review function

using NLTK through a wrapper for scikit-learn, in this section the NLTK models are left behind and focus, instead, turns to the development of models using scikit-learn.

9.3.1 Developing a Naïve Bayes scikit-learn Classifier

Although the development of the scikit-learn model follows a very similar flow to that utilised for the NLTK model, scikit-learn could be considered as a more advanced toolkit. As well as extensive data manipulation functionality, scikit-learn also provides a better selection of learner algorithms though for the investigation, a Naïve Bayes algorithm will be used and then a Support Vector Machine learner is considered.

The first step in the process is to access the data. scikit-learn uses the `load_file` method to import text files. Like NLTK, the subfolder names are used as category labels. An object of datatype *"bunch"* is returned, which is a dictionary-type object. The Python is shown in Listing 13.

Once created, the bunch object can be examined as shown. The data element holds the text of each review.

```
pos_feat = prepare_review(pos_ids)

neg_feat = prepare_review(neg_ids,
                          reviewtype='neg')
```

Listing 11: Calling the prepare review function with default parameter values

```
pos_feat = prepare_review(pos_ids,
                          removepunctuation=1,
                          minwordsize=4,
                          removestopwords=1,
                          stemwords=1,
                          ngramsize=2)
neg_feat = prepare_review(neg_ids,
                          removepunctuation=1,
                          minwordsize=4,
                          removestopwords=1,
                          stemwords=1,
                          ngramsize=2,
                          reviewtype='neg')
```

Listing 12: An extreme example of calling the prepare review function

```
>>> bunch.keys()
dict_keys(['target', 'target_names', 'filenames', 'DESCR', 'data'])
>>> bunch.target[0]
0
>>> bunch.target_names[0]
'neg'
>>> bunch.filenames[0]
'C:/nltk_data/corpora/movie_reviews/neg\\cv405_21868.txt'
```

The next step in the development of the model is to create the training and testing data sets. scikit-learn provides a `cross_validation.train_test_split` operator that will automatically split the data set into random training and testing subsets. The data and target arrays, obtained from the bunch object created earlier, are the first two parameters passed. The third parameter passed is the proportion of the data set to include in the test set. In this case 20% of the data will be held back for the test data set. The final parameter is the pseudo-random number generator state used for random sampling. A random number in the range 1 to 100 is used for each invocation. By convention the returned arrays are

```
Most Informative Features
        ('save', 'grace') = True      neg : pos   =    13.7 : 1.0
        ('matt', 'damon') = True      pos : neg   =    13.7 : 1.0
         ('quit', 'well') = True      pos : neg   =    10.3 : 1.0
         ('four', 'star') = True      pos : neg   =    10.3 : 1.0
        ('famili', 'movi') = True     pos : neg   =     9.7 : 1.0
pos precision:  0.7652173913043478
pos recall:     0.88
neg precision:  0.8588235294117647
neg recall:     0.73
model accuracy: 0.805
g-performance:  0.8014985963805551
Total Time:     360.3829891681671
```

FIGURE 9.8: Performance of NLTK model using the prepare review function.

```
from sklearn.data sets import load_files
bunch = load_files('C:/nltk_data/corpora/movie_reviews/'
```

Listing 13: Loading the movie review corpus using scikit-learn

named X_train, X_test, y_train, y_test where X_train, X_test are the data sets representing the split data array and y_train, y_test are the data sets representing the split target array. Listing 14 shows how this `cross_validation.train_test_split` function is used.

```
from sklearn.feature_extraction.text import TfidfVectorizer
from sklearn import cross_validation
import random
X_train, X_test, y_train, y_test \
   = cross_validation.train_test_split(bunch.data,
                                bunch.target,
                                test_size=0.20,
                                random_state =
                                (random.randrange(1 ,100)))
```

Listing 14: Splitting the data into training and testing data sets

The training and test data sets produced by the cross-validation split function are passed to a TfidfVectorizer function, which performs two main tasks. The first is to convert a collection of text documents, in this case the training data, into a matrix that is a sparse representation of token counts. The second task transforms the count matrix into a term frequency inverse document frequency (TF-IDF) representation.

TF-IDF is a statistical measure of how important a given word is in a collection of documents. Each document is represented as a vector of words, and each word is represented in the vector by a value that is indicative of its importance in predicting the class of the document. The TF-IDF weight for a word i in document j is given as

$$TFIDF_{ij} = TF_{ij} \cdot IDF_i \tag{9.7}$$

where TF is a measure of a words importance in a document and is calculated as

$$TF_{ij} = \frac{n_{ij}}{\Sigma_k n_{kj}} \tag{9.8}$$

where the number of times a word i appears in a document j is represented by n_{ij}, and $\Sigma_k n_{kj}$ is a count of all words in document j. This means that the more times a word appears in a document the larger its value for TF will get. The TF weighting of a word in a document shows its importance within that single document. IDF then shows the importance of a word within the entire collection of documents or corpus and is calculated as

$$IDF_i = log\frac{|P|}{|\{p_j : t_i \epsilon p_j\}|} \tag{9.9}$$

where $|P|$ is the total number of documents in the corpus or collection, and $|\{p_j : t_i \epsilon p_j\}|$ represents the number of documents in which the word, or term, t_i appears. The nature of the IDF value is such that terms appearing in a lot of documents will have a lower score or weight. This means terms that appear in only a single document, or in a small percentage of the documents, will receive a higher score. This higher score makes that word a good discriminator between reviews.

In all, there are over 20 parameters that can be used to customise and fine tune the performance of this operator, but for our purposes here only the following will be examined:

1. **ngram_range**: tuple (min_n, max_n)
   The lower and upper boundary of the range of n-values for different n-grams to be extracted. All values of n such that $min_n <= n <= max_n$ are used.

2. **stop_words**: string 'english', list, or None (default)
   english is currently the only supported string value and this has the affect of removing English stop words.

3. **tokenizer**: callable or None (default)
   Override the string tokenization step while preserving the preprocessing and n-grams generation steps.

Other parameters allow preprocessing of the corpus and more advanced control of the TF-IDF calculation and are beyond the scope of this text.

In order to closely manage the tokenisation of the review text we will develop our own tokenize along similar lines of the `prepare_review` function seen earlier. The tokenizer performs four steps. It first separates each review into a list of individual tokens before removing punctuation, removing purely numerical tokens before finally removing tokens less than the specified length. It would be a simple matter to add an additional steps, stemming for example, if required. The new step to remove purely numerical tokens, 123 for example, was added as it was seen that a lot of the most informative negative features contained numerical values. More on this later.

In Listing 15, the TF-IDF Vectorizer object is created. In this example unigrams, bigrams, and trigrams are considered, and English stop words are removed. The tokenizer just created is utilised. Whereas the training data are transformed into a document/token matrix and the TF-IDF of each token is calculated, the test data are transformed into the sparse matrix format only for use later with the generated model.

```
tfidf = TfidfVectorizer(tokenizer=tokenize,
                        stop_words='english',
                        ngram_range=(1, 3))

X_train = tfidf.fit_transform(X_train)
X_test  = tfidf.transform(X_test)
```

Listing 15: Create TF/IDF vectorizer object

The final step is to fit the model using the training data and then to predict the classes of the testing data. Listing 16 shows the creation and fitting of a Multinomial Naïve Bayes model followed by the class prediction for the training data set. The predicted class for each of the test samples is stored in the `y_predicted` array and can easily be manually compared to the actual class values.

```
>>> y_predicted[:20]
array([1, 0, 0, 0, 1, 0, 1, 0, 1, 0, 0, 1, 0, 1, 0, 0, 0, 1, 1, 1])
>>> y_test[:20]
array([1, 1, 0, 1, 0, 0, 0, 0, 1, 0, 0, 1, 0, 1, 0, 0, 0, 1, 1, 1])
```

```
from  sklearn.naive_bayes import MultinomialNB
classifier = MultinomialNB(alpha=.01).fit(X_train, y_train)
y_predicted = classifier.predict(X_test)
```

Listing 16: Fit the model and classify the training data

The scikit-learn `metrics` package makes it very easy to access the performance measurements of the generated model. Listing 17 shows how the `classification_report` function is used to show the precision, recall, and F1 Measurement values achieved for each class and Figure 9.9 shows the results displayed. The confusion matrix is also calculated. A confusion matrix is a table that describes the performance of a classification model on a set of test data for which the true values are known.

```
from sklearn.metrics import classification_report
print ('\nHere is the classification report:')
print (classification_report(y_test, y_predicted))


print ('\nHere is the confusion matrix:')
print (metrics.confusion_matrix(y_test, y_predicted))
```

Listing 17: Using scikit-learn classification report

```
MODEL: Multinomial Naive Bayes
The precision for this classifier is:  0.768844221106
The recall for this classifier is:     0.801047120419
The f1 for this classifier is:          0.784615384615
The accuracy for this classifier is:   0.79

Here is the classification report:
              precision    recall  f1-score   support
         0       0.81       0.78      0.80        209
         1       0.77       0.80      0.78        191
avg / total      0.79       0.79      0.79        400

Here is the confusion matrix:
[[163  46]
 [ 38 153]]
```

FIGURE 9.9: Performance of the first Naïve Bayes scikit-learn model.

From the classification report the g-performance of this model can be calculated. Using the recall results for the negative review class, 0, and the positive class, 1 the g-peformance for this invocation of the model is calculated as $\sqrt{0.78 * 0.80} = 0.7899$. Examining the confusion matrix further, if we view it as a table of dimensions $2x2$, we can name each of the rows, columns and cells as follows. To top row can be named "actual positive", and the bottom row "actual negative". The left column can be named "predicted positive", and the right column "predicted negative".

Getting the most informative features for this scikit-learn model is a bit more involved than the simple method provided by NLTK. A `show_most_informative_features` function is provided in the complete script available for download from the book website. In the sample shown the most negative informative features are shown on the left hand side and the most informative positive features are shown on the right hand side.

TABLE 9.2: Confusion matrix for a Naïve Bayes scikit-learn classifier.

	predicted negative	predicted positive
actual negative	163	46
actual positive	38	153

```
>>> show_most_informative_features(tfidf, classifier, n=10)
    -14.5308  a-flailing         -6.6783 film
    -14.5308  a-flailing just    -7.1480 movie
    -14.5308  a-ha yellow        -7.5951 like
    -14.5308  a-list cast        -7.6900 does
    -14.5308  a-list following   -7.7257 story
    -14.5308  a-list hollywood   -7.7489 good
    -14.5308  a-list names       -7.7838 just
    -14.5308  a-quarter          -7.7964 life
    -14.5308  a-quarter star     -7.8323 time
    -14.5308  a-trois            -7.8747 characters
```

FIGURE 9.10: Naïve Bayes scikit-learn most informative features.

9.3.2   Developing a Support Vector Machine scikit-learn Classifier

Developing a SVM model requires only a simple two line change to the script just described. Instead in instantiating a Naïve Bayes classifier object, a Linear Support Vector classifier is used instead.

```
# Create the Support Vector Machine model
from sklearn.svm import LinearSVC
classifier = LinearSVC().fit(X_train, y_train)
```

Listing 18: Fit the model and classify the training data

The rest of the script can remain unchanged. The listing available for download from the book website actually contains both options, but the LinearSVC lines are commented out. Figures 9.11 and 9.12 show the performance and most informative features for this model. The g-performance value this SVM model, 0.840, was the best achieved by any model. Reviewing the top most informative features for the negative class it is very conceivable that worst, boring, and stupid are words you would not be surprised to see in a negative movie review. Likewise, great and excellent are words that you would expect to see in a positive movie review.

```
The precision for this classifier is:  0.819512195122
The recall for this classifier is:     0.857142857143
The f1 for this classifier is:         0.837905236908
The accuracy for this classifier is:   0.8375

Here is the classification report:
               precision    recall  f1-score   support
          0        0.86      0.82      0.84       204
          1        0.82      0.86      0.84       196
avg / total        0.84      0.84      0.84       400

Here is the confusion matrix:
[[167  37]
 [ 28 168]]
```

FIGURE 9.11: Performance of the SVM scikit-learn model.

```
>>> show_most_informative_features(tfidf, classifier, n=20)
   -1.3621  worst          1.3872  life
   -1.1779  plot           1.3041  great
   -1.1030  boring         0.9907  truman
   -1.0349  stupid         0.8953  family
   -1.0252  movie          0.8795  excellent
   ...
```

FIGURE 9.12: SVM scikit-learn model most informative features.

9.4 Conclusions

This chapter was a whistlestop tour through binary text classification using Python, NLTK, and scikit-learn. Although testing was not exhaustive, it was found that the scikit-learn Linear SVC classifier provided results that were slightly better than NLTK and scikit-learn Naïve Bayes.

Only the surface of these tools has been scratched and hopefully this chapter encourages you to explore each tool in detail.

Bibliography

[1] The official home of the python programming language.

[2] The natural language toolkit.

[3] The official home of numpy: The fundamental package for scientific computing with python.

[4] The official home of scipy: Scientific computing tools for python.

[5] The home of scikit-learn: Machine learning in python.

[6] Bo Pang and Lillian Lee. A sentimental education: Sentiment analysis using subjectivity summarization based on minimum cuts. In *Proceedings of the ACL*, 2004.

[7] Miroslav Kubat and Stan Matwin. Addressing the curse of imbalanced training sets: One-sided selection. In *In Proceedings of the Fourteenth International Conference on Machine Learning*, page 179186. Morgan Kaufmann, 1997.

[8] Julie B. Lovins. Development of a Stemming Algorithm. *Mechanical Translation and Computational Linguistics*, 11, June 1968.

Part IV

R

Chapter 10

Sentiment Analysis of Stock Market Behavior from Twitter Using the R Tool

Nuno Oliveira

ALGORITMI Research Centre, University of Minho, Guimarães, Portugal

Paulo Cortez

ALGORITMI Research Centre/Department of Information Systems, University of Minho, Guimarães, Portugal

Nelson Areal

Department of Management, University of Minho, Braga, Portugal

Abstract

Sentiment analysis is a hot research topic with widespread applications in organizations. Recently, it has been applied to create investor sentiment indicators that can be utilized in the prediction of stock market variables such as returns, volatility and trading volume.

This chapter presents a use case about sentiment analysis in tweets related to stock market using the open-source R tool. We provide and explain code for the execution of diverse tasks, such as tweets collection, preprocessing tasks, utilization of opinion lexicons, application of machine learning (ML) methods, and respective evaluation. A data set composed by stock market tweets is also provided.

This use case shows that the utilization of ML techniques using manually classified training data outperforms some standard sentiment word lists when applied to test data.

10.1   Introduction

Sentiment analysis (SA) is the computational treatment of opinion, sentiment, and subjectivity in text [1]. In recent years, social media platforms, and in particular microblogging, have enabled an explosion of unstructured content with opinions regarding a huge variety of topics and have provided a valuable and inexpensive source for opinion analysis about organizations and individuals. The analysis of all these data is not feasible without the use of automated computation. The identification and summarization of important information in vast amounts of data is very challenging for the average person [2] and the current amount of social media data makes human processing impracticable. These limitations can be overcome by SA systems that mine large amounts of opinionated content and automatically extract, summarize and classify the opinions about an entity (e.g., product, event, organization) [1]. SA may assign diverse sentiment categories (e.g., positive, negative, or neutral) or attribute a sentiment score. These systems have widespread applications, such as reputation management, sales prediction, stock management, ad placements, products, and services benchmarking.

Diverse machine learning (ML) methods can be applied to learn the correct sentiment value from a set of input features such as the term frequency of unigrams or bigrams, emoticons, or hashtags. Whenever there is insufficient labeled data, the utilization of existing opinion lexicons may allow unsupervised SA to be performed. Opinion lexicons are composed of a list of opinion words and the respective sentiment value (positive, negative, neutral, or a sentiment score). The presence of opinion words in text permits the discernment of the sentiment orientation. For example, the sentence "the computer is good" can be easily classified as positive if the opinion lexicon contains the word "good" as positive. A common text representation is the bag-of-words , which represents the text as a collection of lexical items and ignoring the syntactic structure of sentences. However, particularly in short documents, a more rigorous linguistic approach (e.g., sentiment composition) that considers the interaction between sentence constituents (e.g., negation) may permit better results [3].

SA can be performed at diverse levels such as document, sentence, and aspect levels. Document-level classification is a common approach. It classifies the sentiment of the whole document assuming that the document expresses opinions on a single entity (e.g., customer reviews) [4]. However, it is too coarse for some applications because some documents may include opinions regarding diverse entities or the applications may require the classification regarding various aspects of the entity.

The extraction of investor sentiment indicators from social media data in order to forecast stock market behavior is a very recent research topic (e.g., [5, 6, 7]). These studies suggest that a model that accounts for investor sentiment can potentially be used to predict key stock market variables, such as returns, volatility, and volume. Moreover, it has been demonstrated that individuals' financial decisions are affected by their emotions and mood [8]. Microblogging is a social medium particularly suitable for the creation of investors' sentiment indicators. There are several arguments recommending the usage of microblogging data:

- The analysis of investors microblogging interactions can provide reliable indicators of their sentiment in a faster and less expensive manner than traditional sources (e.g., large-scale surveys)

- The community of investors that utilizes these services has grown and is potentially more representative

- Users react promptly to events allowing a near real time sentiment assessment

- The character constraints require greater objectivity from the author

Diverse studies confirm the informative value of microblogging data for forecasting some stock market variables. Sentiment indicators extracted from microblogging data seems to have predictive value for future market directions [6, 9] and returns [10] and posting volume can improve the forecasts of trading volume [10, 11, 12].

In this chapter, we present a use case about SA in microblogging conversations related to stock market using the open-source R tool. We have significant experience in this topic because we are working in a related project. In the PhD work "Mining Social Media Sentiment to Forecast Stock Market Behavior", we are collecting social media data (e.g., Twitter, StockTwits, message boards) to create sentiment and attention indicators that can be utilized in the forecasting of stock market behavior (e.g., volatility, trading volume, returns). We present and explain some code for diverse steps comprising this process, such as tweets collection, preprocessing tasks, utilization of opinion lexicons, application of ML methods, and respective evaluation. A data set composed by stock market messages from the most popular microblogging service (i.e., Twitter) is provided for this use case. This data set and the R files containing all code utilized in this example are available at `http://www.text-mining-book.com`.

10.2   Methods

R is a free language and environment for statistical computing and graphics [13] that allows the execution of the various tasks required by this topic. It provides a wide diversity of functionalities, and it is easily extensible by applying the diverse available packages. For instance, the package `twitteR` provides an interface to the Twitter web API enabling the collection of a large number of messages filtered by search queries. Additionally, R provides a rich set of Natural Language Processing (NLP) packages that are very useful to perform SA. Packages such as `tm` [14], `RTextTools` [15], `SnowballC` ([16]), `wordnet` [17] or `openNLP` (`http://opennlp.apache.org/`) allows diverse NLP operations to be performed such as stemming, Part of Speech tagging, tokenization, access to lexical databases, easy creation of Document Term matrices, and application of ML methods.

The Comprehensive R Archive Network (`http://cran.r-project.org/`) is a large repository containing up-to-date code and documentation for R. For example, an exhaustive list of packages is presented and described in this platform, and the installation files of current Windows, Linux, or Mac OS X versions of R can be downloaded from its webpage. There are diverse forms to install packages, but an usual and simple manner is to execute the function `install.packages`. For instance, the RTextTools package can be easily installed by executing the command `install.packages("RTextTools")` directly from the R console. This function receives a vector of packages names, downloads these packages from the repositories, and installs them. The `library` function permits the utilization of installed packages (e.g., `library("RTextTools")`). The R online documentation can be accessed by using the command `help.start()`. Further details about the R language can be found in [18].

10.3   Data Collection

To be able to collect Twitter data, it is necessary to sign up on Twitter (https://twitter.com/signup) and create a Twitter application (https://apps.twitter.com/app/new). This account will provide the required information (e.g., consumer key, consumer secret) to connect to the Twitter API. The package twitteR [19] provides the R interface to Twitter API. A data collection example is coded in file tweets_collection.R.

```
### tweets_collection.R file ###
# load package twitteR: provides interface to Twitter API
library (twitteR)
# download cacert.pem
download.file(url='http://curl.haxx.se/ca/cacert.pem', destfile='cacert.pem')
# assign your Twitter application data to R variables
# request token URL
reqURL <- "https://api.twitter.com/oauth/request_token"
# access token URL
accessURL <- "https://api.twitter.com/oauth/access_token"
# authorize URL
authURL <- "https://api.twitter.com/oauth/authorize"
# consumer key
consumerKey <- "your_consumer_key"
# consumer secret
consumerSecret <- "your_consumer_secret"
# create a OAuth object to access to Twitter API
twitter_cred <- OAuthFactory$new(consumerKey=consumerKey,
  ↪   consumerSecret=consumerSecret, requestURL=reqURL, accessURL=accessURL,
  ↪   authURL=authURL)
# execute handshake method to enable connection to Twitter API
# (you must open the provided URL in a web browser and write the code in the
  ↪   Console)
twitter_cred$handshake(cainfo = system.file('CurlSSL', 'cacert.pem', package =
  ↪   'RCurl'))
# save the OAuth object for future sessions
save(twitter_cred, file="twitter_auth.Rdata")
# load the OAuth object
load("twitter_auth.Rdata")
# register OAuth credentials to Twitter R session
registerTwitterOAuth(twitter_cred)
# tweets collection example: last 15 tweets containing the word GOOGLE
tweets_list <- searchTwitter("GOOGLE", cainfo='cacert.pem', n=15)
# each tweets_list element contains several attributes such as:
print(tweets_list[[1]]$id) # tweet id
print(tweets_list[[1]]$text) # tweet text content
print(tweets_list[[1]]$screenName) # user name
print(tweets_list[[1]]$created) # creation time
```

The access to Twitter API requires OAuth authorization. This authentication demands valid Twitter application data (i.e., consumer key, consumer secret, request URL, access token URL, and authorize URL) and "cacert.pem" file, a collection of trusted root certification authorities. Therefore, Twitter application data is assigned to R variables for posterior operations and download.file command downloads "cacert.pem" file. OAuth authorization is obtained by the creation of an OAuth object (OAuthFactory$new command) and the execution of the respective handshake method. Nevertheless, a manual task is needed to enable Twitter API connection. It is necessary to open an URL that appears in the console after running the handshake method, then authorize the application and write the provided code in the R console. This inconvenient last step can be avoided in subsequent automated use by loading a R object with a completed handshake. Therefore, the OAuth object is saved after the successful handshake execution. After loading the OAuth object, the `registerTwitterOAuth` function registers the OAuth credentials to the Twitter R session and permits the start of data collection. Tweet gathering is done with the `searchTwitter` function. Diverse search criteria can be included in this function such as search query (e.g., `searchString="GOOGLE"`), time interval (e.g., `since=2011-03-01`, `until=2011-03-02`), geocode (e.g., `geocode=41.365,-51.1151121,12mi`), and number of tweets (`n=15`). In this example, the last 15 tweets containing the word "GOOGLE" are retrieved. The result is a list of `status` objects composed by diverse attributes such as tweet id, text, creation date, and user name. Tweets text shall be converted to ASCII format because other encodings may compromise code execution.

10.4 Data Preprocessing

This use case provides a data set with 5,000 tweets containing cashtags of a comprehensive set of U.S. stocks (e.g., \$AAPL, \$GOOG, \$GS). Cashtags are composed by the stock ticker preceded by the "\$" symbol. These symbols are commonly used by the investor community in discussions related to the respective security. Concentrating on only these messages results in a less noisy data set. Tweets were collected using the Twitter API between January 1, 2013, and March 31, 2013, and were manually classified as positive or negative. A alternative to this manual classification would be the use of lexicons (as explained in the Introduction). However, we opted for a manual classification given that we also want to test in this work the quality of two lexicons within the financial domain (as describe in Section 10.5). These tweets were manually classified by MSc students from the area of Finance, under the supervision of co-author Nelson Areal (expert in finance). For privacy reasons, all mentions and URL addresses were normalized to "@user" and "URL", respectively. There are three attributes for each message: creation date, text content, and the assigned sentiment label.

Preprocessing is an essential part of text mining because it prepares input data for subsequent analysis. For instance, raw text might be formatted inadequately (e.g., HTML format) or contain many irrelevant terms (e.g., "the", "a"). Thus, preprocessing tasks such as data import, cleaning, and structuring provide an improved input for later Text Mining steps (e.g., application of ML methods) [14]. The file `preprocessing.R` contains the code for data preprocessing.

```
### preprocessing.R file ###
# load R package tm: framework for text mining applications
library(tm)
# load R package RTextTools: Automatic Text Classification via Supervised Learning
library(RTextTools)

# read a CSV file containing tweets about stock market
twt<-read.csv("twt_sample.csv",stringsAsFactors=FALSE)
# convert "created_at" column from character to time
twt$created_at<-strptime(twt$created_at,"%Y-%m-%d %H:%M:%S")
# order messages by creation time
twt<-twt[order(twt$created_at),]

# preprocess some usual expressions in stock market microblog conversations
↪  (punctuation removal will eliminate these expressions)
```

```
# substitute the isolated "@" by "at"
twt$text<-gsub("(^|[[:space:]])(@)([[:space:]])","\\1at\\3",twt$text)
# transform @<number> into "at <number>":
twt$text<-gsub("(^|[[:space:]])(@)([$]?[0-9.]+)([[:space:]]|[[:punct:]]|$)","\\1at
↪    \\3\\4",twt$text)
# substitute "+<number>" by "more <number>"
twt$text<-gsub("(^|[[:space:]])([+])([$]?[.]?[[:digit:]]+)","\\1more
↪    \\3",twt$text)
# substitute "-<number>" by "less <number>"
twt$text<-gsub("(^|[[:space:]])([-])([$]?[.]?[[:digit:]]+)","\\1less
↪    \\3",twt$text)
# substitute "~<number>" by "nearly <number>"
twt$text<-gsub("(^|[[:space:]])([~])([[:space:]]?)([$]?[.]?[[:digit:]]+)","\\1nearly
↪    \\4",twt$text)
# substitute "#<number>" by "number <number>"
twt$text<-gsub("(^|[[:space:]])([#])([[:space:]]?)(([[:digit:]])+)","\\1number
↪    \\4",twt$text)
# substitute "<number>%" by "<number> percent"
twt$text<-gsub("([[:digit:]])([%])","\\1 percent",twt$text)
# substitute all numbers by the word "num"
twt$text<-gsub("[$]?[[:digit:]]*[.]?[[:digit:]]+","num",twt$text)
# substitute cashtags by the word "cshtg"
twt$text<-gsub("[$][[:alpha:]]+","cshtg",twt$text)

# create a list containing the emoticons of each tweet
m<-gregexpr("(^|[[:space:]])(([<>]?[:;=][-o*']?([)]|[(]|[]]|[[]|[dDpP}]|[/:{|\\]))|
↪    (([)]|[]]|[(]|[[]|[dDpP}]|[/:{|\\])[-o*']?[:;=][<>]?))($|[[:space:]])",twt$text)
l_emot<-regmatches(twt$text,m)
# remove these emoticons from text
twt$text<-gsub("(^|[[:space:]])(([<>]?[:;=][-o*']?([)]|[(]|[]]|[[]|[dDpP}]|[/:{|\\]))|
↪    (([)]|[]]|[(]|[[]|[dDpP}]|[/:{|\\])[-o*']?[:;=][<>]?))($|[[:space:]])","\\1
↪    ",twt$text)

# create a list containing the hashtags of each tweet
m<-gregexpr("#\\w+",twt$text)
l_hstg<-regmatches(twt$text,m)
# remove hashtags from text
twt$text<-gsub("#\\w+","",twt$text)

# creation of a Document Term Matrix with stemming, conversion to lowercase,
↪    removal of punctuation and sparse terms and utilization of "Term frequency"
↪    weighting for unigrams
DTM <- create_matrix(twt$text, language="english", removeStopwords=FALSE,
↪    removePunctuation=TRUE, removeSparseTerms=0.99, toLower=TRUE, stemWords=TRUE,
↪    weighting=weightTf)
# save R objects required for future tasks
save(list=c("DTM", "twt", "l_emot", "l_hstg"), file="preproc.RData")
```

The tm [14] and RTextTools [15] packages are loaded by the library function. tm is a framework for text mining applications and RTextTools is a ML package for automatic text classification. The function read.csv reads a CSV file and creates a data frame (R matrix object with column names) from it. In this situation, read.csv imports the Twitter data set.

Diverse operations are executed to reduce dimensionality, such as:

- Convert all words to lowercase

- Perform text stemming , which reduces each word to its stem (e.g., the stem of words "waiting" and "waited" is "wait")

- Remove punctuation and very infrequent terms (i.e., sparse terms)

- Normalize all numbers and cashtags to "num" and "cshtg"

Punctuation and sparse terms removal, stemming, and lowercase conversion are accomplished in the Document Term matrix creation. These matrices contain the frequency of terms in documents and are commonly used in NLP. Rows correspond to documents (e.g., tweets), columns correspond to terms (e.g., unigrams), and each entry contains the frequency of the corresponding term in the respective document.

However, punctuation removal may eliminate informative items such as emoticons and hashtags. Moreover, there are usual expressions in stock market microblogging conversations containing punctuation symbols (e.g., `"@<number>"` means "at <number>", and `"+<number>"` signifies "more <number>"). Thus, some operations are executed in this demonstration before the creation of the Document Term matrix. Two lists holding emoticons and hashtags are created and some expressions (e.g., @<number>, +<number>, -<number>, #<number>) are substituted by identical expressions (e.g., at <number>, more <number>, less <number>, number <number>). For instance, these operations will convert the original message "STO Mar 425 put @ +1.98, $AAPL will fill gap to $500." into "STO Mar num put at more num, cshtg will fill gap to num.".

Regular expressions are an important concept for strings matching, manipulation, and extraction. They are composed by regular characters and metacharacters with special meaning that permit the description of a set of strings. For instance, the regular expression `"a[[:digit:]]"` will match all patterns having the letter "a" immediately followed by a digit (e.g., `"a1"`, `"a9"`). All functions utilized in this example to substitute, eliminate, and extract expressions receive regular expressions as patterns to match. The `gsub` function is applied in all expression modifications, and its inputs are the regular expressions of items to modify (e.g., `"[[:digit:]]+"` for numbers, `"[$][[:alpha:]]+"` for cashtags), the replacement strings (e.g., `"num"`, `"cshtg"`), and the character vector where these alterations take place (i.e., tweets text). The creation of lists of emoticons and hashtags is done with `gregexpr` and `regmatches` functions. The `gregexpr` command receives a character string containing regular expressions to be matched (i.e., `"#\\w+"` for hashtags) and a character vector where these expressions are browsed (i.e., tweets text) and returns a list containing the positions of every match in text. The `regmatches` command extracts these matches from text, taking the list produced by the `gregexpr` command and respective tweets text as inputs. The regular expressions to match emoticons were adopted from Christopher Potts's tokenizing script (http://sentiment.christopherpotts.net/tokenizing.html#emoticons).

The `create.matrix` function creates a Document Term matrix from a collection of documents, including the following arguments:

- **language** - the language used for stemming

- **removePunctuation** - the logical parameter specifying whether to remove punctuation

- **removeSparseTerms** - the maximal allowed sparsity

- **removeStopwords** - logical parameter defining whether to remove stopwords

- **stemWords** - logical parameter indicating whether to stem words

- **toLower** - logical parameter specifying whether to convert all text to lowercase

- **weighting** - weighting function to calculate each entry value (e.g., weightTf for term frequency)

The first Document Term matrix of this demonstration performs text stemming for English language, converts all text to lowercase, removes punctuation and terms absent in more than 99% of all tweets, maintains stopwords, and contains the raw term frequencies in each entry. For example, after performing all preprocessing tasks, the original tweet "$SBUX buy when it clears resistance at 54.5" will have nonzero term frequency in the columns corresponding to terms "buy", "cshtg", "num", "resist" and "when". The `save` command saves R objects required for future tasks.

10.5   Sentiment Analysis

We explore two types of SA: supervised classification performed by ML methods and unsupervised classification by applying opinion lexicons. The ML methods utilized in this demonstration are Support Vector Machines (SVM) and Naïve Bayes (NB). They represent two common and distinct methods applied for text classification. SVM is a discriminative classifier, whereas NB is a generative classifier. A discriminative classifier supplies a model for the target variable conditional on the observed variables, whereas a generative model is a full probabilistic model of all variables, specifying the joint probability distribution of target and observed variables [20].

Lexicon-based SA is supported by existing opinion lexicons and permits the analysis to be performed in an unsupervised manner, thus avoiding the laborious task of classifying data manually. In this approach, each tweet is classified by considering the "positive" and "negative" words that it contains, according to each lexicon. This demonstration uses Harvard General Inquirer (GI) [21], a popular domain independent lexicon, and a financial lexical resource (FIN) created by Loughran and McDonald [22]. GI lexicon comprises more than 11,000 words classified in 182 categories. These categories come from four sources: the Harvard IV-4 dictionary; the Lasswell value dictionary; categories recently constructed, and "marker" categories containing syntactic and semantic markers for disambiguation. This example applies all words of the "positiv" and "negativ" categories. FIN resources contain 6 word lists commonly applied in financial text documents: negative, positive, uncertainty, litigious, modal strong and modal weak words. This demonstration utilize the negative and positive word lists because the other lists do not have a clear sentiment polarity . The file `proc_lexicons.R` codes the download and preparation of these lexical resources to be applied in SA.

```
### proc_lexicons.R file ###
library(tm) # load R package tm: framework for text mining applications
library(SnowballC) # load SnowballC: An R interface to the C libstemmer library
↪    that implements Porter's word stemming algorithm
library(XLConnect) # load XLConnect package: Manipulation of Excel files

# process financial lexicon (FIN) created by Loughran and McDonald
FIN_n<-read.csv("http://www3.nd.edu/~mcdonald/Data/Finance_Word_Lists/LoughranMcDonald_
↪    Negative.csv", stringsAsFactors = FALSE)[,1] # read negative word list
FIN_p<-read.csv("http://www3.nd.edu/~mcdonald/Data/Finance_Word_Lists/LoughranMcDonald_
↪    Positive.csv", stringsAsFactors = FALSE)[,1] # read positive word list
# create a data frame with all words and respective sentiment label (1 for
↪    positive and -1 for negative)
lex_FIN<-as.data.frame(rbind(cbind(FIN_p,rep(1,length(FIN_p))),
↪    cbind(FIN_n,rep(-1,length(FIN_n)))),stringsAsFactors=FALSE)
colnames(lex_FIN)<-c("stem","sentiment")
lex_FIN$stem<-tolower(lex_FIN$stem) # convert to lowercase
lex_FIN$stem<-stemDocument(lex_FIN$stem) # stem all words
```

```
lex_FIN<-unique(lex_FIN) # remove duplicated elements
# write the processed FIN lexicon to a CSV file
write.csv(lex_FIN,"FIN.csv",row.names=FALSE)

# process Harvard General Inquirer (GI) lexicon
download.file(url="http://www.wjh.harvard.edu/~inquirer/inquirerbasic.xls",
↪    destfile="inquirerbasic.xls", mode="wb") # download GI lexicon
GI_book = loadWorkbook("inquirerbasic.xls") # load XLS file containing GI lexicon
GI_sheet = readWorksheet(GI_book,sheet=1,header=TRUE) # read lexicon sheet
# select all words from "Negativ" category
GI_n<-GI_sheet$Entry[!is.na(GI_sheet$Negativ)]
# select all words from "Positiv" category
GI_p<-GI_sheet$Entry[!is.na(GI_sheet$Positiv)]
# create a data frame with all words and respective sentiment label (1 for
↪    positive and -1 for negative)
lex_GI<-as.data.frame(rbind(cbind(GI_p,rep(1,length(GI_p))),
↪    cbind(GI_n,rep(-1,length(GI_n)))),stringsAsFactors=FALSE)
colnames(lex_GI)<-c("stem","sentiment")
lex_GI$stem<-tolower(lex_GI$stem) # convert to lowercase
# process repeated words (e.g., ABOUT#1, ABOUT#2)
lex_GI$stem<-gsub("#(.*)$","",lex_GI$stem)
lex_GI$stem<-stemDocument(lex_GI$stem) # stem all words
lex_GI<-unique(lex_GI) # remove duplicated elements
# exclude stems appearing in both lists
lex_GI<-lex_GI[!(lex_GI$stem %in% lex_GI$stem[duplicated(lex_GI$stem)]),]
# write the processed GI lexicon to a CSV file
write.csv(lex_GI,"GI.csv",row.names=FALSE)
```

FIN word lists are available in CSV format at http://www3.nd.edu/~mcdonald/Word_Lists.html. The read.csv function reads the positive and negative word lists from their URL. GI lexicon can be downloaded in different formats at http://www.wjh.harvard.edu/~inquirer/spreadsheet_guide.htm. In this example, the download.file function retrieves the XLS version. XLConnect [23] package permits the production of XLS files. Its loadWorkbook and readWorksheet functions allow the loading of the GI workbook file and reading of the corresponding sheet. For each lexicon, a data frame containing all words and respective sentiment value (i.e., 1 for positive and −1 for negative) is created. The cbind and rbind functions combines by columns or rows, a series of vectors, matrices or data frames. In this case, the utilization of these functions permits the production of a matrix containing lexical items and corresponding sentiment as columns. The as.data.frame function converts this matrix into a data frame. Both lexicons have their words stemmed (stemDocument function), converted to lowercase (tolower function) and repeated items removed (unique function). SnowballC [16] package implements Porter's word stemming algorithm for collapsing words to a common root. GI lexicon has repeated words represented by the word followed by a "#" character and a sequential number (e.g., ABOUT#1, ABOUT#2). The gsub function removes the "#" character and sequential numbers and maintains the word for every GI item. After this operation and text stemming, GI lexicon has 39 items having both positive and negative labels. These item are excluded from GI lexicon in this demonstration. The write.csv function writes the processed lexicons to CSV files.

SA in Twitter messages about stock market is coded in file sentim_analysis.R.

```
### sentim_analysis.R file ###
library(tm) # load R package tm: framework for text mining applications
# load R package RTextTools: Automatic Text Classification via Supervised Learning
library(RTextTools)
library(rminer)  # load R package rminer: Application of Data Mining Methods
# load R package slam: Data structures and algorithms for sparse arrays and
↪    matrices
library(slam)
```

```r
load("preproc.RData") # load preprocessing objects
total<-nrow(twt) # total number of tweets
n_training<-round(0.75*total) # number of messages of the training set (first 75%)

### machine learning methods for sentiment analysis
# application of Support Vector Machines (SVM) method
# creation of a container using the Document Term Matrix, the sentiment labels and
#     the definition of the training and test set size
container <- create_container(DTM,twt$sentiment,trainSize=1:n_training,
#     testSize=(n_training+1):total, virgin=FALSE)
svm_model <- train_model(container,"SVM") # train SVM model
# predict test set using SVM model
svm_results <- classify_model(container,svm_model)

# application of Na\"{i}ve Bayes (NB) method
# convert Document Term matrix to data.frame
df<-as.data.frame(as.matrix(DTM),stringsAsFactors=FALSE)
rownames(df)<-NULL
df<-cbind(df,as.factor(twt$sentiment)) # add a sentiment column
colnames(df)[ncol(df)]<-"sentiment"
nb_model=fit(sentiment~.,df[1:n_training,],model="naivebayes",task="class") #
#     train NB model
# predict test set using NB model
nb_results<-predict(nb_model,df[(n_training+1):total,])

### unsupervised sentiment classification
# read CSV file containing the processed GI lexicon
lex_GI<-read.csv("GI.csv",stringsAsFactors=FALSE)
# read CSV file containing the processed FIN lexicon
lex_FIN<-read.csv("FIN.csv",stringsAsFactors=FALSE)
# creation of a Document-Text matrix with:
#        - minimum length of letters = 2 (minimum length of GI and FIN words)
#        - without the removal of sparse words to match all GI and FIN items
DTM_lex <- create_matrix(twt$text, language="english", removeStopwords=FALSE,
#     minWordLength=2, removePunctuation=TRUE, toLower=TRUE, stemWords=TRUE,
#     weighting=weightTf)
# creation of a Document-Text matrix containing only GI terms
DTM_GI<-DTM_lex[,which(colnames(DTM_lex) %in% lex_GI$stem)]
# creation of a Document-Text matrix containing only FIN elements
DTM_FIN<-DTM_lex[,which(colnames(DTM_lex) %in% lex_FIN$stem)]
# exclude GI elements absent from all tweets
l_GI<-lex_GI[lex_GI$stem %in% colnames(DTM_GI),]
# exclude FIN elements absent from all tweets
l_FIN<-lex_FIN[lex_FIN$stem %in% colnames(DTM_FIN),]
# order GI lexicon (Document-Text matrix columns are ordered alphabetically)
l_GI<-l_GI[order(l_GI$stem),]
# order FIN lexicon (Document-Text matrix columns are ordered alphabetically)
l_FIN<-l_FIN[order(l_FIN$stem),]
# score each message by summing each word sentiment in that tweet
#              word sentiment = number of occurrences of the word * word
#     sentiment (1 for positive,
#                          -1 for negative, 0 for neutral ou not present in
#     lexicon)
total_GI<-tcrossprod_simple_triplet_matrix(DTM_GI, t(l_GI$sentiment))
total_FIN<-tcrossprod_simple_triplet_matrix(DTM_FIN, t(l_FIN$sentiment))
# tweets with positive score are labeled positive; tweets with negative score are
#     labeled negative
total_GI[total_GI>0]<-"positive"
total_GI[total_GI<0]<-"negative"
total_FIN[total_FIN>0]<-"positive"
total_FIN[total_FIN<0]<-"negative"
```

```
# save R objects required for future tasks
save(list=c("total", "n_training", "svm_results", "nb_results", "total_GI",
  ↪  "total_FIN", "DTM_GI", "DTM_FIN"), file="sent_analysis.RData")
```

The `load` function reads preprocessed data. In this example, ML models are created in the training set composed by the first 75% messages, whereas the evaluation of all methods is performed in the test set containing the remaining 25% tweets. The 75%–25% is a commonly adopted holdout split for evaluating the quality of the ML predictions. Also, only one run is executed for each ML model in order to reduce the computational effort required by the example. However, a more robust validation could be achieved by executing multiple runs and averaging the individual performances and by testing different holdout splits. `RTextTools` package permits easy training (`train_model` function) and classification of (`classify_model` function) SVM models. Both functions receive a container of class `matrix_container`. The `create_container` function creates a container from a Document Term matrix , the corresponding sentiment labels and the size of training and test set. However, this package does not include the NB algorithm. Therefore, the `fit` function from `rminer` package [24] is applied to train the NB classifier. This function does not accept a `matrix_container` or a `DocumentTermMatrix` object as input, so the Document Term matrix is converted to a data frame and the respective sentiment labels are added to this object. The classification is performed by the `predict` function, taking the created NB model and the test set as inputs. To simplify the R code, we adopted the default parameters of the SVM and NB models, which are more likely to be used by non ML experts and that achieved a good classification result in this example data set. Nevertheless, the best parameters of the ML models could be searched using the training data and R functions such as `tune` from `e1071` package [25].

In the lexicon-based models, a message is considered: positive, if the number of "positive" words is higher than the number of "negative" words; negative, if the number of "negative" words is higher than the number of "positive" words; and neutral, if the number of both word polarity types is equal. In order to match all GI and FIN items, a Document Term matrix is created with a lower minimum number of letters and without the elimination of sparse terms. From this matrix a distinct matrix is produced for each lexicon composed only by its terms. Sentiment scores are calculated by the multiplication of the Document Term matrix and the transpose of a list containing the sentiment values of the respective terms (i.e., 1 for positive and −1 for negative) according to the corresponding lexicon. This operation multiplies the term frequency by the respective sentiment value and sums these results for each tweet, producing a sentiment score for each message. The `tcrossprod_simple_triplet_matrix` function from `slam` package [26] computes this matrix cross-product. The applied sentiment lists are created from the lexicon data frames. In order to have a perfect match with the Document Term Matrix, these lists are ordered alphabetically and items absent from all tweets are excluded. Tweets having positive sentiment score are considered positive and those with negative score are labeled as negative. Table 10.1 shows some examples of tweets classification according to each model and the respective sentiment metadata (Sent column).

Lexicon-based models present a significant number of neutral classifications indicating some lack of coverage of these lexical resources. The `save` function saves the R objects necessary for future operations.

TABLE 10.1:   Examples of sentiment analysis according to each model (pos = positive, neg = negative, neu = neutral).

Tweet	SVM	NB	GI	FIN	Sent
$OCZ trying to find a bottom here, like it over 2.20	pos	pos	neu	neg	pos
$OPXA today +12% after my call	pos	pos	pos	neg	pos
Stopped on rest of $GOOG +$1.25	pos	pos	neg	neg	neg
$ADBE Expecting a correction anytime now	pos	neg	neg	neu	neg
$ANAD on 2.14 Launch Pad	pos	neg	pos	pos	pos
$LIFE is a short if it can't hold this 62.30 level	neg	neg	neu	pos	neg
There goes $LIFE short....	neg	neg	neu	neu	neg
$MELA When will it will go UP ?? mmmmm	pos	neg	neu	neu	pos

10.6   Evaluation

Model evaluation is important to assess the relevance of all models. This example compares the results of SA using all models performed on the test set. The evaluation metrics are as follows:

- Classification accuracy (Acc): percentage of messages correctly classified

- For each label, positive (Pos) and negative (Neg), the following are calculated:

    - Precision (Pre_{Pos}, Pre_{Neg}) – measures the proportion of true positives relative to the number of true and false positives

    - Recall (Rec_{Pos}, Rec_{Neg}) – measures the proportion of true positives relative to the number of true positives and false negatives (also known as Sensitivity)

    - $F_1 = 2\frac{Precision*Recall}{Precision+Recall}$ score (F1_{Pos}, F1_{Neg}) – which considers both Precision and Recall under a single measure

- Macro-averaged F-score (F_{Avg}) – averages all F-scores (i.e., F1_{Pos} and F1_{Neg}).

The evaluation.R file codes the model evaluation.

```
### evaluation.R file ###
library(tm) # load R package tm: framework for text mining applications
library(rminer)  # load R package rminer: Application of Data Mining Methods

load("preproc.RData") # load preprocessing objects
load("sent_analysis.RData") # load sentiment analysis objects

# evaluation metrics
svm_eval=mmetric(as.factor(twt$sentiment[(n_training+1):total]),svm_results[,1],
↪   metric=c("ACC","TPR","PRECISION","F1")) # SVM model evaluation
nb_eval=mmetric(as.factor(twt$sentiment[(n_training+1):total]),nb_results,
↪   metric=c("ACC","TPR","PRECISION","F1")) # NB model evaluation
GI_eval=mmetric(factor(twt$sentiment[(n_training+1):total],levels=c("0","negative",
↪   "positive")),as.factor(total_GI[(n_training+1):total]),metric=c("ACC","TPR",
↪   "PRECISION","F1")) # GI model evaluation
FIN_eval=mmetric(factor(twt$sentiment[(n_training+1):total],levels=c("0","negative",
↪   "positive")),as.factor(total_FIN[(n_training+1):total]),metric=c("ACC","TPR",
↪   "PRECISION","F1")) # FIN model evaluation
# create matrix with evaluation results
tab_eval<-rbind(c(svm_eval[c("ACC","PRECISION2","TPR2","F12","PRECISION1","TPR1","F11")
↪   mean(svm_eval[c("F11","F12")])),
```

```
        c(nb_eval[c("ACC","PRECISION2","TPR2","F12","PRECISION1","TPR1","F11")],
        ↪   mean(nb_eval[c("F11","F12")])),
        c(GI_eval[c("ACC","PRECISION3","TPR3","F13","PRECISION2","TPR2","F12")],
        ↪   mean(GI_eval[c("F12","F13")])),
        c(FIN_eval[c("ACC","PRECISION3","TPR3","F13","PRECISION2","TPR2","F12")],
        ↪   mean(FIN_eval[c("F12","F13")]))))
colnames(tab_eval)<-c("Accuracy","Prec_Pos","Recall_Pos","F1_Pos","Prec_Neg",
↪   "Recall_Neg","F1_Neg","F_avg")
rownames(tab_eval)<-c("SVM","NB","GI","FIN")
tab_eval<-round(tab_eval)
print(tab_eval)

# exclude tweets without lexicon items in evaluation metrics calculation
# sum term frequency of GI items for each tweet of test set
num_GI<-rowSums(as.matrix(DTM_GI)[(n_training+1):total,])
# test set tweets without GI items (% values)
print(length(num_GI[num_GI==0])/length(num_GI)*100)
# GI model evaluation
GI_eval_exc=mmetric(factor(twt$sentiment[(n_training+1):total][num_GI>0],
↪   levels=c("0","negative","positive")),as.factor(total_GI[(n_training+1):
↪   total][num_GI>0]),metric=c("ACC","TPR","PRECISION","F1"))
# sum term frequency of FIN items for each tweet of test set
num_FIN<-rowSums(as.matrix(DTM_FIN)[(n_training+1):total,])
# test set tweets without FIN items (% values)
print(length(num_FIN[num_FIN==0])/length(num_FIN)*100)
FIN_eval_exc=mmetric(factor(twt$sentiment[(n_training+1):total][num_FIN>0], # FIN
↪   model evaluation
levels=c("0","negative","positive")),as.factor(total_FIN[(n_training+1):
↪   total][num_FIN>0]),metric=c("ACC","TPR","PRECISION","F1"))
# create matrix with evaluation results
tab_eval_exc<-rbind(c(svm_eval[c("ACC","PRECISION2","TPR2","F12","PRECISION1",
↪   "TPR1","F11")], mean(svm_eval[c("F11","F12")])),
        c(nb_eval[c("ACC","PRECISION2","TPR2","F12","PRECISION1","TPR1","F11")],
        ↪   mean(nb_eval[c("F11","F12")])),
        c(GI_eval_exc[c("ACC","PRECISION3","TPR3","F13","PRECISION2","TPR2","F12")],
        ↪   mean(GI_eval_exc[c("F12","F13")])),
        c(FIN_eval_exc[c("ACC","PRECISION3","TPR3","F13","PRECISION2","TPR2","F12")],
        ↪   mean(FIN_eval_exc[c("F12","F13")]))))
colnames(tab_eval_exc)<-c("Accuracy","Prec_Pos","Recall_Pos","F1_Pos","Prec_Neg",
↪   "Recall_Neg","F1_Neg","F_avg")
rownames(tab_eval_exc)<-c("SVM","NB","GI","FIN")
tab_eval_exc<-round(tab_eval_exc)
print(tab_eval_exc)
```

Preprocessed and SA data is required for this task. The calculation of most evaluation metrics is made by the `mmetric` function of `rminer` package. This function receives vectors of target factors, predicted factors and metrics characters. In this situation, the metrics characters are: `"ACC"` for global accuracy, `"TPR"` for recall (or true positive rate), `"PRECISION"` for precision, and `"F1"` for each class F-score. The macro-averaged F-score is computed by the `mean` function. Functions `factor` and `as.factor` encodes vectors of data as factors. Since GI and FIN models assign an extra class (i.e., 0 for neutral), it is important to include this class in the conversion of target sentiment labels to factors via the `levels` argument. The evaluation metrics of all models are aggregated in a matrix using the `rbind` command. Table 10.2 presents the evaluation measures for all experimented models.

Despite a low recall value for negative messages, the discriminative SVM model obtains the best overall results. For example, it presents the highest values for accuracy and macro-averaged F-score. Moreover, ML models clearly outperform the lexicon-based models. The latter models do not obtain the best value in any evaluation metric. However, many messages do not contain any lexicon entry. Indeed, 58% tweets of test set do not hold any FIN item

TABLE 10.2:   Sentiment analysis results (in %, best values in **bold**).

Model	Acc	Pre_{Pos}	Rec_{Pos}	$F1_{Pos}$	Pre_{Neg}	Rec_{Neg}	$F1_{Neg}$	F_{Avg}
SVM	**76**	76	**92**	**83**	**76**	45	57	**70**
NB	67	**82**	62	71	52	**75**	**61**	66
GI	43	76	45	56	53	39	45	51
FIN	21	78	15	26	45	32	38	32

and 22% do not contain any GI item. This example also evaluates GI and FIN models after excluding tweets without GI or FIN items, respectively. The `rowSums` function permits the summation of each row of a matrix. Therefore, when applied to a Document Term Matrix, it returns the total number of items that each document has. The resulting objects of this operation on the GI and FIN test set matrices are used to select tweets containing lexicon items. The utilization of a condition demanding values greater than zero for these objects (e.g., num_GI>0, num_FI>0) on vectors of target or predicted labels permits to exclude tweets without lexicon items. Table 10.3 shows these evaluation results.

TABLE 10.3:   Sentiment analysis results excluding messages without lexicon items (in %, best values in **bold**).

Model	Acc	Pre_{Pos}	Rec_{Pos}	$F1_{Pos}$	Pre_{Neg}	Rec_{Neg}	$F1_{Neg}$	F_{Avg}
GI	**55**	76	**59**	**66**	**53**	48	50	**58**
FIN	51	**78**	38	51	45	**74**	**56**	53

The evaluation results of ML models remain better than lexicon-based models. The main reason for this behaviour is that there is a lack of opinion lexicons adapted to stock market microblogging conversations. Domain-independent lexicons are not adjusted to the specific terminology and semantics of stock market contents. Many lexical items holding significative sentiment value in stock market conversations are not included in generic lexicons or have opposite sentiment polarities, as shown in [27]. Moreover, the few public domain financial lexicons (e.g., [22]) are not properly adapted to microblogging text. It should be noted that, as previously explained, ML models have the drawback of requiring the use of labeled data, which can be difficult or costly to get (e.g., manual classification).

10.7   Inclusion of Emoticons and Hashtags Features

This demonstration also tests the inclusion of emoticon and hashtags information in the best performing classifier (i.e., SVM classifier). The following features are added to the original Document Term matrix:

- An emoticon score corresponding to the difference between the number of positive and negative emoticons existing in each tweet.

- The presence or absence of a set of hashtags. A matrix, containing all hashtags in columns and all tweets in rows, specifies the presence of each hashtag in each message.

SA applying these features is coded in file `emot_hstg.R`.

```
### emot_hstg.R file ###
library(tm) # load R package tm: framework for text mining applications
# load R package RTextTools: Automatic Text Classification via Supervised Learning
```

```
library(RTextTools)
library(rminer)  # load R package rminer: Application of Data Mining Methods

load("preproc.RData") # load preprocessing objects
load("sent_analysis.RData") # load sentiment analysis objects

# function that calculates emoticon score (number of positive emoticons - number
↪  of negative emoticons)
scr_emot <- function (vec, tab_emot) {
       if (length(vec)>0) {
              vec<-gsub("[[:space:]]","",vec) # remove spaces
              return(sum(tab_emot$sentiment[tab_emot$emoticon %in% vec]))
              } else return (0)
       }
# read a CSV file containing emoticons and respective sentiment polarity
t_emot<-read.csv("emoticons.csv",stringsAsFactors=FALSE)
emot_score<-unlist(lapply(l_emot, scr_emot, t_emot))
DTM<-cbind(DTM,emot_score) # add the emoticon score to Document Term matrix
colnames(DTM)[ncol(DTM)]<-"emot_score"

# function that verifies the presence or absence of each element of a list of
↪  hashtags
prs_hstg <- function (vec, n_hstg) {
       return(as.numeric(n_hstg %in% vec))
       }
hstg<-unique(unlist(l_hstg)) # hashtags vector
DTM_hstg <- unlist(lapply(l_hstg,prs_hstg,hstg))
DTM_hstg <- matrix(DTM_hstg,ncol=length(hstg),byrow=TRUE)
colnames(DTM_hstg)<-hstg
DTM<-cbind(DTM,DTM_hstg) # add hashtag matrix to Document Term matrix

# utilization of SVM method
container <- create_container(DTM,twt$sentiment,trainSize=1:n_training,
↪  testSize=(n_training+1):total, virgin=FALSE) # creation of a container
svm_model <- train_model(container,"SVM")
svm_results <- classify_model(container,svm_model)
# evaluation metrics
svm_eval=mmetric(as.factor(twt$sentiment[(n_training+1):total]),svm_results[,1],
↪  metric=c("ACC","TPR","PRECISION","F1"))
svm_eval<-c(svm_eval[c("ACC","PRECISION2","TPR2","F12","PRECISION1","TPR1","F11")],
↪  mean(svm_eval[c("F11","F12")]))
names(svm_eval)<-c("Accuracy","Prec_Pos","Recall_Pos","F1_Pos","Prec_Neg",
↪  "Recall_Neg","F1_Neg","F_avg")
print(svm_eval)
```

The lists of emoticons and hashtags (i.e., l_emot and l_hstg) extracted in data pre-processing are necessary in this step. This use case provides a file (emoticons.csv) containing a comprehensive list of emoticons and the respective sentiment (1 for positive, -1 for negative) in order to facilitate the identification of positive and negative emoticons. The function scr_emot is created to compute the emoticon score of a tweet. It receives the corresponding l_emot entry and the emoticons data frame and returns the difference between the number of positive and negative emoticons. The function lapply applies scr_emot function to each l_emot element, producing a list of emoticon scores. Unlist converts this list into a vector of emoticon scores and cbind function adds this vector as a column to the Document Term matrix. The function prs_hstg verifies the presence or absence of each element of a list of hashtags in a tweet. The inputs are two vectors containing the hashtags of a tweet and the hashtags to check the presence. The result is a vector of the same length of the latter input vector indicating the presence (i.e., 1) or absence (i.e., 0) of each hashtag in the former input vector. The combined utilization of unlist and unique functions on l_hstg list produces a vector of all hashtags appearing in the data set without duplicated elements. These are the hashtags that are checked in this example. The `lapply` function applies `prs_hstg` function to each `l_hstg` element and passes the vector of hashtags to check as an argument. The `matrix` function transforms the `lapply` result into a matrix having all tweets in rows and all hashtags in columns. This matrix is attached to the Document Term matrix using the function `cbind`. The resulting matrix feeds a SVM classifier. Table 10.4 presents SA results for the SVM classifier with emotions and hashtags features ($SVM_{EmtHsht}$) and without these features ($SVM_{Original}$). As shown in Table 10.4, the addition of emoticons and hashtags features improves the majority of evaluation results. Therefore, emoticons and hashtags demonstrate some informative value.

TABLE 10.4:   Sentiment analysis results with emoticons and hashtags features (in %, best values in **bold**).

Model	Acc	Pre_{Pos}	Rec_{Pos}	$F1_{Pos}$	Pre_{Neg}	Rec_{Neg}	$F1_{Neg}$	F_{Avg}
$SVM_{Original}$	76	76	92	83	76	45	57	70
$SVM_{EmtHsht}$	**77**	76	**93**	**84**	**78**	**47**	**58**	**71**

10.8   Conclusion

This chapter presented a use case about sentiment analysis (SA) in Twitter data related to stock market using the R tool. Mining microblogging data to forecast stock market behavior is a recent and interesting research topic. Some studies showed that sentiment indicators created from microblogging data appears to have predictive value for stock market variables (e.g., [6, 9, 10]). Moreover, the production of these indicators is faster and less expensive than traditional sources (e.g., large-scale surveys). R is a free language and environment that allows the diverse steps within this topic to be performed. There are several packages (e.g., `twitterR`, `RTextTools`, `rminer`) that provide the required functionalities for this tool.

This use case provided and described R code for diverse tasks forming this process and supplied a Twitter data set with stock market messages for the execution of those operations. The addressed tasks were tweets collection, preprocessing tasks, utilization of opinion lexicons, application of supervised ML methods, and respective evaluation.

Overall, the supervised ML models outperformed the unsupervised lexicon-based models. These latter models have insufficient coverage and inferior accuracy than former models. This behavior is due to the current lack of lexicons properly adapted to stock market microblogging conversations [27]. However, it should be noted that ML models require labeled data for the learning procedure (which can be costly to get), whereas lexicon-based models do not. Considering ML models, the discriminative representative (i.e., Support Vector Machine) obtained higher results that the generative representative (i.e., Naïve Bayes). In addition, emoticons and hashtags features have shown to add informative content to SA models, since the inclusion of these features allowed to improve SA results.

Bibliography

[1] B. Pang and L. Lee. Opinion Mining and Sentiment Analysis. *Foundations and Trends in Information Retrieval*, 2(2):1–135, 2008.

[2] M. Hu and B. Liu. Mining and summarizing customer reviews. *Proceedings of the 2004 ACM SIGKDD international conference on Knowledge discovery and data mining KDD 04*, 04(2):168, 2004.

[3] Y. Choi and C. Cardie. Learning with Compositional Semantics as Structural Inference for Subsentential Sentiment Analysis. *Proceedings of the Conference on Empirical Methods in Natural Language Processing EMNLP 08*, (October):793–801, 2008.

[4] Bing Liu and Lei Zhang. A Survey of Opinion Mining and Sentiment Analysis. In Charu C. Aggarwal and ChengXiang Zhai, editors, *Mining Text Data*, pages 415–464. Springer, 2012.

[5] W. Antweiler and Murray F. Is All That Talk Just Noise? The Information Content of Interest Stock Message Boards. *Journal of Finance*, 59(3):1259, 2004.

[6] J. Bollen, H. Mao, and X. Zeng. Twitter mood predicts the stock market. *Journal of Computational Science*, 2(1):1–8, 2011.

[7] P. C Tetlock. Giving Content to Investor Sentiment : The Role of Media in the Stock Market. *Journal of Finance*, 62(3):1139–1168, 2007.

[8] J. R. Nofsinger. Social Mood and Financial Economics Social Mood and Financial Economics. *Journal of Behavioral Finance*, 6(3):144–160, 2005.

[9] C. Oh and O. R. Liu Sheng. Investigating Predictive Power of Stock Micro Blog Sentiment in Forecasting Future Stock Price Directional Movement. In *ICIS 2011 Proceedings*, Shanghai, China, 2011.

[10] T. O Sprenger and I. M Welpe. Tweets and Trades: The Information Content of Stock Microblogs. *Social Science Research Network Working Paper Series*, pages 1–89, 2010.

[11] N. Oliveira, P. Cortez, and N. Areal. Some experiments on modeling stock market behavior using investor sentiment analysis and posting volume from Twitter. In *Proceedings of the 3rd International Conference on Web Intelligence, Mining and Semantics (WIMS '13)*, Madrid, Spain, 2013. ACM.

[12] N. Oliveira, P. Cortez, and N. Areal. On the Predictability of Stock Market Behavior using StockTwits Sentiment and Posting Volume. In *16th Portuguese Conference on Artificial Intelligence (EPIA 2013)*, Angra do Heroísmo, Açores, Portugal, 2013. Springer Berlin Heidelberg.

[13] R Core Team. *R: A Language and Environment for Statistical Computing*. R Foundation for Statistical Computing, Vienna, Austria, 2013.

[14] I. Feinerer, K. Hornik, and D. Meyer. Text Mining Infrastructure in R. *Journal of Statistical Software*, 25(5):1–54, 2008.

[15] T. Jurka, L. Collingwood, A. Boydstun, E. Grossman, and W. van Atteveldt. *RTextTools: Automatic Text Classification via Supervised Learning*, 2012. R package version 1.3.9.

[16] M. Bouchet-Valat. *SnowballC: Snowball stemmers based on the C libstemmer UTF-8 library*, 2014. R package version 0.5.1.

[17] I. Feinerer and K. Hornik. *wordnet: WordNet Interface*, 2014. R package version 0.1-10.

[18] A.F. Zuur, E.N. Ieno, and E. Meesters. *A Beginner's Guide to R*. Springer, 2009.

[19] J. Gentry. *twitteR: R based Twitter client*, 2013. R package version 1.1.7.

[20] A Jordan. On discriminative vs. generative classifiers: A comparison of logistic regression and naive bayes. *Advances in Neural Information Processing Systems*, 14:841, 2002.

[21] P. J. Stone, D. C. Dunphy, M. S. Smith, and D. M. Ogilvie. *The General Inquirer: A Computer Approach to Content Analysis*, volume 08. MIT Press, 1966.

[22] T. Loughran and B. McDonald. When is a liability not a liability? Textual analysis, dictionaries, and 10-Ks. *Journal of Finance*, 66(1):35–65, 2011.

[23] Mirai Solutions GmbH. *XLConnect: Excel Connector for R*, 2014. R package version 0.2-9.

[24] Paulo Cortez. Data mining with neural networks and support vector machines using the R/rminer tool. In Petra Perner, editor, *Advances in Data Mining - Applications and Theoretical Aspects 10th Industrial Conference on Data Mining (ICDM 2010)*, volume 6171 LNAI of *10th Industrial Conference on Advances in Data Mining, ICDM 2010*, pages 572–583, Berlin, Germany, 2010. Springer.

[25] D. Meyer, E. Dimitriadou, K. Hornik, A. Weingessel, F. Leisch, C-C Chang, and C-C Lin. *e1071: Misc Functions of the Department of Statistics (e1071), TU Wien*, 2014. R package version 1.6-4.

[26] K. Hornik, D. Meyer, and C. Buchta. *SLAM: Sparse Lightweight Arrays and Matrices*, 2014. R package version 0.1-32.

[27] N. Oliveira, P. Cortez, and N. Areal. Automatic Creation of Stock Market Lexicons for Sentiment Analysis Using StockTwits Data. In *Proceedings of the 18th International Database Engineering & Applications Symposium*, IDEAS '14, pages 115–123, New York, NY, USA, 2014. ACM.

Chapter 11

Topic Modeling

Patrick Buckley

Institute of Technology, Blanchardstown, Ireland

11.1 Introduction

Topic models can be described as the idea that documents naturally contain a mix of topics where a topic can be described as a distribution over the terms in a corpus of documents [1]. They are desirable where there is a massive amount of textual data stored in large collections and where short descriptions of those documents could be created and used in a variety of ways; to identify similarities across the corpus, to create visualizations of where documents fit relative to others, and also in searching and indexing methods [2]. The main goal is to find short descriptions of the topics in a corpus while still maintaining the statistical relationships in the corpus [3]. In this way, popular tasks like classification, similarity, and summation can be applied.

Topic models are applicable to a variety differing sectors like scientific, political, fraud, software, and Web usage to name a few, all of which benefit from the topic modeling technique of identifying hidden structures in otherwise unstructured text collections [4]. While traditionally accepted to be a text based methodology, topic models have been extended into other applications including images, music and video analysis.

There are a variety of topic modeling techniques but arguably the most popular technique is known as Latent Dirichlet Allocation (LDA), which was developed by Blei et al. [3].

11.1.1   Latent Dirichlet Allocation (LDA)

The LDA topic model can be described as a probabilistic model that makes the assumption that given a corpus of documents, each document is a distribution over the topics and in turn every topic is a distribution over the words in the corpus [3]. It uses a generative model to mimic how documents are created. Simply put, the idea behind the LDA model is that documents can be represented as random mixtures of hidden or latent topics in a corpus. It allows for the reduction in the complexity of the corpus of text, the capturing of key information and their latent underlying statistical relationships.

If you take an example of a collection of scientific documents, there will be a variety of fields of study within the collection so therefore there will be a variety of different topics. Documents sampled from the collection might contain information regarding human anatomy and genetics, another document could contain information on cloning and technology; and another might contain information on genetics and cloning [4]. Figure 11.1 shows a news article extract taken from *The New York Times* (12/04/2014) illustrating this idea at a high level. Since documents when created are formed from a series of topics, a number of potential topics are highlighted in the figure to express this idea. For example, words highlighted in red could collectively be named a topic about "energy", similarly words highlighted in blue could form a topic on "geographic locations" [5].

China Takes On Big Risks in Its Push for Shale Gas

By **KEITH BRADSHER**APRIL 11, 2014

JIAOSHIZHEN, China — Residents of this isolated mountain valley of terraced cornfields were just going to sleep last April when they were jolted by an enormous roar, followed by a tower of flames. A shock wave rolled across the valley, rattling windows in farmhouses and village shops, and a mysterious, pungent gas swiftly pervaded homes. "It was so scary — everyone who had a car fled the village and the rest of us without cars just stayed and waited to die," said Zhang Mengsu, a hardware store owner. All too quickly, residents realized the source of the midnight fireball: a shale gas drilling rig in their tiny rural hamlet. This verdant valley represents the latest frontier in the worldwide hunt for shale gas retrievable by the technology of hydraulic fracturing, or fracking. It is a drilling boom that has upended the energy industry and spurred billions of dollars of investment.

Like the United States and Europe, China wants to wean itself from its dependence on energy imports — and in Jiaoshizhen, the Chinese energy giant Sinopec says it has made the country's first commercially viable shale gas discovery. Its efforts could also help address another urgent issue, as Beijing looks to curb an overwhelming reliance on coal that has blackened skies and made China the largest contributor to global warming.

But the path to energy independence and a cleaner fossil fuel is fraught with potential pitfalls. Threats to workplace safety, public health and the environment all loom large in the shale gas debate — and the question is whether those short-term risks threaten to undermine China's long-term goal. The energy industry around the world has faced criticism about the economic viability of vast shale projects and the environmental impact of the fracking process. But interviews with residents of six hamlets here where drilling is being done, as well as with executives and experts in Beijing, the United States and Europe, suggest that China's search poses even greater challenges.

Topics (multinomials over words)
gas, shale, drilling, fracturing, fracking, coal, energy, fuel, fossil, flames

village, valley, homes, farmhouse, residents, rural, environment, montain

china, united states, europe, beijing, jiaoshizen, country, worldwide

FIGURE 11.1 (See color insert.): News extract topics.

LDA uses probabilistic sampling methods to create a generative model for documents by describing how the words in documents could be created with the use of hidden or latent variables. The main aim of generative models is to find the group of variables that best describe/explain the words observed in documents [1]. In a generative model, the concept of mutual exclusivity doesn't apply, meaning words can be part of one or more topics. In this way, topic models are enabled to capture words that exhibit polysemy.

As the generative model is hypothetical, given that all that is actually observed are the terms in the set of documents, LDA uses a variety of inference techniques to estimate the posterior model distribution. One of these methods is Gibbs sampling [1]. It works by assigning a value to each variable in the model and then taking each word token in a corpus and for each it works on estimating the probability of assigning the current word to each topic. It is from the posterior distribution that we can derive the topics for a corpus.

11.2 Aims of This Chapter

The aim of this chapter is to guide the reader through the process of creating a corpus, right through to the creation of a Latent Dirichlet Allocation (LDA) topic model using the statistical package R. The following are some of the main areas that will be discussed and explained:

1. Creating a corpus in R

2. Pre-processing the corpus

3. Creating a Document Term Matrix

4. Finding the optimum number of topics for the data

5. Creating the topic model

6. Interpreting the models

7. Applying to unseen documents

11.2.1 The Data Set

The data used throughout this chapter is from the UCI machine learning repository and is based upon 20,000 messages taken from 20 newsgroups (http://kdd.ics.uci.edu/databases/20newsgroups/20newsgroups.html). Given the size of the full data set, there is a smaller version of this available which will be used, so depending on the computational power available to you it may make more sense to use that. The mini newsgroup data set contains 2,000 messages from the 20 newsgroups and can be downloaded as a tar.gz file (mini_newsgroups.tar.gz).

11.2.2 R

All of the processing and topic modeling will be performed using the **R** statistical package. The version of R used for this chapter is 3.1.1 (64 bit). There are a number of packages available in R for topic modeling such as **LDA**, **topicmodels**, and others. For the purposes of this chapter the **topicmodels** package is explained and used throughout.

11.3   Loading the Corpus

There are multiple ways to load a corpus depending on where your data source is stored. Two of the more common methods are importing a corpus from a local file repository and importing files from a database.

11.3.1   Import from Local Directory

The first step is to install and load the text mining (**tm**) package library into **R**, this contains the input methods used to create the corpus from the folder of documents. The package can be installed by either using the "Load Packages" option in the "Packages" menu in the R console or by entering the following directly into the R terminal **install.packages("tm")**. R should then ask you to specify a CRAN mirror from which the download can begin.

tm: This package in R allows for a wide range of tasks for text mining including data importation, creation of a corpus, preprocessing of the text data and creation of matrices for the terms and documents that can then be used by other packages to perform topic modeling amongst multiple other things. (http://cran.r-project.org/web/packages/tm/ index.html)

After loading the package, R by default sets a working directory location where it looks for input files and equally where it will store any outputs you may save. If you are unsure where the working directory is, simply entering **getwd()** into the console will give you the file path. If you would prefer to change the default location for the working directory to another location, you can use the set working directly command **setwd("c:/your_preferred_location")**. Note that the forward slash character should be used in the file path and not backslash. After this has been changed, you can use **getwd()** to confirm the directory changes have taken place.

Now that you have set the preferred working directory (or are using the default), unzip the mini newsgroup data and add the newsgroup folder into the directory. The following R code can be used to import the files and convert them into a corpus.

We can use **getSources()** to list the sources and use **getReaders()** to view the document formats that are available to use in the **tm** package. There are different approaches based on the input files you are working with, but since this exercise is dealing with text based files, the following commands point R to a direct source (**DirSource**). By entering the file path to the mini newsgroup folder, R can begin to import the files. Since our data set contains multiple folders with text files, setting the parameter **recursive=TRUE** tells R to look at all the folders within the directory. The **Corpus** command is used to load the documents and create a corpus given the directory source.

```
#LOADING A CORPUS FROM LOCAL FOLDERS:

#Load the text mining package(s)
library("tm")

#Set the working directory
setwd("C:/Users/Documents/R/DATASET/")

#Here the file path is input using a Direct Source command
#which is in turn transformed into a corpus. Also telling R
#to look in multiple folders (recursive)
corpus <- corpus(DirSource(
```

```
directory = "C:/Users/Documents/R/DATASET/mini_newsgroups/",
encoding = "UTF-8",
recursive = TRUE,
mode = "text"
))
```

After running these commands in the R console, by entering **corpus**, this shows the results of the newly created corpus as follows:

```
corpus
> A corpus with 376 text documents
```

Similar to importing files from a local directory, the corpus can be imported through a database connection.

11.3.2   Database Connection (RODBC)

There are also multiple other database connection options including RMySQL, ROracle, and RJDBC, each of which are available from `http://cran.r-project.org`. The **RODBC** package in R was used to perform this connection. In this example, **RODBC** works by creating an open database connection (ODBC) or channel from the client packages (RODBC). In order to establish the connection, the setup of an ODBC (open database connectivity) was required. This involved downloading the required driver for ODBC and mySQL and creating the connection to the database required.

RODBC: is one package that allows a connection to be made to an ODBC database (http://cran.r-project.org/web/packages/RODBC/index.html)

After the initial setup, the package was installed in *R* and the following code can be used to create a connection to where the data in the **mySQL** database is stored. Following on from that the **sqlFetch** command was used to pull the required table from the database into R.

```
#LOADING A CORPUS FROM DATABASE:

#Load the text mining package(s)
library("tm")
library("RODBC")

#Set the working directory
setwd("C:/Users/Documents/R/DATASET/")

#Create connection to your database and then retrieve data
database <- odbcConnect("your_database_connection", "root",
"password")
datatable <- sqlFetch(database, "database_name")
```

In addition to importing the data from the database, some further processing is required to transform the data from its database table format into a structure that can be transformed into a corpus. This first step is to create an R object (e.g., **myReader**) instructing how R should read in the data. Assuming that the data has been stored in the database with the main body of text in one column and the name of the file in another column (amongst other columns of data), the variable **m** is set so that it reads in and sets the "ID" as the "file_name" and the contents as the "text" (note: the names should reflect the column names in your database tables). **m** then becomes an input into the next command, which specifies that R reads the database table as tabular and to map to the requirements stated in **m**. More information on this can be found at `http://cran.r-project.org/web/packages/tm/vignettes/extensions.pdf`.

```
#Converting database tabular structure for text documents
m <- list(ID = "file_name", Content = "text")
myReader <- readTabular(mapping = m)
```

The next stage then is to create the corpus. Whereas in the previous example a **DirSource** command was used, this time the **DataframeSource** command is used as the data in the database is stored as a data frame. This in combination with the previously created **myReader** ensures that the corpus is created.

```
#Creating the corpus from a data frame
corpus <- corpus(DataframeSource(datatable),
readerControl = list(reader = myReader, language = "en"))
```

Now that we have examine some methods for importing data and creating a corpus, the next stage we will look at is preprocessing techniques.

11.4   Preprocessing the Corpus

After importing the data and converting the documents into a corpus, a number of various methods for preprocessing can be applied. These include transformations to lower-case, removal of numbers and punctuation removal of stopwords and white space The package **SnowballC** is one example of a stemmer that can be used and is the only package that is required in addition to the **tm** package that is already installed and loaded.

SnowballC: *Snowball provides a stemmer for the words in the corpus as part of prepro-cessing (http://cran.r-project.org/web/packages/SnowballC/index.html)*

In the R code shown below, each of the commands use the transformation function **tm_map** to transform the corpus text to a more useful format.

The first line of code sets up the stopwords that you would like to remove from the corpus. In addition to the standard English stopwords dictionary that is supplied with the **tm** package, you can further remove custom words as shown by the **"my"**, **"custom"**, **"words"**. The text mining package also contains other stopwords dictionaries in a variety of languages while also providing a second English words dictionary called SMART dictionary which is much more extensive.

Following on from setting up your stopwords, the corpus can then be transformed re-moving; numbers, stopwords, white space, and punctuation. Then the stemmer is applied using the *SnowballC* package.

```
#PRE-PROCESSING THE CORPUS:

#Load the text mining package(s)
library("SnowballC")

#Setting the stopwords dictionaries and custom words
myStopwords <- c(stopwords("english"), "my", "custom", "words")

#Pre-processing and transforming the corpus
myStopwords <- c(stopwords("english"), stopwords("SMART"))
```

```
your_corpus <- tm_map(corpus, content_transformer(tolower))
your_corpus <- tm_map(your_corpus, removeWords, myStopwords)
your_corpus <- tm_map(your_corpus, removeNumbers)
your_corpus <- tm_map(your_corpus, removePunctuation)
your_corpus <- tm_map(your_corpus, stripWhitespace)
your_corpus <- tm_map(your_corpus, stemDocument)
```

After the corpus has been successfully preprocessed, the next stage is to convert the corpus into a document term matrix, which will allow for further inspection.

11.5   Document Term Matrix (DTM)

This is simply a matrix where the documents are the rows and the words the columns, the matrix cells then contain a frequency count of the words (weightTf), which is the default weighting function in the **tm** package. DTMs can also contain different weighting functions such as weightTfIdf (term frequency - inverse document frequency) weightBin (Binary weight a term-document matrix), and weightSMART (weights according to a combination of weights specified in SMART notation). This is a necessary input into the topic modeling package **topicmodels** so that modeling can be performed. The command **DocumentTermMatrix** is used to create the matrix and is part of the **tm** package. More information on this can be found by entering the following **TermDocumentMatrix**. The control list as shown gives you an option to remove terms of less than and greater than a specified number. In this case, the document terms matrix keeps terms that are 3 characters minimum and can be infinite in length.

```
#CREATING A DOCUMENT TERM MATRIX:

#Create a document term matrix (containing between 3 &
#Infinite characters)
myDtm <- DocumentTermMatrix(
your_corpus, control=list(
wordLengths=c(3,Inf)
)
)
```

At this stage, some examination of the DTM can be conducted which gives you a chance to access the quality of the data and to get a feel for the corpus. To simply examine the output of the topic model, entering **myDtm** into the terminal will display information about the matrix created. Examining the output shows useful statistics like the sparsity of the DTM (meaning the level of emptiness or zeros), this shows a very sparse matrix where the majority of entries are zero. In the case of the mini newspaper corpus, we have a corpus with 2,000 documents containing 34,943 terms, with a huge level of sparsity.

```
myDtm

<<DocumentTermMatrix (documents: 2000, terms: 34943)>>
Non-/sparse entries: 194343/69691657
Sparsity           : 100%
Maximal term length: 232
Weighting          : term frequency (tf)
```

Another method to inspect the DTM is to use the Find Frequent Terms function **findFreqTerms(myDtm, 100)**, this looks to find words in the matrix that occur 100 times or more. This displays a list of the terms that occur over 100 times. After examining these frequent terms, there are some terms that are very long in length that don't actually make much sense and haven't been removed as part of preprocessing.

```
findFreqTerms(myDtm, 100)

[55] "cantaloupesrvcscmu"    "car"
[83] "composmswindowsmisc"   "compsysibmpchardwar"
[85] "compsysmachardwar"     "comput"
```

In order to remove theses words, we can create the document term matrix again only this time we can set the maximum length for words to keep to be 15 or under (**wordLengths=c(3,15)**).

```
<<DocumentTermMatrix (documents: 2000, terms: 28039)>>
Non-/sparse entries: 183484/55894516
Sparsity            : 100%
Maximal term length: 15
Weighting           : term frequency (tf)
```

This has reduced the DTM significantly indicating that there were many terms of greater than 15 characters in length. However, the quantity of terms in the corpus is still relatively large and the sparsity level is still 100%, which is understandable given that the matrix would mostly be filled by zeros. Words that occur frequently in documents and across other documents are not good differentiators in topic modeling, words that occur in many documents and many times in a single document are given a lower weighting using TF-IDF (term-frequency - inverse document frequency). This then allows terms with a low frequency to be omitted as they are insignificant to the model and likewise for terms occurring in many documents.

In order to calculate the term frequency-inverse document frequency, the package **"slam"** is required.

slam: *provides data structures and algorithms for sparse arrays and matrices (*`http://cran.r-project.org/web/packages/slam/index.html`*)*

The following code is used to calculate the TF-IDF from the DTM that was created. It will also display a summary of the results as shown:

```
#CALCULATING THE TERM FREQUENCY - INVERSE DOCUMENT FREQUENCY:

library("slam")

#Calculate TF-IDF
term_tfidf <-
tapply(myDtm$v/row_sums(myDtm)[myDtm$i], myDtm$j, mean)
* log2(nDocs(myDtm)/col_sums(myDtm > 0))

#Display results of TF-IDF
> summary(term_tfidf)

   Min. 1st Qu.  Median    Mean 3rd Qu.    Max.
0.00000 0.03821 0.07409 0.09763 0.12750 1.64100
```

Examining the results above, we can determine that we should only include terms with a value of greater than 0.074 as that is slightly below the median number. The median is used as it is not affected by large TF-IDF values in the data whereas the mean would be more influenced. Applying this in the following code and also removing documents where no features a present results in a much smaller DTM with 14, 081 terms.

```
#Retaining features that have a high TF-IDF value
myDtm <- myDtm[,term_tfidf >= 0.074]
myDtm <- myDtm[row_sums(myDtm) > 0,]
summary(col_sums(myDtm))

#Reports the dimensions of the DTM
dim(myDtm)
[1]   2000 14081

#Saving the DTM to local folder
save(myDtm, file = "my_Dtm.Rdata")
```

Another method that can be applied is the removal of sparse terms command, **removeSparseTerms(your_corpus, 0.3)**, this will remove the sparse terms to beyond a specified sparsity level set by the user. This method can sometimes result in most of the DTM being removed leaving only a small percentage of the words so care must be taken not to remove too much. More information on this can be found by typing **?removeSparseTerms** directly into the R terminal.

Based on the above TF-IDF example, a word-cloud can be used to visualize the DTM as shown in Figure 11.2. If when examining the output from the word-cloud shows anomalies or words that you know should be removed (e.g., a person's name or something that a stop-words dictionary has not picked up), adding these to the list of custom stop-words and repeating the preprocessing is advised. The package "wordcloud" is used to create the output.

wordcloud: *used in the creation of word-clouds from text corpus. (http://cran.r-project.org/web/packages/wordcloud/index.html)*

```
#CREATING A WORD CLOUD:

library("wordcloud")

#convert document term matrix to a term document matrix
myTdm <- t(myDtm)

#define tdm as matrix
m = as.matrix(myTdm)

# get word counts in decreasing order
word_freqs = sort(rowSums(m), decreasing=TRUE)

# create a data frame with words and their frequencies
dm = data.frame(word=names(word_freqs), freq=word_freqs)

# plot word-cloud with maximum of 200 words
wordcloud(dm$word, dm$freq,  max.words=200, random.order=FALSE,
rot.per=.2, colors=brewer.pal(9, "Dark2"))
```

11.6   Creating LDA Topic Models

The **topicmodels** package is used throughout this section in performing topic modeling of the data set. The first stage is to install the package which can be completed by entering **install.packages("topicmodels")** into R. Once it has been installed, use the

FIGURE 11.2: Word-cloud of the DTM.

library("topicmodels") command to load the package.

　　topicmodels: *was developed to provide an interface to R for the C code developed by [3]. The package contains capability to create topics models based on Latent Dirichlet Allocations (LDA) but also for the Correlated Topic Model (CTM). It uses Variational EM for estimating the topics but also provides access to Gibbs sampling methods created by Xuan-Hieu Phan and co-authors in C++. (http://cran.r-project.org/web/packages/ topicmodels/index.html)*

　　A Latent Dirichlet Allocation (LDA) will be built using Gibbs sampling, and the following represents the default values for this Gibbs sampling. These are a list of all the possible parameters or controls in fitting an LDA model using Gibbs sampling [6] from the **topicmodels** package. More information on each can be found in the **topicmodels** CRAN document [http://cran.r-project.org/web/packages/ topicmodels/topicmodels.pdf]:

```
R> control_LDA_Gibbs <- list(
alpha = 50/k, estimate.beta = TRUE, verbose = 0, prefix =
tempfile(), save = 0, keep = 0, seed = as.integer(Sys.time()),
nstart = 1, best = TRUE, delta = 0.1, iter = 2000, burnin = 0,
thin = 2000)
```

　　In the next section, some of these parameters for creating an LDA topic model using Gibbs sampling will be explained.

11.6.1　Topicmodels Package

　　To give an overview of the parameters in the package for topic modeling , the following definitions are from the 'topicmodels' paper by [6] and from the topicmodels CRAN package pdf [http://cran.r-project.org/web/packages/topicmodels/index.html]:

- **estimate.alpha, alpha, estimate.beta** - The default value for α is estimated (estimate.alpha = TRUE) and as Griffiths and Steyvers suggested [1], this value should be set at $50/k$, where k is the number of topics. Where α is not set as estimated, it will stay at the initial value. β, the term distribution over topics, is set at estimate.beta = TRUE. If however, the term distribution have been fitted by a previous model, setting estimate.beta = FALSE allows hold-out data or testing data to be applied to the fitted model.

- **verbose**: verbose is set to 0 as default which means during the algorithm, nothing will be printed, if this value changes to a positive integer all iterations during the algorithm will be printed.

- **save & prefix**: save is default to zero meaning no intermediate results are saved to file with prefix

- **keep**: when keep is set to a positive integer, the values for the log-likelihood will be store for every keep iteration.

- **seed**: allows for reproducibility

- **nstart**: shows how many repeated runs there are with random initializations

- **delta**: Parameter of the prior distributions for terms distribution over topics.

- **iter, burnin, thin**: determine how many draws are made over the corpus during Gibbs sampling. The number of burnin iterations that are set indicates the number that will be discarded before each thin iteration after that point is stored for iter iterations.

- **best**: default value is set to TRUE which means only the best posterior likelihood is returned, if value is set to FALSE all draws are returned.

Note that not every parameter requires input from the user when running an LDA model. The main parameters that are used will be discussed in the next section.

11.6.2 Determining the Optimum Number of Topics

One of the main issues with finding topic models in a corpus is determining the optimum number of topics. This is something that is set by the modeler. Perplexity is often used as a method of evaluation for the optimum number of topics and is used on the held-out or test portion of a data set. Perplexity analysis characterizes the quality of the generative model. This method acts as a rough guide to help narrow down the area of focus and does not mean that you will get the precise number of actual topics, this is where the knowledge of the domain expert is required.

A cross-validation is applied to the data in order to gain an insight into the performance of the model. The cross-validation is based on the methodology used in [6]. It makes 10 test and training sets, each set is based on different partitions of the whole data. Each set contains 90% for training and 10% for testing, the result is 10 performances which are then averaged.

The following controls were put in place after installing the 'topicmodels' package, loading the library and setting up the working directory. Firstly the number of topics was set to run from 5 to 35 using the stages set out in the following code, for example 5 times the sequence from 1 to 3, giving $5, 10, 15$ and then 25 and 35 [Note: Topics 2 to 5 are considered later in this section].

```
#SETTING LDA PARAMETERS FOR TOPIC MODELLING:

#Load the text mining package(s)
library("topicmodels")

#Set the working directory
setwd("C:/Users/Documents/R/DATASET/")

#Setting up parameters for LDA topic modeling
topics <- 5 * c(1:3, 5, 7)
SEED <- 20080809
BURNIN = 1000
THIN = 100
ITER = 1000
BEST = FALSE

#Loading your document term matrix
load("my_Dtm.Rdata")
data <- myDtm
```

Following on from this, for each iteration of the Gibbs sampling, the following controls were used. A "burnin" rate of 1,000 was set meaning the model would run 1,000 times before starting to record any results. Then it was set to run for another 1,000 iterations and to record the results for every 100th run. Setting best to FALSE allowed for each log-likelihood value to be returned and not just the lowest value. In this way, plots can be developed to examine how the perplexity of the model looks for the test data. The parameter α was left at its default value, which is $50/k$ with k as the number of topics to be generated. Once this was set, the document term matrix created and saved earlier was then loaded into the model and set as "data".

All of the controls mentioned are used in both the training and the testing models. However, the exception is the addition of the 'estimate.beta' control in the testing models. This is set to FALSE (by default it is set to TRUE) so that the term distributions that were created in the training models can now be used to apply the test data to and a perplexity score can be calculated.

The following code (source [6]) represents the cross-validation portion where the split between training and testing is created and the models are run for both. Each of the models are created using LDA and Gibbs sampling and the results are then saved to an output folder. Creating a folder in your working directory (prior to running the code) called "results" is necessary for the outputs to be saved.

```
#X-VALIDATION TO DETERMINE OPTIMUM NUMBER OF TOPICS (1):

# X-Validation - splitting data into 10 Test data sets
# with remainder used in Training

D <- nrow(data)
folding <- sample(rep(seq_len(10), ceiling(D))[seq_len(D)])
for (k in topics)
{
        for (chain in seq_len(10))
                {
                FILE <- paste("Gibbs_", k, "_", chain, ".rda", sep = "")

                training <- LDA(data[folding != chain,], k = k,
                control = list(seed = SEED,
                burnin = BURNIN, thin = THIN, iter = ITER, best = BEST),
                method = "Gibbs")

                best_training <- training@fitted[[which.max(logLik(training))]]
```

```
testing <- LDA(data[folding == chain,], model = best_training,
control = list(estimate.beta = FALSE, seed = SEED,
burnin = BURNIN,
thin = THIN, iter = ITER, best = BEST))

save(training, testing, file = file.path("results", FILE))
}
}
```

Once the previous process has run, you should end up with a number of files in a folder called "results" in your working directory. This contains all the results from each run through the X-validation. It is from this that comparisons can be made as to which model was generated with the optimum number of topics. Note that the process can take a considerable amount of time (45minutes in my case) as there will be 50 LDA models produced using Gibbs sampling.

The following code (source [6]) then compiles the results and outputs a file displaying the log likelihood for the test data. From this you can see which number produced the lowest perplexity.

```
#X-VALIDATION TO DETERMINE OPTIMUM NUMBER OF TOPICS (2):

topics <- 5 * c(1:3, 5, 7)
SEED <- 20080809
#Set the working directory
setwd("C:/Users/Documents/R/DATASET/")

load("my_Dtm.Rdata")
data <- myDtm

D <- nrow(data)
folding <-
sample(rep(seq_len(10), ceiling(D))[seq_len(D)])

News_test <-
News_alpha <- list()
for (method in c("Gibbs"))
{
        News_alpha[[method]] <- News_test[[method]] <- matrix(NA,
        nrow = length(topics), ncol = 10,
        dimnames = list(topics, seq_len(10)))
        for (fold in seq_len(10))
        {
                for (i in seq_along(topics))
                        {
                        T <- topics[i]

                        FILE <- paste(method, "_", T, "_", fold, ".rda", sep = "")
                        load(file.path("results", FILE))

                        News_alpha[[method]][paste(T),fold] <-
                        if (is(training, "Gibbs_list")) training@fitted[[1]]@alpha
                        else training@alpha

                        News_test[[method]][paste(T),fold] <- perplexity(testing,
                        data[folding == fold,], use_theta = FALSE)
                        }
        }
}
save(News_alpha, News_test, file = "News.rda")
```

The output from this is a file named "News.rda" containing the alpha values used during each model and also the perplexity values calculated during each model build for the given number of topics. The model that minimizes the perplexity value should be chosen as shown:

```
#Find the lowest average log-likelihood
p <- News_test
q <- as.data.frame(p)
rowMeans(q)
```

```
         5        10        15        25        35
  4616.543  4679.822  4782.607  5045.052  5334.478
```

For the mini-newsgroup corpus, the optimum number of topics seems to be minimized at 5 topics as this produced the lowest perplexity from the X-validation. This can be seen in Figure 11.3, it also could be possible that the number of topics is below 5.

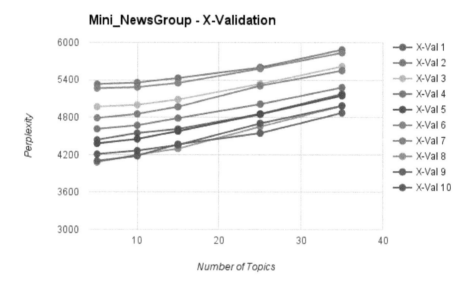

FIGURE 11.3 (See color insert.): Cross-validation — optimum number of topics.

Running the analysis again only this time for topics 2 to 5 shows that there is very little difference found by the cross validation possibly indicating that the optimum number of topics is somewhere in this region, this can be seen in Figure 11.4. In order to run this analysis for topics 2 to 5, the parameters that were set earlier in this section [topics ¡- 5 * c(1:3, 5, 7)] should be changed to [topics ¡- 2 * c(1, 1.5, 2, 2.5)].

Examining the averages for each shows that 5 topics has the actual lowest perplexity score.

```
\begin{minted}[breaklines, fontsize=\footnotesize]{r}
#Find the lowest average log-likelihood
p <- News_test
q <- as.data.frame(p)
rowMeans(q)
```

```
        2         3         4         5
  4647.33   4638.55   4644.35   4639.25
```

In conclusion, we can assume that the actual number of topics in the corpus is low and lies somewhere in the range of 2 to 10.

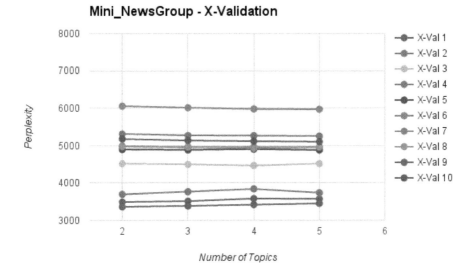

FIGURE 11.4 (See color insert.): Cross-validation — optimum number of topics (2 to 5).

11.6.3   LDA Models with Gibbs Sampling

Once you know the range for the optimum number of topics in your corpus, you can then proceed to build and test the model parameters and start interpreting the results. Since the lowest perplexity score calculated above was for 5 topics, the model is set to produce that number of topics. The following creates an LDA model using Gibbs sampling for topic inference:

```
#CREATE AN LDA MODEL USING GIBBS SAMPLING:

library("topicmodels")
load("my_Dtm.Rdata")

#Set parameters
SEED <- 20080809
BURNIN = 1000
ITER = 1000
k = 5    #number of topics to create

#Create an LDA model using GIBBS Sampling & save the output
model_lda <- LDA(myDtm, k = k, method = "Gibbs",
control = list(seed = SEED, burnin = BURNIN, iter = ITER))
print(model_lda)

save(model_lda, file = "LDA_model.RData")
```

Now that we have created our LDA Gibbs model with 5 topics, we can start to examine the output created by finding the top 10 terms in each topic as follows. Similarly we can find the what topics are associated with what topic by using **topics(model_lda, 5)**, the result is quite long so I have not added the results here.

```
#DISPLAY TERMS FROM POSTERIOR DISTRIBUTION:

#Display the top 10 terms in each topic
```

```
terms(model_lda, 10)

     Topic 1    Topic 2     Topic 3     Topic 4      Topic 5
 [1,] "wire"     "god"       "imag"      "israel"     "game"
 [2,] "car"      "key"       "file"      "drug"       "gun"
 [3,] "jim"      "encrypt"   "window"    "launch"     "team"
 [4,] "sale"     "moral"     "drive"     "station"    "stephanopoulo"
 [5,] "circuit"  "church"    "card"      "mission"    "armenian"
 [6,] "cabl"     "jesus"     "color"     "orbit"      "player"
 [7,] "pin"      "homosexu"  "format"    "arab"       "fan"
 [8,] "insur"    "jew"       "graphic"   "isra"       "steve"
 [9,] "electr"   "clipper"   "jpeg"      "shuttl"     "tax"
[10,] "bike"     "fbi"       "display"   "food"       "turkish"

#Display the top 5 topics in each document
topics(model_lda, 5)
```

Looking at the first 10 terms in each of the 5 topics created, you can inspect whether the topics make sense. A domain specialist may be required to interpret the outputs as sometimes it is not always clear which topic has been produced. In some cases, the model will produce topics that don't make any sense to the human eye. In Topic 5 the word "stephanopoulo" is associated with the topic but unless someone is familiar with the set of documents provided, it is difficult to determine if this is an appropriate word to include or not. If it was deemed to be not relevant, it could be worthwhile removing it from the analysis and the DTM created earlier. In this case, there seems to be a mix of topics within the 5 topics created so it may be worth investigating whether a smaller or larger number of topics would produce a better output. This is where some trial and error is required and where expertise of a domain expert would help to identify the best model fit.

After testing and creating models with topics less than and greater than 5 topics, reproducing the model using the aforementioned techniques, but increasing the number of topics to 7 seems to give better results as shown in the following:

```
#DISPLAY TERMS FROM POSTERIOR DISTRIBUTION:

terms(model_lda, 10)

     Topic 1    Topic 2     Topic 3     Topic 4
 [1,] "window"   "god"       "game"      "gun"
 [2,] "drive"    "moral"     "key"       "car"
 [3,] "card"     "church"    "team"      "jim"
 [4,] "wire"     "jesus"     "encrypt"   "bike"
 [5,] "dos"      "homosexu"  "player"    "batf"
 [6,] "driver"   "fbi"       "fan"       "ride"
 [7,] "disk"     "frank"     "clipper"   "firearm"
 [8,] "monitor"  "koresh"    "insur"     "illinoi"
 [9,] "mac"      "sin"       "canada"    "dave"
[10,] "video"    "jon"       "score"     "bmw"

     Topic 5    Topic 6             Topic 7
 [1,] "imag"     "stephanopoulo"    "armenian"
 [2,] "file"     "drug"             "israel"
 [3,] "format"   "steve"            "turkish"
 [4,] "color"    "tax"              "muslim"
 [5,] "jpeg"     "signal"           "arab"
 [6,] "display"  "food"             "greek"
 [7,] "ftp"      "patient"          "isra"
 [8,] "launch"   "candida"          "islam"
 [9,] "gif"      "pin"              "detector"
[10,] "graphic"  "input"            "jew"
```

In this case, the output of the topics is much clearer, and we can easily distinguish between the majority of the topics produced. For example, Topic 1 is "computer" related, Topic 2 is related to "religion", Topic 5 is possibly related to "images/photographs", Topic 7 is "country/nationality" related. However like in the previous example, Topic 6 shows "stephanopoulo" and "steve" as the 1st and 3rd most important word in that topic but to the reader the meaning of the topic is still unknown.

In order to further examine the outputs, the model outputs can be saved into CSV files which can be examined further as follows:

```
#SAVING MODEL OUTPUTS:

#Save the top 100 terms in each topic to csv.
write.csv(terms(model_lda, 100), file = "model_mini_news.csv")

#Save the topic terms distributions to csv
lda_terms <- posterior(model_lda)$terms
write.csv(lda_terms, file = "LDA_TERMS_mini_news.csv")

#Save the topic  document distributions to csv
lda_topics <- posterior(model_lda)$topics
write.csv(lda_topics, file = "LDA_TOPICS_mini_news.csv")
```

To examine the terms distributions visually, the following can be used to create a quick plot of the terms distributions across the topics Figure 11.5 shows the output for the term distributions (code is based on example used in `https://github.com/OhLookCake/xkcd-Topics/blob/master/scripts/topicExtraction.R`). As can be seen, the first 5-10 words account for the majority of the probability that make up each topic, meaning that only a small number of words define the topic and therefore whether a document fits into it or not based on the words in that document. (Note that each topic assigns a probability to every word in the corpus).

```
#PLOTTING THE TOPIC TERM DISTRIBUTIONS:

require(reshape2)
require(ggplot2)
require(RColorBrewer)

termgenerator <- posterior(model_lda)$terms

###1: relative probabilities of words in each topic ###
termimportance <- apply(termgenerator,1,
↪    function(x)        x[order(x,decreasing=T)[1:20]])
termimportance.longform <- melt(termimportance, value.name="Probability",
↪    varnames=c("TermNumber","Topic"))

#creating the plot
ggplot(data=termimportance.longform,
          aes(
               x=TermNumber,
               y=Probability,
               color=factor(Topic),
               group=Topic)) +
       geom_line()
```

Similarly, the topic distributions can also be examined and used as a physical check against the documents allocated to each topic. Table 11.1 is showing the first two topics and their document distributions for the 1st 10 documents.

Examining the actual documents shows that for Topic 1, the first document subject is on "Electrical wiring FAQ" and is from the sci.electronics collection, the second document is called 'Looking for X windows on a PC' and is from the comp.windows collection.

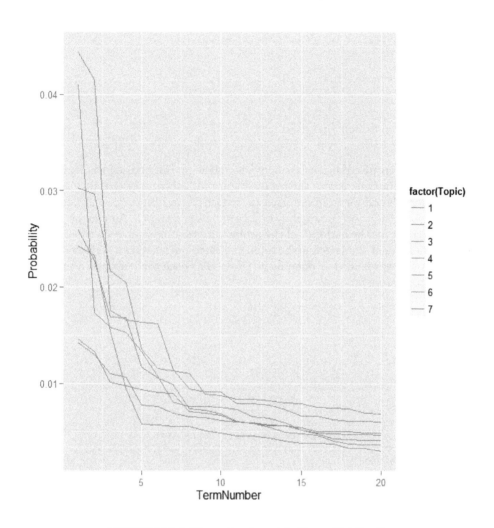

FIGURE 11.5 (See color insert.): Term distribution.

The first document in Topic 2 is called "Americans and Evolution" and is from alt.atheism collection of news, the second document is named "Scroggs" and again is from a religious related group (soc.religion.christian). This is a good way to verify that the documents do actually belong to that topic and acts as a physical check on the accuracy of the topics that were generated.

TABLE 11.1: Topic document distributions.

Document	Topic 1	Document	Topic 2
53,569	0.94	53,564	0.75
68,012	0.80	21,754	0.72
52,090	0.80	20,952	0.69
52,113	0.67	21,597	0.69
76,505	0.64	21,648	0.66
76,117	0.62	21,396	0.62
52,190	0.58	53,351	0.61
51,846	0.57	21,585	0.57
76,851	0.57	20,540	0.57
51,595	0.56	53,623	0.56

11.6.4 Applying New Data to the Model

The **topicmodels** package also allows new data to be applied to the newly created model. This can be useful in the example where you have new documents but would like to categorize them into the predefined topics. The following R code can be used to complete this. In order to apply the new data, the same methods as described earlier are required to turn the new documents into a corpus, preprocess them and finally turn them into a document term matrix (DTM). The DTM then becomes the input into the model as shown. Note that if the new documents contain terms that were not present in the model training, these will not be picked up. To help overcome this, the model should not stay static and should be retrained periodically as new documents become available.

```
#APPLYING NEW DATA TO THE CREATED MODEL:

#Find the posterior for model, option to add in new unseen data
# at this point.
post <- posterior(model_lda, newdata = myDtm)

#PRINT the first 10 topics from the posterior with 4 decimal places
round(post$topics[1:10,], digits = 4)
write.csv(round(post$topics, digit=4), "posterior_newdata.csv")
```

11.6.5 Variational Expectations Maximization (VEM) Inference Technique

The model that was created before used Gibbs sampling as the inference technique for creating the posterior distribution. the **topicmodels** package also allows for another inference technique to be used. By using another inference method, we can then compare and contrast the models. VEM is actually the default inference technique used in creating topics models in the **topicmodels** package. The value for alpha is estimated in the default version (starting at 50/k).

CREATE AN LDA MODEL USING VEM INFERENCE:

```
library("topicmodels")

#Set the working directory
setwd("C:/Users/Documents/R/DATASET/")

#Loading your document term matrix
load("my_Dtm.Rdata")
data <- myDtm

#Setting up parameters for LDA topic modeling
SEED <- 20080809
k = 7

#LDA using VEM inference
model_vem <- LDA(myDtm, k=k, control=list(seed=SEED))
print(model_vem)
terms(model_vem, 10)

save(model_vem, file = "VEM_model.RData")
```

Examining the outputs of the LDA model using VEM inference shows that similar topics are created when looking at the outputs from the Gibbs inference LDA model. Topic 1 seems related to "image/photograph", Topic 4 looks "country/nationality" related, Topic 5 has a "religious" theme and Topic 7 is "computer" related. However there does seem to be less clarity when compared to the Gibbs sampling LDA model outputs. For example, Topic 4 has the terms "car" and "bike" mixed into the "country/nationality" related theme, similarly the term "stephanopoulo" appears in the "image/photograph" topic, again possibly pointing out that this terms should be removed from the analysis.

```
         Topic 1          Topic 2      Topic 3     Topic 4
 [1,]  "imag"           "key"        "game"      "armenian"
 [2,]  "file"           "encrypt"    "wire"      "car"
 [3,]  "jpeg"           "moral"      "team"      "turkish"
 [4,]  "format"         "clipper"    "player"    "bike"
 [5,]  "color"          "jim"        "fan"       "muslim"
 [6,]  "stephanopoulo"  "algorithm"  "circuit"   "turkey"
 [7,]  "display"        "escrow"     "electr"    "armenia"
 [8,]  "window"         "des"        "outlet"    "greek"
 [9,]  "gif"            "jon"        "venus"     "modem"
[10,]  "ftp"            "msg"        "score"     "ride"


        Topic 5     Topic 6      Topic 7
 [1,]  "god"       "homosexu"   "window"
 [2,]  "gun"       "israel"     "card"
 [3,]  "jesus"     "fbi"        "drive"
 [4,]  "church"    "arab"       "dos"
 [5,]  "drive"     "jew"        "disk"
 [6,]  "sin"       "isra"       "monitor"
 [7,]  "launch"    "shuttl"     "driver"
 [8,]  "pin"       "abort"      "graphic"
 [9,]  "firearm"   "insur"      "video"
[10,]  "car"       "orbit"      "scsi"
```

11.6.6 Comparison of Inference Techniques

In order to examine the similarity between the two model outputs, we can use a distance measure using Hellinger distance to calculate how similar topics are to each other. In addition to the **topicmodels** package, the package **clue** is required to compute the distance similarities.

> ***clue***: *used for creating and analyzing cluster ensembles and includes methods for measuring proximity (http://cran.r-project.org/web/packages/clue/index.html)*

The following code is used to calculate the similarity between the two models (LDA Gibbs and LDA VEM):

```
#COMPARISON USING HELLINGER DISTANCE:

library("topicmodels")
library("clue")

#Set the working directory
setwd("C:/Users/Documents/R/DATASET/")

#Load the models saved
load("LDA_model.Rdata")
load("VEM_model.Rdata")

#get the posterior distributions for both models
lda_terms <- posterior(model_lda)$terms
vem_terms <- posterior(model_vem)$terms


#calculate the distance between the term distributions
dist_models <- distHellinger(lda_terms, vem_terms)
matching <- solve_LSAP(dist_models)
dist_models <- dist_models[, matching]
d <- mean(diag(dist_models))

#Order by the best matching
best_match <- order(diag(dist_models))
terms(model_lda, 10)[,best_match[1:7]]
terms(model_vem, 10)[,matching[best_match[1:7]]]

#Order by worst matching
worst_match <- order(diag(dist_models), decreasing = TRUE)
terms(model_lda, 10)[,worst_match[1:3]]
terms(model_vem, 10)[,matching[worst_match[1:3]]]
```

After running this code, the outputs as shown below should give the 3 best matching topic between the LDA Gibbs and LDA VEM models. As you can see, the topics are quite well matched with the themes of "image/photograph", "computer", and "religion" all quite clear. However, as mentioned earlier the Gibbs model seems to have produced better results with more terms in the top 10 seeming to fit the theme, whereas there are more "outlier" terms mixed into the VEM model output (e.g., stephanopoulo in Topic 1)

```
BEST AND WORST MATCHING TOPIC COMPARISONS:

terms(model_lda, 10)[,best_match[1:3]]

     Topic 5   Topic 1   Topic 2
[1,] "imag"    "window"  "god"
[2,] "file"    "drive"   "moral"
[3,] "format"  "card"    "church"
```

```
 [4,] "color"    "wire"    "jesus"
 [5,] "jpeg"     "dos"     "homosexu"
 [6,] "display"  "driver"  "fbi"
 [7,] "ftp"      "disk"    "frank"
 [8,] "launch"   "monitor" "koresh"
 [9,] "gif"      "mac"     "sin"
[10,] "graphic"  "video"   "jon"
```

```
terms(model_vem, 10)[,matching[best_match[1:3]]]
```

```
       Topic 1            Topic 7  Topic 5
 [1,] "imag"             "window"  "god"
 [2,] "file"             "card"    "gun"
 [3,] "jpeg"             "drive"   "jesus"
 [4,] "format"           "dos"     "church"
 [5,] "color"            "disk"    "drive"
 [6,] "stephanopoulo"    "monitor" "sin"
 [7,] "display"          "driver"  "launch"
 [8,] "window"           "graphic" "pin"
 [9,] "gif"              "video"   "firearm"
[10,] "ftp"              "scsi"    "car"
```

Looking at the output for the three least or worst matching topics shows that to the observer there is nothing similar at all between the topics. In fact, it is quite difficult to determine the theme for the majority of the topics shown. In the LDA Gibbs, Topic 7 has a clear enough theme and related terms, Topic 6 and 4 may have a theme that is quite specific so a domain expert might be required to help identify it.

```
terms(model_lda, 10)[,worst_match[1:3]]
```

```
       Topic 6             Topic 7     Topic 4
 [1,] "stephanopoulo"     "armenian"  "gun"
 [2,] "drug"              "israel"    "car"
 [3,] "steve"             "turkish"   "jim"
 [4,] "tax"               "muslim"    "bike"
 [5,] "signal"            "arab"      "batf"
 [6,] "food"              "greek"     "ride"
 [7,] "patient"           "isra"      "firearm"
 [8,] "candida"           "islam"     "illinoi"
 [9,] "pin"               "detector"  "dave"
[10,] "input"             "jew"       "bmw"
```

```
terms(model_vem, 10)[,matching[worst_match[1:3]]]
```

```
       Topic 2       Topic 6      Topic 4
 [1,] "key"         "homosexu"   "armenian"
 [2,] "encrypt"     "israel"     "car"
 [3,] "moral"       "fbi"        "turkish"
 [4,] "clipper"     "arab"       "bike"
 [5,] "jim"         "jew"        "muslim"
 [6,] "algorithm"   "isra"       "turkey"
 [7,] "escrow"      "shuttl"     "armenia"
 [8,] "des"         "abort"      "greek"
 [9,] "jon"         "insur"      "modem"
[10,] "msg"         "orbit"      "ride"
```

For the VEM models, identifying a theme for the topics is more difficult as there doesn't seem to be anything evident and the topics look like a mismatch of terms. Again the inclusion of names seems to be hindering the underlying theme. Although the names can indeed be important to a topic, for someone who is not familiar with the data in the documents, it can be difficult to extract the theme.

11.6.7 Removing Names and Creating an LDA Gibbs Model

As was noted in the previous section, the models produced contain names that can obscure the topic. In this section, some further preprocessing is applied to the data set to remove them from the corpus. In addition to the stopwords dictionaries that were used earlier in preprocessing, names that occurred frequently are added as follows. Note that in the topic models produced, some of the words will have been stemmed so in the case of "stephanopoulo", the full name "stephanopoulos" would need to be added.

```
myStopwords <- c(stopwords("english"), stopwords("SMART"),
"stephanopoulos","frank", "jon", "steve", "jim", "dave", "des",
"brian", "tom", "andi")
```

After preprocessing the data and removing the names, an LDA model using Gibbs sampling was produced for 7 topics and gave the following results:

```
        Topic 1     Topic 2     Topic 3     Topic 4
 [1,]  "imag"      "window"    "game"      "key"
 [2,]  "file"      "drive"     "team"      "encrypt"
 [3,]  "format"    "card"      "player"    "armenian"
 [4,]  "jpeg"      "dos"       "fan"       "clipper"
 [5,]  "color"     "disk"      "tax"       "fbi"
 [6,]  "display"   "driver"    "score"     "turkish"
 [7,]  "ftp"       "monitor"   "trade"     "muslim"
 [8,]  "israel"    "video"     "drug"      "koresh"
 [9,]  "gif"       "graphic"   "abort"     "islam"
[10,]  "arab"      "sale"      "insur"     "algorithm"


        Topic 5     Topic 6     Topic 7
 [1,]  "wire"      "launch"    "god"
 [2,]  "gun"       "station"   "moral"
 [3,]  "car"       "mission"   "church"
 [4,]  "circuit"   "orbit"     "jesus"
 [5,]  "cabl"      "shuttl"    "homosexu"
 [6,]  "pin"       "venus"     "jew"
 [7,]  "bike"      "detector"  "sin"
 [8,]  "electr"    "bbs"       "atheist"
 [9,]  "switch"    "pat"       "mormon"
[10,]  "clock"     "cub"       "pit"
```

Examining the topics show two new topics that up to now had not been picked up. Topic 3 looks to be "sports" related and Topic 6 seems to be related to "space". The "image", "computer" and "religion" topics have remained. Topics 4 and 5 are slightly less obvious and could possibly be a mix of topics. Overall this model looks to be a better fit than the earlier LDA Gibbs and LDA VEM models.

11.7 Summary

In this chapter, the popular topic modeling technique LDA was examined and modeled using the R statistical tool. Using the newsgroup data, the process of loading and transforming a set of document into a corpus was shown. Various preprocessing techniques were applied to the corpus prior to converting it into a document term matrix so that it could be used in topic modeling.

Topic modeling was then applied using the **topicsmodels** package. The analysis showed that small numbers of topics reflected more accurately the structure of the data set. Overall, it was found that the model produced quite good topics that were for the most part coherent. The process for creating a model can involve some trial and error, in that as you develop models you learn more about the corpus, which then helps to inform changes and improvements that enhance the final model.

Bibliography

[1] M. Steyvers and T. Griffiths. Probabilistic topic models. *Handbook of Latent Semantic Analysis*, 427(7):424–440, 2007.

[2] D. J. Hu. Latent dirichlet allocation for text, images, and music. 2009.

[3] D. M. Blei, A. Y. Ng, and M.I. Jordan. Latent dirichlet allocation. *The Journal of Machine Learning Research*, 3:993–1022, 2003.

[4] D.M. Blei and J.D. Lafferty. Topic models. *Text Mining - Classification, Clustering, and Applications*, 10:71, 2009.

[5] D.M. Blei. Probabilistic topic models, available from http://www.cs.princeton.edu/ blei/blei-mlss-2012.pdf, 2012.

[6] B. Grun and K. Hornik. topicmodels — an r package for fitting topic models. *Journal of Statistical Software*, 40, 2011.

Chapter 12

Empirical Analysis of the Stack Overflow Tags Network

Christos Iraklis Tsatsoulis

Nodalpoint Systems, Athens, Greece

12.1 Introduction

Stack Exchange is self-described as *"a fast-growing network of 129 question and answer sites on diverse topics from software programming to cooking to photography and gaming"*, with a current base of more than 5.5 million users and over 82 million monthly unique visitors[1]. By far, the greatest among these 129 sites is Stack Overflow, devoted to questions about computer programming and related topics.

---

[1]http://stackexchange.com/.

Question tags are an essential part of the submitted questions in Stack Overflow, allowing answering users to monitor questions relevant to their field of expertise and to answer promptly to submitted questions. Only users holding an "advanced" status in Stack Overflow are allowed to generate new tags, with the rest of the community limiting themselves in using the existing tags for their questions. Tagging the submitted questions is mandatory (i.e., there is a minimum of one tag per question), and each question can contain up to five tags.

In this chapter, we depart slightly from text analysis proper in order to undertake a task inspired by the recent advances in what is usually termed as "network science" : hence, we carry out an analysis of the Stack Overflow tags viewed as a *network,* or a *graph.* Specifically, we aim to get some insight about the user communities by representing tags and their co-occurrences as a graph, where the graph nodes are the tags themselves, and an edge between two nodes exists if the corresponding tags are found together in the same Stack Overflow question. The resulting network edges are *weighted,* i.e., the more questions exist with two tags co-occurring, the higher the weight of the relevant edge between them will be; for example, if the tag python is found to co-exist with the tag android in 500 questions, the weight of the edge between the nodes python and android in our graph will be 500. In graph terminology, the resulting graph is a *weighted undirected* one.

What is the motivation behind our approach? The recent development of network science [1], largely triggered by the publication of two seminal papers in the late '90s [2, 3], has since made clear that the graph representation of data and processes is certainly of benefit, and can lead to insights not directly or easily achievable otherwise. Our scope is to demonstrate the merit of such a representation in a text-related area and to possibly alert the interested reader for the availability of the relevant principles, tools, and techniques.

There are several introductory textbooks available on network science: Easley and Kleinberg [4] aim for an advanced undergraduate audience and have made their book freely available online;[2] the books by Jackson [5] and Newman [6] are standard graduate-level introductions to the subject, from the perspectives of economics and statistical physics respectively; Kolaczyk [7] provides another graduate-level introduction, with emphasis to the statistical analysis of network data; and Barabási [1] is gradually making available an online introductory book as a work in progress. We also highly recommend the popular book by Duncan Watts [8] for a smooth, non-mathematical introduction to the relevant concepts, notions, and ideas. We will not provide here a formal introduction to graph theory and network science, something that would require a separate chapter by itself; instead, we will introduce rather informally and intuitively the relevant concepts as we go along. For formal definitions, the interested reader can always consult some of the free online resources mentioned above. For the purposes of our discussion, we will use the terms "network" and "graph" loosely and interchangeably, as if they were synonyms (although they are not). The other interchangeable pairs of terms we will use are "node" – "vertex" and "edge" – "link".

We have chosen R [9] for our investigation, as it has become the de facto standard tool for the statistical analysis of data. Among the several available packages for graph and network analysis, we utilize the igraph library [10], a powerful and flexible tool which is already used by at least a hundred other R packages [11].

The rest of this chapter is organized as follows: in the next section, we describe briefly the data acquisition process and present some summary statistics of the raw data; in Section 3 we expose the construction of our first graph based on the whole data set, along with some limited analysis; Section 4 describes the meaningful reduction of our raw data set, which is used in the rest of the chapter; Section 5 deals with various measures of node importance (centrality), and Section 6 we demonstrate the application of some community

---

[2]http://www.cs.cornell.edu/home/kleinber/networks-book/.

Number of records (questions)	7,214,697
Number of unique tags	36,942
No. of tag occurrences	21,294,348
Average no. of tags/question	2.95

TABLE 12.1: Statistics of raw data.

detection algorithms; some attempted visualizations are presented in Section 7, utilizing the communities detected in Section 6; Section 8 concludes the chapter with some general discussion.

12.2 Data Acquisition and Summary Statistics

Stack Exchange makes its updated "data dump" periodically available roughly twice a year (January & September), under a Creative Commons BY-SA 3.0 License.[3] The version we are going to work with is of January 2014. The questions data are available as a large (~ 25GB) XML file, which was downloaded and parsed using BaseX, an open-source lightweight XML database[4]. A separate XML file with the tag frequencies is also provided. The details of the raw data parsing and processing can be found in the Appendix; the results are:

- A list of the used tags, ordered by decreasing frequency

- An adjacency matrix keeping track of the tag co-occurrences, as described in the Introduction.

These results are available as R workspace files (`tag_freq.RData` and `adj_matrix.RData` respectively) from the author's Github repository[5], and they constitute the departure point for our analysis; as said, readers interested in the parsing procedure itself and the construction of these results from the raw data can consult the Appendix; the R scripts used for the parsing are also available at Github, so the whole procedure is entirely reproducible, and even extensible as new versions of the Stack Overflow data dump become available in the future. The summary statistics of the raw data are shown in Table 12.1.

The `tag_freq` dataframe contains two variables: the name of the tag and the corresponding frequency (counts) in the data set. We will load it and add a third variable, to indicate the relative percentage frequency of each tag, and then view the 10 most frequent tags:

```
> load("tag_freq.RData") # needs to be in the current working directory
> tag_freq$rel <- tag_freq$freq/sum(tag_freq$freq)*100
> head(tag_freq,10)
         tag   freq       rel
1         c# 635338  2.983599
2       java 632575  2.970624
3 javascript 605552  2.843722
4        php 573279  2.692165
```

---

[3]http://blog.stackexchange.com/category/cc-wiki-dump/.
[4]http://basex.org/.
[5]https://github.com/desertnaut.

```
5       android 503255 2.363327
6        jquery 468723 2.201162
7        python 297952 1.399207
8           c++ 287483 1.350044
9          html 284234 1.334786
10        mysql 243701 1.144440
```

We can thus see the 10 most frequent tags, along with their absolute and relevant frequencies. Going a little further,

```
> sum(tag_freq$rel[1:10])
[1] 21.28307
```

we can easily see that the 10 most frequent tags account for about 21% of all tag occurrences in the raw data.

We can similarly explore the other end of the list, that is how many tags appear very infrequently in the data set:

```
> length(which(tag_freq$freq < 100))
[1] 26723
> length(which(tag_freq$freq < 10))
[1] 9614
```

We can thus see that the majority of our 36,942 tags appear fewer than 100 times, whereas about 26% of the tags have a rather negligible presence (fewer than 10 times) in our data.

These results suggest a highly skewed distribution, with relatively few frequent tags dominating the data set. Plotting the tag frequencies for the first 100 tags (recall that tags are indexed in decreasing frequency) confirms this intuition, as shown in Figure 12.1 :

```
> plot(tag_freq$freq, xlim=c(1,100),
+ xlab="Tag index", ylab="Frequency (counts)")
```

12.3   Full Graph — Construction and Limited Analysis

Having performed the initial exploration of our tag frequency distribution, we now proceed to construct the full graph using the adjacency matrix already built as shown in Appendix A (file adj_matrix.RData). The igraph library, from version 0.5.1 on, utilizes fully the sparse matrix infrastructure provided by the Matrix package [12], something extremely convenient, since working with dense matrices of size 40,000 x 40,000 can be really cumbersome for most common desktop computers.

```
> library(Matrix)
> library(igraph)
> load("adj_matrix.RData") # contains sparse matrix G
> g <- graph.adjacency(G, weighted=TRUE, mode=c("plus"), diag=FALSE)
> summary(g)
IGRAPH U-W- 36942 2699465 --
attr: weight (e/n)
```

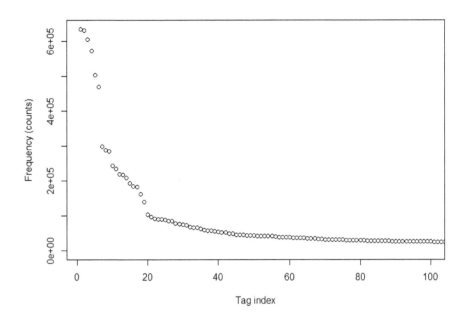

FIGURE 12.1: Tag frequency distribution for the first 100 tags.

The summary() function provides some general information about the graph g, namely, that it is undirected ('U') and weighted ('W'), with 36,942 vertices (nodes) and about 2.7 million edges, and only one attribute (weight), which refers to the edges ('e') and it is a numeric one ('n'). We can decorate the graph with more attributes, such as a name for it as well as names for each vertex (tag):

```
> # set the graph and vertices name attributes:
> g$name <- "FULL TAG GRAPH"
> V(g)$name <- tag_freq$tag  # set tags as node names
> summary(g)
IGRAPH UNW- 36942 2699465 -- FULL TAG GRAPH
attr: name (g/c), name (v/c), weight (e/n)
```

We can see that our graph is now named ('N'), and it contains two more character attributes ('c'), one for the whole graph ('g') and one for the individual vertices ('v').

Clusters and Connected Components

One of the first things in network diagnostics is to check if the network is globally connected:

```
> is.connected(g)
[1] FALSE
```

Since our graph is not globally connected, the next step is to check for its connected components (clusters):

```
> cl <- clusters(g)
> str(cl)
```

```
List of 3
 $ membership: num [1:36942] 1 1 1 1 1 1 1 1 1 1 ...
 $ csize     : num [1:53] 36888 1 1 1 1 ...
 $ no        : int 53
> cl$csize
 [1] 36888      1      1      1      1      2      1      1
 [9]     1      1      1      1      1      1      1      1
[17]     1      1      1      1      1      1      1      1
[25]     1      1      1      1      1      1      1      1
[33]     2      1      1      1      1      1      1      1
[41]     1      1      1      1      1      1      1      1
[49]     1      1      1      1      1
```

From the `csize` attribute of our clusters variable, it is apparent that our graph consists of one giant connected component (36,888 nodes) and 52 clusters with only one to two nodes each. It is trivial to write a short loop, in order to check the tag names in these small isolated clusters (only the first 10 shown here, for brevity):

```
# print isolated tags ("graph periphery")
l <- cl$no # number of clusters
for (i in 2:l) {
    label <- V(g)$name[which(cl$membership==i)]
    print(label)
}
```

```
[1] "untagged"
[1] "beaker-testing"
[1] "arden-syntax"
[1] "zzt-oop"
[1] "ontopia" "tolog"
[1] "ebuild"
[1] "nikeplus-api"
[1] "infinity.js"
[1] "jquery-ias"
[1] "paperless"
```

Even without specific domain knowledge, it is apparent that all the tags in the "graph periphery" listed already are far from common terms expected to be found in a programming-related forum.

Node Degrees

The *degree* of a node is simply the number of its direct neighbors, or equivalently the number of the links in which the node is involved [5, 6]. The degree is very frequently used as a proxy for the importance or the significance of individual nodes in a graph. `igraph` provides a relevant function `degree(g)`, which can be used to compute the degrees of all the nodes in the graph g; nevertheless, it is of no use in our case here, as it does not take into account the weights of the graph edges. The correct `igraph` function for the computation of the *weighted* degree [13] is `graph.strength(g)`. Again, it is straightforward to see the nodes with the highest weighted degrees in our graph:

```
> s <- graph.strength(g)
> V(g)$name[which.max(s)]
[1] "c#"
> s <- sort(s, decreasing=TRUE)
```

```
> s <- as.data.frame(s) # for better display
> head(s, 10)
                    s
c#          1485191
java        1446078
javascript  1359147
php         1192764
jquery      1034841
android      965297
html         705233
c++          639678
ios          621107
python       608211
```

Not unsurprisingly, the above list is similar (but not identical) to the 10 most frequent tags already shown. If we plot the weighted degree, the results are qualitatively very similar with Figure 12.1 (not shown).

Clustering Coefficient, Path Length, and Small-world Characteristics

The *local clustering coefficient* of a node is the fraction of its direct neighbors that are themselves direct neighbors (i.e., directly connected); in a social network framework, for example, it would be the fraction of one's friends that are also friends themselves [4]. The *average* clustering coefficient of the whole graph is simply the average of the nodes' local clustering coefficients [5]. By definition, both coefficients lie between 0 and 1. igraph provides the function transitivity() for the computation of these quantities, as well as a simple function for the computation of the average path length in a graph. For these calculations, we ignore the edge weights, treating the edges between nodes simply as binary entities (present/absent):

```
# Clustering coef & average path length
# Use type="average" argument for average cluster coef
> cc <- transitivity(g, type="average", isolates="zero")
> cc
[1] 0.6099061
> path.length <- average.path.length(g, unconnected=TRUE)
> path.length
[1] 2.341709
```

Thus, on average, the "distance" between any two nodes in our graph is between 2 and 3 hops, making our graph a small-world network [4, 5, 6]. Before commenting on the clustering coefficient, we take a moment to compute the same quantities for a random (Erdös-Renyi - ER) graph with the same number of nodes and edges:

```
# Compare with an equivalent random (ER) graph
> set.seed(42) # for reproducibility
> g.ER <- erdos.renyi.game(length(V(g)), length(E(g)), type="gnm")
> cc.ER <- transitivity(g.ER, type="average", isolates="zero")
> cc.ER
[1] 0.00395176
> path.length.ER <- average.path.length(g.ER, unconnected=TRUE)
> path.length.ER
[1] 2.554753
```

We can see that, compared with a random graph with the same number of nodes and edges, our graph possesses roughly the same average path length between two nodes, with a hugely higher (two orders of magnitude) clustering coefficient. This is a recurrent motif for several real-world networks, including social ones [6], first captured in an abstract network model by Watts and Strogatz in a seminal paper published in *Nature* [2], that partially triggered the subsequent birth of the whole network science field.

12.4   Reduced Graph — Construction and Macroscopic Analysis

We have presented some general analysis for our full graph, but the information revealed so far is rather trivial. To go deeper, we will need to revert to a reduced graph, due to the prohibitively high computational power demanded for the analysis of the full tag graph; due to the highly skewed distribution of the tag occurrences (see Section 12.2), we claim that this reduction still captures almost all of the interesting characteristics of our data set.

We suggest that we proceed with a graph containing only those tags which occur a minimum of 500 times in our data (recall that we have more than 7 million questions and 21 million tag occurrences in total; see Table 12.1). We have taken special care when building our adjacency matrix, so that its columns and rows extend in a decreasing tag frequency; hence, it is a trivial operation to discard the following tags a given frequency in the adjacency matrix:

```
> # select only tags with freq >= 500
> ind <- which(tag_freq$freq >= 500)
> max(ind)
[1] 3711
> tag_freq <- tag_freq[ind,]
> sum(tag_freq$freq)
[1] 19166670
> sum(tag_freq$rel)
[1] 90.00825
> # keep only these entries in the adjacency matrix
> G <- G[1:max(ind), 1:max(ind)]
```

There are thus 3711 tags in our reduced list, or about 10% of all tags used; the sum() functions in the code above show that our reduced tag list contains more than 19 million tag occurrences out of the 21 million in total, i.e., about 90%. Proceeding with a manner absolutely similar to the one presented for the full graph in Section 12.3, we end up with our reduced graph gr, containing about 1 million edges:

```
> summary(gr)
IGRAPH UNW- 3711 1033957 -- REDUCED TAG GRAPH
attr: name (g/c), name (v/c), weight (e/n)
```

We have thus now a much more "lightweight" graph, nevertheless capturing the vast majority of the most frequently used tags. We are ready now to apply some more sophisticated techniques from the toolbox of graph theory and network science in order to reveal possible unexpected information and insights, hidden in the network structure.

General Statistics

```
> is.connected(gr)
[1] TRUE
```

```
> cc <- transitivity(gr, type="average", isolates="zero") #clustering coef.
> cc
[1] 0.4992685
> path.length <- average.path.length(gr)
> path.length
[1] 1.849807
> # Compare with the equivalent ER graph
> set.seed(42) # for reproducibility
> gr.ER <- erdos.renyi.game(length(V(gr)), length(E(gr)), type="gnm")
> is.connected(gr.ER)
[1] TRUE
> cc.ER <- transitivity(gr.ER, type="average", isolates="zero")
> cc.ER
[1] 0.1501704
> path.length.ER <- average.path.length(gr.ER)
> path.length.ER
[1] 1.849801
```

We can see that our reduced graph is now globally connected (i.e., there are no isolated nodes); it has an even lower average path length between two nodes (1-2 hops), and its clustering coefficient is still higher than the one of the equivalent random graph, although this difference is not as marked as with our full graph.

In what follows, we will limit the discussion to the reduced tag network we have just constructed.

12.5 Node Importance: Centrality Measures

We recall from the previous sections that the information revealed so far is rather trivial: taking the weighted node degree as a rough importance measure, the most important nodes essentially coincide with the most frequent tags; clearly, we did not need to go to a graph representation in order to discover something like that.

The graph representation starts paying off when we consider other measures of node importance, which in the networks literature usually go under the label of *centrality* measures (actually, the *degree centrality*, which we have already demonstrated, is just one of them). Furthermore, these measures, in contrast with the *macro* measures considered so far (connected components, average clustering coefficients and path lengths), are in essence *micro* measures, since they do not refer to the graph as a whole, but rather to individual nodes and how they relate to the overall network structure [5].

There are several measures of node centrality in the literature, and most of them are implemented in igraph. We now proceed to have a look to some of them.

Betweenness Centrality

The betweenness centrality, first proposed in the context of social network analysis by Freeman [14], measures the extent to which a node is located in the shortest paths between other pairs of nodes (i.e., "between" them) [5, 11]. As with other centrality measures, igraph provides two ways of calculation: the straightforward betweenness() function, which can be computationally demanding, especially for large graphs; and the betweenness.estimate() function, with a cutoff argument for providing the maximum path length to consider in the calculation. Although the direct calculation of betweenness is not prohibitive for our graph, we will hereby demonstrate the usage of the approximate function, which will most probably be of use in a range of other situations, where the graphs are prohibitively large for the direct application of the `betweenness()` function. In our case, the reader can confirm that the approximate calculation gives results identical to the exact one. Both functions take into account the edge weights [13].

A reasonable value to use as a cutoff value for the path length is the diameter of the graph, i.e., the maximum (shortest) path length between two nodes [5]:

```
# calculate (approximate) betweenness
> diam <- diameter(gr)
> diam
[1] 3
> bc <- betweenness.estimate(gr, cutoff=diam)
> which.max(bc)
[1] 111
> V(gr)$name[which.max(bc)]
[1] "debugging"
```

Keeping always in mind that our node indices are sorted as per their occurrence frequency it the data set, the meaning of the `which.max(bc)` above should be apparent: the node with the highest betweenness centrality in our graph corresponds to the tag `debugging`, which is ranked only 111th in our tag list.

In hindsight, it seems appropriate that the tag linking most of the questions in a computer programming forum should be something that has to do with errors or bugs, but we wonder how apparent this fact could be beforehand.

With a little data manipulation, it is easy to see more of the nodes with high betweenness centrality, and compare their betweenness ranking to the frequency ranking of the corresponding tags:

```
> # see betweenness ranking VS frequency ranking:
> bc.df <- data.frame(bc=bc, freq.rank = 1:length(V(gr)))
> bc.df <- bc.df[order(bc.df$bc, decreasing=TRUE),] #order in decreasing bc
> head(bc.df, 20)   # show the top-20
                       bc freq.rank
debugging         20363.39       111
design            19011.70       198
caching           17694.07       162
exception         17655.67       142
testing           16669.95       183
error-handling    16482.48       370
dynamic           15932.37       223
api               14840.20        78
data              14178.36       261
unit-testing      14144.10       101
user-interface    14009.76       185
parsing           13927.16       105
filter            13884.12       390
web-applications  13834.88       210
optimization      13730.19       201
memory-leaks      13653.39       305
logging           13646.06       207
object            13535.99       144
web               13496.93       254
text              13487.15       230
```

Thus, not only the highest betweenness node is nowhere to be seen in the 100 most frequent tags, but also none of the 10 most frequent tags scores high in betweenness centrality; we can see that, in fact, with the exception of the tag `api`, none of the 20 tags with the highest betweenness centrality is in the top 100 frequency list. We can go a little further, and check in particular how exactly the 10 most frequent tags score and rank in betweenness centrality:

```
> bc.df$bc.rank <- 1:length(V(gr)) # add bc.rank field
> ind <- which(bc.df$freq.rank <= 10) # find the 10 most frequent tags
> bc.df[ind,]  # display them
                    bc freq.rank bc.rank
mysql        7035.926        10     178
html         6295.522         9     226
jquery       5764.672         6     263
android      5645.326         5     269
javascript   4691.252         3     387
c++          4147.752         8     440
python       3967.835         7     465
c#           3665.712         1     511
php          3539.976         4     538
java         2007.629         2     914
```

Hence, we can explicitly see that all 10 most frequent tags rank lower than 100 in betweenness centrality, with the 2nd most frequent one (`java`) barely making it to the top-1000 of betweenness centrality.

Interestingly enough, all the high betweenness node-tags shown above are somewhat "general" ones, in the sense that they are not related with specific software or hardware platforms. This makes perfect sense intuitively, and it demonstrates how the network structure can capture relations and characteristics in the data that are not easily or directly expressed in simple aggregate measures, such as the frequency of occurrence.

As said earlier, the reader can easily confirm that, for our graph, the approximate betweenness coincides with the exact one (which nevertheless would be computationally prohibitive for larger graphs):

```
> bc.exact <- betweenness(gr)
> length(bc==bc.exact)
[1] 3711
```

The last statement means that the condition `bc==bc.exact` is true for all our 3711 nodes.

Closeness Centrality

The *closeness centrality* of a node is a measure of how 'close' a node is to all the other nodes in the network [5, 11]. Since ours is a graph with a rather low diameter (3), we do not expect this measure to be of particular usefulness, but we include it here for illustrative purposes. Following a procedure completely analogous with the one already demonstrated for the betweenness centrality, but using instead the `igraph` function `closeness.estimate()`, we arrive at very similar results:

```
> head(clc.df, 20)
                         clc freq.rank clc.rank
design          0.0001497230       198        1
error-handling  0.0001496110       370        2
```

```
debugging       0.0001485884        111        3
filter          0.0001484120        390        4
caching         0.0001483900        162        5
testing         0.0001483680        183        6
documentation   0.0001483239        593        7
exception       0.0001480604        142        8
logging         0.0001478415        207        9
dynamic         0.0001478197        223       10
web             0.0001477541        254       11
optimization    0.0001476887        201       12
runtime-error   0.0001474926       1021       13
parameters      0.0001474709        339       14
memory-leaks    0.0001474491        305       15
data            0.0001474274        261       16
user-interface  0.0001473188        185       17
frameworks      0.0001473188        429       18
crash           0.0001473188        506       19
design-patterns 0.0001472971        179       20
> clc.df[ind,] # the 10 most frequent tags:
                  clc freq.rank clc.rank
mysql      0.0001414027        10       778
html       0.0001408848         9       915
jquery     0.0001405284         6      1031
c++        0.0001394117         8      1488
android    0.0001385425         5      1944
python     0.0001382361         7      2128
php        0.0001372684         4      2810
javascript 0.0001366680         3      3222
c#         0.0001355381         1      3601
java       0.0001308729         2      3710
```

Eigenvector-based Centrality

Eigenvector-based centrality measures express the importance of a node based on the importance of its neighbors. Since this definition is somewhat self-referential, these measures turn out to be the solutions of some appropriately defined eigenvalue problem (hence the name) [5, 11]. The relevant `igraph` function is `evcent()`, which has a somewhat different interface than the `betweenness()` and `closeness()` centrality functions already used:

```
> eigc <- evcent(gr) # returns a list, not an array
> eigc <- eigc$vector # coerce to array
> V(gr)$name[which.max(eigc)]
[1] "javascript"
```

Following a similar procedure to the one already described for the betweenness, we check the 20 nodes with the highest eigenvector centrality (notice that this measure is normalized to lie between 0 and 1):

```
> head(eigc.df,20)
                 eigc freq.rank
javascript 1.00000000         3
jquery     0.94831551         6
html       0.72171495         9
css        0.51204736        13
```

```
php         0.44673099         4
ajax        0.28340051        22
mysql       0.19656924        10
c#          0.18316147         1
asp.net     0.18129922        12
html5       0.13735764        39
json        0.13219053        28
java        0.10853696         2
forms       0.09822225        46
jquery-ui   0.09133711        84
sql         0.08945679        14
arrays      0.08822174        24
.net        0.08759265        16
android     0.08142784         5
regex       0.07787668        25
css3        0.07391215        83
```

We notice that the results are very different compared to the betweenness and closeness centralities: `javascript` and `jquery` are pronounced as the most important nodes, and the leaderboard is populated by a mix of the most frequent and the less so tags.

12.6   Community Detection

Community detection is both a huge topic and the subject of intense current research: a recent (2010) survey paper in a high-caliber physics journal runs for no less than 100 pages [15], where we read that *"[t]his problem is very hard and not yet satisfactorily solved, despite the huge effort of a large interdisciplinary community of scientists working on it over the past few years"*. The subject also goes under some alternative labels, such as *clustering* and *graph partitioning* [11, 15], although it is advised that the former term be avoided in order to prevent confusion with the clustering coefficient measures mentioned already [6].

Intuitively speaking, the problem of community detection is to uncover a somehow "natural" division of a network into groups of nodes, such that there are many edges *within* groups and relatively few edges *between* groups [6]. Like the measures introduced in the first sections of this chapter, it is a *macro* one, aiming at discovering and understanding the large-scale structure of graphs and networks. Although the first algorithms for community detection and graph partitioning in computer science were proposed in the early 1970's, recent research on the topic was greatly triggered by the publication of a seminal paper by Girvan and Newman in 2002 [16], considered as *"historically important, because it marked the beginning of a new era in the field of community detection and opened this topic to physicists"* [15]. Their method focuses on the concept of betweenness centrality introduced already, and it remains highly popular today. It is implemented in `igraph` by the function `edge.betweenness.community()`, but unfortunately it is computationally very demanding, and we will not demonstrate it here. We will focus on two other popular algorithms instead.

Fast Greedy Algorithm

The fast greedy algorithm was proposed in 2004 by Clauset, Newman, and Moore [17]; hence, it is sometimes referred to as the CNM algorithm. It tries to optimize a modularity measure for the graph [18] by applying, as its name implies, a fast greedy approach. It is available in `igraph` via the `fastgreedy.community()` function:

```
> fc <- fastgreedy.community(gr)
```

All the community detection functions in `igraph` return their results as objects of the dedicated class `communities`, which provides its own special functions and operations for this kind of objects

```
> length(fc)  # how many communities
[1] 10
> sizes(fc)
Community sizes
  1   2   3   4   5   6   7   8   9  10
 32 514 625 506 976 316 521  36 183   2
```

We can see that the fast greedy algorithm returns 10 communities, with the sizes shown above. Before getting for a closer inspection, we can see that most of the detected communities consist of a rather high number of nodes. To get an idea of the quality of the returned communities, we proceed to visually inspect some of the smaller ones:

```
> V(gr)$name[membership(fc)==1]
 [1] "actionscript-3" "flash"          "flex"
 [4] "actionscript"   "air"            "flex4"
 [7] "salesforce"     "adobe"          "flash-builder"
[10] "flex3"          "components"     "swf"
[13] "actionscript-2" "textfield"      "flash-cs5"
[16] "flex4.5"        "apex-code"      "mxml"
[19] "flash-player"   "flexbuilder"    "movieclip"
[22] "visualforce"    "spark"          "red5"
[25] "flv"            "builder"        "loader"
[28] "flash-cs4"      "blazeds"        "flashdevelop"
[31] "swfobject"      "flash-cs6"

> V(gr)$name[membership(fc)==8]
 [1] "excel"                "vba"
 [3] "excel-vba"            "macros"
 [5] "google-apps-script"   "ms-word"
 [7] "automation"           "export"
 [9] "google-drive-sdk"     "ms-office"
[11] "google-spreadsheet"   "range"
[13] "excel-formula"        "excel-2007"
[15] "word"                 "excel-2010"
[17] "powerpoint"           "cell"
[19] "google-drive"         "spreadsheet"
[21] "formula"              "google-docs"
[23] "copy-paste"           "word-vba"
[25] "pivot-table"          "google-apps"
[27] "xls"                  "google-docs-api"
[29] "openoffice.org"       "ole"
[31] "outlook-vba"          "excel-2003"
[33] "shapes"               "powerpoint-vba"
[35] "google-spreadsheet-api" "vlookup"

> V(gr)$name[membership(fc)==10]
[1] "tridion"      "tridion-2011"
```

All three communities exposed above look meaningful: for example, community #1 seems to be about Adobe Flash and related technologies, whereas community #8 contains mostly tags related to "office" applications (by Microsoft, Google, and Apache). Nevertheless, we find it difficult to imagine that the bigger communities, i.e., of size 300, 500, or even higher, may contain such kind of coherent information that could possibly be labeled by a single term (like "Adobe Flash", or "office applications" for our two previous examples).

Could we possibly do better? The answer is not clear beforehand; recall from the discussion so far that, edge weights aside, our graph is densely connected, with a diameter of only 3. It could very reasonably be the case that, given this "tightness" of our graph, we cannot uncover any finer details regarding distinct coherent communities.

To see that this is not the case, we now turn to a powerful, state of the art algorithm, that at the same time is not computationally prohibitive for a common desktop or laptop computer, at least for the size of our graph.

Infomap Algorithm

The Infomap algorithm for community detection was suggested in 2008 by Rosvall and Bergstrom [19, 20]; according to comparative tests, it *"appears to be the best"*, and it is *"also very fast, with a complexity which is essentially linear in the system size, so [it] can be applied to large systems"* [15]. It is available in igraph via the infomap.community() function. Since it has a random element, we first set the random seed for exact reproducibility of the results shown here:

```
> set.seed(1234) # for reproducibility
> imc <- infomap.community(gr)
> length(imc)
[1] 80
> plot(sizes(imc), xlab="Community no.", ylab="Community size")
```

Infomap reveals 80 communities, with the corresponding sizes as shown in Figure 12.2.

Despite the fact that here also we have some large communities detected, we have also a rather high number of smaller ones, with sizes ranging from 2 to about 40 nodes each.

In our case, the only way for validating the communities is by "manual inspection", that is, by going through them and examining if the communities are meaningful. We claim that the communities discovered by the Infomap algorithm are indeed highly meaningful; we leave the complete set of this exercise to the reader, and we will illustrate here only some typical cases.

Before examining the large communities, it makes sense to first examine the smaller ones, as the possible (in)coherences will be much easier to spot. Let us begin with the communities #17-19:

```
> V(gr)$name[membership(imc)==17]
 [1] "facebook"                "facebook-graph-api"
 [3] "comments"                "facebook-like"
 [5] "facebook-javascript-sdk" "facebook-fql"
 [7] "facebook-php-sdk"        "share"
 [9] "facebook-opengraph"      "facebook-c#-sdk"
[11] "opengraph"               "social-networking"
[13] "like"                    "photo"
[15] "facebook-apps"           "facebook-login"
[17] "facebook-android-sdk"    "facebook-ios-sdk"
[19] "access-token"            "facebook-comments"
[21] "sharing"                 "social"
```

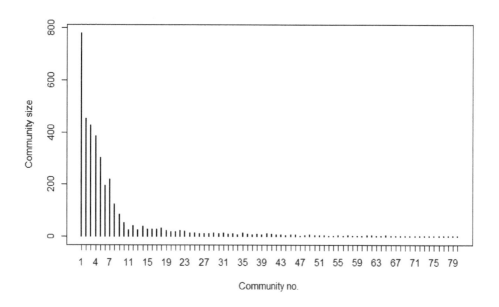

FIGURE 12.2: Communities revealed by Infomap, with corresponding sizes.

```
[23] "facebook-page"          "fbml"
[25] "facebook-oauth"         "facebook-social-plugins"
[27] "facebook-access-token"  "facebook-wall"

> V(gr)$name[membership(imc)==18]
[1]  "r"              "plot"          "ggplot2"
[4]  "statistics"     "latex"         "data.frame"
[7]  "gnuplot"        "time-series"   "markdown"
[10] "visualization"  "aggregate"     "histogram"
[13] "data.table"     "bar-chart"     "data-visualization"
[16] "regression"     "subset"        "plyr"
[19] "legend"         "knitr"         "stata"
[22] "apply"          "rstudio"       "xts"
[25] "heatmap"        "correlation"   "shiny"
[28] "reshape"        "finance"       "igraph"
[31] "labels"         "lattice"

> V(gr)$name[membership(imc)==19]
[1]  "google-maps"       "google-maps-api-3"  "geolocation"
[4]  "maps"              "coordinates"        "google-maps-markers"
[7]  "openlayers"        "gis"                "geocoding"
[10] "kml"               "polygon"            "latitude-longitude"
[13] "distance"          "geospatial"         "google-places-api"
[16] "openstreetmap"     "postgis"            "google-fusion-tables"
[19] "google-maps-api-2" "spatial"            "arcgis"
[22] "google-earth"      "infowindow"
```

Community #18 could very easily be labeled as "R": indeed, plyr, ggplot2, lattice, xts, igraph, reshape, and data.table are R packages; rstudio is the dominant R IDE, while statistics, regression, visualization, and correlation are perhaps the most typical tasks for which R is used; latex could be a possible outlier, but we suspect that its presence is due to the increasing use of the LaTex output option, as facilitated by the knitr and shiny packages in a markdown framework; a similar argument could be brought forward also for stata (questions regarding porting of Stata tasks from and to R); apply is an R family of functions...

Similarly, it is rather straightforward to assign the labels "Facebook" and "GIS" to the communities # 17 and #19, respectively.

How about discovering "new" knowledge from this community structure? We include an illustrative case, as it occurred to us while writing. Community #33 clearly has to do with install/setup tasks in a Windows environment:

```
> V(gr)$name[membership(imc)==33]
[1] "wiz"                "installation"    "installer"
[4] "windows-installer" "setup"           "inno-setup"
[7] "msi"                "installshield"   "nsis"
[10] "uninstall"         "wix3.5"          "custom-action"
```

Having never heard of wiz, we Googled it; it proved to be *"The most powerful set of tools available to create your Windows installation experience"* (see wixtoolset.org).

The list can go on; communities #28 and #35 are devoted to "big data" and "machine learning" respectively, with virtually no outliers at all:

```
> V(gr)$name[membership(imc)==28]
[1] "hadoop"      "mapreduce"  "cassandra"  "hive"      "hbase"
[6] "apache-pig"  "hdfs"       "bigdata"    "thrift"    "piglatin"
[11] "cloudera"   "zookeeper"
```

```
> V(gr)$name[membership(imc)==35]
[1] "machine-learning"        "nlp"
[3] "artificial-intelligence" "neural-network"
[5] "classification"          "cluster-analysis"
[7] "data-mining"             "weka"
[9] "scikit-learn"            "svm"
[11] "mahout"                 "libsvm"
[13] "k-means"
```

We encourage the reader to google possible unknown terms (mahout, perhaps?), in order to confirm that they are indeed relevant with the other members of their respective community.

What about our very small communities? Let us try communities #65 and #69:

```
> V(gr)$name[membership(imc)==65]
[1] "sip"      "asterisk" "voip"      "skype"
```

```
> V(gr)$name[membership(imc)==69]
[1] "neo4j"   "cypher"
```

In community #65, sip stands for the Session Initiation Protocol (SIP) in voip networks (of which skype is the most popular example), while asterisk is *"an open-source telephony switching and private branch exchange service"* (see Asterisk.org). Regarding community #69, neo4j is perhaps the most widely used graph database, and cypher is its dedicated query language [21].

As expected, the situation is not so clear-cut with the larger communities; nevertheless, even in those cases, there is certainly some nontrivial coherence in the communities — for example, there are different and distinct communities for iOS (#6) and Android (#7);

almost each and every one of them are associated with a major programming language or framework. We can easily take a compact glimpse at the first 4 node tags of each of the first 10 communities with the following `for` loop:

```
for (i in 1:10) {
    print(V(gr)$name[membership(imc)==i][1:4])
}
```

```
[1] "c++"  "c"  "arrays"  "linux"
[1] "javascript"  "jquery"  "html"  "css"
[1] "php"  "mysql"  "sql"  "sql-server"
[1] "c#"  "asp.net"  ".net"  "asp.net-mvc"
[1] "java"  "eclipse"  "spring"  "swing"
[1] "ios"  "iphone"  "objective-c"  "xcode"
[1] "android"  "sqlite"  "android-layout"  "listview"
[1] "python"  "django"  "list"  "google-app-engine"
[1] "ruby-on-rails"  "ruby"  "ruby-on-rails-3"  "activerecord"
[1] "git"  "svn"  "version-control"  "github"
```

We think the reader will agree that a certain coherence is already visible from the above list. And as we gradually move towards smaller communities, the picture becomes even more coherent. Here is a similar glimpse of the communities #11-20:

```
for (i in 11:20) {
    print(V(gr)$name[membership(imc)==i][1:4])
}
```

```
[1] "xml"  "parsing"  "xslt"  "xpath"
[1] "excel"  "vba"  "ms-access"  "excel-vba"
[1] "actionscript-3"  "flash"  "flex"  "actionscript"
[1] "opengl"  "graphics"  "opengl-es"  "3d"
[1] "node.js"  "mongodb"  "express"  "websocket"
[1] "unit-testing"  "testing"  "selenium"  "automation"
[1] "facebook"  "facebook-graph-api"  "comments"  "facebook-like"
[1] "r"  "plot"  "ggplot2"  "statistics"
[1] "google-maps"  "google-maps-api-3"  "geolocation"  "maps"
[1] "unicode"  "encoding"  "utf-8"  "character-encoding"
```

The specific setting of the random seed has no effect on the qualitative aspects of the result: the reader is encouraged to perform the previous experiment with several different random seeds, to confirm that the results are indeed robust and stable, although the exact number of the uncovered communities may differ slightly.

12.7   Visualization

It is a common truth between graph researchers and practitioners that straightforward visualizations for graphs with more than 100 nodes are of very little use, and when we move to even a few thousand nodes, as with our reduced graph, visualization ceases to have any meaningful value [11]. Nevertheless, there are still useful and meaningful ways to visually explore such graphs. Two common approaches are [11]:

- To "coarsen" the graph, by merging several nodes together, possibly exploiting the results of an already existing graph partitioning (macro level)

- To highlight the structure local to one or more given nodes, resulting in the so called *egocentric* visualizations, commonly used in social networks analysis (micro level)

We are now going to demonstrate both these approaches with our graph.

Visualizing the Communities Graph

For the first approach, we are going to further exploit here the partitioning into communities provided by the Infomap algorithm from the previous Section, effectively resulting in a dimensionality reduction for our graph, in order to produce a useful visualization. As we will see, igraph provides several convenient functions for such purposes. We demonstrate first the use of the `contract.vertices()` function, which will merge the nodes according to the community to which they belong:

```
> # first, add "community" attribute to each node
> gr <- set.vertex.attribute(gr, "community",
+    value = imc$membership)
> grc <- contract.vertices(gr, V(gr)$community)
> grc <- remove.vertex.attribute(grc, "name")
> for (i in 1:length(V(grc))) {
+    grc <- set.vertex.attribute(grc, "name", index=i,
+        V(gr)$name[membership(imc)==i][1])
+ }
> grc <- set.graph.attribute(grc, "name",
+        value = "Contracted (communities) graph")
> summary(grc)
IGRAPH UNW- 80 1033957 -- Contracted (communities) graph
attr: name (g/c), name (v/c), weight (e/n)
```

The `for` loop aims to give to each node in our contracted (communities) graph the name of the first member of the respective community (usually the community "label"), which will be subsequently used for the graph visualization. From the summary, we can see that we now have only 80 nodes (recall from the previous Section that this is the number of the communities uncovered by the Infomap algorithm), but we still carry all the 1 million edges from the gr graph. That is because, as its name may imply, the `contract.vertices()` function does not affect the edges of the graph. We can further simplify the contracted graph by merging also the edges, summing up the corresponding weights, utilizing the `simplify()` function. This is an important point for visualizing, as one can discover by trying to plot the graph as it is so far, with more than 1 million edges.

```
> grc <- simplify(grc, edge.attr.comb = "sum") # sum edge weights
> grc <- set.graph.attribute(grc, "name",
+    value = "Contracted & simplified (communities) graph")
> summary(grc)
IGRAPH UNW- 80 2391 -- Contracted & simplified (communities) graph
attr: name (g/c), name (v/c), weight (e/n)
```

Thus, we have ended up with a rather simple graph of 80 vertices and only 2391 edges, which should not be hard to visualize. We invoke the `tkplot()` command (the R package `tcltk` needs to be installed, but once installed igraph will load it automatically). The results are shown in Figure 12.3 (for best results, maximize the screen and choose some layout other than "Random" or "Circle" from the figure menu).

```
> tkplot(grc)
Loading required package: tcltk
[1] 1
```

Although our communities graph is still very dense, we can visually distinguish the central nodes from the peripheral ones, and the visualization is in line with what we might expect: nodes representing highly used tools, environments, and tasks are positioned in the central bulk, while nodes representing less widely used tools are pushed towards the graph periphery. We notice that the visualization provided by the `tkplot()` function is interactive, for example, one can move and highlight nodes and edges or change their display properties etc.

We now turn to the second approach mentioned in the beginning of this Section, i.e., the so-called egocentric visualizations focused on individual nodes.

Egocentric Visualizations

We can use egocentric visualizations in order to focus closer on our uncovered communities, keeping in mind the informal visualization rule of thumb mentioned before, i.e., that we should try to keep the number of our visualized nodes under about 100. The following code produces the subgraph of the "R" community (#18) discussed already:

```
> k.name <- "r" # the name of the node of which the community we want to
    examine
> k.community <- imc$membership[which(V(gr)$name==k.name)]
> k.community.graph <- induced.subgraph(gr, (V(gr)$community==k.community))
> k.community.graph$name <- paste(k.name, "community graph")
> k.community.graph
IGRAPH UNW- 32 311 -- r community graph
+ attr: name (g/c), name (v/c), community (v/n), weight (e/n)
```

As expected, we end up with a 32-node graph, which should not be hard to visualize. Although not clearly documented in the `igraph` package manual, it turns out that we can indeed use an `edge.width` argument in the `tkplot()` function, in order to visualize the graph edges proportionally to their weight. Experimenting with the corresponding coefficient (invoking the edge weight as-is produces a graph completely "shadowed" by the edges), we get:

```
> tkplot(k.community.graph, edge.width=0.05*E(k.community.graph)$weight)
```

with the results shown in Figure 12.4.

From Figure 12.4, we can immediately conclude that the vast majority of R-related questions in our data have to do with plotting (and the `ggplot2` package in particular), as well as with the specificities of the `data.frame` structure. Also of notice is the rather strong presence of the relatively new `data.table` package.

We can go a step further, and remove the r node itself from the plot; that way we expect the edge width visualization to be less dominated by the presence of the "central" node (r in our case), and possibly uncover finer details regarding the structure of the particular community. To do that, we only need to modify the `induced.subgraph()` line in the previous code as follows:

```
> k.community.graph <- induced.subgraph(gr,
+ (V(gr)$community==k.community & V(gr)$name != k.name))
> tkplot(k.community.graph, edge.width=0.05*E(k.community.graph)$weight)
```

The results are shown in Figure 12.5. We can confirm, for example, that the presence of `latex` in the "R" community is indeed not spurious, as the subject node is strongly connected with both `knitr` and `markdown`, although our initial speculation for its relation also to `shiny` turns out to be incorrect.

We can easily extend the above rationale in order to examine closer the relationship between two or more communities, as long as we limit the investigation to relatively small communities (remember our 100-node max rule of thumb for visualizations). Say we would like to see how the "Big Data" and "Machine Learning" communities are connected, excluding these two terms themselves:

```
> k.names <- c("bigdata", "machine-learning")
> k.communities <- imc$membership[which(V(gr)$name %in% k.names)]
> k.communities.graph <- induced.subgraph(gr,
+ (V(gr)$community %in% k.communities & !(V(gr)$name %in% k.names)))
> tkplot(k.communities.graph, edge.width=0.05*E(k.communities.graph)$
  weight)
```

The results in Figure 12.6 show that, apart from the mildly strong connections of `mahout` with both `cluster-analysis` and `k-means`, the two communities are practically strangers.

12.8 Discussion

We have provided a brief demonstration of how graph and network approaches and tools can be applied for the analysis of semi-structured text in the form of tags. In summary, the steps we have undertaken in the present chapter are as follows:

- Starting from a raw XML file of about 26 GB in size, we parsed the data and built a graph structure of about 2.7 million edges for the co-occurrences of all 36,942 tags.

- We made an informed reduction of our data, in order to end up with a graph that can be feasibly analyzed using only commodity hardware; in doing so, we retained 90% of our 21 million tag occurrences while ending up with a much more manageable reduced graph of 3711 nodes and about 1 million edges.

- Despite the fact that the relevant metrics (diameter = 3, average path length = 1.85) suggested a very dense and tightly packed structure for our reduced graph, we successfully employed the state of the art Infomap algorithm for community detection, in order to uncover 80 distinct communities that, upon close inspection, look indeed meaningful and coherent.

- Utilizing the detected communities in what stands effectively as a **dimensionality reduction** operation on our reduced graph, we managed to end up with a coarsened graph of only 80 nodes and about 2,500 edges, which could subsequently be visualized and used for further exploratory data analysis.

- Finally, we exploited further the uncovered community structure of our graph, in order to demonstrate how further micro-analysis in the neighborhood of selected nodes is possible and potentially insightful.

There are certainly different choices than can be made in several key points of our analysis;

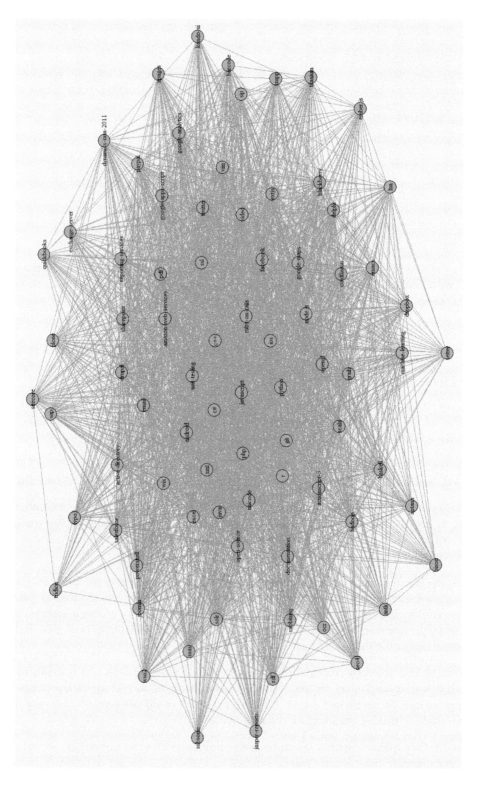

FIGURE 12.3: Visualization of our communities graph.

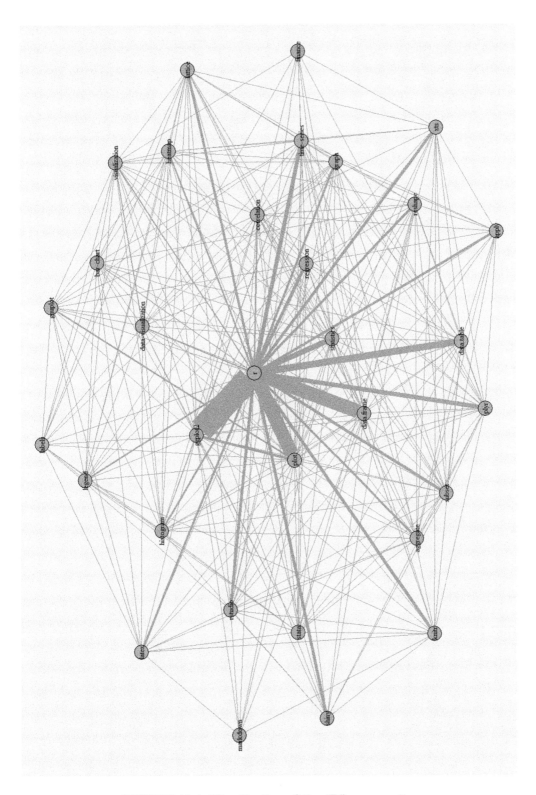

FIGURE 12.4: Visualization of the "R" community.

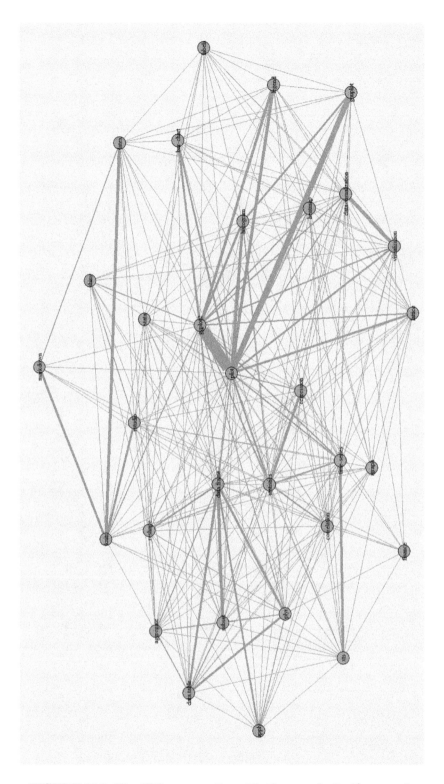

FIGURE 12.5: The "R" community, with the r node itself removed.

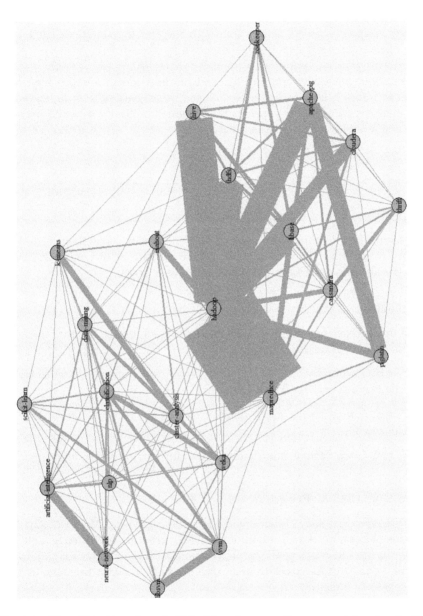

FIGURE 12.6: The "Big Data" and "Machine Learning" communities (excluding these terms themselves).

for example, we could have pruned our initial graph not only according to the frequency of the corresponding tags, but also according to the edge weights (which are also based on a frequency measure). That way, we would have ended with a more clustered and less densely connected graph, with a higher enough diameter and average path length. We chose not to do so mainly in order to fully demonstrate the capabilities of the Infomap algorithm even in such a dense graph, since the community detection is definitely easier for a graph that possesses already some clustering on its own. With the step-by-step instructions and code provided, the reader can easily explore this direction by herself.

We hope that we have presented a convincing case regarding the possible merits of the graph representation, whenever appropriate, and of the handy tools provided by the R language and the `igraph` library. Given the increasing presence of such representations in modern data analysis, we certainly consider that a basic familiarity with the relevant tools and concepts is a must-have skill for the practitioner.

12.9   Appendix: Data Acquisition & Parsing

Here we describe how to obtain the original data and how to parse them, in order to end up with the two R workspace files, `tag_freq.RData` and `adj_matrix.RData`, which are necessary for the analysis described in the chapter's main body.

Data Acquisition

The whole Stack Exchange dump is available from the Internet Archive[6] in `7z` format. The files necessary for our analysis are:

- `stackoverflow.com-Posts.7z` (about 5 GB, which contains the 26 GB uncompressed file `Posts.xml` for Stack Overflow)

- `stackoverflow.com-Tags.7z` (contains the `Tags.xml` file, with the tags and their frequencies)

- `readme.txt` (with various information useful for parsing the data)

Parsing the Tag List & Frequencies

Nowadays, R offers extensive functionality for working with XML files [22], including the XML package. After a quick inspection of the XML structure in `Tags.xml`, it is almost trivial to parse the file and get the individual tag names with their corresponding frequencies (notice that the `Tags.xml` file needs to be in the current R working directory, and the XML package needs to be installed):

```
> library(XML)
> f <- 'Tags.xml'
> doc <- xmlParse(f)
> tag <- xpathSApply(doc, '//row', xpathSApply, '@TagName')
> freq <- as.integer(xpathSApply(doc, '//row', xpathSApply, '@Count'))
```

Subsequently, we just combine the variables `tag` and `freq` in a data frame, we sort it in decreasing frequency order, and we save the resulting data frame in an R workspace file:

---

[6]https://archive.org/details/stackexchange.

```
> tag_freq <- data.frame(tag, freq,
  + stringsAsFactors=FALSE, row.names = NULL)
> # sort in descending frequency:
> tag_freq <- tag_freq[order(tag_freq$freq, decreasing=TRUE),]
> # save in R workspace file:
> save(tag_freq, file='tag_freq.RData')
```

File `tag_freq.RData` should now be in R's current working directory.

Parsing the Tag Co-occurences

In order to parse the tag co-occurrences present in the file `Posts.xml`, we need to download and install BaseX[7], a free open-source XML database. Installation is straightforward, and so is the creation of a new database from `Posts.xml` (although it can take a while); the resulting database is about 19 GB in size.

`Posts.xml` contains all the information about posts, including the answers. From the provided `readme` file, we can see that `PostTypeID=1` refers to questions, while `PostTypeID=2` refers to answers. Since tags are included only in the questions, we are not interested in the latter. After some experimenting in order to arrive to the desired output format (one line of tags per post, with proper separation), we end up with the following simple query (file `get_tags.xqy`):

```
for $x in //row[@PostTypeId="1"]
return ($x/@Tags/string(),'&#xa;')
```

Pasting the above code to the BaseX query window (double-clicking the provided script file also opens the query to a new instance of the BaseX GUI) and running it, we get a sample of the desired output displayed in the relevant window of the BaseX GUI. Although the report window indicates that only 250,000 hits are returned, saving the output results indeed to a text file with the tag co-occurrences of all 7,214,697 posts included in `Posts.xml`.

Building the Adjacency Matrix

Once we have the tag co-occurrences in a text file, we can proceed to build the graph adjacency matrix. It is not exactly a straightforward job, and we will not describe it here in detail - interested readers can always consult the provided script `parse_posts.R`. Here we highlight some challenges that needed to be addressed, using them also as a demonstration of good programming approaches in R.

In theory, with enough memory available (at least 8 GB), it is possible to load the whole `post_tags.txt` file produced in the previous step, and parse it to directly build the (sparse) graph adjacency matrix `G`; unfortunately, it turns out that in practice one encounters the following problem: the sparse matrix `G`, as it gets populated, it gets increasingly "heavier" for incremental updates, leading to unacceptably high execution times, even in machines with powerful processors and lots of memory.

The solution we applied to overcome this issue was twofold: first, we read the `post_tags.txt` file via a file connection, taking in only a bunch of rows at a time in an external `while` loop; second, in each loop iteration, we initialized an all-zeros temporary co-location matrix `G_temp`, which was the one being incrementally updated, and was added to the adjacency matrix `G` only at the end of each loop iteration. This approach speeded up things significantly, since `G_temp` never grew up to sizes that slowed down its

---

[7]http://basex.org/.

incremental updates, while the matrix addition of `G` and `G_temp` proved to be of practically no computational cost.

In our setting, it turned out that a value of 1000 rows per iteration was optimal, leading to 7215 `while` loop iterations; users with slower hard discs may wish to experiment with these settings, since there is a disk read operation in each loop iteration. The resulting solution also has the merit that it is usable to machines with low memory, since the number of rows read at each loop iteration can be as low as desired if the value of 1000 we used turns out to be prohibitive with the memory available.

Been forced to use an external `while` loop for the reasons just mentioned, we aimed to completely avoid any `for` loops in the parsing procedure, since they are notoriously slow in R (see "The Dreaded for Loop" in [23]). We thus made extensive use of the `lapply` family of R functions. Novice R users usually find `lapply` and its relatives rather hard to master initially, but once comprehended, they provide an excellent set of tools for writing efficient R code.

Utilization of the `lapply` functions is also important for one more reason, leading naturally the discussion towards the third ingredient we used for speeding up our code: parallelization, which is rather trivial nowadays in R, even in Windows systems (notice that the `parallel` package is now included by default in any R distribution). Indeed, incorporating parallelization in a multicore machine is almost as easy as the following code snippet indicates:

```
library(parallel)
load("tag_freq.RData")
# initialize parallelization:
num_cores <- 4
cl <- makeCluster(num_cores)
clusterExport(cl, varlist="tag_freq")
```

Now, if we have already put the effort to use `lapply` functions in our code instead of `for` loops, converting them in order to effectively use the existing parallelizatiuon backend is trivial: just compare the single-threaded version shown below, where we build a temporary variable by applying our function `getTags` to the raw file input `doc`

```
temp <- apply(as.matrix(doc), 1, getTags)
```

to its parallel version

```
temp <- parApply(cl, as.matrix(doc), 1, getTags)
```

On the contrary, and despite the functionality available in the `foreach` package, parallelizing `for` loops is by no means that easy and straightforward.

Bibliography

[1] A.-L. Barabási. *Network Science.* 2014. `http://barabasilab.neu.edu/networksciencebook/`.

[2] D.J. Watts and S.H. Strogatz. Collective dynamics of "small-world" networks. *Nature*, 393(6684):440–442, 1998.

[3] A.-L. Barabási and Réka A. Emergence of scaling in random networks. *Science*, 286(5439):509–512, 1999.

[4] Easley D. and J. Kleinberg. *Networks, Crowds, and Markets: Reasoning About a Highly Connected World.* Cambridge University Press, New York, NY, 2010.

[5] M.O. Jackson. *Social and Economic Networks.* Princeton University Press, Princeton, NJ, 2008.

[6] M. Newman. *Networks: An Introduction.* Oxford University Press, Inc., New York, NY, 2010.

[7] E.D. Kolaczyk. *Statistical Analysis of Network Data: Methods and Models.* Springer, 2009.

[8] D.J. Watts. *Six Degrees: The Science of a Connected Age.* W.W. Norton & Company, 2004.

[9] R Core Team. *R: A Language and Environment for Statistical Computing.* R Foundation for Statistical Computing, Vienna, Austria, 2015.

[10] G. Csárdi and T. Nepusz. The igraph software package for complex network research. *InterJournal*, Complex Systems:1695, 2006.

[11] E.D. Kolaczyk and G. Csárdi. *Statistical Analysis of Network Data with R.* Springer, 2014.

[12] D. Bates and M. Maechler. *Matrix: Sparse and Dense Matrix Classes and Methods*, 2014. R package version 1.1-4.

[13] A. Barrat, M. Barthélemy, R. Pastor-Satorras, and A. Vespignani. The architecture of complex weighted networks. *Proceedings of the National Academy of Sciences of the USA*, 101(11):3747–3752, 2004.

[14] L.C. Freeman. A set of measures of centrality based on betweenness. *Sociometry*, 40(1):3–415, 1977.

[15] S. Fortunato. Community detection in graphs. *Physics Reports*, 486(3-5):75–174, 2010.

[16] M. Girvan and M.E.J. Newman. Community structure in social and biological networks. *Proceedings of the National Academy of Sciences of the USA*, 99(12):7821–7826, 2002.

[17] A. Clauset, M.E.J. Newman, and C. Moore. Finding community structure in very large networks. *Physical Review E*, 70:066111, 2004.

[18] M.E.J. Newman and M. Girvan. Finding and evaluating community structure in networks. *Physical Review E*, 69(2):026113, 2004.

[19] M. Rosvall and C.T. Bergstrom. Maps of random walks on complex networks reveal community structure. *Proceedings of the National Academy of Sciences of the USA*, 105(4):1118–1123, 2008.

[20] M. Rosvall, D. Axelsson, and C.T. Bergstrom. The map equation. *The European Physical Journal Special Topics*, 178(1):13–23, 2009.

[21] I. Robinson, J. Webber, and E. Eifrem. *Graph Databases.* O'Reilly Media, Inc., 2013.

[22] D. Nolan and D.T. Lang. *XML and Web Technologies for Data Sciences with R*. Springer, 2014.

[23] Norman Matloff. *The Art of R Programming*. No Starch Press, 2011.

Index

9 781482 237573